Black Powder, White Lace

BECOMING MODERN:
NINETEENTH-CENTURY STUDIES

Series Editors

Sarah Sherman
Department of English
University of New Hampshire

James Krasner
Department of English
University of New Hampshire

Rohan McWilliam
Anglia Polytechnic University
Cambridge, England

Janet Polasky
Department of History
University of New Hampshire

This book series maps the complexity of historical change and assesses the formation of ideas, movements, and institutions crucial to our own time by publishing books that examine the emergence of modernity in North America and Europe. Set primarily but not exclusively in the nineteenth century, the series shifts attention from modernity's twentieth-century forms to its earlier moments of uncertain and often disputed construction. Seeking books of interest to scholars on both sides of the Atlantic, it thereby encourages the expansion of nineteenth-century studies and the exploration of more global patterns of development.

Stephen Carl Arch, *After Franklin: The Emergence of Autobiography in Post-Revolutionary America, 1780–1830* (2001)

Justin D. Edwards, *Exotic Journeys: Exploring the Erotics of U.S. Travel Literature, 1840–1930* (2001)

Margaret M. Mulrooney, *Black Powder, White Lace: The du Pont Irish and Cultural Identity in Nineteenth-Century America* (2003)

BLACK POWDER, WHITE LACE

The du Pont Irish and Cultural Identity
in Nineteenth-Century America

Margaret M. Mulrooney

University of New Hampshire

PUBLISHED BY UNIVERSITY PRESS OF NEW ENGLAND

HANOVER AND LONDON

University of New Hampshire

University Press of New England, One Court St., Lebanon, NH 03766

© 2002 by University of New Hampshire

5 4 3 2 1

LIBRARY OF CONGRESS CATALOGING-IN-PUBLICATION DATA

Mulrooney, Margaret M., 1966–
   Black powder, white lace : the Dupont Irish and cultural identity in
nineteenth-century America / Margaret M. Mulrooney.
     p.   cm. — (Becoming modern)
Includes bibliographical references (p.) and index.
     ISBN 1-58465-273-X (cloth : alk. paper) — ISBN 1-58465-274-8 (pbk. :
alk. paper)
     1. Irish Americans—Brandywine Creek Valley (Pa. and Del.)—Ethnic
identity. 2. Irish Americans—Brandywine Creek Valley (Pa. and
Del.)—History—19th century. 3. Working class—Brandywine Creek Valley
(Pa. and Del.)—History—19th century. 4. Brandywine Creek Valley (Pa.
and Del.)—History—19th century 5. E.I. du Pont de Nemours Powder
Company. I. Title. II. Series.
     F172.B78 M85 2003
     305.891'62074813—dc21   2002006606

FOR MY PARENTS

Patricia Cook Mulrooney

AND

Martin J. Mulrooney, 3rd

CONTENTS

ACKNOWLEDGMENTS

In writing about the various influences that made the du Pont Irish who they were, I have become acutely conscious of the individuals and institutions that made me who I am. It seems only fitting to acknowledge some of them here.

If I can call myself an historian, then Bob Gross must certainly get much of the credit. During his tenure as head of the American Studies Program at William and Mary, he served as my primary advisor and directed the dissertation on which this book is based. Beyond that, Bob is a wonderful role model: a respected scholar and a prize-winning author, he is also a dedicated teacher and a devoted family man. Two other faculty at William and Mary influenced my academic path, as well: Cindy Hahamovitch and Leisa Meyer. Both women had recently joined the History Department when I asked them to serve as readers on my dissertation committee. Their probing questions about class and gender forced me to think much more clearly about these important subjects. Michael Kazin also deserves acknowledgment. He generously agreed to work with me while on sabbatical in Williamsburg, and continued to influence my approach to labor history long after he returned to Washington. At the University of Delaware, Bernie Herman deserves thanks for introducing me to vernacular architecture and material culture. He was my mentor when I was an undergraduate, and he remained a critical presence throughout my doctoral work.

As a researcher, I am most clearly in debt to the staff at Hagley. Of these people, Marge McNinch merits the highest accolades. No one knows the archives better, and no one shares my enthusiasm for the du Pont Irish as she does. Her guidance has been invaluable. Lynn Catanese requires special mention, as well. Always helpful, she readily shared her own research on the du Pont women, and her friendly disposition made my days at the Soda House pleasant ones. Mike Nash read the entire dissertation and encouraged me to think about its public history applications for publication. Before he retired, Rob Howard shared his extensive knowledge of the Hagley property with me, and steered me to the myriad maps, plats, and files in his basement domain. Barb Hall and Jon Williams helped me locate dozens of nineteenth-century images of the powder mill community, while Debra

Hughes and Beth Parker-Miller led me to critical artifacts in the museum's collections. Carol Lockman assisted in administrating my 1994 grant-in-aid, arranged for access to office space, and followed my progress long after the grant period ended. Moving away from the Brandywine, I am most grateful to Donn Devine, who oversees the Diocese of Wilmington Archives and is a veritable fount of local history. For generous and much-needed financial support during the early stages of my work, I would like to recognize the Delaware Heritage Commission, Winterthur Museum and Library, and the National Endowment for the Humanities, which awarded me a Dissertation Fellowship.

Through their constant support of this project, certain people have taught me what it means to be a friend and colleague. These include Anne Verplanck and Gabrielle Lanier, who not only shared chapters, references, and ideas, but tears and laughter, too. Then there is Anne Boylan, who gave me the benefit of her expertise in women's history, evangelicalism, and all manner of things academic. Her encouragement means more to me now than ever. Over the years, Roger Horowitz has become another important confidante; he also went beyond the call of duty and reviewed the entire manuscript for UPNE. Kerby Miller read an early version of this book, recommended it for publication, and gave me invaluable suggestions for revision. At Marymount University, where I am pleased to be part of an amazingly collegial group of scholars, my thanks go especially to Marguerite Rippy, who critiqued the next-to-last version of the introduction to this book, and Chris Snyder, who cheered me on to the finish of this project and guided me through each stage of the publishing process.

People often ask me whether I am descended from a powder mill family. The answer is no, but I have always felt a sense of kinship with my subjects, in large part because I grew up in a wage-earning, Irish Catholic household on the outskirts of Wilmington. There, my siblings especially influenced the person I became. The "big kids," Jeanne, Eileen, Debbie, and Mike, spoiled me rotten and took good care of me; they still do. Nora Mulrooney, the baby of our clan, affably tolerates my efforts to spoil and take care of *her.* More amazing, she shares my fascination with museums, historic sites, antiques, Virginia, and the nineteenth century. As a sister, I am fortunate indeed. Finally, I owe a special debt to my parents. Born at the beginning of the Great Depression and raised in Delaware City, Patsy Cook has always appreciated the "finer things" in life. From her I learned two important precepts: "If you do it home, you'll do it out," and "God never gives you more than you can handle." Marty Mulrooney grew up in the 1930s, too. Descended from Irish immigrants who worked in and around Wilmington's leather shops, he learned his trade from the International Brotherhood of Electrical Workers, and later served as president of L.U.

313. Although proud of his blue-collar background, he gave me this advice: "Be happy," and "Get paid for what you know, not what you do." As a daughter, I took both parents' words to heart.

Mark Hermes deserves the last word. He has been my partner for more than a decade, supporting all of my endeavors and sustaining me through good times and bad. His imprint is on every page. He alone makes me whole.

Black Powder, White Lace

Introduction

Mary McDowell became one of the du Pont Irish in 1888, when she emigrated to northern Delaware to join her husband, William, a laborer already employed by E. I. du Pont de Nemours and Company, the nation's leading producer of gunpowder. Like most nineteenth-century immigrants, she left no written record of her life for posterity. Yet scattered bits and pieces survive in the documents created by others. In fact, much of what is known about her comes from a single paragraph:

> [McDowell] said that there was an explosion at duponts and that she did not know what to do, as she was so frightened, she ran to the woods, and that after walking back to her house her child was born through fright. This last explosion just covered her three children and herself with mortar and stones, she also showing me where she had been cut in the head; three weeks after this explosion occurred she picked a piece of glass out of her little girl's head, but they are all doing well now. She said that when this explosion took place, all her furniture, which was new, was smashed to pieces; but that the duponts were good people and wanted to know what the cost of the furniture was, and that it should be paid for. When her husband and herself reckoned up what it was worth they found it to be 140.00 but that they only told the duponts 90 as its value, thinking it very good of them to even pay half instead of all; the duponts even paid for the repairing of her [sewing] machine. She then said Mr. Dupont even wanted to know if the children wanted clothes; but she told him no.[1]

These few lines appear in a report dated November 11, 1890, and produced by Emily Noble, an undercover detective engaged by Eugene du Pont, then president of the powder company, to investigate an explosion that had occurred several weeks earlier. It is a useful source in that it reveals a great deal about McDowell's daily existence despite its brevity. It is also challenging because the information it contains can be interpreted in several ways.

A labor historian, for example, would likely use it to address questions pertaining to the presence or absence of class consciousness among the powder workers.[2] As other parts of the report make clear, the du Pont company had experienced a spate of mysterious arson attempts just before the explosion referenced. Eugene clearly saw a connection between the two episodes, and like many industrialists at the end of the century, he hired a private detective agency to infiltrate the small, tightly knit community and expose the radicals responsible. McDowell did not know that Noble was a detective, nor were she or her husband suspects. She was simply an ordinary woman who had been engaged in conversation by another ordinary woman, a seamstress newly arrived in the village and curious to know what it would be like to live there on a permanent basis. What the "seamstress" really wanted, of course, was information concerning management-labor relations. In this context, McDowell's comments and behavior indicate that she and her husband were not class conscious in the traditional sense; that is, they did not seem to think their interests fundamentally different from those of their employers. But to a class-oriented scholar, this attitude can be readily explained: McDowell had been manipulated by a clever ploy, the offer of replacement furniture, into thinking the du Ponts worthy objects of her loyalty and affection.

Other historians might use the report to explore questions concerning Irish acculturation. Though recent immigrants to the United States, the McDowells had already acquired a household full of new, probably mass-produced furniture. To an immigration expert, this fact could signify a desire to compensate for material deprivation in Ireland or the modification of America's consumer culture by ethnic households.[3] A scholar interested in gender would emphasize Mary's unique position in the family: that she referred to the new furniture and sewing machine as hers, for example, suggests a sense of proprietorship over the domestic sphere and immigrant women's negotiation of America's feminine ideal.[4] Meanwhile, a practitioner of the so-called "new cultural studies" might stress how the McDowells used consumer goods "to gain identity, dignity, and justice."[5] Interpreted from this perspective, the refusal of these wage-earning immigrants to accept wholly the du Ponts' charity translates into a distinct awareness of and pride in their cultural autonomy.

As this brief discussion suggests, historians of labor, immigration, women, and consumption diverge greatly in terms of the questions they ask and the answers they find. Yet they find common ground in a predilection for historical materialism, a set of beliefs about the nature of human existence propounded initially by Karl Marx. Like many philosophers before and since, Marx endeavored to understand human consciousness or self-hood, which he believed to have two manifestations: one transcendent, ideational, and boundless; the other worldly, relational, and restrictive. He argued that the latter derived from the material circumstances of life, especially the nature of an individual's work, and that a dialectical relationship existed between the two. In an industrialized, capitalistic society, such as the one that characterized Marx's mid-nineteenth-century Germany, an individual's relationship to the means of production had a determining effect on his sense of identity. Since wage earners did not own the factories where they toiled, they controlled neither their labor nor its proceeds, which meant they were axiomatically estranged from their higher, "truer" consciousness. Marx considered this situation untenable. The self-alienation of so many people ultimately precluded the creation of a just society, so, he theorized, there must come a time when the proletariat (the propertyless working class) recognized the cause of its immiseration, organized collectively, and effected a sweeping revolt against the bourgeoisie (the property-holding capitalist class) that liberated everyone. Articulated in books like *The Communist Manifesto* (1848) and *Das Capital* (1867), these theories gained in popularity around the turn of the nineteenth century, when wage earners in many industrialized nations did just what they were supposed to do according to the Marxian paradigm. The results of their revolutions were uneven, however; in many places they failed, in others the new regimes seemed even more despotic than their predecessors. Across the world, scholars critical of the industrial capitalist system looked even harder for proof that a viable alternative existed and could be realized. In the United States, this effort peaked with the New Left in the 1960s, when the upheavals of the Civil Rights era convinced an entire generation of historians to study the past "from below" and thereby foment political change in the future. Although labor historians, heavily influenced by a contemporary decline in union membership, emerged as the earliest and strongest proponents of the New Social History, a similar intellectual project engaged students of specific populations, such as women or immigrants. But if this scholarship greatly expanded knowledge of ordinary people's lives, it confirmed even further their fragmentation and conservatism, and left the distinct impression that any radical, Marxian-style consciousness American workers had was long gone. While historical materialism-minded social historians struggled to make sense of this reality, experts in other disciplines imported a new conceptual framework that promised to explain better why so many people accepted, even embraced, an existentially limiting status quo. Building on the work of French linguists and anthropologists, literary specialists in the 1980s posited the presence of discursive regimes, that is, complex systems of signs or symbols that function in human societies to render economic, gender, racial, and other power hierarchies normative. Because it, too, ultimately sought to free that "unconditioned, abstract kind of selfhood" deemed necessary for a utopian human society, a "linguistic or cultural turn" made considerable inroads among social historians.[6] But the continued power of a "materialist rhetorical common sense" led many proponents to borrow anthropologically based linguistic strategies while neglecting the a-materialist suppositions about culture and consciousness on which they rested. As a result, even many self-proclaimed "culturalists" end up stressing their subjects' identity as workers.[7]

This book takes a different view, rooting culture in shared knowledge as ethnohistorians do and arguing that consciousness is the sum of multiple, frequently contradictory cultural identities deriving from the myriad social positions individuals simultaneously occupy.[8] From this *ethnohistorical-multipositional* perspective, any attempt to interpret Mary McDowell's life would require first and foremost an interdisciplinary methodology. On the one hand, she belonged to a distinct Irish community with a distinct system of values, behaviors, and symbols. As an Ulsterite living along the Brandywine Creek in northern Delaware, her conception of ethnicity surely differed from that of a Corkonian in Worchester, Massachusetts, or Butte, Montana. Indeed, recent scholarship in the field of immigration history debunks the very notion of a typical Irish experience.[9] On the other hand, McDowell also participated in the broader world of American consumers, as her regard for domestic furnishings suggests. Her husband clearly performed manual work for pay, but as material culture scholars have demonstrated, some of their belongings, like the sewing machine, held meanings that transcended socioeconomic status. Meanwhile, her gender and grasp of clothing construction enabled McDowell to communicate effectively with a fellow seamstress. A shared sensitivity to the norms of late-nineteenth-century femininity presumably eased her interaction with other females in the community as well, including perhaps even Eugene du Pont's wife (Amelia): That every married woman who lived within range of the powder yards shared the same fear of losing her husband created yet another kind of solidarity. To use a linguistic analogy, McDowell used her knowledge of each group's grammar and vocabulary to make "understandable utterances."[10] However, her degree of fluency varied as the set of shared symbols, values, and behaviors recognized by each cultural community changed. And since individuals define themselves according to their interactions with multiple populations, her sense of selfhood, the meaning she subjectively ascribed to worldly existence, was necessarily dynamic, fluid, and heterogeneous.

Similarly constituted identities defined the more than two thousand individuals who composed the du Pont Irish in the nineteenth century. Their experiences are of great relevance to the general story of the Irish in America. In the main, scholars of this population stress the difficulties encountered by refugees of the infamous potato famine. Crowded into urban slums, they had few skills, toiled for meager wages, and consequently faced lives of hardship and woe. The Catholic Church, the Democratic Party, the fraternal organization, and the labor union each offered help and comfort. By the end of the century, a small proportion had become shopkeepers, teachers, publicans, civil servants, or craftsmen. These Irish owned their own homes and businesses, dominated urban political machines, and profoundly affected the texture of American life. Yet for all their accomplishments, even these Hibernians remained a breed apart. Conditioned by their conservative faith and agrarian past, historians insist, they endorsed values and behaviors fundamentally at odds with this country's modern, industrial culture. This is a compelling and convincing portrait, for it ennobles the simple Irish peasant and assuages readers' anxieties about capitalism, individualism, and materialism. But focusing on the famine generation obscures the complexities and contradictions that existed within the Irish-American population as a whole. In fact, the majority of Irish emigrants in the nineteenth century fled economic stagnation and sociopolitical oppression, not death by starvation or disease, and they readily adapted to life in an industrializing nation.[11] Many congregated in urban centers, but a significant percentage settled in small, semirural industrial villages or founded farming communities in the heartland. Certainly, some Irish lamented their lot and died unhappy exiles of Erin. Others embraced their new homeland, however, and creatively fashioned a new cultural identity for themselves, one that fused elements of their ethnoreligious heritage with critical components of American national character. In sum, Irish acculturation in the nineteenth century took many forms, and recent studies recommend that greater attention be paid to intra-ethnic diversity.[12] Though few in number, the du Pont Irish address this need.

Interpreted from an ethnohistorical, multipositional perspective, their experiences also inform narratives about American workers. Despite widespread acknowledgment that factors like race, gender, ethnicity, religion, age, skill, and household structure all influence cultural identity, most labor histories remain fixated on the white, male worker and his efforts to resist proletarianization in the workplace.[13] Historians of wage-earning women have repeatedly challenged this orientation. Influenced by the growing body of feminist scholarship and its findings about gender, some argue for a "radical conceptualization" of the field, one that would direct attention to the ways in which cultural identity and consciousness are shaped in the home, the place where personal existence originates. In a post-Communist world, one characterized by an apparently universal faith in the liberating potential of the global marketplace, a household-centered labor history, they insist, might reveal once and for all the link between experience and ideology.[14] Yet no one has heeded this call. The private and public spheres do not divide neatly, and models of domal scholarship are generally oriented toward artifactual, not textual analysis.[15]

In contrast to most studies of Irish wage earners, then, this one centers on the domestic world, broadly construed to include everything from religious beliefs, family structure, ethnic traditions, and gender relations to attitudes about company housing, private home ownership, interior space, consumer goods, yards, foodways, social mobility, and gentility. It concludes that residents of this community developed an undeniable cultural affinity with America's modernizing society even as they labored for wages and retained aspects of their distinct ethnoreligious heritage. Beyond that, it demonstrates how subjective conceptions of identity are, and how they reflect the specific characteristics of an individual's immediate surroundings. Finally, recognizing that the Irish Catholic home of the nineteenth century was a female-centered space, headed by the *bean a ti,* or woman of the house, this study underscores the historic relationship between women's activities (both waged and unwaged) and the construction of cultural identities.

The powder mill community particularly lent itself to a household-centered approach. First, a significant portion of it survives to the present day. In 1952, in honor of the Du Pont Company's sesquicentennial anniversary, E. I. du Pont's heirs established the Hagley Museum and Library, which preserves a portion of the Hagley powder yard, the du Pont family mansion, a foreman's residence, bookkeeper's house, and the Brandywine Manufacturers' Sunday School, plus an extensive collection of corporate records. Thousands of tourists have since visited the property near Wilmington, Delaware, and scholars have produced numerous monographs about the du Ponts and the industry they created. But a complete study of the Irish workforce has never been attempted. "It is such a pity that the workingmen have all been forgotten," lamented a powder man's descendant when she visited the museum. "All these elaborately furnished homes of the wealthy don't give any indication of how the people lived that did the work."[16] Second, there exists a truly unprecedented array of evidence pertaining to the powder workers' domestic lives. In addition to extant houses, primary sources include wage ledgers, rent books, maps and atlases, boarding house accounts, probate inventories, property surveys, historic photographs, archaeological assemblages and reports, artifacts, letters, and oral histories. When cross-linked with quantitative data from census schedules, parish registers, immigration records, and city directories, the volume of these qualitative sources allowed for an unusual depth of analysis. Finally, the community flourished for over a century. Such longevity, coupled with a relatively discrete population, facilitated the study of social, political, and economic forces on wage-earning Irish households over "a considerable historical period."[17] Because of the continuous influx of immigrants into the community, there was no precise, historical moment when residents asserted a single, coherent cultural identity. Instead, the rate and kind of acculturation varied according to each family's length of residence in this country, its size and structure, and the strategies for success it employed. Acknowledging, then, that the nineteenth century wrought profound changes, the following pages note the impact of major events and large-scale forces on powder mill households, but ultimately emphasize the modest transformations that occurred within one or two generations.

Families like McDowell's came to this country in hopes of improving their condition. Unlike most Irish Catholic immigrants, however, they hailed mainly from Ulster, especially counties Donegal, Tyrone, and Fermanagh. Subjugated by England in the seventeenth century, the northern province of Ireland was better developed and far more prosperous than the rest of the country. Still, the best land remained in the hands of absentee English landlords and their Anglican middlemen. Irish Catholics and Presbyterians, who formed the majority of the region's population, leased small and marginally productive plots in the hills. With limited acreage, short leases, low wages, and high rents, they tilled the soil primarily for subsistence and relied on supplementary occupations like flax spinning and linen weaving to pay their landlords. The passage of numerous penal laws added to these indignities by denying the right of religious dissenters to vote, practice their faiths, educate their children, hold political offices, or enter the professions. By the end of the eighteenth century, rising rents, falling prices, and deepening cultural differences compelled many Ulstermen to emigrate to the United States.[18] Over time, emigrants from the south and west of Ireland came to dominate the exodus, but northerners retained numerical significance well into the twentieth century.

The experiences of the du Pont Irish mirrored those of their countrymen elsewhere. Men emigrated first, secured work in the powder yards, then sent for their relatives. Families were large and sometimes extended. Most children went to work at an early age, while married women took in boarders, laundry, and piecework to make ends meet. Du Pont clerks kept careful track of each employee's household income, crediting monthly wages and boarding fees, then debiting expenditures for rent, fuel, medical services, and goods purchased at local stores. Accustomed to the rhythms of rural life, entire households adjusted to industrial time. Factory bells signaled the beginning of each work day, and once inside their respective mills, operatives performed their tasks according to strict guidelines. In the powder yards, a typical shift lasted ten hours, but if a large order needed to be filled, the men labored around the clock. Although work "in the powder" offered steadier and better-paid employment than farming, danger loomed everywhere. Explosions occurred frequently and produced a sizeable percentage of female-headed households. Like other Irish communities in industrializing America, this one, too, had high rates of geographic mobility and labor turnover. Despite these obstacles, a stable core of skilled men and their kin established themselves by the 1820s, and the presence of this core enabled the perpetuation of Irish Catholic folkways on American soil.

The longer an Irish family remained in this community, the more it acculturated and the more its members' values, beliefs, and behavior diverged from those of their newly arrived neighbors. The du Ponts preferred to hire and promote from within; wage accounts show that once a common laborer became a powder man, his earnings and savings increased steadily. A portion of each family's annual income still paid the rent on its company-owned house, put food on its table and fuel in its firebox, but stability endowed many Brandywine households with money to spend on education, church memberships, parlor furnishings, fashionable clothing, and leisure activities as well. Residents did not devote much time to fraternal associations, political parties, or religious sodalities. They also failed to exhibit any behavior that might be construed as "radical"; that is, they never challenged the capitalist wage system.[19]

From the founding of the powder mills in 1802 to the company's centennial celebration, there occurred only two episodes of organized labor protest. The first took place in 1835, when independently contracted coopers working in the powder yards joined their counterparts in Wilmington and struck for higher wages.[20] The second came more than fifty years later, when a small group of recently laid-off carpenters formed a secret society and exacted their revenge against the company by burning its barns and issuing threats of physical violence against its managers.[21] If the yard foremen, powder workers, refiners, colliers, common laborers, wheelwrights, millwrights, blacksmiths, and masons employed by the du Ponts sympathized with the cause of their brother coopers and carpenters, they left no record of it. On the contrary, sources like Emily Noble's report, submitted shortly after the barn burnings, make collective action appear aberrant.

Daily life in this community cannot be understood apart from management's attitude toward labor. Unlike most nineteenth-century industrialists, the du Ponts successfully maintained a personalized, affective form of paternalism. They did so not only because their firm dominated its market, but because the volatility of its product and the correspondingly small size of its workforce before 1902 successfully insulated both managers and workers from the rigors of technological and organizational development.[22] E. I. du Pont de Nemours and Company also differed in terms of its owners' patrician origins and cosmopolitan outlook. As titled members of the French aristocracy, the du Ponts honored the code of noblesse oblige; as heirs to the intellectual teachings of their patriarch, Pierre Samuel, the famed economist and proponent of Physiocracy, they sustained the egalitarian ideals of the Enlightenment. Beginning with the founder, Éleuthère Irénée, in 1802, and continuing until the death of his son, Henry, in 1889, managers of the firm pledged to uplift their workmen through various policies of direct assistance. These included good wages, interest-bearing savings accounts, free or low-cost housing, education for children, opportunities for advancement, and impressive benefits for widows. The family facilitated the emigration of its workmen's kin from Ireland, and it did so in numbers that went well beyond the firm's need for labor. At the same time, the du Ponts encouraged the formation of new Catholic parishes. In contrast to other manufacturers in the region, the Deist leaders of the company declined to promote evangelical Protestantism, and practiced religious tolerance instead.

Like Mary McDowell, the Irish responded with gratitude and loyalty, persuaded by a preponderance of occurrences, great and small, that their interests and the du Ponts' were one and the same. Writing to Eleuthera du Pont Smith from her new home in Seymour, Indiana, in 1873, Catharine Davison expressed typical sentiments:

> I hope yourself and all the Dupont famely is well. I long to hear from you all for with the exceptions of my own family thare is no one this side of the sea that feels so near to me as that name[.] [I]t was my first home in America and now in my old adge your frienship seems more dear to me than ever.[23]

Davison's letter went on to relate how well her children were doing in the west, especially daughter Eleuthera, whom she named in honor of her patron. Some people felt differently, of course. Company records do contain references to absenteeism, sabotaged equipment, and drinking and smoking on the job. Yet such passive resistance pales in comparison to Irish labor protests elsewhere. Most of the literature concerning wage-earning Irish immigrants pertains to industries or communities marked by large-scale strikes, coordinated violence, or significant union activity.[24] Even the new cultural studies, which emphasize workers' nonproductive lives, stress populations that openly confronted industrial capitalism and its attendant values.[25] The majority of Irish in the nineteenth century never organized, however, nor did they reject America's market-oriented culture in its entirety.

Indeed, the experiences and attitudes of powder workers, different from yet akin to other Irish, support the opposite conclusion: some wage earners identified strongly with their economic superiors, seeing in their lives values and behaviors consonant with their own.[26]

Inured to the reality of social stratification, the du Pont Irish accepted a degree of subordination as a condition of everyday life "in the powder," but they did not do so naively. Like most immigrants who came to the United States in the nineteenth century, they first encountered modern capitalism and its attendant modes of social and political organization in their homeland.[27] Since conditions in Ireland precluded their economic and social advancement, Catholics and dissenting Protestants alike left to better themselves in industrializing America. While individual members of powder mill households seldom committed their thoughts, beliefs, or aspirations to paper, a close reading of their *behavior* suggests that they were not axiomatically opposed to, alienated from, or immiserated by the capitalist wage system. An insistence on this point does not deny the greater social, economic, and political power of their employers. Industrial paternalism, like all forms of paternalism, grew out of a need to justify an economic arrangement in which some people lived off the labor of others.[28] Rooted in the seigneurial world of medieval Europe, it was resolutely patriarchal and hierarchical, yet the system also imposed reciprocal demands and obligations. In this respect, paternalism bore a remarkable similarity to the communitarian ethos that ideally bound different social strata together in rural Ireland.

Over time, residents of this community manipulated paternalism to their own advantage. They created a stable enclave that allowed them to preserve the vitality of their affiliative networks, regulate the importation of new workers into the community, assert the dominance of a home-centered, vernacular spirituality over the official, parish-centered faith of the Roman Catholic Church in America, and reaffirm the central role of women both at home and in the larger community. Despite hostility from America's native-born, Anglo-Protestant majority, the du Pont Irish continued to wake their dead, drink whiskey, eat potatoes and cabbage, and christen their children with ancestral names like Bridget and Patrick. These folkways clearly defined the Irish as a distinct ethnic group with a distinct ethnic identity. Paradoxically, they simultaneously exhibited folkways associated with America's "dominant liberal social and political ideology of progress."[29] Like their native-born, white-collar counterparts, powder mill households amassed substantial savings accounts, and a sizeable number purchased real property. Irish families also signified their shifting identities through the purchase and use of various consumer goods. Workers' dwellings seldom had a separate parlor, but many powder mill homes boasted mahogany bureaus, tea sets, and other objects associated with respectability and gentility. While it restricted tenants in terms of what they could do to alter interior spaces, the company did allow residents of company-owned housing to appropriate certain exterior spaces for their exclusive use. Designed to strengthen worker loyalty to the company, this act had an added side effect: it reinforced the tenants' respect for "private" property rights. And finally, the du Pont Irish avidly pursued social mobility. All of the powder workers started out as common laborers, as did many skilled craftsmen and independent businessmen. More important, residents of this community eagerly embraced self-culture, the project of character building so dear to nineteenth-century hearts, because they astutely grasped its relationship to social advancement. No matter how insignificant to twenty-first-century sensibilities, steady work, decent wages, and a high expectation of achieving property, occupational, and upward mobility constituted dramatic gains for Irish immigrants; a greater spur to their bourgeois identity was the corresponding sense that they had finally acquired some control over their own lives.[30]

It has long been understood that individuals need a sense of self-agency in order both to interact effectively with others and reach their full potential as social beings. Moreover, that sense of self-agency must be nurtured from without as well as from within. Marx argued that wage earners necessarily lacked the capacity for independent egoism because the relations of production rendered them "purely material in their being."[31] This view, advanced to explain human behavior at a specific moment and place, now seems clearly reductionist. Today, social theorists contend that a person's sense of selfhood is a complex entity derived from a combination of factors, some material and biological, some relational, and some purely psychological.[32] Moreover, it is apparent from a large body of evidence that life in a modern, capitalist society mysteriously works to deflect alienation and immiseration. The definitive explication of this phenomenon is left for another author. Nevertheless, it seems reasonable to venture that high rates of upward mobility, home ownership, and literacy seem to have combined in this country with religious freedom, a decent standard of living, and political liberty to foster the average American worker's sense of personal autonomy, which, in turn, promoted a kind of empowerment. "Power," as one historian argues, "need not be a term applied exclusively to class analysis. Power can be measured much more subtly in terms of the goals held by immigrants and their ability to achieve them. No matter how insignificant the goals, the smaller the distance between ambition and achievement—at least from the immigrant's perspective—the greater the power held by an immigrant over his own life."[33] In other words, agency is a quality of life issue.

The lives of the du Pont Irish illuminate in a new way the presumed link between lived experience and self-agency. Like so many other groups of Irish Americans, Mary McDowell and her neighbors came to this country in search of life, liberty, and the pursuit of happiness, what might otherwise be termed self-determination. Above all else, social thought in the nineteenth-century United States stressed the right of *all* free persons to choose and shape autonomous selves, including wage-earning immigrants.[34] Though somewhat hindered by their economic condition, powder workers understood this dominant aspect of modern American culture and embraced it wholeheartedly.[35] From *their* perspective, then, it was not at all contradictory to hang lace curtains—the stereotypical Irish symbol of bourgeois domesticity—at the windows of their company-owned houses, or to harvest new potatoes for the community's Fourth of July celebration. These behaviors proclaimed the inhabitants' sense of themselves as simultaneously "Irish" and "American," "proletarian" and "bourgeois"; other actions evinced identities as "parents," "Catholics," "neighbors," or "consumers." How these various dimensions of consciousness actually came together is, of course, "a very complex business," and scholars "might be well-advised not to think we can really get to the bottom of it."[36] That said, the following chapters move simply in that direction.

CHAPTER I

Mutual Interests

Born in 1874, the son of an Irish saltpeter refinery worker and his wife, Philip Dougherty grew up in the powder mill community and eventually worked for the Du Pont Company himself. In a 1955 interview, he emphatically declared:

> I liked them all. All the du Ponts. I'll tell you why. Especially those fellows I worked under. I knew them all. I had a reason to like them. We called them by their first names. These du Ponts were good men. All of them. All that I saw around here. They were brainy. Didn't take any back step. They were good men. They were smart men, too. I don't believe we would ever have had this country if it hadn't been for Du Pont. I believe they saved this country, myself. I really do.[1]

Incorporated in 1801, Du Pont is one of the oldest continuously operating firms in the United States. It also has a long history of uninterrupted family control. During their first hundred years in America, the du Ponts worked hard to promote a sense of mutual interests between management and labor, and as Dougherty's statement suggests, they largely succeeded.[2] In fact, Du Pont's particular brand of paternalism has come under attack only in recent decades, and in places like Delaware, where Du Pont is still one of the largest private employers in the state, many people remain fiercely loyal.[3]

Since the word *paternalism* has many connotations, its use here deserves comment. Although rooted in the agrarian world of medieval serfdom, the concept was appropriated by Americans to describe the social and economic relationships that existed between slaves and planters, then apprentices and master craftsmen, and eventually, wage workers and industrialists. Over time, its interpretation and use have evolved considerably. For example, one historian has identified three distinct forms of industrial paternalism: *familiar,* like the face-to-face relationships that characterized small, semirural, industrial villages such as those along the Brandywine; *fraternal,* like the mid-sized manufacturing neighborhoods of Philadelphia; and *formal,* like the highly structured, impersonal environment of Lowell, Massachusetts, and other single-industry cities.[4] At the dawn of the nineteenth century, when the du Pont company began its operations, prospective industrialists shared an implicit understanding that, "Even in Republican America, where no nobility or rigid system of classes arrogated to itself a monopoly of rank, there was a visible social order based on the exercise of power by men of capital. With that power came a responsibility to use one's position as God's steward on Earth: to punish those who made mistakes or behaved wrongly, as parents punished children, and to reward the virtuous and competent."[5] Like parental authority, then, early industrial paternalism involved overlapping spheres of provision, protection, and control. In its initial stage of development, it also embodied a genuine commitment to fair dealing and reciprocal obligations.[6] As the industrial revolution progressed, however, rising competition from firms in the same product line forced many employers to change their approach. Seeking to maintain profits, they imposed speed-ups, cut wages, and implemented labor-saving technologies, practices only beneficial to management. Embittered wage earners retaliated with strikes and walk-outs. By the end of the century, mutualism had largely disappeared.

Along the Brandywine Creek, where the du Ponts established their home plant in 1802, various circumstances combined to nurture a familiar, mutualistic form of paternalism until at least the 1890s. The nature of the industry itself dictated a soft touch. Making black powder was a dangerous, highly skilled occupation, one that resisted mechanization and mass production. To recruit and retain a stable, knowledgeable workforce, officers of the du Pont company offered good wages, steady employment, opportunities for advancement, and benefits that included free housing, education, pensions, and interest-bearing savings accounts. In return, they expected employees to be loyal, subordinate, and deferential. Most workers accepted this arrangement as a condition of employment, yet they demanded fair treatment, respect, and autonomy, both at home and at work. The small size of the community enabled the du Ponts to know most of their employees by first name, and spatial proximity provided management and labor with intimate knowledge of each other's domestic life and problems. In addition, the mutualistic compact mirrored the reality of life as experienced both by Irish Catholics in Ireland and the du Ponts in France. In Ireland, deference to authority originally stemmed from the rundale system of land ownership, in which individuals received a share of communal property in exchange for their fealty to the head of the clan. While repeated invasions changed the ethnic and religious character of Ireland's landholders, the reciprocal obligations of landlords and tenants stayed the same.[7] As for the du Ponts, membership in the French nobility entitled them to receive the same deferential treatment as the landed gentry in Ireland, and imposed upon them the tradition of noblesse oblige. Although clearly hierarchical, the familiar, reciprocal nature of industrial paternalism resulted in a remarkable sense of community solidarity.

Like textile workers in New England and the southern Piedmont, residents frequently used a family analogy to describe everyday social relations.[8] Powder mill families employed this imagery to convey the very real networks that linked their households together, but it also encompassed the fictive bonds that tied them to the du Ponts. "All a sociable crowd and everybody seemed to be satisfied. . . . All the people knew each other," recalled one employee. "The men really loved Mr. Alfred," said another. In the past, historians interpreted these kinds of affective metaphors in terms of social control or simple nostalgia. From the worker's perspective, however, the allusion to kinship bespeaks a highly developed sense of place and attachment. By the end of the century, the Irish inhabitants of the waterside community actually referred to themselves as "crickers," a self-conscious label symbolizing their newfound identity. The du Pont company's approach to paternalism thus worked on many levels to initiate acculturation: Because it encouraged the social and economic advancement of Irish immigrants, mutualism inspired the allegiance of wage earners, linked their interests with those of the company, and facilitated their accommodation to life in industrial America.

Éleuthère Irénée du Pont de Nemours established his manufactory for black powder in 1802, only two years after his arrival in America. A bookish and rather shy sort of fellow, the twenty-five-year-old fled France after the Reign of Terror along with his wife, Sophie, and their three small children, his father, Pierre Samuel, his elder brother, Victor, and Victor's family.[9] The senior du Pont, a famed economist and a leading figure among the French Physiocrats, served as inspector general of commerce under Louis XVI and received a patent of nobility in 1784.[10] When revolutionaries challenged the ancien régime, Pierre Samuel defended his king and narrowly escaped the guillotine himself. By 1797, the du Ponts agreed that emigration offered their best hope of survival and chose the United States as their destination. Pierre Samuel had been corresponding with Thomas Jefferson for years and saw a young country teeming with opportunities; the family had also heard fascinating stories about the United States from Victor, who had been there twice on diplomatic missions. They sailed from La Rochelle on October 2, 1799, and landed on New Year's Day, 1800.[11]

Once settled in Bergen Point, New Jersey, the refugees quickly set about making a living for themselves. Before leaving France, they had optimistically formed the firm of du Pont de Nemours, Père et Fils et Cie. Pierre Samuel hoped ultimately to establish a rural, utopian commune based upon physiocratic principles, but in the meantime, he opened a commission house in nearby New York City to promote trade between Europe and America. Victor supported the project wholeheartedly, for the business world suited his gregarious personality. His younger sibling had other plans. E. I. du Pont, known familiarly as Irénée, preferred the natural world. As a child, he roamed the fields and forests of the family's estate, Bois de Fosses, gathering specimens for further study, and in 1786, he went to the government powder works at Essonne to study under Lavoisier, the great French chemist. Soon after his arrival in the United States, Irénée went hunting with a friend and discovered firsthand the poor quality of American-made gunpowder. When a little sleuthing indicated that American methods of manufacture were hopelessly outdated, he resolved to build his own powder mills. With some difficulty, Irénée convinced his father and brother to back the venture. He then returned to France to seek additional sponsors from among the family's many political acquaintances. On April 21, 1801, he filed papers in Paris organizing a new firm, E. I. du Pont de Nemours and Company, with a capital investment of $36,000 in eighteen shares of $2,000 each. Authorized to act on behalf of the stockholders, Irénée assumed full responsibility for the undertaking and returned eagerly to the United States to begin construction.[12]

During the fall of that year, du Pont visited Delaware to investigate a site on the Brandywine Creek, near Wilmington, as a possible location for the powder works. Although called a creek, the Brandywine is actually a river that originates in the hills of southeastern Pennsylvania. Cascading down through the rolling farmlands of northern New Castle County, it joins the navigable Christina River at Wilmington and from thence flows on to the Delaware River and bay. Between the Pennsylvania line and Wilmington, it falls one hundred feet in a course of four miles, providing an excellent source of water power.[13] By the time du Pont scouted its narrow, rock-strewn valley, an assortment of textile, grist, saw, and snuff mills already lined both banks. Additional mills flanked the Christina's two other tributaries, the Red Clay and White Clay creeks, making northern Delaware one of the young nation's leading industrial centers and Wilmington an important processing and distribution center.

Though a newcomer to America, Irénée knew a good place to build when he saw one. Delaware laws prohibited the sale of land to foreigners,

Fig. 1.1. Exterior view of powder mills after an explosion in 1890. The blast and resulting fire destroyed the light timber roofs and front walls, but left the distinctive stone structures intact. (Courtesy of Hagley Museum and Library)

so between April and June of 1802, he arranged for William Hamon, a naturalized Frenchman living in Wilmington, to purchase a site three miles north of the city. The ninety-five acre property belonged to Jacob Broom, a Quaker miller, who had previously operated a cotton factory there. In Wilmington, as in nearby Philadelphia and its hinterlands, Quakers controlled the milling, mercantile, and shipping industries, and Broom had a special knack for canny business deals.[14] True to form, he charged the Frenchman $6,740, well above the going price for real estate. Broom's own textile mill had burned down several years earlier, but, he maintained, the site still contained numerous support structures plus an impressive system of dams and races. Locals laughed aloud when they heard what du Pont paid. The rugged terrain clearly negated cultivation, and rebuilding the mill seemed ludicrous given the amount of local competition. As construction began that summer, their amusement quickly turned to curiosity.

Irénée wasted little time. Wilmington had a small colony of French-speaking émigrés from the West Indies, and he promptly recruited some of

Fig. 1.2. Drawing of Eleutherian Mills by E. I. du Pont's brother-in-law, Charles Dalmas, 1806. The du Pont mansion with its two-story piazza is shown on the hill overlooking the original powder yard. (Courtesy of Hagley Museum and Library)

them to dig foundations, cut timber, and haul materials. For the actual construction of the powder rolling mills, however, he turned to skilled local craftsmen, who found his plans puzzling. Using the good, blue granite that outcropped along the river banks for walls made sense. But each structure would have only three masonry sides. The fourth, which paralleled the Brandywine, required timber framing, as did the roof, which angled down toward the water. In his limited English, Irénée carefully explained how the unusual design served to minimize damage in the event of an explosion: A lightweight façade and sloping roof would direct the full force of any blast over the river and away from other buildings (fig. 1.1). As a further precaution, the mills would be built in pairs with open stretches of land between them. Irénée also allowed room for a network of fast-flowing races; these not only provided power, but a source of water to extinguish fires. Inside each mill, he planned to install a system of gears and shafts that transferred energy to a series of massive wooden pistons, each fitted into a shallow, cylindrical receptacle. Once the equipment became operational, trained powder men would pour into the receptacles various amounts of charcoal, sulphur, and saltpeter, which had been processed elsewhere on the property, and monitor the pistons as they pounded the raw ingredients together. With these plans made clear, the workmen easily followed Irénée's directions and began laying the foundations that summer.

Despite an auspicious start, the company's early years were fraught with difficulty. Bad weather, malaria, and material shortages caused numerous delays, and when the construction phase ended, Irénée still had to recruit and train operatives. As a result, the manufacture of gunpowder did not begin until May 1, 1804. Irénée proudly christened his first powder yard "Eleutherian Mills" (fig. 1.2) and by the end of the year the workmen produced 1,500 barrels of powder weighing 45,000 pounds. Most of it went to ordinary farmers, trappers, and sportsmen, but after rigorous tests by the federal government confirmed its superior quality, du Pont won a lucrative contract to supply the Army and Navy.[15] Still, the company seemed perpetually broke. Many customers, especially the federal government, failed to pay their bills promptly.[16] Then, on August 15, 1807, the first explosion rocked the powder yard. Although no one died, the damage severely slowed production and added to du Pont's financial burden. Ordinarily, he would have turned to his father and brother for help, but by this date, they were bankrupt, too. When another explosion occurred in 1811, the firm's financial prospects dove sharply downward.

The War of 1812 offered a welcome reprieve. As government orders poured in, Irénée channeled all of his profits back into the company and daringly purchased another thirty-two acres of previously developed land along the river. The Hagley yard opened on this property in 1814, bringing the number of men working in and around the powder mills to nearly a hundred. By interrupting the importation of British manufactured goods, the war stimulated other American enterprises as well, particularly textiles. Seizing the new opportunity, Irénée invested in two new ventures: the Du Pont, Bauduy, and Company woolen mill, which he established for Victor's benefit on the opposite bank of the Brandywine, and Duplanty, McCall, and Company's cotton manufactory, which a friend operated downstream at Hagley.[17] The textile mills provided an important supplementary source of employment for the community, and many families had members in both industries. During the war years, however, most Brandywine men worked in the powder yards, where high wages offset the threat of explosion.

An extremely volatile craft, powder manufacturing required cool heads and practiced hands. For this reason, Irénée initially recruited several experienced powder men from France, but they demanded outrageous salaries and challenged him at every turn. Frustrated, he considered training some of the common laborers employed around the property. In addition to the émigrés from San Domingo, who spoke French but comprised a finite labor supply, Irénée had begun hiring Irish immigrants, who spoke English but outnumbered other wage-earning populations and accepted lower wages to boot. Despite these advantages, he questioned the Irish aptitude for powder making, saying, "It will be, I believe, impossible to educate a skilled worker from the race of Irish workers which they have in this country. I have employed nearly a hundred of them this last year and in this quantity there were no more than two whom I would want to work for me in the mill."[18] Market forces prevailed. In April 1804, Irénée hand-picked seven apprentices, including four Irishmen.[19] Their success surprised and pleased him. Training from within became an official company policy, and the French and French-speaking workmen soon faded into the background.

After 1805, the company assigned all new hands—with the exception of masons, wheelwrights, coopers, and other craftsmen—to either general or outdoor labor. General laborers shoveled materials, cleaned equipment, hauled supplies, dug foundations, erected buildings, excavated races, cleared land, and mended fences. Outdoor laborers tended livestock, planted and harvested crops, maintained orchards, and cleaned the stables. "No worker was admitted to the powder yard unless he had been a considerable time at our outdoor work," Irénée later wrote. This trial period allowed new employees to familiarize themselves with the layout of the property and the flow of industrial time. More important, it exposed them to the hazards of the job. General laborers, in particular, worked in close proximity to the powder mills, but even the outdoor men faced tremendous risks. The system also gave du Pont an opportunity to assess their potential and ability to take orders. Because he personally supervised the yards, Iré-née came to know his employees well. He readily accepted those who seemed "peaceful," "steady," and "good-natured," and who "behaved faithfully and conducted themselves well." He deliberately rejected men who believed "that because they have crossed the ocean they ought to make a rapid fortune" and made all immigrants commit to a considerable length of employment before they struck out on their own.[20] In exchange, a promising candidate could expect to be made a helper at the saltpeter refinery, the press house, the charcoal house, the pounding mill, or the rolling mills. In time, he might advance to second workman, then head workman. Alternatively, du Pont hired some on as company clerks or storekeepers, and apprenticed others to company coopers, millwrights, and machinists. Implemented under the tenets of mutual interests, in-house training benefited labor and management alike.

Workmen who espoused the mutualistic contract could expect a steady income, too, one that rose according to occupation. In the 1810s, du Pont's common laborers started out at $10 per month, but skilled powder men received anywhere from $23 to $27. After the war years ended, wages throughout the United States fell and the gap between du Pont's common laborers and powder workers narrowed. By the 1830s, the former earned a monthly base wage of $15.50 and the latter got $20 or $24 depending on the nature of their position. Local textile workers, by comparison, received $18 or $19, whereas farmhands, who worked on a seasonal basis, averaged about $10. Twenty-five miles away, Irish men digging the Chesapeake and Delaware Canal counted themselves lucky to bring home $8–9 for the same period of time.[21] Because the mills often ran around the clock when a large order had to be filled, powder men accrued overtime pay as well. Thus laborer William Green went "to the powder" in 1820, and within a few years, his base income reached $20 per month. Like other long-term employees, he also enjoyed the benefit of free housing, which raised his real earnings considerably. On January 12, 1835, the Irishman advanced again; as foreman of the Upper Yard, a position he held until his death in 1847, his monthly earnings exceeded $40 per month, not counting income from his wife and children.[22] Of course, not all men achieved this level of success. Highly skilled, foremen comprised a small, elite group. Still, the example provided by Green and others led many unskilled Irish immigrants to believe that they, too, could rise in American society.

By training and promoting its own workmen—a policy that persisted throughout the nineteenth century—the du Pont company intended more than social control; it aimed ultimately to stimulate upward mobility. This goal reflected the influence of Irénée's father. Though a titled member of the nobility, Pierre Samuel du Pont de Nemours began life as the son of a common Paris watchmaker and shopkeeper. His early experiences as an apprentice convinced him that there were only two kinds of people in the world, wage earners and profit makers. Anyone could move up into the profit-making class (as his own father, Samuel, had done), but real wealth required land. The young artisan regularly expounded upon his theories to the minor intelligentsia, and he eventually came to the attention of Diderot, Voltaire, and other *philosophes*. In 1763, he wrote the first of many influential pamphlets, "Reflections on the Wealth of the State," which neatly encapsulated not only his own ideas about the value of property, but those of other notable French economists.[23] "Reflections" soon caught the eye of Dr. François de Quesnay, personal physician to the Marquise de Pompadour and one of the most influential men at Versailles. Quesnay took the twenty-three-year-old under his wing and encouraged him to produce other articles, reports, and theoretical essays on the subject of laissez-faire economics. By the end of 1764, Pierre Samuel had become editor of the *Journal de l'Agriculture, du Commerce et du Finances* and a protégé of Turgot and Mirabeau as well as Quesnay. The following year witnessed the publication of his most ambitious work to date, *Physiocracy*. Drawn from the classical Greek, the new term referred to du Pont's belief in a political economy based upon the natural, physical laws of the universe. Adherents hoped that by applying these laws to existing, man-made systems they could create a world of peace and plenty. When the Physiocrats' dream fell victim to the guillotine, du Pont drew up a prospectus for a utopian commune, Pontiana, which he intended to establish across the Atlantic. In keeping with Physiocratic principles, every member would be a free person, every man would be a self-sufficient tiller of the soil, and everyone would work together to guarantee mutual security and economic well-being. Laborers would have access to land, and by farming it collectively, they would rise in society and become independent freeholders themselves. Where better to launch his new enterprise than the United States, he argued, "where liberty, safety and independence really exist in a temperate climate, [and] where land is fertile and bountiful."[24] Unfortunately, only a few of du Pont's influential acquaintances came forward to invest, and rising land values in America greatly exceeded the little money he amassed for the venture. Undaunted, Pierre Samuel passed his beliefs on to his son, instead. "All workmen who are wise have large savings and buy farms," he told Irénée.[25]

E. I. du Pont shared these republican convictions and in the tradition of noblesse oblige promised to assist all those in his employ, saying, "It is my intent as well as my character to better their situation as much as possible."[26] It was not an idle boast. Around 1813, Irénée instituted a savings plan whereby workers in the powder yards accrued 6 percent interest on balances with the company of more than $100. If a workman could not amass enough capital, du Pont helped him establish credit and buy property in the vicinity. When and if employees opted to leave Delaware, he wrote them letters of recommendation and urged them to check in periodically with his agents in other cities.[27] Through these and other policies, the company founder established an important precedent for the future.

Another demonstration of du Pont's paternalism came in June 1815. While the men labored to fill a large government order, the pounding mill exploded, causing $20,000 more damage and the firm's first fatalities.[28] Eight workmen died instantly, but a ninth, Patrick Dougherty, lingered, horribly, for several days. Born near the port town of Malin, in the northernmost tip of County Donegal, he had come to the Brandywine in the spring of 1807. Within a few years, Patrick became a press man, compacting the loose powder into the hard, flat cakes that comprised stage two of the manufacturing process. It was dangerous work—like all jobs in the powder yards—but it paid $18 per month. Because he boarded with his older brother, Richard, and sister-in-law, Ann, Dougherty's personal expenses were few, and most of his earnings went straight into a company-sponsored savings account. As death approached, Dougherty carefully dictated his will to his trusted employer, Irénée du Pont, and Thomas Ritchie, a fellow powder worker. The two men later signed an affidavit indicating that,

> The said Patrick desired . . . that in the case of his death . . . he wished all the money he had in the hands of his employers and all other property of which he should die possessed, should go to and be given for the use of the wife or widow and children of his brother, Richard Dougherty, who likewise lost his life by the accident aforesaid, excepting however that in case two of his nephews for whom he had sometime since written, should come from Ireland, then and in that case it was his desire that their passages might be paid for out of his estate.[29]

Du Pont readily complied with Dougherty's wishes. After laying the thirty-five-year-old immigrant to rest beside his brother and taking the necessary deductions for his funeral expenses, Irénée transferred a balance of $761.96 from Patrick's account to Ann's. It was a princely sum, especially when added to the $601.25 that she inherited from Richard. The other widows also received their husband's earnings. Nevertheless, a one-time windfall provided no assurance for the future, and several of the company's best men quit in response to the explosion. Like Patrick Dougherty, they feared for their families' long-term security. In keeping with his mutualistic ethos, Irénée responded with a new policy: He promised each widow a pension of

$100 a year plus free housing for as long as she remained unmarried and lived on company property.[30] The new practice persuaded several men to return and convinced the majority to stay as well. Most of the jobs available to Irish immigrants in nineteenth-century America carried the risk of death or disability, but with du Pont, workmen had at least some insurance for their dependents.

The workmen soon faced another test of loyalty. On March 19, 1818, the graining house, pounding mill, and powder magazine exploded in swift succession.[31] The force of the blast, which reverberated for miles, uprooted nearby trees and hurled rocks and debris through the air, damaging buildings and breaking windows as they went. The community mobilized quickly. A group of women, including du Pont's adult daughters, tended the wounded in a makeshift hospital. Two fortunate men, who had been thrown over a hundred yards, received minor bruises. Thirty-six others died, including a workman's wife and a child. Only eight of the bodies could be identified, and a detail formed to pick up the scattered remains of the others. It was gruesome work. Bits of human flesh landed all the way at Louviers, Victor's home across the river; his houseguest at the time, a veteran of the Napoleonic wars, felt so sickened that he removed to a hotel in Wilmington. But of the sixty-odd powder workers, only two decided to quit. The rest remained faithful, insisting that since every man had to die eventually, he might just as well "go across the creek"—their euphemism for being killed in an explosion.

Away on business when the tragedy occurred, Irénée raced back to the Brandywine, where he learned that the overseer had been absent and that the yard foreman, who had been drinking, had ordered the operator of the graining mill to run the machinery too quickly. In the graining mill, men used machines of various sizes to break cakes of compressed powder into chunks, which were then sifted through sieves into various sized grains of powder. When the equipment overheated, the powder in the mill ignited. Shocked at this blatant disregard for safety, Irénée fired the foreman, a Frenchman named Augustus d'Autrement, and ordered his eldest son, Alfred Victor, home from college to take d'Autrement's place. Thereafter, he stipulated, at least one male family member must be present in the yard at all times. By this means, du Pont hoped to enforce safety regulations and prevent further accidents; by putting himself and his sons directly in harm's way, he cemented further the bond between employer and employee.

In hindsight, policies like these undoubtedly enhanced the firm's long-term viability, but du Pont was no seer. In fact, Irénée remained deeply in debt, and a lesser man might have succumbed to the temptation to exploit his employees. He certainly had many reasons to do so. Over the years, he had borrowed heavily from several Philadelphia banks, and he still owed money to creditors and shareholders in France. Incensed at the paltry dividends du Pont paid out, one came personally to the Brandywine to investigate and another sent his eldest son. In addition, one of the firm's local investors, a Haitian-born planter named Peter Bauduy, had been accusing Irénée of financial mismanagement since 1806; in 1816, Bauduy finally filed suit in the Delaware Court of Chancery to dissolve the powder company altogether. Even du Pont's subsidiary ventures were failing. After the Treaty of Ghent, Great Britain flooded American markets with cheap textiles and the du Pont, Bauduy, and Company woolen mill fell into arrears along with the Duplanty, McCall, and Company cotton factory.[32] To make matters worse, Pierre Samuel died in 1817 and Irénée assumed the debts of du Pont de Nemours, Père et Fils et Cie. Despite these problems, he refused to cut wages. Instead, he slashed dividends. Believing that his primary economic responsibilities owed to his creditors and employees, Irénée directed all revenue toward interest payments and fixed costs. Even his own share, as director of company, totaled a mere fraction of the amount to which the terms of incorporation entitled him.

Irénée's familial responsibilities weighed heavily as well. Before her death in 1828, Sophie du Pont bore her husband a total of seven children, all of whom came of age during the powder company's most tumultuous years. Daughter Victorine, the eldest, had married Peter Bauduy's only son in 1816, but his sudden death after the honeymoon returned her to the Brandywine, where she eventually took her mother's place as mistress of Eleutherian Mills. Also dependent upon Irénée's largesse in the 1810s were: daughter Evelina, her husband, James Bidermann, and their child, James, Jr.; son Alfred, his wife, Margaretta Lammot, and their six children; daughter Eleuthera and her husband, Dr. Thomas Mackie Smith; daughter Sophie, who planned to marry her first cousin, Samuel F. du Pont, the future Rear Admiral; sons Henry and Alexis, who also meant to wed soon; his brother-in-law, Charles Dalmas; and Victor's family, who seemed needier than ever.

Fortunately, the next decade brought stability. The Brandywine mills continued to produce the highest quality black powder in the United States. With the proceeds, Irénée finally managed to repay one of his major French benefactors, his father's old friend, Tallyrand. Meanwhile, Victor handed over his woolen mill to the care of his son, Charles, and entered the political arena. An advocate of high protective tariffs and an admirer of Henry Clay, he used his Gallic charm to form a local Whig party. Always the soberer of the two brothers, Irénée steered clear of elected offices, but gladly became a director of the Bank of the United States, where he advised Nicholas Biddle on matters of economic policy. In 1829 du Pont's own finances took a turn for the better when the courts settled Bauduy's suit in his favor.[33] He celebrated by refinancing his outstanding debts and breaking ground for a third powder yard.

Everyday life in the community improved as well. Expansion produced new opportunities for advancement as well as new jobs. Even more profound changes occurred in the area of employee benefits. Like other manufacturers in the region, du Pont built and largely subsidized a voluntary Sunday school. Here, the Irish children could learn to read and write and cipher alongside their American neighbors. Here, too, they could study theology, but without fear of proselytizing. A Deist, Irénée tolerated all denominations and made sure that each pupil encountered the requisite catechism for his or her faith. Attendance at the Brandywine Manufacturers Sunday School rose significantly after du Pont inaugurated another new program. Aware that many of his Irish workmen left wives and children behind, he allowed them to charge trans-Atlantic tickets against a prepaid account and work off the debt after the passengers arrived. Very quickly thereafter, the Irish also received permission to bring out parents, siblings, nieces, nephews, cousins, and neighbors. As Alfred I. du Pont later explained to one of the immigration agents, the practice clearly caused "trouble and responsibility," yet the company "was indebted to the men for their good conduct" and it was "but a small regard for the attachment" workers demonstrated toward their employers.[34]

A related policy required the company to locate heirs when employees died. According to a ca. 1820 list of explosion victims and their next of kin, du Pont's clerks sometimes had difficulty doing so. A notation next to powder man John Brady's name read, "inquire of J. Brady in town." Other entries included "ask William McGraw," "has a brother here," "father and mother in Ireland," "sister in Cork," and "widow."[35] The case of Henry Kyle is particularly revealing. An Irish immigrant who went "across the creek" in 1834, Kyle "entered the service of Messrs du Pont in 1825" and managed "by his industry and saving" to accumulate a considerable amount of personal property "amounting at present including interest to upward of $2000." Because Kyle died intestate, the du Ponts contacted his mother and only legal heir, Anne Mullin, in Ireland. When a man claiming to be Kyle's father came forward to contest the award, the company retained the services of several lawyers and detectives in Ireland and tried to sort out the matter. Their investigation revealed that Kyle was illegitimate and that the plaintiff, Henry Kyle, Sr., had had little or nothing to do with his offspring during his lifetime. After Mullin's death, her three other children continued to litigate for ten years. During this period, Alfred I. du Pont and William Warner, a company agent, held the money in trust. It eventually went to the deceased man's siblings.[36]

Not long after Kyle's death, the community finally lost its *pater familias*

*Fig. 1.3. Portrait of Éleuthère Irénée du Pont, founder
of E. I. du Pont de Nemours and Company.* (Courtesy
of Hagley Museum and Library)

(fig. 1.3). While in Philadelphia to meet with his creditors on the morning of October 31, 1834, E. I. du Pont de Nemours suffered a heart attack and collapsed on the sidewalk. He died later that day, far from his beloved Brandywine and doubtful that the company could survive without him at the helm. According to family legend, Irénée considered his eldest son and heir an unlikely successor. At thirty-six, Alfred Victor du Pont was a brilliant chemist but meek and unsure of his managerial abilities. Ordered home from Dickinson College in Philadelphia following the great explosion of 1818, he served a full apprenticeship in the powder yards, and then became superintendent of the Upper Yard. Following his father's funeral, he surprised everyone by insisting that his brother-in-law, James Bidermann, take control temporarily. Bidermann accepted. The son of a Swiss banker, he had been Irénée's right-hand man since 1814 and knew well the firm's daily affairs and financial problems. He soon managed to pay off all of the firm's

French debts, including those of Pierre Samuel.[37] Meanwhile, the heir apparent spent his days in the office, learning the administrative aspects of the business and preparing to take over.

When Alfred finally assumed control in 1837, he naturally vowed to fill his father's shoes. As predicted, he proved ill-suited to the task. Despite several years under Bidermann's tutelage, he showed little interest in management or finance, preferring instead to conduct experiments in a lab he had had built beside the company office. The day-to-day operations of the powder yards gradually fell to his younger brothers, Henry and Alexis. Alfred had his hands full directing sales, signing letters, paying bills, and keeping books for the growing concern.[38]

During the 1830s and 1840s, the Delaware plant grew to include four powder yards with structures and land worth nearly $500,000. Western expansion, the rising demand for coal, and conflicts like the Mexican War all boosted demand. Before his death, Irénée began experimenting with new equipment to make the production process faster and safer; consequently, each new powder mill housed within its distinctive, sloped-roof structure a massive pair of eight-ton, marble wheels seated vertically in a large, round, wooden basin. As the wheels rotated, the powder men poured in the appropriate amounts of sulphur, charcoal, and saltpeter, and carefully monitored the texture and temperature of the resulting mixture.[39] Because of their size, these new rolling mills proved especially efficient. In 1849 alone the Brandywine yards produced 89,855 kegs, which the company then distributed among the fifty-seven agencies that sold du Pont products throughout the United States. By that time, the company also owned five textile mills, a keg mill, and several farmsteads in surrounding Christiana and Brandywine hundreds (fig. 1.4). But with this growth came new debts and difficulties.

The problems were manifold. Another terrible explosion had occurred on April 14, 1847, killing eighteen men and causing the worst property damage in the company's history. The number of widows receiving pensions and free rents rose accordingly. At the same time, the company's expenditure for prepaid passages out of Ireland reached an all-time high: When word of the Great Hunger reached American shores, du Pont employees scrambled to save their kin, and by mid-century, the population of the community had risen to more than 2,000 souls.[40] Strangely, however, many of the firm's financial difficulties seemed to stem from mismanaged funds and resources. After repeated requests, the family ordered Alfred to produce detailed balance sheets. They revealed that the company's new debts totaled in excess of $500,000, that Alfred had repeatedly used the company's cash, credit, and workmen for personal projects, and that he just could not keep accurate accounts. Disturbed and disappointed, his siblings asked Alfred to cede control to his younger brother Henry.[41]

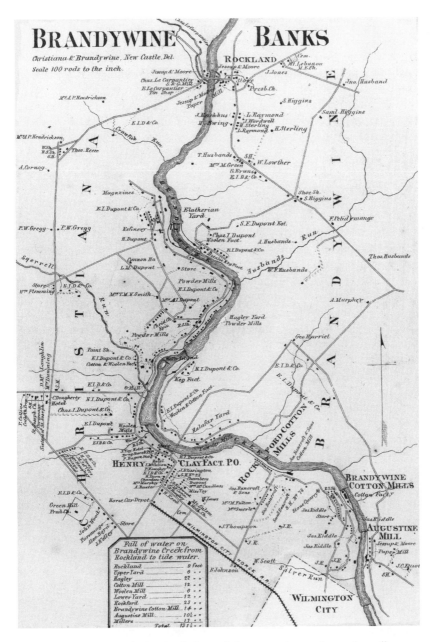

Fig. 1.4. Map of "Brandywine Banks," one of the names given to the powder mill community in the nineteenth century. Taken from D. G. Beers, Atlas of the State of Delaware (1868). (Courtesy of Hagley Museum and Library)

The sixth of Irénée du Pont's seven children, Henry assumed the presidency of E. I. du Pont de Nemours and Company in 1850. Daguerreotypes show a short, stocky man with his grandfather's bulbous nose; the du Pont family's characteristic cleft chin hid behind a fiery red beard. A graduate of West Point, a staunch Whig, and an avowed Deist, he was a shrewd businessman and a born leader. Like his brother, Henry served a complete apprenticeship, working his way up from laborer to powder man, and he readily supported the tenets of mutual interests. Unlike his predecessor, however, the new, thirty-eight-year-old director constantly monitored the yards. In truth, no aspect of the business escaped his notice, whether the need for a new foreman or the assignment of company housing. The men took to calling him "Boss Henry," a sure sign of the power he wielded (fig. 1.5).[42]

Charged with correcting the firm's finances, the new president moved decisively into action. First, he cut transportation costs by purchasing Conestoga wagons to take the powder to market. In the past, the company paid others to carry its kegs. Then he bypassed additional middlemen by constructing his own wharf and warehouses along the Delaware River. Within the powder yards themselves, he laid railroad tracks and commissioned special push-carts to facilitate the efficient transfer of materials. When explosions occurred, as they inevitably did, Henry used the opportunity to build larger structures and install new equipment. Other practices were purely symbolic: He continued to use inexpensive candles and quill pens in the office, and on his long walks around the powder yards he picked up random twigs of willow to add to the charcoal pile.[43]

Recalling how his father had handled hard times, Boss Henry decided not to touch wages or the production process. This strategy had important consequences for the powder workers. Elsewhere in the United States and in other industries, increasing competition encouraged many firms to implement supervision, time-keeping, and labor-saving devices as part of their efforts to increase productivity, reduce fixed costs, and raise profits. By the 1850s, these employers typically viewed workers as an abstract "labor pool," not as individuals.[44] With this change in perception, working conditions deteriorated. Long hours, low wages, unsafe surroundings, and limited occupational mobility became the norm, and laborers expressed their frustration by staging more frequent strikes and demonstrations. But not those along the Brandywine. Du Pont's dominant position in the gun powder market protected the company from pressures to rationalize, economize, and organize. The du Pont plant also remained relatively small compared to other manufactories, with a combined workforce of fewer than 200 men. Moreover, most employees were Irish immigrants from western Ulster, rural folk who may have welcomed the economic and

*Fig. 1.5. Portrait of "Boss" Henry du Pont, sixth
child of E. I. du Pont and third president of E. I.
du Pont de Nemours and Company.* (Courtesy of
Hagley Museum and Library)

social protection that a familiar, mutualistic form of paternalism provided.
And finally, the volatile nature of powder manufacture precluded most attempts to boost output. As a result, du Pont employees enjoyed a high degree of autonomy.

Whether at work or at home, residents of the powder mill community
found many ways to assert their independence. For example, there are frequent accounts of men skipping work because they wanted to attend social
events, travel, or fulfill personal and familial obligations.[45] Others came and
went as their finances dictated. Thus Michael Callahan worked at the Upper
Yard from June 29 to August 24, 1818, then again from December 2, 1818, to
September 9, 1824, and again from October 21, 1824, to October 18, 1825.
He continued to work sporadically through the next two decades. Alcohol
consumption remained a crucial part of Irish culture, and despite rules prohibiting drunkenness on the job, some men indulged anyway, certain in the
knowledge that repeat offenders would eventually lose their jobs.[46] More
rarely, company records reveal acts of industrial sabotage and espionage.

One powder man, evidently smarting from a recent reprimand, caused a minor explosion in 1852, and another offered his services to a du Pont competitor in 1857.[47] Workers proved equally self-directed away from the powder yards. Despite free access to the Brandywine Manufacturers Sunday School, parents had different ideas about education and often put their children to work. Being Irish, they held different religious beliefs as well. While most of E. I. du Pont's heirs had converted to Episcopalianism by the 1850s, their employees remained staunch Catholics or Presbyterians. And finally, a significant percentage of families simply moved away. Some individuals bought farms, moved west, served apprenticeships in Philadelphia or Wilmington, or accompanied relatives to other manufacturing communities.[48] The vast majority stayed, however, suggesting that service to the du Pont company continued to offer a reasonable expectation of success.

The distribution of power among the company's partners and the policies they enacted directly affected the persistence of this expectation. After Alfred Victor's death on October 1, 1856, his siblings reorganized the company. Henry received eighteen shares and Alexis fifteen. The remaining twenty-four were divided evenly among Victorine, Sophie, Eleuthera, and Alfred's eldest son, Éleuthère Irénée. Henry remained president, but Alexis controlled the production side of the business. A warm, outgoing man, the baby of the family, Alexis favored experimentation and innovation much more than his brothers. Given the distribution of shares, the du Pont company might have had a very different history had he not suffered an untimely death. Instead, while Alexis was helping several workmen remove a large, heavy, wooden, mixing box from a rolling mill on August 22, 1857, a spark ignited the powder residue in the bottom of the box and caused a chain reaction of explosions in the Upper Yard. The force of the flying debris crushed his leg and chest. When he died the following day, there remained no one to question Henry's control of the company or its conservative direction.[49]

The community soon faced another turning point: The Civil War. Strong nationalists, the du Ponts opposed the very thought of secession. During the Nullification crisis of 1832, Irénée refused an order for gunpowder from South Carolina, and when the same state opened fire on Fort Sumter in 1861, Henry canceled all sales to his southern agents. Neither did the family favor war. Henry's oldest son, Henry Algernon du Pont, stood ready to graduate from West Point that spring, and Sophie's husband, Samuel F. du Pont, the future Rear Admiral, commanded the Philadelphia Naval Yard. As the fighting escalated, both men saw active duty. The other male du Ponts, along with 214 full-time employees, received special exemptions from the federal government and dedicated the powder yards to the Union cause.

Sales to the Army and Navy quickly exceeded $1 million. Because of the time and effort required to build new mills, production increased primarily through overtime, and wages rose along with profits. In 1863 powder men received $25 to $30 a month as their base salary alone. In just six months, Darby McAteer earned $158, while his foreman, William Gibbons, earned $238.[50] Residents of the community undoubtedly enjoyed the extra income, but they could also take pride in the unique contribution they made to the war effort. After the battle of Antietam in western Maryland, rumors abounded that Southern spies and saboteurs might target the Brandywine complex. In response, Henry petitioned the legislature in Dover for military protection and quickly organized his least essential workmen into two armed units. As Lee's army moved northward in the summer of 1863, the Governor of Delaware made Henry du Pont Major General of the state militia and stationed the home guards at the powder yards for the duration of the conflict.[51]

The mills operated more or less continuously by this point. In addition to the federal government, the company also supplied most of the domestic market for powder, especially in the west. As a result of this speed-up, the packing room exploded on February 26, 1863, destroying 10,000 pounds of powder and killing thirteen men. Following custom, Henry organized a detail of men to collect the bloody bits and pieces, and closed the yards for the mass funeral. Two other explosions followed later that year, bringing the death toll to forty. By June of 1864, the Bureau of Army Ordnance owed more than $350,000 and Henry had to raise prices in order to meet the soaring costs of wages, materials, and repairs.[52] The demands of wartime production, then, laid the foundation for renewed attention to safety and expenses during Reconstruction.

In the 1870s, three trends developed that would have enormous repercussions for management-labor relations. First, the du Pont company began aggressively expanding and consolidating its role as leader of the American powder industry. Dozens of small powder mills had arisen during the war years, and beginning in 1865, the federal government began to auction its surplus powder at rock-bottom prices. Du Pont still controlled 42 percent of the market, but falling prices and rising competition aroused the need for some stability and order within the industry. In 1872 Henry convinced nine other firms to join a new Gunpowder Trade Association, or "Powder Trust," which set wages and controlled production. Lammot du Pont, Alfred Victor's second-oldest son, served as its first president. Under his leadership, the trust forced many independent powder companies out of business. One by one, the du Pont company bought out its smaller competitors and secretly acquired a controlling share of its major rival, Hazard Powder. By the 1890s, the firm owned full or controlling interests in powder mills in California, New York, Georgia, Pennsylvania, New Jersey, Tennessee, Massachusetts, and Iowa, making du Pont the largest powder concern in the United States, if not the world.[53]

Second, family members began to question whether periodic wage increases, free housing, pension plans, and other forms of direct assistance should be based on economic considerations or on the continuing welfare of workers. Widows' pensions posed special problems. The du Ponts genuinely felt that they owed widows compensation, but the financial commitment was taxing. During the Civil War years alone, forty men died on the job; by the early 1870s, the company owed lifetime pensions and free housing to thirty women. Under pressure from his relatives, Henry finally decided to hold widows' pensions to a lump sum of $500, and limited annuities and free housing to a period of five years. By 1880, only twelve widows remained on the company rolls.[54]

The third trend concerned the company's production process. Lammot du Pont, Alfred Victor's son, conducted several studies of labor efficiency in the powder yards. He concluded that too many powder workers shirked their duties and neglected safety precautions. According to his cousin and colleague, Francis Gurney du Pont, the powder men had become "a set of lazy rascals who think themselves hard worked to do 1/4 hour work out of every hour."[55] Although prohibited from taking any kind of metal into the powder yards, workers sometimes used copper and iron hammers instead of the wooden ones required. The company also banned matches, tobacco, coins, penknives, and shoes with nailed soles, but workmen found ways to smuggle these items into the mills. Further reports indicated that some employees ran equipment too quickly and that others knowingly used improper procedures. Most workers simply viewed these policy violations as shortcuts. To the company, such negligence could and often did cause explosions. Based on these findings, Henry authorized additional safety precautions as well as several new labor-saving machines, yet he refused to adopt any of the time-saving measures.[56] Crucial aspects of the powder-making process thus remained the domain of highly skilled, autonomous workmen even as other aspects of production became increasingly streamlined.

When Boss Henry died in 1889, the company's administrative structure changed again. The new partners were: Alexis's three sons, Eugene, Alexis I., Jr., and Francis (Frank); Boss Henry's eldest son, Henry Algernon; Alfred Victor's grandson, Alfred I.; and Victor's grandson, Charles Irénée. Though the presidency passed to Eugene, he actually shared control of the business with Frank. Both men preferred the laboratory over the powder yards, and consequently the brothers were "not [as well] liked by the working people" as their father or Uncle Henry.[57] It was in recognition of this fact that their cousin, Lammot, had been groomed for the presidency, but conflicts with Boss Henry over the direction of the company had compelled Lammot to found a subsidiary of his own in 1880. Technically a joint venture between du Pont, Hazard, and Laflin and Rand, the Repauno Chemical Company manufactured dynamite in New Jersey. Because everyone expected that Lammot would eventually return to take his rightful place along the Brandywine, his death during an 1884 explosion inaugurated a power struggle among the male members of the family. Henry Algernon du Pont, who had long headed the sales division, assumed that he would succeed his father. His brother, William, blocked this move. Boss Henry's two sons were fourteen years apart in age, and a deep-seated antagonism existed between them. As a result, the mantle of leadership fell to Eugene, the company's general manager and eldest of the three remaining partners.[58]

Eugene first joined the company in 1863 at the age of twenty-three, but his years of service had not prepared him for the role of president. A quiet, even aloof man, he adored research and received two patents for an improved type of charcoal. Eugene also authorized the construction of a new plant at Carney's Point, New Jersey, for the development and production of a smokeless gunpowder. Despite these contributions, scholars characterize his administration as "stagnant." Like Boss Henry, Eugene hated to delegate authority, yet he lacked his uncle's confidence and forcefulness. Having lived most of his adult life in the shadow of others, Eugene contentedly maintained the status quo.[59]

While Eugene assumed the administrative duties of the presidency, Frank took charge of day-to-day operations. Second only to Lammot du Pont in terms of his chemical knowledge, Frank was "conservative," "authoritarian," "pious," and "demanding."[60] Also like Lammot, Frank believed that management should direct the manufacturing process, and his efforts to tighten control and boost efficiency raised the level of "ill feeling" among the workmen. He stopped paying wages during slack periods, laid off twelve long-standing employees, and brought in outsiders to construct a new building on company property. Seldom present in the powder yards, Frank asked an assistant, Pierre Gentieu, to keep him informed of the men and their problems.

The era of "mutual interests" was ending and workers knew it. A small minority responded by forming a secret society, the "Never Sweats," and turned to arson, threats of violence, and anonymous letters for redress. The protesters held Frank du Pont personally responsible for reneging on his family's pledge of security, and on December 26, 1889, they set fire to one of the company's barns. Additional fires soon followed, and sources have even suggested that the Never Sweats caused an explosion in 1890. "Arson," said

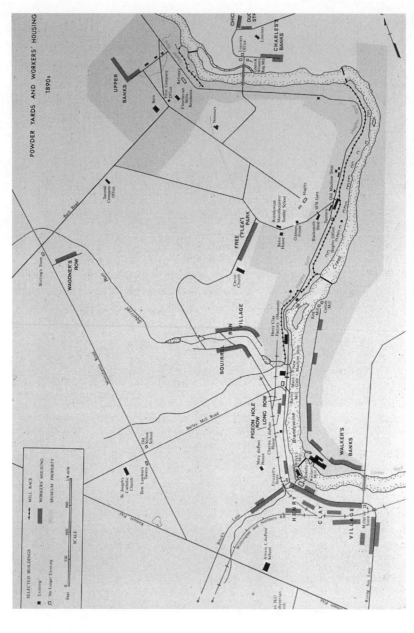

Fig. 1.6. Conjectural map of the powder mill community in the 1890s, showing the location of all four powder yards and the major clusters of workers' housing. Taken from Glenn Porter, The Workers World at Hagley (1981). (Courtesy of Hagley Museum and Library)

convicted barn-burner Edward Clark, "was the only way to get square as you were not sure of employment from one day to another with Frank du Pont."[61] No more than a handful of employees participated in the violence, and the three men convicted were a farm tenant, a former mason, and an unemployed carpenter, not powder men. Nevertheless, the 1890s marked an important shift in employer-employee relations.

Increasing contact with the city of Wilmington accelerated the decline of familiar paternalism at the du Pont powder mills. E. I. du Pont deliberately chose a secluded spot for his manufactory, but the community was never isolated or self-sufficient. The Wilmington City Railway Company extended its horse-drawn trolley service to Rising Sun Lane in 1864, and the Wilmington and Northern Railway ran a spur line to Wagoner's Row in 1884 (fig. 1.6). By the 1890s, monthly wages averaged from $40 to $50 and, with house rents ranging between $24 and $60 per year, many families used their discretionary income to shop, dine, and socialize in town. As rows of inexpensive and moderately priced housing arose along the railway lines, some workers bought property within city limits and commuted to the powder mills. Cheap public transportation also encouraged the employment of unskilled Italian laborers, whom the new managers increasingly preferred to the established Irish workforce. In Alfred I. du Pont's opinion, "An Italian will do what he is told, whereas an Irishman is apt to get to thinking of some way to do it better."[62] Some of the Italians moved their families out of the city and into the newly vacant company houses of the upwardly mobile Irish, but others preferred Wilmington's ethnic neighborhoods. At the same time, residents of the Brandywine began commuting to jobs in the city. After the Civil War, Wilmington's most significant industries included ship and railroad car building, foundry work, tanning, and carriage making. These offered well-paying and safer alternatives to work in the powder mills.[63] James Toy's father, a second-generation Irish-American, worked as a carpenter in the downtown railroad car shops. "You couldn't get him into powder," Toy recalled. Richard Rowe's father, the son of a Fermanagh family, became a carriage painter. "I don't know the name of the man he learned his trade with," Rowe said in a 1968 interview, "but I do know he had to walk to town." Eleanor Kane's uncle and cousins also learned their trades in Wilmington. "I don't think they ever worked in the powder mill. Uncle Huey came to a leather morocco factory at Second and Madison. . . . I think the training period was two or three years." Her grandfather, powder man Dan Dougherty, gave Huey carfare for the trolley, but he saved the money and walked both ways. Eventually, Huey "had Bar and Dougherty Leatherworks at Sixth and Church and it was, well, he was successful. The other son was a molder."[64]

Other events also affected management-labor relations. On October 7, 1890, the Upper Yard exploded again. The blast injured twenty people and killed twelve, including a grandmother and her two-year-old grandchild. As one resident recalled,

> I was a mile and a half from the yard. When we heard the explosion we were let out of school, and we ran to the Upper Yard to see it. The houses were all demolished. I saw a lady out on the roof of a house on a bed tick, as we called them. She was dying. Her name was Rose Ann Dougherty. She had a boardinghouse there. Her husband had been killed in the powder [mills] years before.[65]

The force of the explosion practically leveled the mills and most of their support structures, including the entire Upper Banks community of workers' houses. Du Pont offered pensions to the victims' families and reimbursed them for medical care and funeral expenses. This time, it did not rebuild the yard. The decision typified both the company's new management and the times.

During the 1890s, E. I. du Pont de Nemours and Company continued to produce the best black powder in the United States, but it bore little resemblance to the enterprise Irénée founded in 1802. For one thing, the firm now encompassed five plants located throughout the United States. For another, the home plant in Delaware looked its age. Some of the younger partners, especially Pierre S. du Pont and Alfred I. du Pont, recognized the need for new machinery, newer building designs, and a more efficient and rational system of movement for materials. They also saw new opportunities for growth in the manufacture of high explosives and smokeless powder. The senior partners, by contrast, preferred to improve the manufacture of gunpowder for the average American sportsman. Despite the importance of army and navy contracts during wartime, the general public remained the company's leading customer, and as long as the Delaware mills were able to satisfy this demand, they deemed many innovations unnecessary. As assistant superintendent of the Upper Yard, Alfred I. du Pont implemented certain mechanical improvements, often without the approval of either Eugene or Frank, yet for the most part, "the dead hand of the past laid heavily upon all operations."[66]

The opportunity for change came when Eugene du Pont suddenly died on January 28, 1902. Once again, the family members had difficulty deciding who should take over next. Neither Frank nor Alexis, Eugene's brothers, enjoyed good health, so the family offered the presidency to Henry A. du Pont, Boss Henry's son. This time, Cousin Henry declined, preferring to pursue his political career. As the remaining partners squabbled, rumors began to circulate that the firm would be sold to a competitor, Laflin and Rand. Upon hearing this rumor, Alfred I. du Pont, the eldest son of the eldest son of the founder's eldest son, claimed the presidency as his birthright. He offered to buy the company, but the partners considered him too young and inexperienced for the job. They relented only after Alfred convinced two of his older cousins to join him at the helm. Frank and Alexis resigned and on February 26, 1902, the heirs of E. I. du Pont formally reorganized the firm with T. Coleman du Pont as president and Pierre S. and Alfred serving as vice-presidents.[67] Under their dynamic leadership, the powder company would soon become a chemical giant.

The Du Pont Company celebrated its centennial on July 4, 1902. Festivities at the home plant included a picnic, shooting matches, music, dancing, games, and fireworks. To commemorate the event, 248 men, representing the total full-time workforce at that site, presented the new managers with a signed document, which resolved "That the record of one hundred years in the manufacture of gunpowder made by the Du Pont Company as a family is also shared with pride by many of the employees whose fathers and grandfathers have been identified with the history of the works."[68] With sixty-six years to his credit, octogenarian Gilbert Mathewson, Jr., had the longest record of service among the document's signers. Mathewson and his brother, George, began working in the powder yard in November 1837. Their father, Gilbert, Sr., came to the Brandywine from Ireland and had established himself with the company by 1809. Although an accident in 1824 or 1825 prevented Gilbert, Sr., from becoming a powder man, his namesake eventually became superintendent of the Lower Yard.[69] In keeping with the paternalistic, mutualistic ethic that governed life and work in the powder mill communities, four generations of the Mathewson family enjoyed long and distinguished careers with the company. Like Pierre Samuel du Pont, they benefited from the benevolence of their patrons and lifted themselves and their families out of one social category and into another. In exchange for this assistance, the Mathewsons offered the du Ponts loyalty, gratitude, and respect. Other Irish families followed the upward path as well. An enterprising lot, they abandoned the land of their birth and knowingly risked their lives in pursuit of the American dream. Because the company's policies fostered that goal, powder mill families identified their interests with those of their employers. But by 1902 the shift toward more modern methods of labor management and production was well underway. E. I. du Pont de Nemours and Company's familiar, nineteenth-century brand of paternalism had finally come to an end.

POSTSCRIPT

Between 1902 and 1907, the Du Pont Company absorbed an additional 108 competitors and increased its number of plants from five to more than fifty. The number of employees also swelled, rising from approximately 900 in 1902 to 7,400 in 1912.[70] Although the company had never faced a legitimate challenge from organized labor, Du Pont had its first unionized plants by this time, acquired when it bought out competitors. Believing that unions undermined their authority, Alfred I. du Pont and his cousins took steps to reestablish the mutualistic compact along the Brandywine.[71] "Never had no union at all in my time," recalled John Peoples. "Never had no trouble, even after an explosion."[72] John A. Dougherty, grandson of the aforementioned Rose Ann Dougherty, agreed.

> Union organizers never got to first base. I only know of one case where they tried it, and my dad was in on that, and they couldn't get him. This Charlie Godfrey lost out on it. . . . Godfrey was practically an illiterate. Well, they started this union business. This was stuff that was more or less under cover that the outsiders didn't know. Being a sort of an ignorant chap, he started to shoot his face off, and what they were going to get, and my Dad told him, he said, "Dodgie,"—that's what they called him—"You'd better damn sight keep your big mouth shut." Well, he didn't. He went out on strike but he never came back. Never got back in the company.[73]

Workers at the home plant went out on strike in 1906, seeking an eight-hour day, better pay, and union representation. They lost. It was the only significant effort to organize in the history of this community. By 1910, an insurmountable gulf existed between Du Pont managers and workers.[74] The demands of World War I and the postwar recession only intensified the company-wide drive for efficiency and control, and in 1921 Du Pont decided to close its original Brandywine powder yards. As the director of the Hagley Museum and Library commented, "they and the way of life they represented had both become something of an anachronism."[75]

CHAPTER 2

The Ties That Bind

Edward Beacom began working at the saltpeter refinery on March 2, 1872. A farmer by trade, with a good education and a talent for making "rapid calculations," he came to the Brandywine from County Fermanagh in northern Ireland (fig. 2.1). His married sister, Elizabeth Ward, already lived in the powder mill community, where she ran a small boarding house along Squirrel Run. It was her letters that had persuaded him to come, and it was she who provided his first home in America. Later, Beacom married and raised a family of his own, but he never forgot the friends and relations left behind. On the contrary, his daughter, Elizabeth, recalled that,

> He wrote them and sent them newspapers and he brought a lot of relatives over here. My cousin, Sarah Cordner, came over and went to work for Mrs. Henry du Pont and Miss Evelina du Pont. Then there were three sisters who came over and my mother brought them to our place. Then John Cordner, who was Sarah's brother, came to our house. Maggie Martin wrote to my father and asked him to let her come over, and he said she had to ask her mother if she could come, and if her mother said she could come, then my father would let her come. She came and often tells about how she came. She had a sheaf of wheat on the top of her hat and she carried a cloth bag in her hand. That was all the baggage she had. She walked up Rising Sun [Lane] and along the Brandywine. She walked all the way [from Wilmington]. My father was to meet her but she got in too soon. She came on by herself and she recognized Mrs. Stevenson because she had come from Ireland and she asked [her] for directions."[1]

Maggie Martin, in turn, helped her mother and father emigrate to the Brandywine. They eventually lived along Squirrel Run, too.

Like Edward Beacom, Sarah Cordner, and Maggie Martin, most Irish immigrants came to the United States through a process called chain migration.

Fig. 2.1. Metal trunk marked "steerage." Brought to the Brandywine by Edward Beacom in 1872. (Courtesy of Hagley Museum and Library)

Linked to one another by blood, marriage, or friendship, they emigrated in continuous succession, sometimes singly but usually in groups of two or more. In most cases, they came because they had a job or a relative waiting for them. The two were often linked. Families formed the primary occupational network for immigrant communities, and they helped pre-industrial peoples accommodate themselves to the rhythms of factory life.[2] Because of this connection, social historians often stress the economic aspects of chain migration, but kinship systems served important noneconomic functions, too. By promoting the resettlement of family and close friends in this country, they sustained cultural ties between the "Old Country" and the United States, reinforced certain traditional beliefs and behaviors, and contributed to the inculcation of new ones.

With the help of people like Edward Beacom, roughly 4.9 million Irish men and women immigrated to this country in the nineteenth century.[3] By historians' accounts, they had much common. The majority came from densely populated rural districts where impoverished families sublet small farms in a complex web of tenancy spiraling out from largely Protestant land owners. Overwhelmingly Catholic, they appeared to American observers "clannish," "superstitious," and "backward." Many could not speak English, for example, and those who could were functionally illiterate. Compared to other immigrants, the Irish also displayed a distinctly premodern mentality. Rooted in "a shared identity based on religion (whether practiced regularly or not) and a legacy of defeat and proscription at the hands of British and Irish protestants," this deep-seated outlook promoted "passive, communal, and pre-capitalist norms, such as continuity, conformity, and mutuality, while devaluing individual action, ambition, and the assumption of personal responsibility." Within this context, the decision to seek a better life abroad caused particular consternation, symbolizing as it did a fundamental rejection of Irish culture and identity. In response, voluntary migrants seized upon the rhetoric of exile and attributed their departure to British tyranny. But if this rationalization satisfactorily explained their behavior to kith and kin in Ireland, it adversely affected their ability to acculturate. As one scholar concluded, "the exile motif and its underlying causes led Irish emigrants to interpret experience and adapt to American life in ways which were often alienating and sometimes dysfunctional."[4]

A tendency to view their situation as exile especially characterized the so-called Famine generation. Beginning in 1845 a mysterious new fungus appeared and proceeded over the next five or six years to destroy part or all of every single potato crop Ireland produced. The potato, introduced to the island by Sir Walter Raleigh in the seventeenth century, had become by this time the chief food of a majority of the population. British relief measures proved ineffectual, and as hunger and disease stalked the land, over 2.1 million Irish embraced emigration as their only hope of survival. Of these, nearly 1.5 million made their way to the United States, where they ended up in the worst jobs and the worst slums. In large measure, these misfortunes reflected the fact that, as refugees, they arrived penniless and demoralized. But arguably their origins in Ireland also affected their chances for success: Drawn primarily from Munster and Connaught, the most agrarian, tradition-bound regions of the country, Famine emigrants lacked not only the practical skills needed to succeed in an industrial society but the temperament; that is, they "seemed oblivious, even antagonistic, to bourgeois ideals and leadership."[5]

While popular and scholarly fascination with this group is understandable given their sheer numbers and trials, this emphasis tends to obscure other aspects of the Irish-American experience, especially the making of an ethnic "middle class" who shared America's "dominant liberal social and political ideology of progress."[6] It minimizes differences, too, in geographic origin. Prior to 1845 the majority of Irish immigrants came from Ulster, the most commercialized province in the country. American port officials recorded in 1820 that artisans comprised 22 percent of recent arrivals, farmers 20 percent, tradesmen and professionals 10 percent, and common or agricultural laborers 21 percent. By 1828 this demographic pattern had shifted and a whopping 48 percent of the Irish passengers who disembarked in

New York City identified themselves as artisans. Influenced in part by the recession that followed the Napoleonic wars, they left their homeland in search of an "independence," which they increasingly defined in terms of upward mobility.[7] As their occupational category suggests, most were highly skilled and literate. Presbyterians and Anglicans predominated, yet many Catholics immigrated, as well. These early pioneers contributed to the emergence of an Irish-American "middle class," and while fewer in number than their Protestant counterparts, the successes of a Mathew Carey, a Marcus Daly, or later, a Joseph Kennedy attest to the affinity that some Irish Catholics had for the capitalist system. In addition, these so-called "lace-curtain" Irish exerted a great deal of influence over their "shanty" neighbors.[8] Through their position as employers, landlords, and community leaders, they furnished jobs, housing, aid, and information; as parents, siblings, cousins, and in-laws they provided all these things plus a prepaid ticket to America. In both cases, these "respectable" individuals served as powerful role models whose very success encouraged recent immigrants to embrace modern values.

Recognizing this point, scholars of immigration recommend further exploration into the ways in which chain migration "shaped the aspirations, opportunities, strategies, fortunes, and accomplishments" of foreign-born populations.[9] In most cases, a lack of documentary evidence makes it virtually impossible to reconstruct these familial networks. Happily, the reverse is true for the powder mill community. E. I. du Pont de Nemours and Company maintained standing accounts with various agents in Philadelphia and Wilmington until the Civil War. Their surviving correspondence provides detailed information about the immigration procedure, along with the names of passengers and sponsors, dates of immigration, and fares. Moreover, sources like cemetery records and oral histories pinpoint the immigrants' actual place of birth. The result is a deeper appreciation not only of the arduous journey, but of the regional culture and identity the powder workers brought with them.

Irish immigration to the Brandywine began with the construction of the first powder mills. On July 8, 1803, Irénée du Pont boasted to his brother Victor that the "work of building is proceeding rapidly," and that he had been "urged on by the arrival of three boats of Irishmen, which have furnished all the workmen we needed."[10] Despite his initial doubts about the Irish aptitude for black powder manufacturing, du Pont quickly approved their performance and took steps to retain their labor. Like other nineteenth-century industrialists, he considered married men more stable than single men. He also recognized that his Irish workmen could furnish him with a cheap and extensive supply of potential laborers. As a result, Irénée soon offered to help his employees bring out family members from Ireland.

In keeping with Irénée's broader policy of direct assistance, the first efforts were personal in nature, but as demand rose, the company served as an intermediary. John Barrett's case typifies the firm's involvement. An Irish immigrant, Barrett began working in the powder yards on September 16, 1808. Eight months later, E. I. du Pont de Nemours and Company sent forty guineas to William Warner, a Philadelphia shipping agent, and asked him to arrange passage for seven members of Barrett's family. According to company receipts, Samuel, Joseph, Elizabeth, Richard, Edward, Abraham, and Hugh Barrett sailed from Londonderry aboard the ship *Helena,* probably sometime in August 1809. They arrived in Philadelphia in early October but had to await passage on one of Warner's packet ships to Wilmington. On October 19, Warner sent du Pont the following letter:

> Esteemed friends—I herewith send pr. Capt Byrnes Sloop Julia the Irish family which I by your directions became security for the passage of—I enclose the only bill the owners handed me & and have at foot added their expenses for boarding.[11]

The total cost of passage for all seven people was $448.32. According to Warner's note, John Barrett owed $261.52 plus $6.75 for the cost of his family's boarding in Philadelphia. At this point, the powder company intervened. E. I. du Pont paid the balance to John Warner, William's brother, who ran a Wilmington shipping office, and then charged John Barrett's wage account. Although Barrett earned only $10 per month in 1809, he repaid his employer in regular installments.[12]

An organized system emerged in the 1820s. Whenever an employee wanted to bring out a relative, du Pont contacted one of the company's transportation agents and requested an order of passage for that particular individual. Upon receipt of the request, the agent debited the fare from the company's prepaid account and sent the order back to the Brandywine. Passage orders, sometimes called vouchers, expired eight months to a year after issue and in theory applied only to the person named on the margin. In reality, agents frequently added the words "or bearer" to reduce identification problems at dockside.[13] Du Pont gave the order to the employee, or subscriber, who mailed it to the prospective passenger in Ireland. Meanwhile, the American agent, usually in Philadelphia, sent a letter to his counterpart in either Londonderry or Liverpool indicating that an order had been issued and for whom. The foreign agent then reserved a passage on the next available ship and sent a letter to the passenger indicating when the ship would sail. Passengers had to get to the ship on their own, so the subscriber in Delaware would arrange to have a draft, or money order, sent as well. The procedure was the same, but clerks issued, logged, and sent drafts separately. The Philadelphia agent regularly notified du Pont when a ship left port, which passengers it carried, when and where in America he expected it to arrive, and when and where it actually did arrive. Then, du Pont notified the subscriber, who often met the ship and personally brought his passengers to the powder mill community. Although the agents considered embarkation sufficient to fulfill the passage contract, du Pont waited until the passenger reached the Brandywine before debiting the subscriber's wage account. In many cases, the passenger went to work in the powder yards, repaid his subscriber, placed an order for another relative, and the cycle began all over again. More than 1,200 individuals came to the powder mill community by this method.[14]

Despite the du Ponts' involvement, British entrepreneurs largely dictated the terms of emigration from Ireland. From the lodging-house keepers and booking agents to the ships' masters, mates, and owners, profit was the name of the game. The great bulk of Irish immigrants traveled in ships of considerable age and marginal serviceability. Nevertheless, officials carefully choreographed the movement of men and women from ports in Ireland to ports in England and beyond. As in any business, the efficiency of the system needed constant supervision. Clerks accounted costs and changed them to correspond with the seasons and with demand. Still, the Byzantine structure of the emigrant trade hid extensive abuses. Widespread illiteracy before the 1870s made it difficult, if not impossible, for prospective passengers to read tickets and flyers, tell time, and handle cash transactions. Many Irish fell prey to fraudulent agents and crooked authorities. In response to persistent charges of corruption, Parliament passed seven protective Passenger Acts between 1842 and 1855, but the high demand for tickets in this period limited their effect.[15]

The determination of space in steerage posed especial problems. The committees responsible for passenger legislation tried repeatedly to establish and enforce a maximum number of "souls" that could be carried per registered burden. Ships could carry two souls per five tons under the American code and three souls per four tons under the British version. On paper, then, a ship of 400 tons could carry 160 people under one code and 300 under the other. Either way, overcrowding prevailed. Politicians debated whether the laws referred to the *total* amount of space for cargo or to the amount of *unoccupied* space available for passengers. Anxious to maximize their profits, the agents, ship captains, and ship owners generally booked passages in accordance with the former figure.[16]

Additional concerns arose about provisions, fitness for travel, and fares. In the 1830s, standard provisions for the voyage included "two 1/2 pounds navy biscuit, one pound wheaten flour, five pounds oatmeal, two pounds rice, half pound sugar, half pound molasses, two ounces tea & 21 quarts pure water each [adult] weekly." Fully aware that stores of food aboard ship were meager and of poor quality for the price, agent A. J. Catherwood advised du Pont to tell the subscribers that they "would need to find some provisions of their own together with their cooking utensils & bed & bedding."[17] In general, the cost of provisions continued to rise along with the demand for passages, and Parliament passed several laws to regulate their distribution. By 1848, Parliament even debated whether to add rations of beef and pork to the requirement, but the high cost of providing meat provoked great opposition from ship captains and agents. The agents always informed the company when changes occurred. "I enclose you a schedule of the provisions as required by the new law. And all our passengers will get full allowance." But, Catherwood added primly, "Some people you cannot satisfy. No matter if you give them *pound* cake every day."[18]

Another consideration entailed the health of the passengers. Medical officers stationed dockside examined all ticket holders for signs of disease and rejected those of advanced age or infirmity. Even a temporary illness could prevent passengers from having their tickets honored. Thus Patrick Donahue and his family arrived at their ship in December 1830, but failed to embark "on a/c [account] of ill health of Pat."[19] A similar letter from J. & J. Cooke, the Londonderry agents of A. J. Catherwood in Philadelphia, reported that, "Sarah Doherty aged 3 years who is in the ticket with Sarah Doherty adult (No. 1575) does not proceed to Philadelphia with her mother in consequence of illness."[20] Faced with overcrowded conditions and inadequate supplies of fresh food and water, healthy immigrants often fell ill aboard ship. Lice and outbreaks of typhus and cholera were common. During epidemics, doctors quarantined Irish vessels within sight of American ports. Many passengers died on board these "coffin ships," with mortality rates generally rising and falling in proportion to the numbers sailing.

Employed to ensure the passengers' good health, medical officers also determined whether the proper fare had been charged. Throughout the first half of the century, ticket prices reflected the age of the individual traveling. Regulations specified that anyone over the age of twelve was an adult and had to pay the going rate for a single "soul." Those under the age of twelve counted as children and paid the equivalent of a "half-soul."[21] Fares fluctuated, but by 1850 the passage had dropped to $21 for the former and $15 for the latter.[22] With no passports or other identifying materials, however, determinations of age were often vague. In May 1851, for example, the du Ponts wrote agent A. J. Catherwood contesting the assignment of a child's fare. Catherwood politely yet firmly replied:

> Messrs—In your letter of yesterday you say that Mary Jane Allison is eleven years of age. Now all that we know about it, we get from the manifest of passengers p. *Mary Ann* which is made out at the Custom House at Derry by the Doctor, who examines the passengers & reports their ages to the officer before the ship leaves. And she is marked nineteen on that manifest for we have it in our possession.[23]

Ship captains and agents wanted to minimize the number of "half-souls" booked and thereby maximize their profits. The Irish wanted just the reverse and soon learned to present their teenagers as children. Since the du Pont company paid for most passages up front, it too preferred the lower fare.

Despite these efforts to reduce the number of children traveling to the United States, a substantial number of passengers fell under the age of twelve. Moreover, many of these children traveled without adult supervision. In 1847 Catherwood wrote, "In the barque *Royal Saxon* arrived yesterday from Londonderry, came three children named McConnelogue who say their father was, when he wrote them, in your employment. If he is there still, will you be good enough to let him know that the children have arrived that he may come for them or that they may be sent down to your place."[24] By 1850 Catherwood pleaded with the du Pont company, "Don't send any single children unless there is a grown person paid for to come with them to take care of them." Three days later he again wrote, "You must be careful about these large families. We are better without the children than with them unless you can get $20 each for them. If it was late in the season we would not care so much, but it is the spring when we can get almost any price we choose to ask in Derry."[25] Children's fares remained a problem until the 1870s, when improvements in steamship technology lowered the cost of trans-Atlantic travel in general.

Given the difficulties of the voyage, pre-Famine migrants did not take the decision to leave Ireland lightly. Various forces conjoined to impel their departure, including the enclosure movement, the commercialization of the countryside, the shift toward impartible inheritance, and rising rents. But going abroad seemed a drastic solution, and most would-be travelers needed some assurance that the rewards outweighed the risks. Typically, it came in the form of letters written by friends and relations already in America. Like their counterparts elsewhere, du Pont employees sent regular missives, sometimes through the company and sometimes through the local priest or tavern keeper.[26] In general, Catholic writers were more likely to encourage and assist their kin than Protestants.[27] By the 1810s, exposure to modern, capitalistic values meant that members of both faiths sanctioned emigration and upward mobility, but in different ways. Protestantism, with its greater emphasis on individual salvation and self-reliance, led adherents to view advancement in terms of personal gain. Increasingly afraid that dependent relatives would retard their progress, these emigrants sent letters filled with warnings, and eschewed responsibility for those who came anyway. Catholic emigrants, by contrast, actively promoted chain migration. Their belief system, which stressed communalism and the sacramental nature of human relationships, prompted individuals to conceptualize mobility and success in group terms. To this end, powder mill letters not only boasted of high wages and social fluidity, but they carried the sender's pledge to secure the recipient a prepaid ticket and a paying position in the community.

The Great Famine accelerated this pattern. Indeed, the entire community responded to the sudden crisis, opening their pocketbooks as well as their homes to the victims. Robert Taylor warned the du Ponts in November 1846 that "late letters from Londonderry say the emigration will be large, and ships or freights high, and that therefore the price must be raised to $24 for full passengers, and no half ones under $20."[28] Beginning in 1847, powder men authorized voluntary deductions from their wage accounts "for the poor of Ireland and Scotland."[29] They also placed fully 51 percent of their passage orders between 1845 and 1849. Although circumstances likely stranded some refugees in Philadelphia or Wilmington, most seem to have made it to the Brandywine, where the newcomers quickly stretched local resources to the limit. Astonished by the sudden deluge, Alfred Victor du Pont's wife, Margaretta, wrote to her son that "A fresh Irisher threw himself from delirium into the creek this afternoon and they were nearly two hours bringing him to. No end to the applications for work & there are now 250 men at work."[30] In fact, the number of residents rose from approximately 1,500 in 1840 to more than 2,000 in 1850, with 40 percent reporting nativity in Ireland and 22 percent claiming at least one Irish-born parent. The du Ponts and their associates hired as many of the refugees as they could, but the small size of area manufactories effectively limited employment opportunities.

Truth be told, northern Delaware had little to offer Famine migrants in and of itself. The rise of manufacturing industries along the Brandywine and Christina rivers, coupled with the construction of the Chesapeake and Delaware Canal, the New Castle and Frenchtown Railroad, and several turnpikes in the 1820s and 1830s attracted earlier immigrants, but after 1840, the region developed a specialized industrial economy in which iron, steel, shipbuilding, railroad car manufacturing, and carriage making predominated.[31] Most employers required skilled labor, and consequently, Wilmington attracted fewer Irish than other parts of the mid-Atlantic region. In 1860, for example, foreign-born persons comprised only 18.9 percent of Wilmington's population, compared with 24.7 percent of Baltimore's and 28.9 percent of Philadelphia's.[32] Thus it was family ties, not jobs, that pulled so many Irish to the powder mills.

Kinship networks influenced post-Famine arrivals, as well. In contrast to the panic-stricken Famine generation, most of those who left Ireland after 1855 fled the effects of rural commercialization, not death and disease.[33] William Flemming's case is typical. Faced with falling crop prices and shrinking acreage, he decided that his family would have a better life in Delaware and emigrated in the 1860s. The procedure remained the same. His brother, Andrew, financed his passage and found him a job in the powder yards. William then sent for his wife, Faith Lyttle, and their children. According to the couple's granddaughter, Faith Betty Lattomus, "He was only over a year, I guess, because Aunt Mattie was only about seven years old and my grandmother came over on a sailing boat and it took her six weeks to come, with a family of two girls."[34] James Cheney, another farmer, came to the Brandywine from County Fermanagh in the early 1880s. His brother-in-law, Edward Beacom, and sister-in-law, Elizabeth Ward, already lived in Squirrel Run, along with their maternal uncle, George Hurst. With their help, Cheney also secured a position in the powder yards and sent for his wife and four children two years later.[35]

After they settled along the Brandywine, immigrants like Beacom, Flemming, and Cheney dispatched thousands of dollars home to Ireland. These remittances, usually sent in the form of a money order, served several purposes. Sometimes they supported the everyday subsistence needs of the subscriber's family in Ireland. Sometimes they financed another passage or procured gifts and services. Catholics generally felt obligated to send money home. In his 1868 book, *The Irish in America,* author John Maguire especially emphasized the sacrifices made by Irish Catholic women. They considered remittances a filial duty, "which they do not and cannot think of disobeying; and which on the contrary they delight in performing." December and March were the busiest months for banks and immigration offices because the Irish wanted to send money home for Christmas and Easter. In Maguire's opinion, "misery and want are not in accordance with the spirit of these festivals, nor with the feelings which ought to prevail with those who believe in their teaching."[36] This sentiment surfaced in Wilmington, too, where in 1866 passenger agents Grimshaw and McCabe urged Irish immigrants to "Call at 301 Market Street and send your friends a Christmas present."[37]

Money orders frequently afforded "little comforts" for the holidays, yet most drafts financed the trip to America. There are many examples in the company records, but one will suffice to explain the practice. Henry Doran, a mason and local innkeeper, sent a draft of $15.75 to his mother, Catharine Doran, on February 22, 1841. At the same time, he ordered passages for three of his children: Michael (probably aged 12), Rose (10), and Francis (8). The draft defrayed the incidental costs of his children's voyage. The little Dorans had lived with their grandmother since March 1835, when their mother, Margaret, and several older siblings emigrated to Delaware. On March 21, 1842, Henry sent his mother another draft for $21.00. Additional drafts and a ticket eventually followed. When the federal census taker visited the Brandywine in July 1850, he listed Catharine Doran as an occupant in Henry's household. She was eighty years old at the time.

In spite of these efforts to ensure adequate funds for the journey, some immigrants ran out of cash before reaching their final destination. On May 11, 1848, A. J. Catherwood wrote John Peoples, the du Pont company clerk, that "Alice McKenna has arrived here today . . . & has no funds to pay her lodging or fare to Wilmington. She says she has a daughter in the city but cannot find her address. Will you inform John McKenna—the person who paid you the passage—of these facts and let him send the old woman some relief." Two years later, Catherwood again wrote Peoples that "[Patrick] Murphy & [Julia] Brady arrived p. *Euxine* from Liverpool yesterday and are in want of money. Please inform James Murphy the engager that they are stopping at the Leeds House, No. 119 South Water Street above Dock Street."[38] In some cases, the sheer volume of remittances and the difficulty of obtaining precise mailing addresses meant that money orders never reached Ireland at all. When questioned by the du Ponts about this problem, agent Robert Taylor admitted that his bookkeeping system was faulty, saying, "It is possible however that some odd one or two [orders] may have miscarried and the person who remitted the bill should write to her parents inquiring particularly whether they have received it."[39]

As these examples suggest, most immigrants came to the Brandywine under the financial auspices of a close relative. Indeed, Irish Catholics had a unique reputation in America for their "clannishness" and the concerted efforts they made to reunite their families. These Irish also tended to maintain bilateral, extended, kinship networks; that is, they recognized ties to the maternal and paternal lines, by marriage as well as blood, and on both sides of the Atlantic. A typical emigrant's family thus included his parents, siblings, aunts, uncles, cousins, spouse, and children *plus* a wide assortment of in-laws.[40]

The small size of the powder mill community and the richness of its surviving data provide a good opportunity to reconstruct these affiliative relationships. Nearly 28 percent of the 1,258 known immigrants to the Brandywine had a consanguineous relationship to the subscriber. In most cases, local records identified them as wives and children, but parents and siblings appeared as well. Patrick Dougherty, for example, ordered the passage of Mary Cole and Owen Dougherty, aged eight, on January 25, 1845. Their date of arrival is unknown, but in October 1848, the local priest recorded the baptism of a child born to Patrick Dougherty and Mary *Mc*Cole, evidence indicative of their true relationship. In fact, many married women traveled under their maiden names, including Jane O'Donnell and Bridget Boner, the wives of Philip Dougherty and Daniel Dougherty, respectively. This practice conformed to Irish custom but obscured spousal relationships between passengers and subscribers. Other women used their husband's surname. Catharine Lynch (42), for example, left Ireland sometime after June 1847 accompanied by her children, John (15), Hugh (13), Mary Ann (10), Ellen (5), and Sarah (2). Once in Delaware, she quickly joined her firstborn, Patrick Lynch (17), a laborer and future priest, and her husband, John Lynch (47), then Sophie du Pont's gardener. Another 27 percent of the passengers bore the same surname as the subscriber, suggesting an equally close though as yet undetermined degree of kinship.

Some relationships involved in-laws. Consider the Blessington family, for instance. John came first and brought out his brothers, James and Michael, in the fall of 1839. Then James arranged passage for Margaret Begley in 1844 and Catharine Begley in 1846. His wife, identified in church records as Rosanna Begley, must have been their sister. Similarly, Peter Conaway, Jr., assisted some of his relatives in 1847, including Peter, Mary Ann, James, Hannah, Bernard (10), and Rose (5) Conaway. One year later, he and John Peoples, a company clerk, co-sponsored the passages of Bernard, Edward, John, Mary, Joseph (9), and Thomas (7) Sweeney. Then, in 1849 Conaway pooled resources with his father, Peter Conaway, Sr., and a man named Hugh Sweeney to finance the passage of Michael Sweeney, his wife, Catharine, and their children, Patrick, Michael (15), John (8), Charles (5), and James (1). A look at the baptismal registers and 1850 census schedules shows that Peter's sister, Mary, was married to Hugh and that Peter Conaway, Sr., resided with them. Bernard and Michael Sweeney must therefore have been Hugh's brothers.

Many of the passengers (17 percent) had no kinship tie to the subscriber, who served instead as an intermediary or sponsor for someone else in the community. Members of the du Pont family most frequently fulfilled this function, but merchants, ministers, priests, farmers, innkeepers, and other manufacturers in the community also did so. Immigrant James Conley, a stone mason by trade and the du Pont company's primary contractor for construction and repairs, sponsored the passage of thirty-two people between 1847 and 1853.[41] Other notable sponsors include James Peoples, an Irish-born company clerk; Rev. John S. Walsh and Rev. Patrick Reilly, Irish pastors of the local Catholic churches; Sarah Donnan, an Irish tavern keeper and widow of a former du Pont employee; and American Robert Young, who leased and operated a du Pont–owned textile mill.

Under the du Pont company's system, all passage vouchers had to be ordered directly by a powder mill employee or a reputable person in the community. Whereas 28 percent of the 1,258 passengers bore a different surname from the subscriber, the need to stand security for the cost of the ticket meant that a congenial relationship must have existed between the parties. In some of these cases, the passenger accompanied a known relative of the subscriber's and likely hailed from the same village. Peter Collins, for example, ordered passages for his sister, Margaret Collins, and an unidentified man named Dennis McGonigal, while Patrick Dougherty ordered passages for a female relative, Nancy Dougherty, and a woman named Biddy Donohue. Bernard McManus, a laborer, ordered a passage for Catharine Gallagher in 1846. Although Gallagher's relationship to McManus remains unclear, she knew him well enough to be godmother for his son, John, born the following year.

The strength of family ties also accounts for the high number of individuals emigrating from the same part of Ireland. Scholars recognized this point long ago, yet few provide more than a passing reference to their subjects' geographic origins. The problem is usually a lack of precise evidence. Federal census records note merely the country of birth for foreign-born persons, and few Irish immigrants left additional documentation of their own. Recently, some historians have resorted to surname analysis, where the prevalence of certain patronyms in certain regions of Ireland suggests a general pattern of nativity.[42] The powder mill community, by contrast, is fortunate to have fairly specific surviving data, leaving little doubt as to the residents' place of birth.

Oral histories, for instance, consistently point to the northern province of Ulster. In a 1964 interview, James F. Toy stated that his great-grandparents, Daniel Toy and Rose Coyle, came to the Brandywine from County Tyrone in 1814. Eleanor Kane's grandfather, powder man Daniel Dougherty, left Invershone, County Donegal, in the 1830s. Robert Betty, a carter for the du Pont company, emigrated from the Clogher valley of County Tyrone in the early 1840s, and eventually married a woman from County Fermanagh. Other families moved around Ulster before emigrating abroad. John Peoples, who worked in the keg mill, was born on February 28, 1871, in County Donegal, and emigrated to the Brandywine around 1881. His older brother, powder man Robert Peoples, had been born in the Belfast area of County Antrim.[43] Significantly, several of these individuals appear as subscribers in the immigration agents' letters. Given the propensity for chain migration in this community, it is probable that many of their relatives also reached the Brandywine.

Other sources confirm the numerical dominance of Ulster emigrants. Company records sometimes indicate an Irish mailing address for passages or money orders. Grace Gallagher, for example, left Cash, County Donegal, sometime after May 18, 1832 and arrived in time for Christmas that year.[44] With the help of Alfred du Pont, Mrs. Owen McGuire arranged for the passage of Thomas Roe (36), his wife, Elizabeth (37), and their children Catharine (15), William (13), Elizabeth (11), and Mary (9) in mid-April 1836. A loose memo from agent Robert Taylor in Philadelphia indicates that the Roes (also spelled Rowe) lived in or near "Castle Asdale, Irvinstown Post Office, Co. Fermanna." Taylor sent the passage orders, and the family arrived by June 15, 1836.[45] Records also note Glennalla, County Donegal, and King's Court, County Cavan.

Additional information can be found in the local Catholic cemeteries that served the community. In the 1930s, historians employed by the Works Progress Administration transcribed all of the tombstone inscriptions in St. Mary of the Assumption (Coffee Run) and St. Joseph on the Brandywine churchyards.[46] Some record the decedent's county of birth, and a few note the specific parish or townland as well. At Coffee Run, which served Catholics in the powder mill community before 1840, nine individuals emigrated from County Cork, including James Moynihan, a native of the Parish of Balleyvourney. Irénée recruited these men from the Ballincollig Royal Gunpowder Mills, which operated in that parish until 1815.[47] Three other decedents came from Donegal, including brothers Richard and Patrick Dougherty, who died in the explosion of 1815. Tyrone, Louth, Kerry, Cavan, and Dublin each appeared once. At St. Joseph's churchyard, established by powder workers in 1841, 159 out of 803 stones record a birthplace in Ireland. Fifty list Donegal, twenty-two Tyrone, seventeen Cork, sixteen Galway, and ten Fermanagh. Nineteen other counties are represented, each with fewer than six references. Despite the greater variety of birthplaces in this sample, ninety, or almost 57 percent of the total, specified a county in Ulster.

These origins profoundly shaped the way immigrants to the Brandywine acculturated. In the past, historians and sociologists used the "melting pot" metaphor to describe the transformation immigrants underwent in America. This theory, which persisted until the 1960s, held that foreign-born populations assimilated into the host society and lost their distinctive ethnic identity in the process. Later historians celebrated ethnic persistence. In actuality, immigrants acculturate, that is, they retain critical aspects of their Old World culture as they embrace values and practices reflective of their new country. Prior to emigration, the Irish in nineteenth-century Ulster, like other rural populations at other times and in other places, tended to affiliate along local lines, with most individuals deriving their primary identity from their family group and place of residence. The typical settlement, often merely a collection of cottages and turf sheds, was itself a congerie of blood relatives who traced their ancestry to a handful of families. Thus tied to their neighbors, the Irish also tied themselves to the land.[48] As every person in the community received a name that evoked his distinct genealogy, so every hill and dale received an appellation designed to recall its unique history. Consequently, the process of chain migration did more than resettle people in northern Delaware; it transplanted with them a particular regional identity based on specific modes of cultural expression, values, and beliefs. For most powder workers, this identity emanated from a triangular area encompassing the extreme north and east of County Donegal, the west of counties Tyrone and Londonderry, and the north of Fermanagh (see fig. 2.2).

The triangle in question covered a rich agricultural region characterized by the production of grain, flour, meat, and butter. At its center lay the Foyle valley, which had one of the highest living standards in pre-Famine Ireland. The land here was generally good, though interspersed with hills and bogs, and contributed to local prosperity. So did the northern custom of the tenant-right, which, by perpetuating "fair rent, fixity of tenure, and free sale," essentially gave renting farmers greater security on their holdings and thereby provided an incentive for investment and improvements. However, a great part of area farmers' success stemmed from the linen trade.[49]

Beginning in the 1780s, the Irish textile industry expanded well beyond its traditional manufacturing area around Belfast. As it did, the northern province became the most commercialized part of Ireland, and travelers commented frequently on its "numerous and busy" market towns. By 1810 nearly every household in the south and west of Ulster grew flax, spun yarn, or wove cloth. These activities enabled agricultural families to purchase trade goods when times were good and to pay the rent when they were not. Yet the transformation happened slowly and unevenly. Much of the development occurred in the east, a trend that accelerated in the 1820s. With the rise of mechanized factories, urban centers expanded dramatically. The population of Belfast alone mushroomed from 20,000 in 1800 to over 75,000 in 1840. As other towns grew, they disseminated powerful new values and behaviors. Many northerners, including some Catholics, began to define their goals in entrepreneurial, proto-capitalistic terms. During the depression years of the late 1810s and early 1820s, they fled Ireland altogether.[50] Others clung to tradition, especially in the far west, where Gaelic

Fig. 2.2. Map of Ireland indicating the region that produced the du Pont Irish. Drawn by author, 2001.

speakers and Catholics predominated. There, the enclosure movement, the contraction of the linen industry, and a bleak and rugged terrain led to profound displacement. The Rosses in west Donegal, for example, deteriorated into one of the most impoverished places in all of Ireland. Residents there, "largely isolated from dictates of market," had to be self-sufficient.[51] The same could not be said of their immediate neighbors to the east.

Exposure to modern values generally reflected proximity to a commercial district, and many Brandywine households originated in or near substantial market towns. Powder man Richard H. Rowe, for example, who died in 1873 at the age of forty-three, came from Ballyshannon, a prosperous seaport, market, and post town in southern Donegal. Situated at the head of the river Erne, where there is a natural harbor, Ballyshannon functioned as a major export center sending grain and farm produce to England.[52] Farther north lay Malin, another port and the site of an important local shrine. Brothers Richard and Patrick Dougherty were born here, but went "across the creek" in 1815. According to the terms of Patrick's will, the company reserved enough money from his estate to finance the passage of two nephews. One of them, James, finally claimed his inheritance in 1833. At least six other individuals are also known to have emigrated from the Malin vicinity: Charles Dougherty, Daniel Dougherty, Edward Dougherty, Ellen Houtton, Michael Houtton, and Patrick McKenny.[53] By 1850, sixty individuals named Dougherty lived at the powder mills along with four Houttons and eleven McKennys. Some or all of these individuals might be tied to Malin, as well. And finally, there is Letterkenny, the most frequently mentioned place of origin. Located along the Swilly River in eastern County Donegal, it was a substantial post and market town with 358 houses, a courthouse, a market square, a school, a dispensary, a work house, and a Roman Catholic chapel. Letterkenny served the surrounding Parish of Conwall, which had 10,611 inhabitants and more than 45,000 acres by 1870. Although the town itself had only 2,161 residents, its impact on the Brandywine appears great.[54]

Imagine the anticipation that Hugh Creeran and William McCarron felt as they left Portebelsame, in the Letterkenny vicinity. It was the early spring of 1837, and two of Hugh's relatives, who already worked in the powder yards, had sponsored their passages to Delaware. The men had married two sisters, Mary Ann and Rosanna Gibbons. Over the next decade, the new powder men brought out their wives and children, as well as John Gibbons, their brother-in-law and a future Hagley Yard foreman. Gibbons, in turn, sponsored his brothers Charles and William. John's gravestone simply says "County Donegal," but his family must have lived in the Parish of Conwall, too. By 1850 there were four Creerans, one McCarron, and twenty-three Gibbonses living and working along the Brandywine.

There are several other family networks with ties to Letterkenny. In 1836 powder man James Haughey ordered a passage for Thomas Gallagher, who lived in or near the town. Haughey began working in the yards on April 16, 1835, and sent for his wife, Sarah Gallagher, soon after. Thomas, Sarah's son by a previous marriage, was only seven at the time, and she had to leave him with her kin. They returned his 1836 ticket, perhaps because noone else could come, and received another later. By April 1844, sixteen-year-old Thomas was working in the powder yards and boarding with his mother and stepfather. If we assume that James Haughey met and married the Widow Gallagher while living in the Letterkenny vicinity, then he and the twenty-eight other Haugheys living around the powder mills in 1850 had roots there, too. Likewise, the gravestone of Thomas Lynch, killed in the explosion of 1847, reads "Parish of Conwall, County Donegal." Lynch began working for the du Ponts in December 1837 at the age of seventeen. Given his age, he probably received a prepaid ticket from his brother, Hugh, with whom he first boarded. Thomas eventually helped bring out his parents, Hugh and Catherine, along with at least five identifiable siblings, all of whom had spouses and children. Then, in 1846, Lynch married a young woman named Julia McGeady. When her husband went "across the creek" the next year, Julia took her infant daughter and went to live with her parents, Hugh and Fanny. As it turns out, Thomas had also sponsored them and two of Julia's siblings. Julia and another sister migrated separately; the fact that the company charged their passages to James Haughey, introduced above, suggests further linkages.

Of course, many families sprang from the countryside, not market towns. But even they had some exposure to the capitalist marketplace prior to emigration. Take the Hollands, who traced their roots to the Parish of Ardstraw in County Tyrone. John arrived first, in 1822, and sent for his brothers, Thomas and Patrick, five years later. Earning $15.50 apiece as common laborers, the Holland men sent regular drafts of money to their relatives back home. Located in the extreme west of the county, Ardstraw was one of the "best and most fertile" parishes in Tyrone at the time, producing oats, wheat, and barley for export. After the harvest, farmers could process their grain at one of the county's seven corn mills and transport it via one of several good roads that crisscrossed the area. Newtown-Stewart, the largest town in the parish, held a general market every Monday and a "cloth market" every other week. Like other parts of Ulster, Ardstraw participated actively in the linen trade, and boasted five flax mills, a tuck mill, and a bleach works. The spinning and weaving took place in private homes, with wives and daughters engaged in the former.[55] During the Napoleonic wars, many rural households came to depend on this supplementary income, especially Catholics like the Hollands, who generally occupied marginal lands in the parish's mountains. When linen production fell into decline after Waterloo, the number of emigrants began to rise. Protestants predominated, but port officials in Londonderry in 1826 estimated that 25 percent or more were Catholics.[56] By the spring of 1829, the rest of the Holland family had resolved to leave, as well. The party that landed in Wilmington that summer included Patrick's wife, Eleanor McMackin, and their two children, John (5) and Nancy (2); a sister, Anne Holland; and the family patriarch, Patrick Holland, Sr. The clan quickly expanded. John Holland had already married the daughter of a French powder maker in 1824; Thomas and Anne chose Irish spouses. In the meantime, Patrick and Eleanor had two more children, and other relatives continued to emigrate from Ardstraw. By mid-century, more than thirty people named Holland lived and worked along the Brandywine.

The chains that led from northern Ireland to northern Delaware persisted for so long that many immigrants in the 1880s and 1890s originated in the same region as their predecessors had in the 1810s and 1820s. The majority of powder mill families thus shared a common cultural hearth where they learned to meld the demands of an increasingly market-oriented society with premodern or traditional values and folkways. As the commercialization of Ulster progressed, improved transportation and communication networks fostered knowledge of other places and people. Then, when economic conditions soured, many ambitious and forward-looking individuals emigrated voluntarily to the United States. Their cultural transformation continued at sea. Packed prior to 1880 into overcrowded steerage compartments and often segregated by sex, immigrants needed qualities like competitiveness and adaptability to survive. Poles of leadership shifted from the old and wise to the young and healthy. A large family, oral communication skills, and a good memory—traits cultivated in rural, preliterate communities—ill-suited the new environment.[57] Experiences associated with the passage itself thus indicated which values and behaviors would be compatible with life in the new world and which would not.

Once safely ensconced along the Brandywine, the immigrants' process of acculturation continued apace. Because they could tell time, read, perhaps even make "rapid calculations," Ulstermen like Edward Beacom adapted to life in industrial America better than other Irish immigrants. Contemporaries believed that the Protestantism of the region, especially the Presbyterianism of the Scotch-Irish, encouraged a spirit of enterprise that men and women in the south rarely exhibited. This religious explanation remains problematic; northerners *in general* had distinct advantages over southerners, including marketable skills, education, and exposure to capitalist values.[58] Catholics from Ulster also benefited from their bilateral kinship networks. Already indebted to their siblings, cousins, or in-laws for the price of passage and remittances, immigrants continued to rely on their sponsors after arrival. Some of the sponsors were relative newcomers themselves, and performed common labor for day wages in the powder yards. Still, they served a vital function: by providing jobs, housing, and information they eased the sense of uprootedness greenhorns felt and helped them adjust to life "in the powder." Other sponsors had advanced to positions of respectability and authority. Bound to the rest of the community by blood and marriage, these seasoned veterans of the capitalist marketplace became role models par excellence. Their occupational mobility, coupled with their sizeable savings accounts, church memberships, fashionable clothing, and quality furnishings, confirmed newcomers' perception that mobility was possible and oriented them to life in industrializing America. By these means, migration networks fostered acculturation and, ultimately, Irish *embourgeoisment*. Because these Ulster families were Catholic, however, they only adopted some modern values, not all.

CHAPTER 3

A Distinctive Faith

☙

Patrick Kenny rose early on the morning of July 4, 1817, and after performing his regular ablutions, he walked to the little log chapel next door and
said Mass. A Catholic priest, Kenny performed the ritual every day, but on
this particular day, he offered a special prayer "that all Irish Catholicks taking shelter in the United States, may be spiritually more faithful to their religious principles, than enamour'd with the political constitution of the
country."[1] The Dublin native came to northern Delaware in 1804 to serve
the region's growing Catholic population, and by 1817, Irish powder workers and their families composed a significant proportion of his flock. An
immigrant himself, Kenny could appreciate the temptations that life in an
egalitarian society offered his fellow countrymen. But he also believed that
too much personal autonomy could lead to licentiousness and atheism.
And so, on a day that commemorated American independence, Kenny
prayed for the strength of the Irish to withstand its secularizing influences.

Author John Maguire expressed similar sentiments in his 1868 book,
The Irish in America. Maguire's stated purpose was "to see what the Irish
were doing in America," that is, "whether reports were true that peasants
continued to live in slums until they lost their prospects, or if they were
prosperous." Yet he included an assessment of Irish Catholicism because
he firmly believed that any "loss of faith or indifference to religion would
be . . . fatal to their material progress, would disastrously interfere with the
proper performance of their duties as citizens, and would be certain to
turn the public opinion in America against them." After carefully compar-
ing their conduct in Ireland and in America, Maguire concluded that some
Irish had, indeed, fallen away from their faith, but not nearly as many as
critics contended. "Fortified by suffering and trial at home," he wrote, "in-
heritors of memories which intensify development rather than weaken fidelity, the Irish brought with them a strong faith, the power to resist as
well as the courage to persevere, and that generosity of spirit which has

ever prompted mankind to make large sacrifices for the promotion of their religious beliefs."[2]

Writing expressly for those Irish contemplating migration to the United States, Maguire seemed far more optimistic about their religious prospects than Rev. Kenny, but he shared the latter's basic concern: Could Irish Catholics maintain their distinctive spirituality on American soil? The question demanded consideration because Catholicism was more than a religious system to the Irish. Unable to vote, hold office, own property, or receive an education, Catholics in Ireland cleaved to their faith, and by the early nineteenth century, religion had become inextricably intertwined with Irish conceptions of national identity and culture. In America the constitutional separation of church and state technically precluded institutionalized religious prejudice, but Irish "papists" still faced hostility and suspicion. Prior to the Civil War, most Americans believed that "Popery" merely hindered social, economic, and political advancement. After about 1865, this attitude changed, and native-born Anglo-Protestants typically considered Catholics incapable of assimilating at all.[3] While few Irish immigrants actually converted as part of their acculturation process, a pervasive anti-Catholic atmosphere reinforced the idea that apostasy was not only possible, but probable.

The issue of Irish faithlessness challenges common beliefs about Irish and Irish-American piety. Popular wisdom holds that all Erin's children had a deep, abiding relationship with the Catholic Church, that their spiritual lives centered on the neighborhood parish, they meekly obeyed clerical directives, and they routinely favored denominational interests over class. These traits certainly characterized many Irish families, especially those living in cities like San Francisco, Chicago, Boston, New York, or Philadelphia at the end of the nineteenth century. But it is equally true that, in both Ireland and the United States prior to 1870, Catholicism bore little resemblance to the faith promulgated from the Vatican.[4] How, then, did Irish immigrants become such devout *Roman* Catholics—and perhaps even more important, why?

Sociologists, theologians, and anthropologists contend that the primary function of a religious system is to help individuals make sense of the world around them. More concretely, a religion is "a system of symbols which acts to establish powerful, pervasive, and long-lasting moods and motivations in men by formulating conceptions of a general order of existence and clothing these conceptions with such an aura of factuality that the moods and motivations seem uniquely realistic."[5] Religions thus serve human societies by attributing inexplicable phenomena to supernatural powers, and people practice a particular religion because its interpretation of the cosmos, as revealed in a specific set of symbols, enables them to understand, accept, or endure their everyday experiences. And because religions are socially constructed, a decision to affirm and observe the meaning of a particular faith's symbols, whether consciously or unconsciously, will profoundly affect an individual's identification with that society.[6]

Given this relationship between religion and group affiliation, close attention to the way powder mill families used, observed, manipulated, embraced, and discarded religious symbols can tell us much about the way they viewed themselves. One ubiquitous Catholic symbol is the crucifix, which denotes the same thing whether talked about, visualized, shaped in the air, displayed on an altar, or worn at the neck.[7] Along the Brandywine, signs of Catholic identity included affiliation with a parish, participation in public rituals like baptism, marriage, and confirmation, the perpetuation of specific naming patterns, and the use of Catholic material culture. Analyzed together, they confirm what Kenny and Maguire suspected: exposure to America's modern, capitalistic culture did affect Irish spirituality. But instead of abandoning their faith, the majority of immigrants embraced it, becoming more orthodox, more pietistic, than they had ever been back in Ireland. Moreover, their "conversion" experience constituted an important part of the acculturation process. In Tridentine or Roman Catholicism, immigrants from Tyrone, Fermanagh, and Donegal found a way to transcend regional differences and forge a new spiritual identity. Arguments about other Irish notwithstanding, these people did not embrace organized religion because of ethnic persecution, clerical coercion, or opposition to industrial capitalism.[8] They did so because it enabled them to reconcile past and present experiences with future goals. For along with seemingly "traditional" expressions of Irish ethnicity like St. Patrick's Day celebrations, the American Church actively encouraged immigrants to adopt bourgeois values and behaviors. To many Brandywine residents, then, becoming a good, practicing Catholic offered a means of comprehending their place not only in God's plan, but in American society.

Patrick Kenny must have cut a strange figure when he first arrived in northern Delaware. At forty-one years of age, the short, "rather robust" priest wore a black suit notable for its "too-short, too-wide trouser legs." This distinctive costume might simply have been the result of bad tailoring. It more likely accommodated his severely ulcerated leg, the unfortunate result of a bout with "the spotted or putrid fever." Despite his affliction, which caused a great deal of pain and gave him a pronounced limp, Kenny took his pastoral duties seriously and made every effort to tend his widespread flock.[9] Stationed at a working farm along Coffee Run, a tributary of

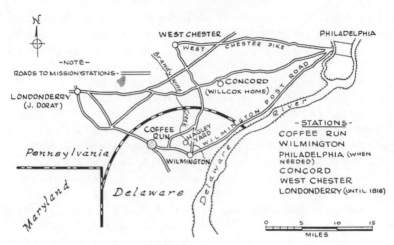

Fig. 3.1. Map showing the mission stations attended by Rev. Patrick Kenny from 1814 to 1827. Taken from Coffee Run (1960).

the White Clay Creek, he served a total of six missions in Pennsylvania, Maryland, and Delaware (fig. 3.1). People in New Castle County soon grew accustomed to the sight of the intrepid little Irishman racing along the country roads in his "faithful Dearborn," and came to value his kindness, wit, and candor.

Kenny brought to the region a distinctly Irish attitude toward religion, one shaped by his country's long and intensive colonial experience. Beginning in the late sixteenth century, Ireland's English conquerors embarked on a deliberate program to impose the "religion, the arts, the civilization of Protestant Britain over the fanaticism, the ignorance, and barbarism of Rome."[10] Over the decades, crown officials closed Irish monasteries, unroofed chapels, evicted bishops, abolished "papist" schools, and prohibited the public practice of Catholicism. Many clergy fled to the continent. Those who remained established outdoor stations at the homes of well-to-do farmers where on a rotating basis they held secret masses and administered the sacraments. Stories of these courageous "outlaw" clerics, who moved through the countryside under cover of darkness, cleverly eluding capture by English soldiers, helped forge a unique bond between them and the faithful. By 1800, the English offensive had relaxed considerably, but the damage was done: the ratio of priests to people stood at 1:1,276 — a significant problem for such a ritual-intensive religion.[11]

Without a strong ecclesiastical presence, Catholics in Ireland took to worshiping when, where, and how they saw fit. They actually practiced a vernacular faith that dated back to the Middle Ages. While acknowledging the symbolism of Saint Patrick's battle with the snakes, experts agree that Christian beliefs and observances did not replace Celtic paganism so much as they augmented it. In fact, early missionaries encouraged a certain degree of spiritual syncretism as a means of facilitating the conversion process. Thus Brid, the pagan goddess, became St. Bridget, the three-leafed shamrock symbolized the Trinity, and the harvest festival of Samhain, with its bonfires and carved gourds, became the feast of All Saints (All Hallows). Such admixture also produced the "pattern," a communal rite that combined prayer, fasting, and self-mortification with drinking, fighting, dancing, and fornicating.[12] Once held to mark various points in the agricultural cycle, the event began with a procession to a site associated with a pagan spirit, now saint. Virtually every rural settlement had its own supernatural patron whose aid and benediction villagers sought and celebrated. In 1815 a Protestant minister described a pattern in the Parish of Cloncaugh, County Donegal, home to many future powder workers:

> The patron days of the place are Saint John's Eve [formerly Midsummer's Eve] and the Assumption of the Virgin [formerly the harvest festival of Lughnasa] and they are celebrated here by the most disgusting drunkenness and debauchery, under the pretence of paying adoration to saint Moriallagh, the patron of the well. This saint is not acknowleged in the calendar; and the clergy of the church of Rome have, very properly, forbidden the offensive orgies by which he is worshipped; it is, however, to be regretted, that his votaries have not attended the salutary advice of their pastors on the subject.[13]

Beneath the unifying veneer of Christianity, Irish religious practices remained so localized that it is somewhat misleading to speak of an "Irish" Catholicism at all, especially before 1830.

Patterns, like wakes and crossroads dancing, reflected the chthonic origins of Irish spirituality. Ancient Celts inhabited an enchanted landscape populated by fairies (the people of the hill), ghosts, and witches. In addition, the earth itself had animate qualities, activated whenever would-be desecrators sought to alter it, divide it, objectify it, or deny its inherent power. To those who lived near them, caves and wells served as portals to the netherworld, and the spirits associated with them became their express intercessors. Early Christians co-opted these holy places in the name of favored missionaries, but even the new "patron saints" were autocthones; that is, they served the local countryside and its people.[14] Believers consequently construed their site to be a symbol of community ties, and so nominal Catholics living in, say, the northeastern Donegal parish of Cloncaugh only partially shared the spiritual identity of Catholics in Glencolumbkille to the southwest. For that matter, Catholics *within* Cloncaugh subdivided according to a complex sacred geography. A particularly enlightened person might go to Lough Derg for the annual pilgrimage honoring Saint Patrick's purgatory, but the typical layman did not embrace generalized devotions until several decades after the Famine.

After Parliament repealed the penal laws in 1829, the Catholic Church in Ireland initiated a new crusade to standardize religious beliefs and practices. This "devotional revolution" also attempted to relocate the sacred from open fields to newly built chapels. Its success was mixed. The Bishop of Raphoe, whose diocese included half of the powder workers' cultural hearth, found it impossible to effect real reform. Isolated in the far west, he had in 1842 only fifty priests at his disposal, and they themselves lacked full knowledge of Catholic dogma.[15] These conditions, coupled with few roads and lay resistance, contributed to the persistence of certain "Hibernianisms" throughout the nineteenth century.

The weak institutional status of the Catholic Church in America enabled the Irish to perpetuate their vernacular faith after they emigrated. Although the first amendment to the Constitution guaranteed the separation of church and state, it did not yet endorse religious liberty as we know it. Only four states actually sanctioned Catholicism: Maryland, Pennsylvania, Delaware, and Virginia. Georgia and Rhode Island grudgingly tolerated the "Papists" in their midst; the remaining seven states actively opposed them. Much of the hostility reflected widespread fears of "foreign influence." In the wake of the XYZ affair and the Alien and Sedition Acts, some Americans saw in Catholics' allegiance to Rome an active plot to infiltrate the new nation and subvert its historic Protestant mission. Others simply doubted whether Catholics could exercise civic virtue if they bowed to a distant authority. Faced with seemingly insurmountable legal and cultural prejudices, the fledgling Church adapted to the republican context.

Among other things, accommodation meant vesting control of Catholic parishes in secular hands. In the northeast in particular, statutory laws required that parishes be incorporated by lay trustees, not clergy, while disestablishment worked to promote clerical dependence on the voluntary contributions of affluent pew renters. The resulting system, called trusteeism, proved a mixed blessing. On one hand, it allowed Catholic churches to exist where they would not otherwise have been possible. On the other hand, it teetered uncomfortably close to congregationalism. With only seventy priests and eighty churches to serve them, the estimated 70,000 lay Catholics living in the United States around 1800 seized the initiative and established their own parishes.[16] Most of this ecclesiastical growth took place in urban centers, and American and English-born Catholics comprised the largest proportion of the faithful at this time. In deference to canon law, which vested authority over all temporalities in the episcopacy, some trustees petitioned their bishop for a pastor, but more typically they appointed their own clergy. Since the trustees held title to parish proper-ties, collected money from parishioners, paid the bills, provided salaries for the clergy, and administered the parish's legal affairs, they often viewed themselves as employers, with all the rights and prerogatives that that posi-tion implied.[17] Bishop John Carroll, metropolitan for the United States, generally condoned trusteeism on practical grounds: he lacked the institu-tional infrastructure required to enforce compliance with canon law, and he recognized the need to adapt the traditional Catholic polity, with its em-phasis on hierarchy and clerical control, to a democratic climate. As a result, early American parishes enjoyed considerable autonomy.

Because of these two preconditions, Catholics living along the Brandy-wine initially adhered to Irish heterodoxy. Probably fewer than 40 percent of them attended Mass on any given Sunday, for example. Historians tradi-tionally attribute high rates of absenteeism to either the Irish countryman's ignorance of his Sunday obligation or his inability to pay pew rent.[18] A more likely explanation is indifference to that particular ritual. As late as 1851, the majority of rural Catholics in Ireland neglected their canonical duty; in the specific geographic area that produced the powder workers, the rate of nonattendance ranged from 65 to 68 percent.[19] This is not to say that du Pont employees lacked reverence for their faith. On the contrary, they voluntarily authorized regular deductions from their wage accounts to support Fr. Kenny's mission. A surviving 1818 list of subscribers to St. Mary's, Kenny's chapel at Coffee Run, gives forty-six names along with the amount they contributed. Single men gave $1 per year, married men $2, and men with families $3. A few men even paid $5, the same amount do-nated by their employer, E. I. du Pont.[20] They received all major sacra-ments, and when they considered it worthwhile, they even went to church. On Sunday, April 5, 1818, Kenny happily recorded a particularly notewor-thy event in his diary:

> Great rain all morning opened passage to a great number who attended church. 18 communicants, 4 masses ordered for Pk Brady's son & 1 mass in particular for John Brady—1 mass by Js Brady for Sl [soul] of Hugh Brady— 3 masses for Sl [soul] of Philip Gallagher 3 masses Sl [soul] of Edward Brad-ley—Jas Brady paid for what I already celebrated.[21]

Offered especially "for the Sls of all that were swept off [in an explosion] on the 19 of March 1818 at du Ponts' powder mills," the April 5 service drew an unusually large crowd because the community needed to grieve collec-tively and publicly. Still, these circumstances were unusual. To reach St. Mary's, Brandywine Catholics had to hike three miles uphill. To reach St.

Peter's, founded by Fr. Kenny on 4th Street in Wilmington in 1816, they faced a four-mile trek along the river. As a consequence, most families observed their Sabbath at home, but sensibly joined local parishes to receive home visits from the pastor and bury their dead in consecrated soil.

That Kenny continued the Irish practice of stations contributed to their canonical laxity. Victor du Pont's wife, Gabrielle de la Fite de Pelleport, attended St. Mary's, where she often sat in the front pew with her three children, Charles, Amelia, and Frank. Yet she often invited the priest to say Mass at her home, Louviers. Kenny also held large, open-air celebrations for the powder workers from time to time, and he regularly administered communion wafers to the sick. According to his diary, a typical trip to the powder mills went something like this:

> Started about 10 A.M. for Hagley Brandywine. Arrived over rocks, through woods, amidst stumps, down precipices, up perpendicular (almost) steeps and bumping loose stones against my wheels at every step, across Squirrel Run, until I got out at Edward Doherty's house. Administered him. From thence through abominable rocky, loose, stoney roads through Hagley tanyard, down Brandywine Creek to Hugh Bogan's mother. Administered her. From thence to Peter Quigley's on a bank as high as the third story of the big cotton factory, gave private baptism to his infant child. From thence to Wilmington where I sent my horse and Dearborn to Mrs. McGee's.[22]

The dying received communion at home as part of the sacrament of extreme unction, and Kenny often heard confessions, performed marriages, and christened children there as well.

Even so, many pious Irish believed in witches, prophetic visions, evil curses, banshees, and fairies.[23] Picture, for example, eighty-year-old powder man Patrick Brady insisting to his neighbors that his cows had been bewitched and that "if we would get the priest to come and say a few prayers over them, they would get well; [because] 'that was the way they did it in Ireland.'" Or imagine him standing "bent over his stick, muttering his prayers as fast as he could, while old Ann Lovell was milking, because he thought her a witch."[24] Other immigrants shared these beliefs. Nancy Kelly, a domestic who worked for Evelina du Pont, thought herself possessed by an evil spirit, and powder man Mickey Mullin heard the voice of his dead mother shortly before his own demise.[25] Even Father Kenny practiced "white magic" from time to time. "My fine cow Hannah seems strained in the kidneys—no mark of hurt," he wrote. "Rubb'd her back with a stick then with a coarse rag & train oil, slit her tail & put in a clove of garlic. Seems better this evening."[26]

As the number of Irish immigrants living in the antebellum United

States began to rise, American clergy embarked upon a concerted campaign to eradicate these practices. They intended, however, to make wild "Hibernians" good Americans as well as good Catholics. Everything about the new arrivals seemed threatening: they were poor and unemployed during an era of economic expansion, illiterate and boisterous when the nation prized education and decorum, and servile and immoral in a self-governing republic of virtuous citizens.[27] Despite their canonical laxity, they also made up the majority of the laity. In light of rising nativism, prelates had to find a way to make both Catholicism and the Irish more tolerable without jeopardizing the Church's integrity or unity. The episcopacy opted to modify lay behavior. Most bishops—and many native-born lay Catholics—attributed Anglo-Protestant animosity to an Irish penchant for drinking and brawling. They also blamed such "dissolute pastimes" for Irish indifference to devotional rituals. Thenceforth, clerics agreed to stress the importance of frugality, punctuality, honesty, sobriety, and industry, fully cognizant that a well-regulated life was as conducive to the regular discharge of religious duties as to Americanization. There was only one catch: reaching the mass of lay Catholics required an array of new parishes and priests, all of which would have to be under episcopal control. Fortunately, the Irish tended to support clerical authority. Because of earlier British policies, few of Ireland's sees had sitting bishops when the nineteenth century began. In many communities, well-to-do lay men stepped into the void and imposed the continental custom of patronage, which exchanged certain episcopal prerogatives for financial support. They also monopolized the spiritual services of local clergy, and the majority of Irish Catholics, typically landless cottiers and tenant farmers, greatly resented elite interference. The influx of Irish immigrants after the Napoleonic wars thus gave American bishops a power base against trustees they had not had before.[28]

Events in northern Delaware illustrate how the emergence of an Irish American Catholicism began. The American episcopacy's efforts to assert its authority over the laity accelerated in the 1820s, when "trustee fever" raged uncontrollably. Even Father Kenny became embroiled in conflict between 1825 and 1829. Although he tried to maintain a reasonable visitation schedule for his six parishes, each set of trustees demanded his presence for Sunday Mass.[29] The leaders of St. Peter's and St. Mary's pressed especially hard; both groups insisted that they represented the majority of his flock and deserved special treatment. Kenny stood his ground. A Sulpician by training and hence a stickler for religious protocol, he requested an assistant from his bishop, Rev. Hugh Conwell of Philadelphia. But Conwell could do little to help; he had no priest available, let alone one capable of pleasing both Kenny and his embattled constituents. For example, when Rev. Shanon Keenan came to serve temporarily at St. Peter's and failed to pay his respects at Coffee Run, Kenny fumed to his diary that "he is above reporting himself at headquarters, and not above carrying off all the stole could muster for him." Keenan eventually made amends for the gaffe, but Kenny always held a dim view of the young man's ministerial efforts, saying at one point, "In fine, it has been a bungled, ill handed transaction. When all mischief was done (mass celebrated, etc.), then Rev. Keenan, bearing no scrip, walks in."[30] Other priests also incurred the pastor's wrath, especially the itinerant ones who traveled through New Castle County en route to and from Baltimore and supplied sacraments for cash on demand.[31] Meanwhile, with no permanent help in sight, the trustees at St. Peter's cut Kenny's minimal salary several times in quick succession. He retaliated with stern sermons and private reprimands. When these tactics failed, Kenny withdrew his spiritual services completely.

In July 1826 the trustees filed suit against their pastor in civil court—no doubt for breach of contract—yet Kenny refused to be intimidated. While the court convened, he wrote a carefully worded letter in which he offered to resume his original Mass schedule, for a price. The cleric announced that,

> I would be in Wilm tomorrow, & if upon examination I should find all matters square, I would officiate in Wilm providing that ALL the trustees that were elected 7 July would sign a document purporting they regretted the occurrences and that they would use their best efforts, whilst in office, to prevent a repetition thereof.[32]

The trustees refused. Clearly, they wanted Kenny's services, but they insisted that their administrative role gave *them* the right to decide where, when, and how often the sacraments should be administered. Kenny disagreed. The absence of an official Church hierarchy in Ireland had vested parish priests with sole authority over religious affairs, and his actions conveyed an intention to uphold the Irish system. Four months later, Rev. Keenan and a trustee named Thomas Larkin paid a visit at Coffee Run. "This too busy gentleman assur'd me, that there would be blood spilled on Sunday next in Wilm if I should give Mass, as he was inform'd I intended," Kenny wrote. "[The trustees] thought it more prudent that I should not attend St. Peter's until the next court decision."[33] Undaunted, Kenny went to William Larkin's store, a popular Irish meeting place in Wilmington. There, he boldly proclaimed that he would indeed offer Mass on Sunday and further, that he would be available for the next two days to meet with any member of the parish who wished to speak with him. As a steady stream of parishioners filed into Larkin's, the trustees realized the extent of the priest's appeal in the community and reopened their own negotiations with him. Though the conflict did not end officially until a permanent assistant, Rev. George A.

Carrell, arrived at St. Peter's in 1829, Kenny had won an important victory. By taking the matter straight to his flock, he diminished the power of an American innovation—the voluntary parish with its lay trustees—and reinforced the traditional Irish relationship between priest and people.

This shift in the locus of parish authority especially pleased Kenny and his superiors because of other developments in the region. In the 1820s a series of religious revivals swept the mid-Atlantic states. Always concerned about Irish apostasy, church officials watched in horror as evangelical Protestants launched a crusade to convert all "infidels" in their midst, especially Catholics.[34] Drawing upon the Reformed tradition, evangelicals believed that Catholicism deprived its adherents of the crucial, life-changing encounter with God. This encounter or "conversion" could only come about through a close reading of scripture. Since, in their view, Catholicism did not encourage either Bible study or individual interpretation, it necessarily prevented its adherents from developing a personal relationship with the Almighty. Evangelicals therefore concluded they had a duty to help Catholics "come out from darkness into the light of the true faith in Christ."[35] Believing further that Roman Catholic influence might substantially delay the Second Coming, millenialists advocated an aggressive activism. They adopted promulgation of the gospel as a necessary corollary, for Catholics had to be re-educated to achieve conversion. Biblicalism became the cornerstone of anti-Catholicism, but it also reflected a very different attitude toward salvation. To Protestant eyes, Christ's crucifixion made good works, the sacraments, and prayers of intercession unnecessary. Salvation occurred by faith alone. As a result, "evangelical anti-Catholics had a strong hostility to all aspects of the Roman church that seemed to them to imply that there were intermediaries between the believer and Christ, such as papal authority, the Mass, and veneration of saints."[36]

Spread by the force of the Second Great Awakening, these beliefs appealed to many souls along the Brandywine, including some du Ponts. Victorine Bauduy, E. I. du Pont's eldest child, became an Episcopalian after the sudden death of her husband in 1814. Sophie, eighteen years Victorine's junior, embraced her sister's faith as a teenager and went on to convert her Catholic cousin, Frank du Pont (the future Rear Admiral), after their 1833 marriage. Eleuthera joined them after wedding Thomas Mackie Smith in 1834, and Alexis converted after he married Joanna Smith, Thomas's sister, two years later.[37] Despite their common denomination, the Episcopalian members of the family seldom agreed on matters of religion. Sophie, Frank, Eleuthera, and Victorine ascribed to low-church, or evangelical, beliefs while Thomas Mackie Smith and Joanna Smith du Pont espoused high-church, or Tractarian, principles.[38] Alexis wavered between the two, but had leanings toward the latter.

On some level, the evangelical du Ponts hoped to convert the entire community. They chose as their instrument the Brandywine Manufacturers' Sunday School (BMSS). Established by E. I. du Pont in 1816 and subsidized largely by him and his heirs, it deviated sharply from the broader Sunday school movement. The children began in Alphabet classes, where they learned their letters, worked through various levels of reading, writing, and ciphering exercises, and ended with lessons in the catechism and Bible of their choice.[39] Since attendance cost nothing, nearly 1,200 students representing every major Christian denomination enrolled between 1817 and 1852.[40] Ever the Deist, Irénée insisted upon a nonsectarian program, but Victorine (fig. 3.2) supervised the curriculum, and her correspondence, coupled with that of her sisters, who also taught at the school, reveals an overt desire to awaken their little charges.

The du Pont women fervently believed in the nineteenth-century ideology of female moral influence and well understood "how much is placed in the power of a S. School teacher."[41] In addition to their lessons, students received from them copies of the Ten Commandments "to hang up in their houses and learn," as well as monthly premiums for perfect attendance. These included small books of moral tales, religious tracts, embroidered pen-wipers, or hand-made collars. The sisters also visited their pupils at home. "Immediately after dinner I went over Squirrel Run to see some of my Sunday scholars. I had a charming walk," wrote Victorine.[42] These "pastorals" generally worked to cement the teacher-student relationship. Sometimes the women paid purely social calls. More often they discussed religion. "Yesterday I spent the afternoon visiting those at the cotton factory. First E. McVey—had very satisfactory converse with her, from what she said & M. Aiken said of her, I trust she is on the way to salvation."[43] Mindful of their father's mutualistic brand of paternalism, Victorine and Sophie (fig. 3.3) tried to respect the authority of their students' parents in matters of faith, but they found it hard to countenance infidels. "Mrs. Rigby talked so much I could not speak to Martha as I wished. . . . I do not altogether like Mrs. Rigby," Sophie admitted. "She talks a great deal about religion but I fear she dont *feel* what she says."[44] Alexis duplicated his sisters' efforts in the powder yards. After his conversion, he became an increasingly active proselytizer, arguing that men engaged in powder manufacture must be prepared at any moment to meet their maker. He even continued his exhortations from his deathbed, using his own wounds to impress the operatives that filed through the room to pay their respects.[45]

The directors of the powder company, by contrast, openly disdained organized religion and authorized no corporate policies concerning it. Like their father and grandfather, Alfred and Henry believed only that a somewhat vague kind of divine order governed the universe.[46] In accordance

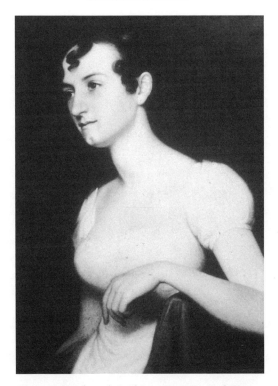

Fig. 3.2. Rembrandt Peale's 1813 portrait of Victorine (du Pont) Bauduy, eldest child of E. I. du Pont and director of the Brandywine Manufacturers' Sunday School from 1816 to 1852. (Courtesy of Hagley Museum and Library)

with the mutualistic compact, however, both men felt obligated to tolerate the religious inclinations of others, and they graciously accommodated the Baptists, Methodists, Presbyterians, Episcopalians, and Catholics in their employ. Each denomination received donations of cash and building materials, for example. Most got to buy land on the periphery of the community for a ridiculously low price, and most received quarterly payments deducted from workmen's earnings. In all, the firm contributed to the formation of at least eight different congregations.

Equitable treatment by their employer allowed individual working people to follow their own path to God. Some were genuinely reborn. When the Methodists held revivals at William Young's nearby textile village, Rockland, in 1832, many Brandywine residents "came forth, crying, weeping, etc.," to be baptized, including (much to Sophie's chagrin) young Martha Rigby.[47]

Fig. 3.3. Rembrandt Peale's 1831 portrait of Sophie Madeleine (du Pont) du Pont, the fifth child of E. I. du Pont, who used her extensive diaries and letters to record valuable information concerning everyday life in the powder mill community. (Courtesy of Hagley Museum and Library)

Additional conversions took place among textile operatives living at Rockdale and Crozerville, on the Pennsylvania branch of the Brandywine, and at Kentmere, just south of the powder mills. Consequently, at least one historian contends that all wage workers in the region became "Christian soldiers," transformed by the "triumph of evangelical capitalists," and their wives and daughters. In the absence of direct testimonials from the workers themselves, this conclusion seems implausible, especially when applied to the region's Irish Catholics. Consider Sophie du Pont's comment that "a good many Catholics go to hear Mr. Love preach at the S[unday] school, because it is not a church, & is a house open to all denominations."[48] Rev. Thomas Love, a well-known Presbyterian minister, regularly visited the Brandywine. On the basis of this quote, one might conclude that Catholics truly preferred his message to Fr. Kenny's. Or, given the distance to St. Mary's, perhaps they simply considered Love an acceptable alternative. After all, the Irish had long suffered the established Church of Ireland, and with the dearth of Catholic chapels in nineteenth-century Ulster, attending Protestant services might not have been so novel. Maybe their presence at the Sunday school reflected an attempt to curry favor with the female du

Ponts. Although they did not directly participate in the manufacture of black powder, Victorine and her sisters had each inherited a sizeable share of company stock, which gave them a voice in all manner of company policies, including hiring and firing. Since the du Pont women held some authority in their own right, supporting their special interest, religion, might bring rewards. Moreover, the building was not an actual church. As Sophie's language suggests, local Catholics did not recognize the Sunday school as a consecrated space, and so their presence there posed no moral dilemmas. But they eschewed outright conversion. "There were but two persons confirmed at Trinity [Episcopal Church], Mr. Breck and a lady," Victorine lamented. "Mr. Breck told Eleu that his wife did not come forward, because she feared it would distress her mother as she had been confirmed in the Catholic Church."[49] Likewise, immigrant Ann McGran participated in numerous theological exchanges with both Sophie and Victorine, yet became a nun around 1836. Many years later she boldly wrote, "It does not become a scholar to instruct her teacher [but] . . . I hope you will not die before embracing the true faith, which is Catholic, you know that good marks are not sufficient."[50] Clearly, the waves of pressure against apostasy surged just as strong as the ones for it.

After nearly four decades in a kind of spiritual limbo, a group of powder workers finally resolved in 1840 to build their own parish. Led by an immigrant named Peter Brennan, the organizers enlisted the aid of Father Kenny, who supported the idea wholeheartedly. When he died later that year, they conscripted his successor, Rev. George Carrell. Our veteran chronicler, Sophie du Pont, noted the event in her diary:

> Yesterday I heard that there is plan on foot to build a Catholic church here— it was quite *news* to me, but not at all to Amelia [her cousin and sister-in-law]. she said she had heard of it long ago. it originated she thinks with priest Carrol. Peter Brennan is one of the most zealous promoters of it— Amelia said Alfred had promised to give the land, if funds enough to build the church were collected—no fear but that they will very soon be collected!—The Catholics put us protestants to shame completely by their superior zeal and devotedness.[51]

Brennan typified a new breed of Irish Catholic. Born in 1817, he came to the Brandywine as a young child and began working at the Louviers textile mill while just a teenager. After suffering a crippling accident of uncertain nature, he became a bookkeeper, keeping track of bolts woven and wages paid. By 1840 he earned a respectable $600 per annum. This amount easily enabled him to become a trustee, still a position of some repute. Brennan persuaded his employer, Charles I. du Pont, to support the venture and sell the diocese a prime plot of land along the edge of the powder mill community for $100.[52] The other Irish trustees had similar stories: Brothers Edward and Charles Dougherty emigrated in the 1820s and advanced from common laborers to powder men; so did Michael Dougherty (no relation). A new phase of Irish Catholicism had begun.

Though Alfred, Henry, and Charles du Pont contributed to the church fund and served as trustees to safeguard their investment, their Catholic counterparts directed the venture. The wage-earning trustees organized a voluntary drive to finance the building's construction, and many powder workers bought $100 shares at 6 percent interest. Then they commissioned the company's master mason, Presbyterian James Goodman, to supervise the construction. Goodman likely drafted the basic plan, and du Pont employees, on temporary leave from their duties in and around the powder yards, performed most of the labor. The structure incorporated Brandywine granite for the walls, oak for the rafters and joists, and pine for the floors, pews, altar, and wainscoting. By the following December, the "neat and commodious" church appeared ready for its dedication; the congregation chose St. Joseph, patron saint of carpenters, as their guardian.[53]

The new parish encapsulated some of the dramatic changes taking place within the community. On one level, it symbolized economic prosperity.[54] Though clearly wage earners, the congregants' actions advertised the fact that du Pont employees had enough discretionary income to build an appropriate edifice and retain the services of their own pastor, the Rev. Bernard McCabe. Most of their financial support still came in the form of voluntary pew rents. Like his predecessor, Father Kenny, McCabe assessed parishioners' minimum contributions on the basis of marital status, and he relied on the du Pont company to make the necessary deductions.[55] Along with rising subscriptions came rising attendance rates, helped along, no doubt, by the arrival of Famine refugees. Within five short years of the dedication ceremony, there were enough people crowding into the church on Sundays and holy days to justify enlarging the nave by one-third its original length. Additional improvements followed, including the acquisition of several rental properties and the establishment of a school in 1850.[56]

St. Joseph's also facilitated an important shift in spiritual orientation. Stations and home visits ended as parishioners embraced new liturgical and devotional practices. In relocating the sacred from their homes to the church, powder mill families demonstrated their growing communion with Rome. However, the character of Tridentine Catholicism in the United States differed significantly from that in Italy. The Forty Hours devotion, for example, took on special significance in this country. The idea to display a consecrated host in remembrance of the forty hours Christ's body lay in the sepulchre originally served to focus the believer's attention on the doctrine of the real presence. Bishop John Neumann of Philadelphia introduced the devotion into this country in 1853, and established a rotating schedule of exposition for every church in the diocese, which still included Delaware. His actions reflected the fact that anti-Irish and anti-Catholic sentiments had increased in intensity; Philadelphia experienced some of the worst nativist-inspired violence in American history in 1844, and the Know-Nothings (American Party) campaigned actively throughout the mid-Atlantic region. Viewed in this context, Forty Hours has been called an "intentionally and aggressively Catholic" devotion, one that publicly celebrated a doctrine Protestants spurned. Indeed, American apologists promoted veneration of the Blessed Sacrament for two reasons: it offered the laity another way to receive grace, and it enabled them to make reparations to God on behalf of those who rejected the true church.[57] Thus, when the Irish of northern Delaware participated in this ritual, as they did at St. Peter's in 1864, they self-consciously asserted an emerging identity as *American* Roman Catholics.

The parishioners' conceptions of ethnic identity were changing, too. In Ireland, individuals tended to affiliate along local lines, forming attachments to families and factions, that is, groups organized on the basis of geographic territory. The importance of having shared national origins emerged only after migration abroad, and recent research suggests that definitions of "Irishness" varied considerably from place to place.[58] Whether in Canada, the United States, or Australia, newly formed Catholic parishes fostered the construction of a generalized Irish identity because they acknowledged certain Old World saints, festivals, and customs even as they promoted Roman ones. For urban dwellers, in particular, the physical church became a potent symbol of ethnic community, and Catholics learned to place one another culturally and geographically by asking strangers to name their parish. In Wilmington, for example, the answer "St. Anthony's" long served as a kind of linguistic shorthand for "person of Italian descent living in the center of Ward 5." This attachment to place also characterized the Germans at Sacred Heart, the Poles at St. Hedwig's, and the Irish at St. Ann's, St. Patrick's, St. Mary's, and St. Peter's. Thus, a layman who joined St. Joseph's in the 1850s not only allied himself with American Roman Catholics, but with Irish Catholics who lived and worked in the shadow of the du Pont powder yards.

Whether heterodox or orthodox, lay people found myriad ways to preserve their ethnic heritage within the American Church. The sacraments served as especially potent vehicles for Irish identity. Catholic catechisms define a sacrament as an "outward sign of grace received" and recognize seven different rites: baptism, first communion, reconciliation, confirmation, marriage, holy orders, and extreme unction.[59] All seven sacraments are deemed necessary and conducive to the supernatural life of Man, but baptism is especially important because it purportedly removes the stain of Original Sin and marks one as a child of God. In the nineteenth century, the ritual usually occurred within a few weeks of birth. In some locales, however, the difficulty of reaching a priest postponed the official ceremony for months or even years. In that case, the Church authorized lay persons to perform the rite, with the understanding that the ceremony would be supplied by a priest as soon as possible. Baptism could also be administered by a lay Catholic if a child seemed in danger of death; the frequency of Brandywine babies baptized *ob periculum mortis* underscores the very real threat of infant mortality. Registers at St. Peter's and St. Joseph's carefully note whether a priest or a lay person had performed the ritual and where it occurred. Prior to about 1850, most baptisms followed Irish practice: they took place at home under a priests' direction.

The selection of a child's godparents reflected Irish customs, too. The role of a sponsor was to testify on behalf of the infant and rear the child in the Catholic faith should the parents be unable or unwilling to do so. Because of the tremendous responsibility retained by this position, parents did not choose sponsors lightly. The Church required only that they be Catholics "in good standing"; that is, they had to be men and women who practiced their faith in accordance with official dogma. Brandywine couples preferred blood relatives, generally their siblings or parents, followed by in-laws, cousins, and close family friends. Old Patrick Brady's family illustrates this pattern. His eldest child, John, married a woman named Ann Carrol. When their only son received baptism on July 5, 1818, almost four months after John went "across the creek," Mary Brady, John's sister, stood as godmother. The young widow reciprocated by witnessing Mary's marriage to Henry Gagan in May 1821. Ann Carrol then married Owen McQuaid in September 1821, but her ties to the Brady clan held fast. Terence Brady, her former brother-in-law, witnessed her wedding to Owen, and Ann became godmother to one of Mary Brady Gagan's children. Through the selection of godparents, then, Irish Catholics symbolically used baptism to strengthen familial and communal ties as well as spiritual.

The patterned use of personal names extended the affiliative function of the baptism ritual to include certain outsiders. For the most part, Irish immigrants along the Brandywine maintained the traditional naming practices associated with patron saints, but increasing contact with different ethnic and cultural groups meant that a few new names did slip into the community over time. Significantly, workers who developed close, personal relationships with their employers often borrowed the du Pont nomenclature. François Jeandelle, for example, who worked in the powder yards from 1804 through the 1840s, gave the name Irénée to his eldest son, and named another son Alfred, for Alfred Victor du Pont.[60] Irish American Tom Mathewson, a machinist in the 1870s, and later an electrician, was a close friend of Alfred I. du Pont's. He named his oldest son Alfred Irénée, "but they never put the I in. It was just Alfred."[61] Other examples include Victorine Finegan, the daughter of Hugh Finegan, a laborer and weaver, and Evelina Hannah Holland, the daughter of powder man John Holland.

The bestowal of names like Victorine, Evelina, Alfred, and Irénée on the children of Irish powder mill workers helped reinforce ties between employer and employee, yet the practice reflected more than a simple bid for preferential treatment. Only a small number of the children in the baptismal registers bore du Pont names. Although other sources confirm their use, there is no evidence that children named for du Pont family members received special consideration. Indeed, if children named Irénée or Victorine received privileges like better-paying jobs, then more parents would have adopted this practice.

Given the importance of patron saints in Catholic naming rituals, it is more likely that some workers considered the du Ponts appropriate role models for their children. In 1835 Joshua V. Gibbons wrote to Victorine Bauduy from his new home in Brownsville, Pennsylvania, that, "I have a fine healthy daughter nine months old, whom we call Victorene [*sic*] and I earnestly pray that she may imitate in every trait of character, the lady after whom she is named. (I am not certain that I spell the name properly, when you write please inform me.)"[62] Similarly, Catharine Davison had a daughter named Eleuthera, and in an 1872 letter, she informed Eleuthera du Pont Smith that "I gave hir [*sic*] your letter to read and she said she would be so happy to see the lady she was named for." Eleuthera Davison, in turn, married and had a daughter, whom she named "Catharine Victoreen [*sic*] Bean."[63]

Most Irish parents, however, named their children for close relatives. When asked about naming practices among the powder mill families, Eleanor Kane, the granddaughter of Daniel Dougherty and Ellen Gibbons, said,

> Well, I thought it was just in my family, but I did hear that we were all named for grandparents, and they named them in regular order. . . . It was the custom in Irish families to name the first boy for the paternal grandfather and the first girl for the paternal grandmother, and then the next two were maternal grandfather and maternal grandmother. And in my family they did that, and when you see all these William Gibbonses, I can see why some of these others, why, they would put the initial in sometimes when they're identifying them.[64]

When several brothers named their eldest sons for a common grandfather, they reinforced group and family solidarity. In the process, they also created confusion in the historical record, for the pattern typically produced several individuals with the same personal name and surname in a single generation. Brothers Thomas, John, and Patrick Holland, for example, all named their firstborn sons John. That their father answered to "Patrick" points to variations in the pattern.[65]

The custom applied to girls as well as boys. Historians typically argue that Christian parents had no compunction about naming female infants for their mothers or grandmothers because the eventual assumption of a husband's surname would sever a daughter's ties to her family of orientation. But women in nineteenth-century Ireland typically kept their patronym after marriage, and even those who did not maintained a close relationship with their birth families.[66] That parish priests in northern Delaware consistently identified Irish Catholic mothers and godmothers by maiden name suggests that the custom continued here. In addition, parents selected godparents from and named children for relatives on both sides of their nuclear family, thus honoring bilateral kinship ties. By these methods, powder mill families used the Roman ritual of baptism to assert their ethnocultural identity as well as their religious affiliation.

The sacrament of holy matrimony functioned the same way. In contrast to most Christian denominations, Catholicism defines marriage as a sacred covenant, one insuperable to civil divorce. Prior to 1962, the Church prohibited interfaith marriages on the grounds that spiritual exogamy fostered marital discord and jeopardized the propagation of Catholic beliefs to the next generation. The du Pont Irish agreed. Of 786 children baptized at St. Joseph's between 1846 and 1856, only twenty-eight resulted from a "mixed marriage."[67] The intense pressure to conform forced some couples to elope. Sophie duly related the scandalous behavior of one enterprising duo to her brother, Henry:

> On Wednesday, the fair Mary Green took a stroll to Wmn [Wilmington] to buy herself a gown—as she did not return that evening, her father dispatched her brother after her next day—when, oh horror & dismay to all the Greens both great & small! they found she was *married,* actually *married* the night before to *your* hopeful squire James Mullin! Now to conceive the indignation of the clan, you ought to know that there has been a feud since a year or more between Mullen & all her relations because he had presumed to court her— He is a *Catholic,* too; & they are staunch protestants—All the *verdant* tribe are in the state of a disturbed anthill & as for the groom, he looks *quite pensive* & scratches his head twice as much as usual.[68]

Faced with similar opposition, Eleanor Ramo eloped with Alexander Bradburn, and Nancy Andrews eloped with William Fisher that same year.[69] That the ban cut both ways undoubtedly reflects the long-standing hostility between Catholics and Protestants in Ireland. Nor did this animosity toward mixed marriages ease over time. When William Buchanan's mother, a Catholic, wed his father, an Episcopalian, in the 1880s, "all her people turned against her."[70] Even American-born Irish families saw interfaith marriage as a rejection of family and community ties.

Material culture offered another means of preserving Irish Catholic identity. During the severe repression of Catholicism in Ireland, the laity began using symbolic objects to sanctify their homes. The Church still refers to candles, prayer books, rosaries, crucifixes, sacred images, bells, incense, fonts of holy water, scapulars and other spiritual aids as sacramentals; their purpose is "to excite good thoughts and to increase devotion" among the faithful.[71] Premodern rural folk usually hung a special cross near the fireplace—the symbolic "heart" of the home—every February 1st in honor of St. Brigid's feast day. Woven from straw or hay, the cross merged folk custom and Catholic faith by blessing the house in preparation for a new agricultural season.[72] By the early nineteenth century, many Irish households owned inexpensive prints with religious themes, Catholic devotional books, crucifixes, and lives of the saints books, all of which could be purchased from traveling pedlars.[73] St. Brigid's cross remained a popular fixture, as did the small, wall-mounted "shrine shelf," which also hung in proximity to the hearth. Flanked by sacred prints and certificates, the shrine served as an important focal point for domestic rituals.[74]

Immigrants used a variety of religious objects in northern Delaware. Patrick Kenny, for example, purchased in 1811 "2 doz. vade mecums, Bousset's *Expo[sition]*, Eng[land]'s *Conv[ersion]*" and assorted other Catholic works, along with a framed print of Pope Pius VII, two seals with Pope Pius' image, a copy of O'Halloran's *Ireland,* and a framed view of Dublin's lighthouse.[75] Likewise, Catholic students at the BMSS read Catholic catechisms and received Catholic prayer books as premiums for good work. Elsewhere in the community, du Pont laborers blessed a new workers' dwelling by placing a Miraculous medal into the builder's trench, and in Wilmington, Irishmen displayed statues, holy water fonts, and iconographic engravings.[76] As the number and kind of Catholic artifacts available to Brandywine families increased over time, Irish households found additional ways to sanctify their homes. Powder man Anthony J. Dougherty, Jr., proudly displayed his 1868 First Communion certificate in an elaborate frame. Similarly, the Gibbons family owned a linen tablecloth with a woven image of the Last Supper, and members of the Toomey family used devotional books to record births, deaths, and marriages. By the turn of the century, the Irish were also commemorating confirmations and weddings with studio portraits.

Although sacramentals appeared in Catholic homes throughout the Western World, native-born Americans associated them exclusively and pejoratively with the Irish. The problem lay in the *kinds* of objects Catholics used: crucifixes, not crosses, and chromolithographs and statues, not Bibles and religious mottoes. Ancient charges of idolatry surfaced anew with the rise of nativism in the mid-nineteenth century. The popular press played up the issue with derogatory cartoons and engravings. "The Very Image of Pat," for example, an 1860 image from *Harper's Weekly*, showed the interior of a supposedly typical cottage in Ireland. Aside from the clearly impoverished family group, the scene included a dresser with chickens roosting in the bottom half, and a crucifix and rosary nailed conspicuously to the hearth wall.[77] Another artist showed a one-room tenement where hogs rutted happily beneath several saints' portraits that had been haphazardly tacked to the wall.[78] Like the literary caricature of Paddy, which used specific facial features, postures, and dress to convey Irish ethnicity, these images conveyed the presumed "backwardness" of the average Irish immigrant, who could not separate himself from either the pigsty or the Papacy.[79]

Catholic apologists acknowledged this negative domestic stereotype and took various steps to combat it. Prelates like Bishop Gibbons of Baltimore patiently and repeatedly explained that Catholics did not actually worship religious objects, but "by the images which we kiss, and before which we uncover our heads or kneel, we adore Christ, and venerate his saints, whose likeness they represent."[80] Meanwhile, the authors of Catholic novels, newspaper columns, and advice books began to articulate a domestic ideal that closely resembled the prevailing Protestant version. They encouraged the laity to create not only "visibly Catholic" homes, but orderly, clean, cheerful, refined, hierarchical, and moral ones as well. Irish wives bore the brunt of responsibility for the transformation. A typical pro-Irish lithograph from 1872, for example, portrays a family preparing to celebrate St. Patrick's Day.[81] In contrast to mainstream depictions of the holiday, which featured drunken men in public places, this scene focused on a mother and her two children, a boy and a girl, and depicted them in the midst of their comfortable parlor, enjoying the parade outside from the safety of their window. A prominently placed portrait of Daniel O'Connell flanked by flags of Ireland and the United States heralded their hybrid Irish-American identity, while a nearby statue of the Blessed Virgin signaled their faith. The number of positive depictions increased further with the publication of Catholic magazines like *Sacred Heart Review, Ave Maria,* and *Catholic*

World. At the local level, even diocesan newspapers began to feature domestically oriented columns and articles.[82] The clergy also insisted that the home no longer serve as the primary locus of spirituality. Despite the rise of several new, domestically oriented devotions, the official heart of American Catholicism had shifted to the parish.

Acceptance of these innovations came, like the Irish themselves, in waves. For every immigrant who embraced his parish as a sign of bourgeois respectability and Roman orthodoxy, four or five others clung to the old ways. St. Joseph's first two decades of existence coincided with the arrival of hundreds of famine refugees, including families from rural Connaught and Munster. By mid-century, the population of the powder mill community exceeded 2,000 inhabitants. According to the 1857 Wilmington City Directory, Fr. John S. Walsh, the church's fourth pastor, claimed all 2,000 as parishioners, but only several hundred actually had that status and, judging from their behavior, a great many of them seemed ambivalent.[83] Though higher than it had been in the 1820s, Sunday attendance remained a problem, and many immigrants reneged on their voluntary contributions. Imagine Walsh's frustration in 1851 as he wrote to John Peoples, one of the company's Irish-born clerks, concerning powder man Thomas Devine:

> He says, at least he, like some others, told you it was a mistake on my part. There was no mistake on my part. Thomas Devine, Peter Conway and others took pews for themselves and friends but, I suppose, when they failed in getting paid from those friends, they endeavored in getting out of paying themselves by fastening a mistake on me.[84]

Another letter, dated seven years later, notified Peoples that,

> The late Anthony Doherty, Lewis Vache, and John McClafferty, having paid no pew rent, owed for the burying ground. Please let me know if they had any money in the office and if anything could be done towards getting something.[85]

By 1858 pew rents had risen to $4 for single men and $6 for married men, paid in two installments.[86] As they had in the past, company clerks made regular deductions from Catholic workers' wage accounts, but the pastor had to submit periodic lists of parish members for this purpose and clever workers found ways to manipulate the system. Hence, Thomas Devine tried to split the cost of one pew with several other families. Others claimed to be bachelors so they could pay a lower sum. Walsh admitted to James Peoples, another clerk, "I sometimes am not aware that some are married. I would be thankful if you corrected such mistakes." If a dispute arose, the priest might turn a secular authority. Addressing "Boss" Henry, then president of the company, Walsh wrote, "I understand that Daniel Haley is about to leave here. He owes us $23 rent and I expect nothing from him. If you could secure it for us you would confer a great favor."[87] For recent arrivals like Devine and Haley, the benefits of belonging to "an organized, Rome-centered, religious community which emphasized the parish, the Mass, and fulfillment of religious duties" did not yet outweigh the costs.[88]

Their children were another story. As early as 1829, the First Provincial Council of Baltimore announced, "We judge it absolutely necessary that [Catholic] schools should be established in which the young may be taught the principals of the faith and morality, while being instructed in letters."[89] At the powder mills, Irish parents took advantage of the free instruction provided at the BMSS, and did not begin worrying about their children's religious socialization until the 1840s. Rev. Daniel McGorian, an Irish immigrant, became pastor of St. Joseph's in 1842. Shortly thereafter, the "comments" column of the BMSS receiving book records the withdrawal of Catholic children from the Sunday school "by order of Mister McG." "Mister" was the common honorific applied to Catholic clergy in the nineteenth century and it is likely that McGorian established a day school in the church basement at this time.[90] Many parishes in the region were establishing schools in church basements, including St. Xavier (1842) in Philadelphia and St. Vincent de Paul (1849) in Madison, New Jersey.[91] Founded by priests, not parishioners, they were a direct, institutional response to the growing nativism and evangelical fervor sweeping the country. By 1850, forty students attended classes at St. Joseph's. As a local newspaper reported, however, "most of the children of the neighborhood resort to the district School, which is near by; . . . as two or three teachers in this school are Catholics, it is not liable to the same objections as most schools of the kind."[92]

Clearly, powder mill households did not automatically support the concept of Catholic education. Parishioners still tell the story of one Mrs. Russell, who fell suddenly ill and called for extreme unction sometime in the 1850s. The priest arrived, but refused to administer last rites until she promised to withdraw her children from the BMSS and enroll them at St. Joseph's. After the poor woman consented, she made a miraculous recovery, and when she went to make good her word, she told Victorine Bauduy, with tears in her eyes, that she would never have made such a promise if she thought she was going to live![93] There were several reasons for Catholic "disloyalty" to parish schools. Although Delaware established free public schools in 1829, the state did not mandate attendance until 1921.[94] In addition, many Irish parents needed their children to work, while others, barely literate themselves, placed little value on book-learning.[95] Nor were Brandywine residents unusual in their attitudes. Only thirty percent of all parishes in the northeastern United States had educational facilities before the Civil War.[96]

Prior to the so-called "bricks-and-mortar" phase of American Catholicism, those parents securing a formal Catholic education for their children were the upwardly mobile, affluent members of their communities. By 1855, enough powder mill families fit this description to necessitate building a separate school building (fig. 3.4). Constructed of stone and erected adjacent to the church, it accommodated 126 students. The parish brought in three sisters from the order of St. Joseph in Pennsylvania to teach them to read and write and cipher. Students also received instruction from the Baltimore Catechism. Few graduated, however; a belief in the necessity of child labor meant that the average pupil attended for four or five years only.[97]

Public schoolers benefited from an active Sunday school, and in 1857, the community's first confirmation classes began. The latter event particularly manifested the transformation taking place at St. Joseph's. According to an antebellum Catholic catechism, "Confirmation is the sacrament through which those already baptized are strengthened by the Holy Ghost, in order that they may steadfastly profess their faith and faithfully live up to it."[98] Then, as now, the ritual marked the onset of Catholic adulthood. Before 1896, however, *confirmandi* in northern Delaware professed their faith at the age of twelve, after two full years of preparation. They also made their first communion at this time. Administered in 1859 by Bishop John Neumann of Philadelphia, the ceremony inspired communal celebration and affirmation. As the Catholic *Herald* exulted,

> The children had been preparing for a long time both on Sundays and throughout the weekend. There is no doubt that the instructions they received, both from their pastor and the sisters of St. Joseph qualified them for the important ceremony, and strengthened them to bear their faith worthily throughout life. The weather on the occasion was agreeable but notwithstanding that the church was crowded to excess by the Catholics of Brandywine and the surrounding country.[99]

Because of the ritual's spiritual significance, the Church encouraged each adolescent to choose a new patron saint whose name would be added to their baptismal name and surname. Many of the parish's early records disappeared in 1866, when a fire nearly destroyed the rectory, but an 1872 list of *confirmandi* shows the dramatic shift underway. Of the seventy-two girls listed, fully 91 percent bore traditional Irish names (such as Mary, Margaret,

Fig. 3.4. Exterior view of St. Joseph's Sunday School students, 1887. (Courtesy of Hagley Museum and Library)

and Ann) that had been given to them at baptism.[100] The names the girls chose for themselves, however, differed greatly. The majority (69 percent) selected names like Agnes, Theresa, Cecelia, Walbarga, and Dolorosa, which honored Italian saints. Their choice spoke volumes. Having been born in the United States and reared entirely within the province of the American Catholic Church, with its increasing emphasis on an official or Tridentine version of the faith, this generation had a much closer relationship with Rome than its predecessor.

A new spirit of parochialism flourished toward the end of the century. The necessity of fighting and recovering from the Civil War temporarily redirected local institution-building efforts, but notable events in the 1870s included the construction of a tower over the entrance to the church and the establishment of various religious confraternities including the Ancient Order of Hibernians (AOH) and the Sodality of the Blessed Virgin Mary. Despite links to the Molly Maguires in nearby Pennsylvania, the AOH in the Reconstruction era shook off its radical roots, becoming a symbol of Irish Catholic patriotism, progress, and social uplift. At a national meeting in 1876, the organization's leadership even passed resolutions saying, "it is the most earnest desire of the AOH to think, judge and act in accordance with the government, teachings, and practices of the Holy Catholic

Church, [and to] to disown, denounce, protest against, and ignore any connection with organizations, societies or bodies or individuals that hold, advance, or do anything contrary to what their Church and Country demand of them."[101] The women of the community were equally dedicated. The Sodality promoted reverence for Mary through devotion to the rosary. An intensely private act when done at home or during the Mass, saying the rosary could become a powerful symbol of communal identity when performed by a group publicly. Members of the Sodality also demonstrated their parochialism in other ways. These women raised funds for the parish by organizing bazaars, festivals, and raffles, and preparing the food and goods to be sold there. They also performed much of the congregation's charity work, made the pastor's vestments, and cleaned the church.[102] In contrast to the Hibernians, who elected their own officers, the Sodality accepted leaders chosen by the pastor. Both organizations reflected the social hierarchy of the community, however, drawing their members from the families of prosperous, long-term employees.

As St. Joseph's became the center of religious life, parish activities increasingly merged Irish, Catholic, and American identities together. "We had very little social life, except what we had at church," recalled one parishioner.[103] When the parish erected a steeple in 1887, for example, locals eagerly came out to watch the construction, bringing oil lamps on dark mornings (fig. 3.5). The most notable social event of any year was the parish's Fourth of July celebration. Inaugurated in 1869 by Father George Kelly, a native of County Cavan, it lasted until 1926. Like the ancient pagan pattern, the festivities began with a procession from the church to a shady spot along Squirrel Run. There, families from throughout the community gathered to sing, dance, and hear patriotic lectures. Depending upon their cultural tastes, parishioners could attend church-sponsored dances that featured Irish music or join the Brandywine Catholic Literary Association (no. 143) and read books like *Valentine McClutchy, the Irish Agent*. Then there were the church ladies' periodic bazaars, including at least one that featured stereopticon slides of Ireland along with ethnic food.[104]

By the close of the century, local Catholics stood ready to proclaim publicly their new sense of spiritual identity, and they did so by completely remodeling the interior of the church. The beautification effort focused on a new, high altar of marble. A gift from the descendants of Peter Brennan, the Irish immigrant who helped found the parish in 1841, it came with flanking angel statues and an elaborate reredos. Additional embellishments included shrines to St. Joseph and the Blessed Virgin, two stained-glass windows, red carpeting, and a paneled ceiling of Florida pine. Although the church reopened in June 1894, the real celebration came five months

Fig. 3.5. Exterior view of the Church of St. Joseph on the Brandywine, 1898. (Courtesy of Hagley Museum and Library)

later with the four-hour consecration ceremony on November 11. It was a "red-letter" day for the congregation; the church, finally free of debt, became a sanctified space.[105]

Approximately a decade later, an anonymous parishioner sat down and composed a poem to commemorate St. Joseph's distinctive past. Entitled "A Country Churchyard," it eloquently conveys Roman Catholicism's new place in the community's collective psyche:

> I know a quiet churchyard;
> The mounds they cover sons of toil—
> Men whose early years were nurtured
> In distant lands of foreign soil.
> Side by side the Celt and Latin
> Rest in peace beneath the sod—
> Sturdy builders of this nation,
> Earnest, faithful sons of God.
>
> From across the restless ocean
> Came these men so brave and true—
> Sons of France and Sons of Ireland,

The work of God and man to do,
Earnest in their search for freedom,
Upholding it whate'er the loss;
Sustained in all their high endeavor
By fervent trust in Jesus' cross.

Side by side with their home dwellings
Builded they a temple fine,
Where every morn to God was offered
The sacrifice of bread and wine.
Thus they builded old St. Joseph's
Of rugged rocks from out the glen,
Symbolic of the faith of Peter,
An ark of hope to earnest men.

Small their work in the beginning,
Proudly stands their work today—
Their children marvel at their courage,
The fathers long since passed away.
On the hillside stands St. Joseph's,
The schoolhouse nestles at its side;
All around the church and schoolhouse,
Sleep the founders who have died.

Down in the canyon roars the river—
Rushing, whirling through the glen—
Not more restless in its madness
Than the minds of wordly men.
In the world is dire confusion—
Men and women all at sea—
Wondering if there's God or heaven;
Doubting if there's life to be.

But the children of St. Joseph's
Those who to their faith are true—
Ever have a lamp to guide them,
Always know just what to do.
Jesus present at the altar,
Listens to their prayer, their cry;
Peace to them while they are living,
Never fearful when they die.

Oh, the peace the faith brings to us!
Overcoming noise and sin,
As we kneel before the altar
and our hearts cry out to Him.
When your hearts are bowed in sorrow,
Wearied by the world's loud din,
Go to Jesus—ask his blessing—
Seek Him in the twilight dim.

Oh, ye children of St. Joseph's
When in the church at setting sun,
Ponder o'er your fathers' labors,
Their battles fought, their victories won.
Prize your faith o'er worldly treasures—
Live it as the years go by;
It will joy your living moments
And bring you solace when you die.

Remember all your worthy fathers
As the years do onward roll;
Imitate their earnest actions—
Pray for rest unto their souls.
Strolling on the Brandywine,
O'er field, or hill, or dell,
Pray for all your noble sires
When you hear St. Joseph's bell.[106]

As these stanzas suggest, the Irish never abandoned their faith, as Fr. Kenny and others feared; on the contrary, through their veneration of certain saints, and their preference for Irish Catholic spouses, names, and consumer goods, they merged the ethnocultural distinctiveness of their religion into a new identity as Irish-American Catholics. For a people who had once been denied the right to practice their religion at all, their transfiguration is remarkable indeed.

CHAPTER 4

The Bean a Ti
(Woman of the House)

Mary O'Connor lived in the powder mill community for nearly twenty years. When she died in 1876, her loving family erected a tombstone with the following inscription:

> A noble, pure, tender Mother,
> She gently hushed our griefs to rest
> And her low whispered prayers
> Our slumbers blessed.
> She put her trust in heaven
> Worked well with hand and head.
> What she gave in charity sweetened
> Her sleep and daily bread.
> If of need a friend was she
> That was her creed.[1]

These moving, evocative words honor Mary's life by conjuring up a specific image: they portray a pure, pious, hard-working, charitable, helpful, and above all, maternal woman. Because it stressed these particular traits, the poem suggests that her Irish-born family embraced Gilded Age America's ideal of femininity.[2] But the gender acculturation remained incomplete, as other parts of the tombstone indicate. Mary's survivors considered it important to record her exact origins, for example. The second and third lines identify her as "daughter Michael O'Connor and Margaret Maloney of Faha, County Clare," thereby acknowledging not only her ties to a specific place in Ireland, but to both her paternal and maternal kin. Her relationship with her husband, by contrast, is muted. The first line reads simply "Mother Mary O'Connor." She is identified by her maiden name, and aside from three little words, "wife Peter Ford," there is no hint of wifely love and devotion, let alone that quintessential female virtue, submissiveness.

91

Since Peter survived Mary by nearly twenty years, these omissions are particularly striking, and provide important clues about behavioral norms for Irish women in the United States.[3]

Stereotypes offer additional clues, resting as they frequently do on minor truths. In most written accounts, then as now, Irish women appear brash, independent, even domineering.[4] Jokes frequently privilege "Herself" over "Himself," while memoirs written by Irish and Irish-American authors stress relationships with their mothers, not their fathers. Frank McCourt's 1996 paean to his mother, *Angela's Ashes,* is but a recent example of this tendency. American popular culture also stresses the matrifocal nature of Irish family life. John Ford's classic 1952 film, "The Quiet Man," depicts the courtship between a bold, assertive Irish woman and a mystifying American come back to Ireland to reclaim his family's ancestral home. It is not a coincidence that the lady's hair is red, that her name is Mary Kate, and that the man who wins her heart turns out to be a prizefighter. But marriage does not entirely tame the shrew: husbands and wives in Ireland typically occupied separate spheres and the movie version ultimately implies a partnership between equals more than a patriarchal conquest. Movies about the Irish in America continue the maternal theme.[5] Thus, Katie Nolan is the glue that binds her family together in "A Tree Grows in Brooklyn" (1945), while Rose Muldoon dominates her policeman-son in "Only the Lonely" (1991).

Historians, by contrast, typically argue that Irish immigrants espoused a bourgeois conception of the family, complete with male breadwinner, subordinate wife, and dependent children, as they acculturated to American society. If some Irish women appeared assertive or self-directed, like the ones who organized unions, then it was purely economic motives that made them so.[6] Though widely maintained, these conclusions rest on certain assumptions about human behavior and male-female relationships. They presuppose that individuals are autonomous beings who only establish social contracts in order to advance their own self-interests, and further, that a man's greater earning potential always makes a father the supreme authority figure in a family. However, these theories of self-interest and male domination often contradict the lived reality of men and women in the past.[7] Consider rural Catholics in nineteenth-century France. They defined the family as an indivisible entity comprising a series of concentric spheres with power, authority, and prestige emanating from the core. Like paternalism, the system stressed hierarchy and reciprocity; it required the person at the center—typically the father—to guide and protect the whole, while it obligated other members of the household—usually his wife and children but sometimes other kin—to ignore their self-interests and subordinate their individual will for the benefit of the common good. Strange and exotic today, this concept of a family interest formed a powerful ideology that shaped male-female relations in many societies.[8] And it did not necessarily render married women meek and dependent. If a French patriarch could not or would not fulfill his role, for example, his female partner could legitimately usurp the center herself. Similar role-reversals took place in colonial New England, where married women served as "deputy husbands" when circumstances incapacitated their spouses, and in the slaveholding South, where bondswomen typically headed families instead of bondsmen.[9] Just so, married Catholic women in nineteenth-century Ireland upheld the rhetoric of male authority and status even though English rule effectively emasculated their spouses.[10] They did not consider "subordination" an inherent part of being female, nor did they relinquish their domestic authority after emigration. On the contrary, while various forces in the United States conjoined to promote male dominance in both the public and private spheres, Irish Catholic families remained matrifocal because they considered strong, assertive women integral to the perpetuation of Irish identity. And so a "tender" mother like Mary O'Connor came to husband her community as well as her household.

Immigrants like the Fords derived their initial notions of womanhood from premodern Irish attitudes toward the family. Whether they lived in Clare, Tyrone, or Dublin, prior to 1800 most rural Irish derived a significant part of their self-identity from membership in a specific kinship group. Rooted in the ancient Celtic concept of the *derbfine*—a social, legal, and economic body comprising all the adult male descendants of a common great-grandfather—the strength of these family networks survived not only in the *clachans* or villages that still dotted the landscape in the nineteenth century, but also "in the Irish countryman's proverbial passion for genealogy and his belief that ties with even remote kin were paramount in enabling him to cope with life's trials." Within this context, the Irish, like the French, viewed the family as a corporate body in which individuals subordinated their self-interests to those of the collective. Their tacit acceptance of communal values in no way precluded intrafamilial conflict. Individuals often disputed whether a specific decision really favored the group interest, yet they generally "strove to present a united front to the outside world." Indeed, the sense of interdependence that governed family life proved so strong that the Irish defined only kin as "friends" *(cairde)*. Nonrelated persons, regardless of intimacy, could only be "acquaintances" *(lucht aitheantais)*.[11]

Gender divided Irish families along strict lines. Members used the old Gaelic term *fear ti* (far chee) to designate male household heads. This title

originally signified membership in the *derbfine,* and by extension, participation in the broader economic and political system. His female partner
answered to *bean a ti* (bon a chee), or "woman of the house," a phrase that
merged wife, mother, cook, and housekeeper together.[12] Her social position reflected his. In keeping with the legacy of the *derbfine,* premodern
Irish society retained an emphasis on male inheritance rights, hierarchy,
and patriarchy. But the *fear ti*'s power owed little to economics. Male
status and authority derived from a prestige system that endowed men's
activities with greater social worth than women's, and their higher social
status endowed whatever resources men controlled with market value, not
vice versa.[13] By the end of the eighteenth century, English domination of
the public sphere, coupled with strict laws preventing land ownership by
Irish Catholics, effectively abrogated the authority of the *fear ti*s and enabled wives to assume new responsibilities. True to the dictates of their
family interest, Irish women did not use this opportunity to recast the
basic patriarchal framework. Instead, they effected subtle changes from
within it.

One shift concerned the nature of work. Although Irish women had always made vital contributions to the domestic economy, the amount and
kind of female labor increased significantly under English rule. Potato cultivation, for example, required that every member of the family toil in the
fields at various points in the agricultural year. Among landless cottiers and
tenant farmers, who together comprised almost 70 percent of the Irish population in 1841, women planted, harvested, and fertilized crops, cut peat for
fuel, wove fishing seines, and tended livestock, all tasks once designated
solely for men. The devastation of several famines reinforced the practical
necessity of women's work. By the time of the Great Hunger, women accounted for 50 percent of Ireland's predominantly agricultural labor force.
Since much of rural society favored partible inheritance, a small number of
daughters even received portions of their father's holdings.[14]

In Ulster the linen industry gave women an opportunity to earn cash, as
well. There, married women and their elder daughters scutched flax and
spun thread, which they then sold to male weavers at local markets. When
Lieutenant R. Stotherd visited County Tyrone in the early 1830s, he noted
that this income superseded men's agricultural labor, and in good times
made small farmers' families feel "independent and comfortable."[15] The introduction of mechanized spinning frames greatly reduced this important
cottage industry, especially in and around the eastern Lagan Valley, where
most factories concentrated. Women who lived in the western counties of
Donegal, Tyrone and Fermanagh continued to scutch and spin, albeit for
less money; after 1845, they also finished shirts and knit stockings.[16]
Whether great or small, women's economic contributions gave them some

say in family financial decisions, including if and when members should emigrate abroad.

Religion afforded the *bean a ti* a second sphere of influence. Celtic mysticism gave prominence to goddesses like Brid, Roi, and Anu, and early Christian missionaries incorporated elements of this feminized spirituality into Irish Catholicism. Later, during the English Reformation, celebration of the Mass shifted to secluded hillsides while administration of the sacraments moved to humble cottages. Religious beliefs completely permeated the domestic sphere between 1800 and 1840, when Catholics started to favor new devotions, especially those emphasizing individual prayer and contemplation. At this time, the Church consciously encouraged housewives to maintain visibly Catholic homes, which they did by displaying appropriate religious pictures, statues, or crucifixes, and by setting up small home altars or shrines.[17] Each time domestic space incorporated the sacred, the *bean a ti* acquired new responsibilities and respect.

Of course, the Great Famine altered this pattern. Commercialization, well underway in Ulster, dramatically transformed other parts of the Irish countryside by 1845, but many rural folk, especially Catholic cottiers in Connaught, Leinster, and Munster, clung to traditional values and practices. After starvation, disease, and emigration removed the vast majority of these people, a more modern, market-oriented culture spread quickly. Faced with a severely diminished supply of hands to work the land, for example, surviving agriculturalists adopted less labor-intensive methods of farming, while others simply switched to raising livestock. In the process, women lost much of their ability to effect directly their families' subsistence. Then, to protect their hard-won assets, the post-famine Irish embraced impartible inheritance, late marriage, and the dowry, practices that further undermined women's position within the family.[18] Changes in religion occurred as well. The devotional revolution that began in the 1820s swung noticeably in Rome's direction and began in the 1870s to reorient lay spirituality toward newly built churches and their parish priests. But however dramatic the transformation, married women did not lose their status overnight. Guided by their notion of a family interest, "traditional-minded" Irish Catholics continued to uphold customary gender norms, and many of these individuals joined the stream of migrants heading for to the United States.[19]

Favorable demographic conditions in the powder mill community reinforced gender conventions brought from Ireland and enhanced the likelihood that women would continue to direct Irish households long after arrival. Most notably, the steady influx of immigrants like Mary O'Connor shifted the numerical balance toward the "weaker" sex. In 1829 Irénée du Pont commissioned a private census of all hands living on company property. At that time, adult males outnumbered adult females by two to one.

The 127 men, 59 women, and 149 children occupied 59 households, each headed by a married couple, plus a company dormitory. By mid-century, the total population exceeded 2,000 souls, and with the dramatic increase came a marked difference in the sex ratio (see table 4.1). Because of the company's need for male labor, the community still had a preponderance of men between the ages of twenty and forty, but females now outnumbered males. The fundamental social unit remained the same: a simple nuclear family, defined as a married couple and their natural children. Of the 365 households that made up the powder mill community in 1850, for example, 212 consisted of such families living by themselves, and 148 of these included Irish-born parents. Other possible living arrangements included married couples whose children had not yet been born or who had died or moved away, and households headed by widows or widowers. Only three individuals lived alone. The social and economic burdens of bachelorhood and spinsterhood prevented the vast majority from establishing independent residences. For most Brandywiners, as for most nineteenth-century Americans, survival and advancement strategies clearly hinged on their relationship to a nuclear family.

Indeed, conventional wisdom held that the quickest way for an individual to improve his station in life was to marry and thereby form an economic and emotional partnership. The key word in this statement is "partnership," for it implies an equitable relationship between the parties. Although feminist scholars often stress the negative impact of marriage on a woman's status within the family, Irish powder men's wives had a different experience. The average Irish bride was 25.11, with a median age of twenty. Some scholars contend that the spread of late marriage through post-Famine Ireland contributed to the subordinate stature of Irish wives, but residents of this community found little need to wait. Moreover, as the population table shows, men of marriageable age (roughly 20–40) outnumbered women of a comparable age. In a time and place where people put a high value on matrimony, women's low numbers afforded them a strong bargaining position. Finally, when they did consent to marry, Brandywine colleens preferred spouses the same age or slightly younger.[20]

Once married, Irish women took up the oldest female occupation: keeping house. This term usually implies the everyday business of cooking, cleaning, and childcare, but these activities actually subsumed a variety of related tasks. Food preparation, for example, included baking bread, raising poultry, preserving homegrown produce, picking local fruits and nuts, and, in the early part of the century, helping to slaughter the family's own livestock. Women also made most of their family's clothing and bedding, though falling textile prices in the Federal period soon absolved them of spinning yarn and weaving cloth. Laundering these items required at

TABLE 4.1
The Population Distribution of the Powder
Mill Community (1850)

Age	Males	Females
90–100	0	1
80–89	2	2
70–79	8	13
60–69	23	26
50–59	42	48
40–49	82	66
30–39	164	128
20–29	231	207
10–19	211	255
0–9	264	290
Totals	1,027	1,036

least two full days, one for washing and one for ironing. Dirty dishes needed daily washing, whereas light cleaning (sweeping, dusting, and so forth) occurred every Saturday in preparation for Sunday's visitors.[21] Heavier spring and fall house cleanings, by contrast, entailed everything from whitewashing walls to beating rugs, and turned entire households upside-down.

Opportunities for remunerative work abounded as well. The mid-Atlantic region's famed "butter belt" included northern Delaware, and Brandywine women actively participated in this cottage industry.[22] Some sold eggs or tallow, and a surprisingly large number worked for the powder company. In 1806 Irénée hired Sally Campbell, Mary Creighton, Ann Dougherty, Bell Murphy, and several others to pack powder, then cut and paste labels onto the filled kegs.[23] Initially implemented for lack of male hands, female employment soon became routine. Following the explosion of 1847, Alfred du Pont told one the company's sales agents that, "We have the powder all made but cannot well get the wrappers served on the kegs just now—This branch of work is done by women who are almost all widows—We cannot well ask them in the magazines so soon and we do not want to transfer their work to others."[24] Women still labeled kegs when Philip Dougherty worked in the Eagle Packing House in the 1880s. As he explained, "This lady came in after we would get a certain amount of canisters packed. Her father also worked in the yard. They would tell her what time to come in and she would label whatever we had at that time. She made the paste in her own home and brought it with her. I guess they thought the job was more suitable for a woman."[25] Other suitable jobs for women could be found in the textile mills (fig. 4.1), where their children could also find employment, or in the various homes of the du Ponts and their wealthier neighbors.[26]

Like other immigrant women, Irish wives preferred the kind of piecework they could do at home.[27] Typically, they sewed powder bags, press cloths, aprons, and wagon covers for use in the powder yards. One day in 1832, for example, Eleuthera du Pont Smith wrote her sister, Victorine, that, "Brother sent loads of powder sheets to mend to day; he sent word the dry house was at a stand for want of them, so I did not know what to do." Home alone when the piles of sheets arrived, Eleuthera quickly delegated the work to several women in the community.[28] The company also paid Irish women to take in laundry, punch holes in leather to make powder sieves, and peel willow branches for charcoal (fig. 4.2). The daughter of one powder man recalled, "I used to peel willows under that big tree down by the cannon house. We would go up with my mother. I don't remember my father ever doing it. There would be a lot of women and children from the village and we'd all meet there. . . . My parents would get the money."[29] Boarders brought in money, too, even as they increased the quantity of meals to prepare and clothes to wash.

The du Pont company maintained separate boarding books for its employees, and though most accounts bore men's names, women did all the work.[30] Thus, in June 1810, Irénée credited Billy Martin's account with $165.26, "by balance due your wife for her services at the boarding house to this day."[31] Martin, an Irish immigrant, ran the company farm while his wife, Fanny, managed the company's dormitory. When the number of bachelor workmen exceeded that building's capacity, du Pont placed them with families. By the 1840s, the company's rate had reached eight dollars per person per month, and some households regularly hosted seven or eight boarders at a time. Through piecework, then, Irish women turned their homes into production spaces, but boarders enabled them to parlay company-owned housing into a kind of capital.

Upon closer inspection, the practice rested on more than economics: boarding merged a wife's role as cook, maid, and laundress with that of "kin-keeper."[32] Few boarders lived with strangers. Take Thomas Gallagher for example. He commenced work as a common laborer on April 1, 1844, soon after his arrival from Letterkenny, County Donegal. At that time, the sixteen-year-old earned $10 per month and resided with a man named

Fig. 4.1. Exterior view of women workers at Walker's Mill, ca. 1890–1900. (Courtesy of Hagley Museum and Library)

James Haughey. Each month, the company deducted $7.50 in boarding fees from Gallagher's account and credited it to Haughey's. In January 1846, Gallagher became a powder worker, and in April, he went to live with William Green, the foreman of the Upper Yard, presumably to learn his new craft. By September, he earned $20 per month and paid $8 board to John Wier. As it turns out, neither Haughey nor Weir were strangers to young Tom: the former had married his mother and the latter, his sister.[33] Other men also boarded with cousins, brothers, fathers, and uncles, yet their sisters, mothers, and aunts made the arrangement possible.

The *bean a ti's* duties included keeping tabs on money as well as kin. If work "in the powder" made her husband the primary wage earner, then it made her the primary wage spender. This role entailed the acquisition of household goods she could not make at all, like furniture or coffee. It also encompassed items she could not produce cheaply, like soap and fabric. Over the course of the nineteenth century, industrialization and mechanization brought a vast array of goods within the price range of working people. Brandywine women could purchase small, mass-produced items at several local establishments, and they usually did so on credit. Andrew Fountain, for example, ran a small company-owned store at Louviers, the textile mill complex associated with Victor du Pont's family. Every month

Fig. 4.2. "Peeling Willows," by Stanley Arthur. (Courtesy of Hagley Museum and Library)

or so, Fountain submitted a bill to the appropriate clerks, who then debited the appropriate wage accounts. Other purchases required actual money. Thus "Mrs. Ferguson" attended a local estate sale in 1852 and paid $2.70 for a set of six chairs. Women also used currency when itinerant peddlers came through the community.[34] In fact, company wage ledgers show frequent deductions of cash. Much of it undoubtedly ended up in female hands, especially since the company always credited a wife's earnings to her husband's account.

Fiscal responsibility gave mothers control over their children's earnings. Widow Bridget Dougherty always signed for her adolescent son's wages during the Civil War, for example.[35] Women with husbands managed their children's earnings, too. "We used to turn everything we made over to our mother," noted William Flanigan.[36] Elizabeth Beacom offered a similar statement:

> My mother was a good manager. She paid cash for everything and never had a bank account until we went to work. When my sister went to work, she first gave up her money and then she paid board. Then when I went to work and my brother was going to the University of Delaware, we gave her the money. . . . Mother never kept written accounts—just the sugar bowl."[37]

Irish mothers even decided whether, when, and where a child could work. When Victorine du Pont Bauduy needed a new maid, she wrote to her sister, Sophie, that "I was thinking of asking Mrs. Cavender for Mary Jane[.] [S]he would be large enough to do my work and she is a very clever child."[38] Twelve-year-old Mary Jane Cavender began working for Victorine in January 1838, at a rate of thirty-eight cents per week, yet she had to have her mother's permission to do so.[39] She left the position and was replaced by Mary Toy on October 28, 1840. Three years later, when Toy left, Victorine wrote, "I saw Mrs. Toy about Mary. [F]eel very sorry to part with her but think it is for the best."[40]

Irish mothers likewise determined how much and what kind of schooling their children received. Before 1852, most children in the community attended the Brandywine Manufacturers' Sunday School, which offered many local families their first real opportunity to achieve basic literacy.[41] Because it was both nondenominational and free, Irish Catholics actively supported the school. Many children missed classes, however, because they had to work at home or in the textile mills. Sophie du Pont taught one of the girls' primer classes and her diaries record the problems she and other teachers had getting students to attend regularly and do their assignments. More important, the diaries reveal that Sophie addressed her concerns to the students' mothers, not their fathers. On February 17, 1832, for example, she noted,

> Stopped to see S[ophia] Boyd—A very unsatisfactory visit—the old mother was in the room, with Sophia, Matilda, and Elisa—they would not speak before her—When I spoke of recitation, [the mother] said she "wasn't for slaving her children at learning their tasks, they had education enough, etc." and when I quietly attempted to explain to her the reasons why we wished them so particularly to learn their testament lessons, she ended by saying, "Well, well, I reckon the testament's as easy learned as any other book you'd give them."[42]

Almost two decades later, Victorine wrote in her diary that "William Holland was not [in school], nor at Church; I must go see his aunt & speak to her about his coming."[43] Despite repeated entreaties, teachers quickly found that education took a back seat to practical considerations.

Made on Sundays, when Irish women themselves went visiting, Victorine's and Sophie's "pastorals" ostensibly provided time for one-on-one instruction, but the hectic atmosphere of powder mill households often prevented any useful interaction between student and teacher. After a typical attempt, Sophie recorded: "Went after dinner to see S. Kirk with Nora—ushered into a room full of women & children . . . and therefore I could not speak to Susan as I wished."[44] At another time she wrote, "Yesterday afternoon I went to see M. Rigby & took her two capes—They were cleaning up the house, so I could not set long because it hindered them. Mrs. Rigby talked so much I could not talk to Martha as I wished."[45] Some mothers meddled so much that Sophie had to ask a fellow teacher for advice: "Do you not find the presence of the mothers of the scholars at times a great difficulty? Most of them, I have found, talk so incessantly that I can scarcely say a word to the children & they seem to think the best thing they can do, is to praise their children's smartness at learning."[46] Historians of bourgeois American families attribute a mother's authority in this area to the widespread belief that women's caring nature suited them to direct their children's education. Irish Catholic immigrants upheld this belief, too, but the strength of the family interest meant that few women saw their children graduate.

Childbirth was another inherently "female" area of expertise. Although three male doctors served the community in the nineteenth century, women attended and directed many deliveries.[47] Some may even have been paid for their professional services. As Victorine explained sometime in the 1850s, "Joanna and Eleu have agreed to paid Mrs. Rigs for nursing Mrs. Dunbar in her approaching confinement—a very good idea as it will do good two ways."[48] Mrs. Riggs worked as a domestic in the home of Lammot and Mary du Pont, and likely attended other women in the community. After the Civil War, the field of medicine became increasingly professionalized and masculine, but Irish mothers continued to rely on midwives. Katie Farren, for example, delivered babies into the 1880s and had a special black bag that she used to house her instruments (fig. 4.3).[49] Nor was she alone. "Now, Mom used to go to all the baby matinees," recalled Richard Rowe. "When the doctor wasn't around they always called Annie Rowe until someone else got there. She always took care of everybody else."[50]

Having at least one adult female on hand not only eased the physical aspects of delivery, but it helped prospective mothers cope with the psychological burdens of maternity.[51] Irish wives in the powder mill community, unlike their native-born American counterparts, generally gave birth every other year, and each pregnancy brought new feelings of fear and anxiety. As various experts have shown, parturition caused an astonishing number of deaths among reproductive-age women in the nineteenth century. Biddy (Bridget) Callahan, old Patrick Brady's daughter, a consumptive, was "brought to bed" on January 17, 1825, delivered twin boys, and expired from her exertions several days later. Other women died in childbirth, too, including healthy twenty-five-year-olds like Ann Curran Toy in 1849, and her husband's niece, Annie A. Toy Gunn, in 1893.[52] Those who survived often had serious gynecological problems, such as perineal or cervical lacerations, prolapsed uteruses, and postpartum infections. Pregnant women also feared for the safety of their infants, especially if they had lost one previously. Some

Fig. 4.3. Kate Farren, a noted midwife, ca. 1890.
(Courtesy of Hagley Museum and Library)

powder men's wives, like the unfortunate Mrs. Rambeau, experienced late-term miscarriages. A few confronted strange deformities. Irish-born Letitia Aiken, for example, had four teen-aged children and a rambunctious five-year-old when she became pregnant again in her mid-forties. That fetus, de-livered on a cold February night in 1824, suffered from encephaly; that is, it lacked a fully-developed brain and cranium. Still births occurred as well. Thus Margaret Boyd, the head carpenter's wife, gave birth in 1826 to frater-nal twins: "une fille vivante et une garson mor [*sic*]."[53]

While producing a healthy child seemed a daunting task, rearing one to adulthood proved even tougher. Bridget McCullion Toy learned this lesson the hard way: of the twelve children she bore during her first sixteen years of marriage, five died before reaching their first birthday.[54] In addition to ordinary colds, scrapes, and bruises, Irish mothers battled serious diseases. Typhus, cholera, and measles made repeated visits to the Brandywine, and in the absence of modern vaccines, each claimed its share of young victims. During the spring of 1843, when scarlet fever began to spread through the community, worried women prudently kept their children home from the Sunday School for fear of contagion. According to Victorine, the strategy worked quite well.[55] Mothers could not stave off consumption, however, which seemed especially prevalent in families with textile workers. Nor could they foresee freak accidents like the ones John Peoples remembered: "There was a good many boys worked in the keg factory, you know. . . . You had to be a pretty quick worker around them machines. About once every two weeks a boy would get his finger cut off if he didn't watch himself."[56]

Explosions brought additional problems. Before her death in 1852, octogenarian Mary Brady, Biddy Callahan's mother, buried four of her five sons: the two eldest died in the blast of 1818; Terence died of injuries suffered when a cannon blew up on the Fourth of July; and Peter died at sixteen, the victim of an unknown accident.[57] The du Pont company locked the gates to each powder yard after the men arrived each morning, partly to keep women and children out of harm's way, and partly to keep them from rushing in after an explosion. Still, a big blast always brought fearful family members running. "I'll never forget those scenes I witnessed," recalled Katherine Collison, a bookkeeper's daughter who lived on Blacksmith's Hill near the Hagley Yard. "The people used to flock down . . . past our house. It was just terrible! You would hear those Irish women crying out, 'Worra! Worra! Where's my John?' Just ring in your ears afterward. And then they would come up and you could tell by the way that woman was supported by another woman that that woman's husband was gone."[58] One can only imagine how fifty-two-year-old Ellen Gibbons must have felt upon hearing of her husband's injuries following an explosion on May 2, 1888. Local newspapers reported that powder man Daniel H. Dougherty "was thrown outside . . . the top and back of his head badly mangled." For seven weeks "he lay between life and death," while Ellen hovered at his bedside. "A large splinter was taken out of the back of his neck the 4th week and the 8th week one was found in his eye." Although Dougherty eventually recuperated, his sight had been nearly destroyed.[59] Other men suffered terrible burns or lost limbs. Although the company always provided a doctor's services in these instances, a man's wife or mother or sister supplied the critical, day-to-day care.

When death came, as it often did, women took charge again. They washed and dressed corpses, sewed shrouds, provided refreshments for mourners, and, in keeping with Irish custom, dominated local wakes.[60] Held at the home of the deceased, a typical wake focused on the corpse, which rested in a plain, wooden coffin set on chairs or a table in the front room or parlor. There, eulogies for the dead alternated with episodes of loud wailing from female keeners. These women could be family, friends, or paid professionals, whose howls lamented both the passing of the deceased and human mortality in general.[61] Men, by contrast, quickly paid their respects and went into a back room to drink, smoke, and tell stories. In January 1838, Victorine sent Evelina an arch note that said, "Poor old Pat Brady died this morning. . . . I expect there will be no small quantity of whiskey drunk at his wake tonight, for he was quite the Patriarch of the Catholics in this settlement."[62] Evangelical Protestants might disapprove, but drinking, dancing, game playing, courting, eating, and storytelling emphasized the vitality of life in the face of death, while a large gathering of friends assured the deceased of his popularity and enabled his spirit to rest in peace. The wake thus served as more than an outlet for grief.

Too many wakes marked the early occurrence of widowhood. Bridget O'Brien, for example, was only twenty-nine when her husband, Michael, went "across the creek" in 1847, and Ann Conners, twenty-five.[63] Widows headed 13 percent of powder mill households in 1850 and 14 percent in 1870. Despite the risks posed by powder manufacture, these figures compare favorably with those of other Irish communities.[64] Some widows braved the altar again. Elizabeth King wed Fergus Rhynes or Ryans fewer than five years after William King's death in 1847. The match may even have caused a stir; Fergus had been a boarder of Elizabeth's since *before* her husband died, and he was seven years her junior, to boot. Not all women felt the need to remarry, however. Margaret Holland lost her husband, Thomas, in the same explosion that took William King yet remained a widow for more than forty years. She lived rent-free in a four-unit stone building called the Widow's Asylum, where she reared six children on her own.[65] Her neighbors, Rosanna Toy, Catherine Baxter, and Rosanna Connor, also declined to remarry. The du Pont company's pension plan, when combined with their husband's estates and the money they earned from boarders or piecework, allowed some widows to subsist quite comfortably without a male partner.

The patterns of migration, work histories, boisterous public behavior, and active family lives of Irish women in America clearly deviated from the nineteenth century's celebrated "cult of true womanhood."[66] Since the "cult of true womanhood" reflected elite Protestant ideals of femininity, this difference is not surprising. Yet the Irish women's assertiveness also contradicted Catholic prescriptive literature of the period. In the 1840s and 1850s a unified and largely American-born group of Catholic reformers began encouraging Irish women to relinquish their control of domestic affairs to their husbands. Articulated and disseminated through advice books, prayer books, newspapers, journals, sermons, catechisms, and novels, this effort to bolster the patriarchal authority of married Irish men paralleled the promotion of a new, idealized conception of Catholic domesticity. In their public discourse, these writers claimed to uphold an eternal, aristo-cratic, European model of family life, but the rituals, virtues, and symbols they promoted had far more in common with the Anglo-Protestant ideal of domesticity that characterized bourgeois American society.[67] While Irish immigrants avidly embraced some of those bourgeois rituals, virtues, and symbols, they struggled with American gender conventions. Unlike cloth-ing, language, or other outwardly discernable markers of ethnic identity, at-titudes about masculinity and femininity reflect deeply held, often subcon-scious cultural norms. As a consequence, powder mill families not only continued to encourage the assertiveness of Irish-born women, but they instilled it in their American-born daughters.

Naming practices within the powder mill community confirm this con-clusion. The system of appellations chosen by a specific society usually re-flects the virtues and powers its members admire, the pursuits they value, and the supernatural forces they cultivate.[68] Because names are assigned on the basis of sex, an analysis of personal naming patterns can also reveal in-formation about gender roles. Irish Catholic parents along the Brandywine tended to name their children after close kin, thereby strengthening ties on both the maternal and paternal sides of the family. But they also subscribed to a belief in patron saints. Indeed, Irish Catholics perceived "otherworld-liness" as a lived phenomenon, not an abstraction.[69] During the sacrament of baptism, then, a child received the name of a particular saint, who would serve as both a guardian and an intercessor with God. Deharbe's catechism further emphasized that "The name of a saint is given in baptism in order that the person baptized may imitate his virtues."[70] As a result, local chil-dren bore names laden with rich, multilayered, cultural connotations (see table 4.2).

Nineteenth-century Irish Catholics showed great devotion to their pa-tron saints and frequently displayed pictures of them, said special prayers to them, and carefully observed their feast days. Hence, Annie Haughey, born in 1843, would have grown up knowing that her name honored the mother of Mary. According to scripture, St. Anne bore Mary in her old age, after she and St. Joachim had given up all hope of having children. Several years later, when Mary suddenly disappeared in the temple one day, she instantly recognized the holy nature of her only offspring and humbly accepted the loss as God's will.[71] "Anne" also resembled *Anu,* the name of Ireland's ancient Earth Mother, that is, the Gaelic goddess of health, fertil-ity, and plenty. Kate Bogan, by contrast, born in 1856, looked to St. Catha-rine of Sienna. A tradesman's daughter, like many of her namesakes, St. Catharine dedicated her life to God as a child, taking a vow of celibacy at

TABLE 4.2
Leading Names for Irish Catholic Girls

	1805–34	1846–56	1876–86
Top three female baptismal names (Mary, Anne, Catharine), %	50	46	47
Top ten female baptismal names (Mary, Anne, Catharine, Elizabeth, Margaret, Sarah, Ellen, Bridget, Jane, Rosanna), %	86	87	85
Total baptisms in sample	312	786	490
% Female infants baptized*	49	49	53

Sources: These data were compiled from baptismal registers at the three Catholic churches patronized by Irish powder workers in the nineteenth century. The first sample (1806–1834) came from a register begun at Coffee Run in 1796 and maintained by Fr. Kenny. It is now kept at the Diocese of Wilmington Archives in Greenville, Delaware, but microfilmed copies are available at the Archives and at the Family History Center of the Wilmington Stake, LDS. The second sample covers the years from 1846 to 1856, and includes all of the children baptized at St. Joseph's on the Brandywine during this decade. The third and final sample was also from St. Joseph's and included the years from 1876 to 1886. Samples two and three were both taken from a single register running from 1846 to 1895. The original volume is kept at St. Joseph's rectory. Copies are available at the Archives and Family History Center.

*Percentages that do not total 100 reflect difficulties determining the sex of some children on the basis of their first names alone.

the age of seven and refusing to marry. She eventually entered the convent, but being exceptionally well educated and highly outspoken, she soon left to become a papal advisor and a militant defender of the faith.[72] Her Gaelic counterpart was likely *Cath Badb,* the female war goddess, who assumed the form of a crow or raven during battle.

At first glance, these examples suggest that Brandywine parents distinguished between two opposing sets of behavioral traits for their daughters. These included motherhood and chastity; obedience and autonomy; humility and pride; acquiescence and strength; reservation and assertiveness. The saints can also be divided into two opposing groups. On the one hand are Mary, Anne, Margaret, Elizabeth, Sarah, and Helena, women known chiefly for their actions as wives and mothers. Catharine, Bridget, Rose of Lima, and Joan of Arc, on the other hand, espoused virginity and devoted themselves to God. To secular eyes, marriage and celibacy afford wildly divergent vocations, and modern observers, mindful as well of the twentieth-century's feminist sensibilities, tend to associate the former group of saints with the first of each behavioral polarity and the latter with the second set. But the specific traits outlined above did not correspond neatly to either group of holy women. Instead, all ten of the chief female role models for this community manifested traits from both lists. Irish Catholic womanhood ultimately conflated dedication to family and to God.

The overwhelming popularity of the name Mary reflects this paradox. The Catholic Church has long upheld the Blessed Virgin as its ideal of Christian womanhood. One popular nineteenth-century prayer book exulted, "The best devotion we can practice towards her . . . is to imitate her excellent virtues; to abhor sin, to love God tenderly, and copy her humility, her purity, and her heroic patience, in the different occurrences of our lives."[73] But Mary actually offered a mixed message. On the one hand, she was pure and virginal; on the other hand, she bore and reared a son. An obedient Hebrew housewife in some accounts, she is lauded as the Queen of Heaven in others. Despite this dichotomy, the Church called Mary "the most perfect mirror" of feminine behavior and urged women to follow her example.[74] Based on their widespread devotion to Mary, powder mill families had little difficulty reconciling the disparate traits that she and other celestial beings exhibited.

Strangely, there is no male counterpart to Mary. There is, of course, St. Joseph, her husband and earthly father to the child Jesus. Presented with the miraculous pregnancy of his betrothed, Joseph humbly accepted the will of God and, without complaint, protected and provided for his holy charges.[75] Little else is known about him, but the Church emphasized his obedience, fidelity, and sense of duty. Because he had been a carpenter, he eventually became the patron saint of workers. But the traits he embodied contradicted Irish conceptions of masculinity.

Brandywine Catholics consistently named their sons for celibates who eschewed family ties to follow Christ and whose life stories emphasize an aggressive defense of the faith (see table 4.3). In fact, the Church has long promoted celibacy as the most perfect state for Christian men and women. As the future saint Alphonsus Liguori explained in 1851, "He that is without a wife is solicitous for the things that belong to the Lord, [and] how he may please God. But he that is with a wife is solicitous for the things of the world, how he may please his wife, and he is divided."[76] Recognizing, however, that only a special few would ever be called to holy orders, the Church encouraged the faithful to marry and become as devout as the demands of family life allowed. Though Catholics in pre-Famine Ireland eagerly wed, Irish husbands rejected domesticity and showed little interest in religion. Male culture revolved around the fields, the local pub, and perhaps a secret political society; after emigration, it simply shifted to America's factories, saloons, and Irish fraternal organizations. Catholic reformers, however, deplored the new immigrants' rowdy public behavior and, blaming it for nativist hostility, they touted St. Joseph as the ideal of Catholic manhood,

TABLE 4.3
Leading Names for Irish Catholic Boys

	1805–34	1846–56	1876–86
Top three male baptismal names (John, James, Thomas), %	42	37	34
Top ten male baptismal names (John, James, Thomas, William, Michael, Charles, Daniel, Francis, George, Patrick), %	70	67	67
Total baptisms in sample	312	786	490
% Male infants baptized*	50	45	47

Source: Boys' names were taken from the same baptismal registers as the girls'. For the meanings attached to these boys names, consult Butler, 99, 261, 387; Hoever, 99, 282, 381, 498, 506, and 508; Woulfe, 203.

  *Percentages that do not total 100 reflect difficulties determining the sex of some children on the basis of their first names alone.

hoping on some level to promote a new, domestic orientation among Irish men.[77] The scheme failed miserably.

Brandywine parents continued to name their children with the expectation that while both sexes would marry, only girls need be domestic. None of the top ten role models for Irish sons had families, for example, compared to five of the corresponding female saints. And unlike Italian or other saints, the paragons of Irish Catholic womanhood were neither submissive nor dependent.[78] St. Margaret, for example, an eleventh-century Queen of Scotland, used her influence over her husband and children to direct state affairs. St. Helena, Empress of the Holy Roman Empire, found the cross of Christ and built a magnificent church on Mount Calvary. Sarah, the wife of Abraham, is not technically a saint, but the combination of her desire for a child, her forceful personality, and her acquiescence to God's will made her a popular role model. From their patron saints, then, Irish girls learned how and why women asserted themselves in the past. Their mothers, aunts, and grandmothers brought the lesson up to date.

The importance Brandywine parents attached to female assertiveness stemmed from the *bean a ti*'s historic obligation not only to safeguard the family but to defend the faith. This mandate explains the one trait that characterized both male and female patron saints: a courageous, frequently aggressive piety. Catholic reformers expected boys alone to advance the Church and its mission in Protestant America. Consider Rev. Bernard O'Reilly, for instance, who admonished mothers to take "special care in educating boys," because "Catholic men must go forth from their mothers' homes filled with the spirit of the ancient martyrs and the more recent crusaders."[79] O'Reilly deliberately chose martyrs and crusaders as male role models, for he considered "fearlessness in the cause of Truth" the leading attribute of Christian manhood. Mixing time and place with abandon, he also invoked the rules of medieval chivalry: "1st. Before all, with pious remembrance, every day to hear the mass of God's passion. 2d. To risk body and life boldly for the Catholic faith. 3d. To protect the holy Church, with her servants, from everyone who would attack her."[80] His modestly popular book listed nine other rules endorsing virtues like charity, loyalty, and honor, but all used equally assertive language. Finally, O'Reilly linked anti-Catholicism in nineteenth-century Ireland and America with the Christian persecutions of the early Church and the Crusades. Warning that, "Our dangers are many; our enemy is formidable," he exhorted every Catholic man to "Be the soldier of truth."[81] Yet piety seemed conspicuously lacking in nineteenth-century Irish males. As one Irish observer explained in 1868, "The Irish nature is impetuous and impulsive and passionate, and the young are too often liable to confound license with the display of manly independence; hence even the light yoke of the Church is occasionally too burdensome for the high-mettled Irish youth, [and] in an especial degree, the American-born sons of Irish parents."[82] In actual practice, reproducing Catholicism remained the responsibility of women.

Despite its official emphasis on patriarchy and celibacy, the Catholic Church in America relied on women in general, and married women in particular, to propagate the faith. This role sometimes led female immigrants into open conflict with their employers and benefactors. Author John Maguire gleefully recounted the story of a domestic servant named Kate who dumped a tureen of soup on the head of a Protestant preacher when he ridiculed her religion.[83] The preacher was a guest in her employer's home and Kate could have been fired for her actions, but she valued faith over rational economics. A similar episode occurred on the Brandywine. Sometime between 1894 and 1900, the two daughters of a Catholic powder man named Charles Deery joined a sewing class at the local Presbyterian church. At work that week, Alfred du Pont teased Deery about his daughters' "conversion" from Catholicism and threatened to inform Father Bermingham, then pastor at St. Joseph's. Deery came home and told his wife, also named Kate, about the joke, but she failed to see any humor in the situation and marched right over to the powder yard to set du Pont straight.[84] To pro-Irish supporters, such willingness to challenge authority affirmed the piety and virtue of Erin's daughters in America. Irish women also asserted their spirituality by participating in Catholic religious services, Sunday schools, voluntary associations, and sodalities to a much greater extent than did Irish men. Maguire likened them to "a strong but delicate chain of gold," which bound the wayward and headstrong to the Church of their fathers.[85] In so doing, Irish women bound their families to the culture of Ireland.

That the female traits symbolized by saints like Mary, Anne, Catharine, and Margaret mirrored those of the *bean a ti* suggests that Irish Catholics in the powder mill community used naming patterns not only to validate assertive female behavior but to symbolize the important role of married Irish women in preserving their ethnic identity in America. The equation of Irish nationalism with Roman Catholicism, and the perpetuation of certain folk customs, like the wake, are among the most obvious cultural defense mechanisms that scholars have studied; yet preserving the autonomy of married Irish women may have been an equally effective strategy. Distressed by the cultural, political, and ideological dominance of Anglo-Protestant landholders, Catholics in Ireland responded by focusing their attention on the household, and charging the *bean a ti* to defend the Irish family and its attendant cultural values. In accordance with these values, all members of the household worked together for a mutual subsistence. While Irish society extolled the waged and unwaged contributions that Irish women made to the domestic economy, it subsumed woman's work under her broader cultural mandate to safeguard the family. With a similar social reality of Irish Catholic wage earners and nominally "Anglo-Saxon," Protestant employers, conditions in the United States perpetuated the perceived need for strong, assertive Irish women throughout most of the nineteenth century.

Over time, changing material and social circumstances modified gender roles in powder mill families, but the process was slow and gradual. For the most part, necessity and custom allowed wives to retain control of the household, even as husbands increasingly asserted themselves in the marketplace. America's economic system endowed male labor with value, its political system gave men political power, and its social system emphasized a resource-based conception of patriarchy. The emerging ideology of separate spheres brought these forces together and justified male dominance at home and at work. But despite the assertions made by some scholars, the Irish family's acceptance of certain bourgeois values did not necessarily indicate a complete acceptance of Victorian femininity. On the contrary, selective acculturation was a logical response to their minority status, one that also demonstrates the complexity of cultural identity. Because Irish Catholics remained committed to their distinctive ethnic and religious heritage, they continued to endorse the central role of women in their homes and communities, even if it brought them criticism. Sure, the *bean a ti* was alive and well in nineteenth-century America.

CHAPTER 5

Habitations

Motorists passing through Wilmington's old Seventh Ward today barely register the modest, three-story brick structure at 1907 Lincoln Street (fig. 5.1). Set slightly back from the sidewalk and shielded by several tall bushes, it shares a deep, narrow lot with its conjoined twin at number 1909. The surrounding blocks are full of similar structures that, when built in the 1880s and '90s, attracted considerable attention. These substantial, present-able houses, purchased mainly by Irish immigrants, symbolized to the original occupants upward mobility and acculturation. Their neighborhood, known as Forty Acres for the small farms it replaced, occupied a slight rise just north and west of the central business district downtown. Though imperceptible to the eye, this elevated position enabled successful Irish families to look down, literally if not figuratively, on their "shanty" counterparts, many of whom congregated in the Third Ward near the city's burgeoning leather goods factories. The priests at St. Ann's Roman Catholic Church, situated at the western edge of the community, frowned on such behavior. The poor Irish were not as different as their "lace curtain" counterparts liked to think; indeed, many of the newly affluent parishioners had only recently left the morocco shops. But others, like "Big Dan" Dougherty, the first owner of No. 1907, owed their success to the du Pont powder yards, located a short trolley ride to the north. Neither he nor his neighbors really needed the clerical reproof; all of them were self-made men and women, well aware of what it took to succeed in industrial America. From their standpoint, however, they had crossed an important line, and though intimately connected to the Irish masses, they considered themselves a group apart.

The house at 1907 Lincoln Street surely meant a great deal to its first owner. Daniel H. Dougherty hailed from County Donegal, specifically a small clachan near the town of Invershone. In 1849 he emigrated to the Brandywine, and the big, powerful farmer, "a six-footer," soon became a

Fig. 5.1. Exterior view of 1907 N. Lincoln Street, once the residence of powder man Daniel Dougherty. Taken by author, 1995.

powder man. A wife and children followed in due time. Then, shortly after the Civil War ended, Dougherty moved his growing household to Wilmington. Presumably, he sought to achieve his "independence" at this time, but by 1870, the family had returned to the Brandywine. Still, Big Dan remained undaunted. In 1876 he bought a farm in Pennsylvania, near two of his sisters. The following year witnessed a critical downturn in the national economy and he once again reverted to his rolling mill. The next time he acted, Dougherty proceeded with caution. In 1887 he bought the house on Lincoln Street, but opted to rent it out and save the income for his eventual retirement. That event came earlier than anticipated: Dougherty's mill had exploded on May 2, 1882. Although he recovered from the blast, it left him virtually blind in both eyes. Aided by a generous pension from his employers, the fifty-two-year-old Irishman moved with his wife, Ellen, and their seven children to Forty Acres, where he lived until his death in 1904.[1]

Dougherty's experience is not surprising. Nineteenth-century Irish immigrants proved especially "assiduous and successful" in acquiring real estate. By 1900, they enjoyed occupational parity with native-born Americans, and higher wages coupled with easy credit facilitated their ability to buy property.[2] Nor were they alone. The accessibility of cheap land, vast stands of virgin timber, and a predilection for self-building meant that rates of home ownership in this country greatly exceeded those of other nations. Observers recognized the cultural ramifications of this propensity immediately. In a society heavily influenced by the tenets of Jeffersonian republicanism, property afforded security, respectability, and autonomy, traits critical to the success of democratic republican government. It had the added benefit of transforming immigrants into Americans and elevating wage laborers into the ranks of capitalists and yeomen farmers.[3] Residents of the powder mill community concurred with this assessment. As one hopeful fellow wrote to Alfred du Pont, "A little money laid out in land soon raises a person to independence by the raise of land."[4]

Despite the general recognition that property holding "loomed large in the eyes of laborers," historians continue to debate its "objective" meaning, especially where the cultural affiliations of Irish immigrants are concerned. Some say it is "the most unambiguous indicator of well-being and status," a sign that "emergence is emergence indeed." Others insist that buying real estate actually limited advancement by forcing wage-earning families to forgo the skills and education needed to enter the nonmanual professions, the "true" indicators of class affiliation.[5] This endeavor is complicated by the fact that a significant number of Irish in the nineteenth-century United States resided in semirural industrial villages and company towns.[6] The availability and meaning of real estate to immigrants in these communities, where employers typically held a monopoly on all houses and property, remains unclear.

When employers held the lease on their employees' homes, they secured a level of control that transcended normal management-labor relationships. In 1865, for example, anthracite coal operators in Pennsylvania successfully pressured their representatives into authorizing legislation that legalized the first ten-day eviction notice clause. Under this law, a company could justifiably evict an employee if he failed to uphold his part of the labor contract for any reason whatsoever. Some employers merely stipulated that occupation of company-owned housing must terminate upon cessation of employment with the firm and gave tenants no notice of eviction at all. Company ownership also permitted employers to practice extreme racism and favoritism by reserving certain kinds of houses for certain kinds of workmen. By the turn of the century, state and federal commissions openly denounced these practices and concluded that company ownership not only resulted in a denial of civil liberties but undermined traditional American values like independence and self-reliance.[7]

Not all of the nineteenth-century firms that provided workers' housing built company towns, however, and not all of them exhibited such a blatant disregard for their employees' civil rights. In fact, most of the manufacturing communities built before the Civil War can best be described as industrial villages. Located primarily along the waterways of the northeastern United States, they were small, self-contained, and somewhat isolated with populations that rarely exceeded several hundred persons. Several dozen stone or frame cottages, scattered haphazardly around the mill and its races, represented the typical layout. Mill owners usually lived within these communities, as well, and spatial proximity reinforced the genuine sense of paternal obligation that many felt toward their employees. Company towns, by contrast, owed their existence to absentee owners, and chiefly arose during the Gilded Age. Carefully laid out in grid or linear plans, they incorporated a clear hierarchy of architecture that separated management from labor and segregated workers by ethnicity as well as occupation. With an average of between 2,000 and 5,000 inhabitants, they substantially exceeded mill villages in both size and population. As its operations expanded beyond Delaware after 1902, the Du Pont Company also built company towns, often with allusive names like Nitro, West Virginia. Yet the Brandywine site retained its village-like atmosphere well into the twentieth century.[8]

Living conditions in the powder mill community promoted Irish acculturation. In keeping with his paternalistic outlook, Irénée du Pont initially provided free accommodations to all workers. Bachelors lived in a dormitory, whereas men with families received free use of a house, a garden, and a cow pasture.[9] By the 1820s, rising operating costs compelled du Pont to charge married employees rent. He kept the amount well within the average household budget, however, and he continued to reward many long-term and high-status workers with free housing. After 1815, he also exempted the widows of men killed by explosions. While only a portion of households enjoyed this privilege, few of their neighbors had cause for complaint. The quality of free houses differed in no measurable way from other houses on company property, and even the worst rentals surpassed the old stone cottages of rural Ulster. Unlike other employers, du Pont and his heirs did not segregate workers on the basis of occupation, ethnicity, or religion, and seem to have assigned housing on the basis of family size or proximity to relatives. The company's savings plan held out the possibility of owning one's own home, and like Daniel Dougherty, many Irish managed to buy property on the edge of the community, in the surrounding countryside, in Wilmington, or in the West. In some cases, members of the du Pont family helped certain households get sound titles. In 1843, for example, Alfred du Pont personally secured a deed for a favorite employee

saying, "I am bound to protect the interest of the people in my employment."[10] In sum, decent habitations combined with a high expectation of
property mobility reinforced Irish immigrants' perception that their social
status had improved. That perception, in turn, enhanced their affinity for
modern American culture.[11]

⚜

The desire for "a place to Stop that I can call my own" figured prominently
among the motives behind Irish emigration to the United States.[12] Catholics, in particular, had been denied the right to own property since 1700. As
the native-born population of Ireland swelled in the late eighteenth century, access to arable land became even more competitive. The movement
toward enclosure, the series of famines that occurred after 1800, and widespread poverty only compounded the problem. By the 1830s, living conditions for the majority of Irish families had deteriorated noticeably, even in
prosperous Ulster. The 8,120 inhabitants of the Parish of Dromore,
County Tyrone, for example, crowded into 1,044 small, one-room cottages
of "very wretched description . . . built of mud, with miserable thatch."[13]
Those who sought to escape by emigrating often found equally bad accommodations in the congested slums of Great Britain and America. But many
nineteenth-century Irish immigrants made their way to semirural industrial
villages, where opportunities for advancement seemed to abound, and
where houses were larger, better built, and frequently more comfortable
than the ones they had known in Ireland.

    The domestic architecture of rural Ireland changed very little over the
course of the seventeenth, eighteenth, and nineteenth centuries. Most Irish
families occupied windowless, chimneyless, one-room cabins, which contemporary visitors called "hovels." Unable to buy lumber or stone, the
rural poor constructed a framework from the trunks and large branches of
nearby trees. They then wove smaller pieces through the frame to make
walls and laid pieces of sod or turf over the whole structure to enclose and
insulate it. A hole at the apex allowed smoke from their cooking fires to escape. Although some families managed to construct more substantial,
thatched-roof cabins of rubble, these so-called "mud" cabins predominated. As late as 1861, a national housing census found 579,042 mud cabins
still standing.[14]

    That same survey revealed severe overcrowding. At the lowest level of
society, more than one million families occupied only 89,374 one-room
cabins that year. The national averages had deteriorated, as well: the typical house in 1861 sheltered two families, and the typical family had five
members. These conditions arose partly as a result of the Great Famine.

As the potato blight spread, thousands of Irish families lost their primary source of income. Unscrupulous landlords used the opportunity to effect more "efficient" methods of land use; they evicted their starving tenants for nonpayment of rent, and unroofed the empty dwellings to preclude their use. Other cabins and houses fell into ruin when the inhabitants died or emigrated. Urban living conditions worsened as well; by 1861, an average of eleven people occupied each dwelling unit in Dublin, Ireland's largest city.[15]

The deplorable living conditions of the poor rightly dominate the accounts of visitors and government officials; however, most of the 4.8 million Irish who emigrated during the nineteenth century came from the middling ranks of Irish society and consequently occupied substantially better accommodations.[16] Prosperous laborers and small holders, for example, typically occupied stone houses with one or two rooms, clay floors, whitewashed interiors, glazed windows, and masonry chimneys. Strong farmers and minor gentry had even larger dwellings, with multiple floors, slate roofs, and a complex of outbuildings that expanded, divided, and gendered their use of domestic space.[17] Like their poorer neighbors, however, to whom they often had blood ties, even middling households typically rented their lands and dwellings. Hence, the quality and character of the homes they occupied varied with the degree of local prosperity and the attitude of local landlords.

In northern Ireland, nineteenth-century landowners continued to respect the "Ulster custom," which guaranteed their tenants fair rent, long leases, and adequate compensation for any improvements they made prior to departure.[18] Theoretically, this practice gave lessees a tangible incentive to upgrade the property, and thereby shifted the burden of upkeep away from the landlord. In practice, farmers often declined to develop their holdings. Government officials surveying the region in the 1830s readily explained why: "the desire and inclination of the labouring class to improve their houses almost exceed our expectation . . . [but] heavy rents and taxes are great preventatives."[19] Consequently, cottages in Tyrone, as in neighboring Donegal and Fermanagh, often appeared "mean and shabby," their dooryards in disorder and their fields in disarray.

Ireland's colonial economy, coupled with the severe dislocations that accompanied the Great Famine, meant that substandard living conditions continued to characterize much of the nation until the 1860s and 1870s. At that time, a few enlightened landlords began to build model tenant houses, but most simply made repairs and additions or built new cottages in the traditional manner.[20] Villages, towns, and cities with industries like weaving and shipbuilding experienced more substantial regrowth. There, new houses for skilled artisans and low-income professionals sprang up by the hundreds. Surviving examples in Letterkenny, County Donegal, and Belleek, County Fermanagh, are two-story, double-pile structures of brick or stone with slate roofs and glass windows. Arranged in long, contiguous rows or terraces, they had a minimum of four small rooms, plus a small rear yard with an outside water closet. Though far superior to "mud" cabins, urban houses, too, reflected economic considerations. Indeed, speculator-owners typically ordered them built as quickly and as cheaply as possible.

Similar principles governed the acquisition and construction of workers' housing along the Brandywine. Like other early-nineteenth-century industrialists, Irénée du Pont understood that he would have to provide housing in order to attract and maintain a stable workforce. In fact, he found Jacob Broom's sixty-five-acre property appealing in part because it had already been developed. Along with the burned-out shell of Broom's cotton factory, a saw mill, a store house, a blacksmith shop, and a barn, it contained in 1802 a stone house with a cellar, two frame houses, two small log cabins, and two two-story log dwellings.[21] Du Pont installed his own family in the stone building, which he grandly referred to as the "director's residence," and allocated the remaining structures for workmen. Within months, the dozens of laborers filled the buildings to capacity. Although Irénée managed to place the overflow with local farmers, he knew that permanent quarters had to be built on site. First, he commissioned two boarding houses. One contained "two or three small, separate lodgings for the head workmen, the cooper and the carpenter." Built from the granite that outcropped across the property, it had two stories with four "apartments" on each floor, plus a garret and cellar. The other building, sometimes referred to as the "barracks," was a two-story, frame structure with a large, open dining room on the ground floor and sleeping space for single men above.[22] When he learned that many workmen wanted to bring their wives and children to the Brandywine, Irénée added four semidetached and two detached stone houses to the property.[23] Built between 1806 and 1814 and arranged in an L-shaped cluster just above the powder yard, they accommodated ten families (fig. 5.2).

The topography of the valley dictated where every building went. Du Pont wisely reserved the flat land along the Brandywine for the mills and their support structures. He relegated all new residences to the river bank, including his own. The two-room "director's residence" functioned well enough for temporary housing, but the aristocratic Frenchman envisioned something far grander for his new family seat. Uncertain of his own architectural abilities, however, he consulted Peter Bauduy, a French-speaking refugee from Saint Dominique, who resided in nearby Wilmington and who had designed its new city hall. Together they arrived at a suitable plan, one large enough and sophisticated enough to meet the family's needs and tastes, yet one that local craftsmen could erect and maintain. Built of the

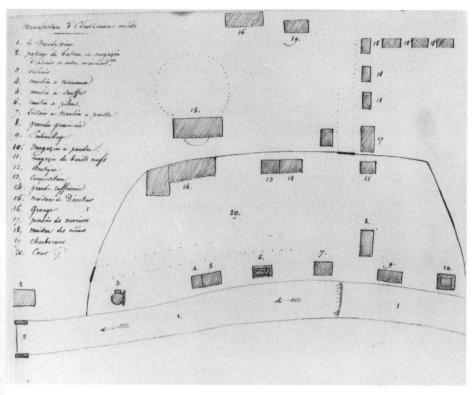

Fig. 5.2. Map of Eleutherian Mills by Gabriel Denizot, 1818. Note the location of the Brandywine (1), the fence surrounding the powder yard and its relevant structures (3–14), the du Pont mansion (15), and the Upper Banks cluster of workers' housing (18). (Courtesy of Hagley Museum and Library)

same blue granite as the rolling mills and set into the hillside above the powder yard, Eleutherian Mills welcomed its new tenants in the summer of 1803. Inside, the house contained a formal dining room, a parlor, several bedrooms, and on the first floor, Irénée's office, the first administrative center of E. I. du Pont de Nemours and Company. Outside, a spacious, two-story piazza stretched across the rear façade. The director found that feature especially useful; it allowed him to communicate with workmen in the powder yard below via trumpet.[24]

Irénée also built a home for his elder brother. In 1810, Victor finally abandoned his failing mercantile business in rural New York and moved to the Brandywine, where he became a partner in Du Pont, Bauduy and Company. This firm, organized with Irénée's assistance, set out to dominate the American textile industry through the production of fine Merino woolens.[25]

Located directly opposite the powder yard, the new woolen mill, its race, and ancillary structures occupied all of the land along the river bottom. Victor's own residence, which he called Louviers in honor of his mother's ancestral home in France, stood on the bank above. The complex also included forty-five workers' houses that accommodated the families of powder men as well as textile operatives (fig. 5.3).

The acquisition of the Hagley property increased further the number of dwelling units. Situated south and east of the upper yard, past a sharp bend in the river, the sixty-two-acre parcel originally belonged to one Rumford Dawes, who operated a merchant mill, slitting mill, and blacksmith's shop there in the 1790s. When advertised for sale in 1803, it included "a large, well-finished stone dwelling house," a coal house, wagon house, carriage house, stables, cooper shop, poultry house, smoke house, a spring house, and "a number of dwelling houses for workers and their families, with every other requisite building."[26] A second notice in 1808 featured "seven comfortable houses for work people, some of stone." After Irénée purchased the property on March 9, 1813, he incorporated several of the existing structures into the new Hagley powder yard, including the old blacksmith's shop. He then erected an eight-foot safety fence around the perimeter, and built two access gates, one on "Blacksmith's Hill" and one to the south along the river road. A new cluster of two-story, frame workers' houses arose at the top of the hill.[27]

By 1820 the community had begun to take on a distinctive appearance. Grist, snuff, and saw mills were familiar features of northern Delaware's rural landscape by the Revolution, but the factories that arose in the Federal period bore them little resemblance. Textile and paper mills followed a new pattern imported from England; they had massive masonry walls, three or more floors, and monumental stair towers. While functional in appearance, their simple yet well-proportioned exteriors adhered to certain basic design principles. They had large, evenly spaced windows, for example, symmetrical façades, and cupolas to mark the main entrance.[28] The dwellings built for mill operatives seemed equally strange. Clustered near their respective factories, they were strikingly similar in appearance—too similar, in fact, to account for a native building style.

In their physical appearance, early industrial communities not only reflected practical considerations about space and money, but they addressed strong prejudices against manufacturing establishments. Despite the growth of new industries in this country, many Americans adhered to the tenets of Jeffersonian republicanism. These people believed that agriculture should remain the basis of the young republic's economy. To them, working the land imparted moral as well as material benefits. Since civic virtue flowed from private virtue, the model citizen had to maintain his inner

Fig. 5.3. Eleuthera du Pont's sketch of the Louviers cotton mill and its associated workers' housing, ca. 1822–27. (Courtesy of Hagley Museum and Library)

compass, yet he could only do so if he remained "independent." In this context, as distinct from the Irish immigrants' use of the term, "independence" meant heading a household, owning one's own home, working on one's own account, and thereby sustaining a fair living or "competence" that allowed the exercise of free will and mature judgment in both politics and social life. Opponents of manufacturing rightly feared the loss of autonomy that would inevitably come when men labored for others in large, impersonal surroundings, and for an example they pointed across the sea to England, where by the 1810s cities like Manchester and Lancashire had already become "filthy sewers."[29] To critics, nothing could be worse than to gather up hordes of ill-paid, insecure working people under miserable conditions, in order to produce riches for the few. Advocates countered that the evils of industrialization could be avoided by locating American factories in the countryside and by instituting a strict system of moral supervision. They also pointed out that farmers would gain a new market for their products if industrial centers developed. During his presidency, even Thomas Jefferson himself finally admitted that "manufactures are now as necessary to our independence as to our comfort," but many others, especially Southern planters and yeomen, still believed that wage work would only degrade the laboring classes and thereby undermine American social and political ideals.[30]

In response to these fears, conscientious manufacturers like du Pont took steps to ensure that their employees would neither become a permanent proletariat nor lose their moral standards. As a Frenchman and a maker of explosives, du Pont's pro-industry rhetoric seemed doubly suspect, yet his patriotism during the War of 1812, his superior gunpowder, and his policies of direct assistance—especially his efforts to help workmen buy property—eventually relieved his opponents' concerns. The semirural nature of the powder mill community helped, too. Believing that the physical environment affected the development of certain character traits, critics carefully scrutinized the appearance of industrial districts and concluded that the degradation of labor largely resulted from relegation to city slums. To combat this negative perception of wage workers' living conditions, the Society for the Encouragement of Domestic Manufactures urged all would-be industrialists in America to locate their factories in the countryside, "on chosen sites, by the fall of waters and the running stream, the seats of health and cheerfulness, where good instruction will secure the morals of the young and good regulations will promote, in all, order, cleanliness, and the exercise of civil duties."[31] A member of the Society himself, du Pont willingly followed this directive. Since all of the Brandywine factories utilized water power, they produced little in the way of noise, smoke, ashes, or waste to spoil the landscape. Their reliance on water power also limited the size of each mill complex, as did the rudimentary state of transportation networks. Compared to the mining and manufacturing landscapes of Great Britain and Europe, then, the powder mill community seemed not only clean and quiet, but picturesque.[32]

This salutary environment appeared to have the desired effect. As one foreign visitor to the Brandywine remarked around 1820:

> It is very pleasant to see the cleanliness and prosperity of Mr. du Pont's workers. I took several short walks to inform myself about their conditions, for workers in Sweden are so miserable. Here each one has his own neat house and little garden; everywhere in the colony I met contented people.[33]

More than twenty years later, a reporter for the *Delaware State Journal* attended a political meeting at Louviers and echoed the enthusiastic response of previous visitors:

> The place itself is beautiful beyond description: the high hills on either side, covered with lofty trees rich with verdure, bright with brilliant sunshine on their towering tops, and rich in their dense shadows below; the lucid stream gently gliding over its stony bed, its glassy surface reflecting its woody sides and the bright cerulean sky; high on the hillside peered out some ornamental

dwelling while numerous smaller habitations, neat, commodious, and comfortable, showed where industry and virtue live in peace and happiness.[34]

Not everyone shared this view. In 1860, another reporter likened the powder yards to a "grim, slumbering monster, whose chief ailment is villainous saltpeter, which has laid full many a tall fellow low."[35] Still, most visitors found the combination of danger and beauty strangely appealing. As William Cullen Bryant's *Picturesque America* declared in 1872, "Too often, labor mars the landscape it enters, but the [brook-side] mill seems to partake of the spirit of its surroundings, to gain a charm from woods and waters and to give one. This is particularly true of the factories along the Brandywine ... [where] the romance of the adventure is heightened by the proximity of the powder mills, built expressly to burst out upon the water."[36]

Brandywine industrialists encouraged this romantic vision through the imaginative, evocative names they gave the mills and their surrounding communities. When cotton manufacturer William Breck married Gabrielle Josephine du Pont in 1836, her uncle, Victor's son, Charles I. du Pont, built them a large, new house overlooking the valley. Inspired by one of Sir Walter Scott's poems, the couple christened their home "Rokeby," and quickly extended the name to the small factory below. Other manufacturers followed suit. There was "Rockland," to the north of the du Ponts, "Rockford" to the south, and "Kentmere," named for an English estate, in nearby Wilmington. Similar naming practices also characterized the Chester Creek textile manufacturing district in southeastern Pennsylvania, where workers lived in communities called "Rockdale," "Parkmount," and "Lenni" (for the Lenni Lenape tribe).[37] Meanwhile, powder workers resided in clusters of housing dubbed "Squirrel Run," "Duck Street," and "Free Park," among others.

The uniqueness of these names suggests that each cluster of du Pont workers' housing had a distinct personality, but they actually had a great deal in common, particularly architecture. In 1902 the company sent one of its employees, George Cheney, around the property to survey every housing unit it owned.[38] His notebook records detailed data for 143 separate units, nearly all of them built in the first half of the century. Most (60 percent) stood two-and-a-half stories high, including garrets. Fifty-three percent were frame, 33 percent stone, and fifteen a combination of the two. Nearly half had shingle roofs (49 percent), although some featured multiple materials, as in the entry that read "shingle roof, porch roof slate, summer kitchen roof tin." Other possibilities included slate (9 percent) or shingle and slate (13 percent). Tar paper, a relatively new product in 1902, appeared only rarely. Inside, most units had either three or four rooms (22 percent and 23 percent, respectively), although Cheney also counted two one-room structures and thirteen large, detached dwellings with seven or more apiece.[39] These variations aside, the community as a whole contained only four distinct forms of housing: the boardinghouse; the detached, single dwelling; the one-third Georgian-plan house; and the back-to-back.

The boardinghouse is perhaps the best known form of workers' housing from the nineteenth century. Its mere mention invariably calls to mind Lowell, Massachusetts, where, in response to critics' fears of proletarianization, the Merrimack Manufacturing Company deliberately hired young women from the surrounding countryside and housed them in large, brick, dormitory-style structures. Run by older female housekeepers, these accommodations supposedly offered the mill girls safe, clean living conditions until such time as they decided to return home. In the 1840s, however, immigrants from Ireland and French-speaking Canada began to replace the native-born women, and the mill owners converted the boardinghouses into single-family homes. Although historians have spent considerable time and energy studying them, the massive, institutionalized boardinghouses of New England never spread beyond their regional cradle. Du Pont's dormitory typified the form as it tended to appear elsewhere: small and compact, it housed fewer than twenty hands at any given time and fell into disuse as the company switched to married men.

Like most American employers, Irénée preferred men with wives and children because he considered them more stable and reliable. This population mandated single-family dwelling units. Some employers went so far as to build detached houses for their operatives. These occasionally mimicked the domestic architecture of the local area. More typically, they clustered closely together like urban houses, and copied each others' size, shape, and appearance as much as hand tools allowed. Despite a common plan, single homes usually proved too costly to build. That is, most wage workers simply did not earn enough to pay the rents required for employers to recoup their expenditures for land, labor, and materials. Irénée understood this relationship very well, and so he owned no detached dwellings apart from those commissioned for his own family or acquired by purchase of a neighboring property. These latter dwellings usually went to master craftsmen and professionals. Ordinary powder workers occupied far different accommodations.

The dominant form of workers' housing in the community was a two-story, semidetached structure containing two four-room, single-family units. Built all over the United States, in all kinds of industrial communities, this particular form surfaced first in the anthracite coal fields of eastern Pennsylvania and western Maryland.[40] Early examples of stone survive, but savvy mine operators soon switched to cheaper vertical-board and balloon-frame construction. Irénée utilized the latter method. The Free

Park, Breck's Lane, and Keg Mill clusters, for example, all featured semidetached, frame houses. Around 1890 or so, Albert "Yaba" Buchanan's family
moved to 174 Breck's Lane. "We had what we called the parlor," his son,
William, recalled. "And then there was your kitchen. Well, that's where we
lived, that's where we ate. You only got in the parlor when you had special
company." A one-story ell, "where they done their washing," extended beyond the kitchen proper, and a winder stair led from the kitchen to two
bedrooms on the second floor. The attic contained bedroom space as well.
The adjacent structure, house number 172, was a mirror image of 174 (figs.
5.4 and 5.5).[41]

Previous research highlights the British antecedents of this distinct,
double-pile configuration, yet it also bears an intriguing resemblance to a
specific Georgian form that characterized the mid-Atlantic region. The
standard Georgian house, which made its appearance in this country in the
late eighteenth century, had a double-pile plan with two rooms on either
side of a central stair hall. Several modifications were also possible. The
most common one entailed subtracting two rooms, leaving what has been
called a "two-thirds Georgian" plan, that is, two rooms and a side passage.[42] Farmhouses throughout Delaware, southeastern Pennsylvania, Maryland, and New Jersey often followed this format. Urban dwellers found it
equally appropriate and made it the dominant townhouse in the region.
Subtracting the side passage produced yet another option, the "one-third
Georgian" plan. This version often appeared as one-half of a semidetached
dwelling. Narrow and deep, it also made up the familiar urban rows that
still define Wilmington, Philadelphia, Baltimore and various other
towns.[43] The "one-third Georgian plan" house particularly suited the small
lots, crowded conditions, and low-income households that characterized
city life. For these reasons, manufacturers in the hinterlands adopted it,
too. Whether built as a semidetached dwelling or combined into rows of
four, six, eight, or ten units, this form dominated workers' housing in the
Delaware Valley.

Since one-third Georgian-plan workers' houses also characterized industrial communities in Great Britain, their presence in this country should
come as no surprise. The widespread popularity of English pattern books
helps account for their use here. More important, most of the men who invested in, operated, and worked at American industrial sites had English,
Welsh, Irish, or Scottish roots. The owners of Parkmount, for example, a
textile mill in the Rockdale district of southeastern Pennsylvania, hailed
from Belfast. They commissioned a stone row for their workers in 1830.
Built into the hillside above the road leading to the mill, the two-story,
single-pile, ten-bay structure probably housed five families. John Price
Crozer erected similar stone structures for his English-born textile workers

Fig. 5.4. Exterior view of "Windett's House" on Breck's Lane, ca. 1890–1900. The semi-detached structure, which included two rental units, once accommodated the Buchanan family. (Courtesy of Hagley Museum and Library)

at West Branch, another Chester Creek complex.[44] When American manufacturers decided to build workers' housing, they looked to their experienced British counterparts for guidance. Although the du Pont company relied mainly upon French investors, its housing stock followed established Anglo-American patterns.

Row houses did not characterize the powder mill community, but several of note existed. Two rows, called Duck Street and Chicken Alley, stood on the hill above Louviers textile mill. The former, a single structure containing four contiguous dwelling units, is no longer extant. The latter, now a single, one-and-a-half-story residence, once incorporated six separate units consisting of two rooms apiece. Three additional rows could be found on the opposite side of the creek: Long Row, a substantial, two-story, stone structure; Diamond Row, a modest frame building, and the Widow's Asylum, a four-unit structure of unknown construction. When built in the 1810s, these rows housed workers at the Rokeby cotton mill. By the 1840s, powder mill families made up the majority of tenants.

Further inland, at the northern edge of the du Pont company's property, stood Wagoner's Row, a four-unit stone structure originally constructed on

Fig. 5.5. Exterior view of Albert Buchanan and family, ca. 1890–1900. (Courtesy of Hagley Museum and Library)

land owned by William Donnan, who operated a local watering hole called the Buck Tavern. An Irish immigrant, Donnan started out as a common laborer in the powder yards on August 15, 1815. He soon captured Irénée du Pont's trust and approbation and rose to become manager of the company farm. Donnan eventually saved enough money to purchase several tracts adjoining his employer's land. Despite his growing wealth, he continued to run the farm, while his wife, Sarah, ran the tavern. When Donnan died in 1828, she inherited his entire property, which by then included several structures besides the tavern, including Wagoner's Row. After Sarah's death in the early 1840s, the complex passed to her daughter, Mary C. Donnan Flemming.[45] Despite its name, the chief residential structure accommodated more than cartmen and teamsters. In 1846 the tenants of Wagoner's Row included brothers Charles and Michael O'Brien, both powder men, John McPherson, a collier, and Malcolm Baxter, a laborer. Irish-born wagoner Robert Betty let one of these units in the 1890s. A daughter recalled that "There were four in a row and then there was a space in between then there was a double house . . . that's four, five, six; then there was one; seven, eight; then there was nine, ten and one up high . . . there was eleven houses down there at that time." The Betty family's unit had a large basement kitchen with a small "cellar" adjoining, a "setting [*sic*] room and parlor" on the first floor, and two bedrooms above.[46] This description suggests that Wagoner's Row was a three- or three-and-a-half-story, double-pile structure built into the hillside. The cluster included several other dwellings, too.

British building practices likely explain the other significant form of workers' housing that defined the Brandywine: the back-to-back. Back-to-back housing emerged in England during the mid-eighteenth century as a deliberate response to high-density land use in industrialized cities like London, Manchester, Birmingham, and Leeds. Sometimes referred to as double houses, and not to be confused with semidetached structures, they conspicuously lacked a back door, window, or any other form of cross-ventilation. Like the modified Georgian forms described above, the two-story back-to-back originated in the countryside. Initially a one-story, one-room cottage, the new house type arose in the eighteenth century, when builders began lining the walls of back lots and infilling courtyards. This development of interior spaces only assuaged the demand for low-cost housing until 1780. After that date, speculators annexed adjacent land in the countryside and charted new streets. Since English farmers traditionally laid out their fields in long, narrow bands, the most appropriate houses to build on these lots were rows of economical and efficient back-to-backs. Small and identical in appearance, units facing neighboring streets shared the same back walls. Each unit had one room on the entrance level and one above, measuring approximately fifteen by fifteen feet. Most had garret space, in addition, but each unit's cellar was actually a separate residence. Reformers widely criticized the back-to-back for its lack of adequate light and air. Still, they became the primary form of housing available to low-income, unskilled households in Great Britain by 1850.[47]

Because back-to-back houses made such efficient use of available land and resources, industrialists in outlying industrial districts adopted them, as well. Built into the steeply sloping hillsides, they especially characterized the coalfields of Wales, Shropshire, and Northumberland, where the rugged terrain sometimes required a slightly different arrangement of units. There, builders devised "dual rows" that had a lower range with access from the downhill side and two rooms that extended back into the hill, plus an upper range with doors on the uphill side and two rooms situated directly above those below. Unlike urban versions, which tended to be brick, these used rubble that had been excavated from the mine shaft. Whether oriented vertically or horizontally, back-to-back stone terraces can also be found in the manufacturing regions of West Riding, Staffordshire, Durham, Cumberland, and Cornwall among others.[48]

Back-to-backs sprang up in Delaware Valley mill villages, too. One of the surviving stone tenements at West Branch, John Crozer's Chester Creek mill complex, has a back-to-back configuration, as does the shell of an additional building that stands on the banks of Mill Creek, near the historic district now known as Gladwyne.[49] Further south, on Squirrel Run, a small stream that flows into the Brandywine, two similar structures arose in conjunction with John Hirons' cotton mill. Like many Brandywine manufacturers, Hirons began operations during the textile boom of the 1810s. Faced with a flood of cheap, imported textiles after the Treaty of Ghent reopened trade with Britain, Hirons soon declared bankruptcy. Advertisements from the sheriff's sale in 1821 described his complex as "A farm containing about 85 acres and adjoining the land of E. I. du Pont & Co., McClane and Milligan and others." Improvements included "a cotton factory of stone with 1,000 stone spindles and the necessary buildings to accommodate the number of hands necessary to keep it in operation."[50] Irénée managed to acquire the property himself in 1824, and immediately made several improvements designed to attract new tenants. These included the addition of a newer, larger water wheel to the mill, plus "a new building opposite Squirrel Run factory containing 8 dwellings."[51] This structure, often referred to in company rent books as the "New Block," mimicked the form of an earlier structure, the eight-unit "Grand Block" that Hirons presumably built. The du Pont company demolished both buildings when it razed the entire Squirrel Run cluster in the 1920s, but surviving evidence confirms their back-to-back configuration. Photographs, for example, record the basic form: two rooms deep, two-and-a-half stories high with interior chimneys and low-pitched, gable roofs pierced by two dormers per side (fig. 5.6). Built of stone, each structure had two sets of porches running the full length of both the front and rear façades. The former porch gave entry to the ground-level rooms, while the latter accessed the second floor. That there would have been no internal communication between the two tiers is confirmed by the placement of windows in the gable end. Census records echo this conclusion. When the federally appointed enumerator came to the powder mill community during the summer of 1850, he found the "new block opposite Squirrel Run factory" occupied by forty-two people. His language here is significant; within the local lexicon, a "block" conveyed a higher density of units per structure than either "house" or "row." Moreover, the residents belonged to eight households headed by Charles A. Gibbons (28), a powder manufacturer; Charles Gibbons (27), a laborer; Hugh Haughey (30), another powder worker; Peter Massey (40), also a laborer; Catharine Althaus (33), a widow; Francis Ryes (35); Dennis Rowe (48); and Mary Mullen (48), another widow. Wage records place most of the men in the Hagley powder

Fig. 5.6. Exterior view of stone back-to-back houses in Squirrel Run, ca. 1890–1900.
(Courtesy of Hagley Museum and Library)

yard, and company rent books confirm their tenancy. More important, the rent books clearly differentiate between the "upper" and "lower" sides of the Squirrel Run blocks. The four units on the "upper side, New block," which likely consisted of one main room on the second level, two on the third, plus garret space, let for $2.75 per month in the 1840s and '50s. The four lower tier units, by contrast, would have contained only three rooms, and rented for $2.25.[52]

Hugh Haughey lived at the "New Block" for many years. Born in Ireland, he commenced working in the powder yards on June 21, 1839. After boarding in the homes of his brothers, Owen and Patrick, for several years, he set up housekeeping in 1843 with his wife, Jane, and their four children, Peter, Francis, Barney, and Jane. As a laborer, Hugh earned $15.50 per month. After April 16, 1846, Peter Haughey, then aged about sixteen, brought in an additional $12.50.[53] The family's rent during this period amounted to only $2.25 per month. According to company records, it occupied "No. 15, New Block" from March 1, 1843, to March 25, 1850, and a unit on the "lower side" of a block in Squirrel Run from March 25, 1850, to October 15, 1851.[54] Since the company did not have a uniform system of numbering houses, it is probable that the Haugheys occupied the same three-room unit for all eight years. Most of the other units in the building, by contrast, changed hands at least five times between 1840 and 1850; some families stayed for fewer than six months. Only two other households resided there for more than five years.

Although there may have been as many as ten back-to-back blocks in the powder mill community, only one survives to the present. Known today as Walker's Banks, it was associated with a textile mill erected on the Brandywine in 1814 by Philadelphia merchant Joseph Sims. Like John Hirons, Sims clearly hoped to capitalize on the new and expanding industry. He initially leased the complex to John Siddall, who manufactured cotton yarn, muslins, checks, and plaids. An 1816 tax assessment listed seven tenements owned by Sims and three by Siddall, who declared bankruptcy the following year. Originally called "Simsville," the complex changed hands several more times until the du Pont company acquired it around 1843. In 1848 Joseph Walker began renting the property. His name still graces the site, although several other firms succeeded him.[55]

The Walker's Banks cluster contained at least two and possibly four blocks built into the banks behind the mill. Each had three-and-a-half stories and originally contained eight back-to-back units (figs. 5.7 and 5.8). A tenant who occupied one of the four units that made up the lower range in the 1840s entered from the river side and had three rooms on the first or "ground" level. The front room, measuring approximately 15' 6" by 14' 9", served as the kitchen. At the back, a second door gave access to two small storage rooms, measuring 10' 6" by 10' 6" each. A winder stair, built into the space between the exterior wall and the chimney breast, led to a bedroom on the second level. Oriented directly above the kitchen, this space once measured 15' 6" by 12' 6", but later tenants divided it into two unequal-sized bedrooms and a hallway. Another winder stair led to a bedroom on the third level, which measured 15' 6" by 13' 3". A tenant who occupied a unit in the upper range occupied four rooms arranged in a complementary fashion. His guests entered from the hill side into the kitchen, a 15' 6" by 13' 11" space on the second level. From that room, a winder stair led to a sleeping chamber on the third floor. It initially measured 15' 6" by 13' 3" although later alterations subdivided it into two smaller spaces and a hallway. Another set of winder stairs led to the garret, where a vertical board wall partitioned the space into two more bedrooms. Each measured 15' 6" by 13' 3" and received natural light from a single dormer window. Period photographs show an identical eight-unit, stone structure located immediately downriver, and two six-unit, frame back-to-backs at the Keg Mill cluster, just to the north. William Flanagan's family lived at the Keg Mill in the 1890s. "This side of Walker's Mill they were all frame houses," he recalled. "There was a kitchen with a slanted roof to it and a coal or wood stove. There were two rooms down on the first floor, one on the second floor, and one on the third floor. Then there was an attic with a bed in that. There

Fig. 5.7. Exterior view of stone back-to-back houses at Walker's Banks, ca. 1890–1900.
(Courtesy of Hagley Museum and Library)

were seven of us living there at that time."[56] His comments describe an L-shaped, back-to-back configuration and suggest how Irish families utilized interior space.

The presence of back-to-back and row housing in the powder mill community is ironic given the stated aims of American manufacturers. Like his counterparts throughout the northeastern United States, E. I. du Pont envisioned industrial villages as a kind of middle landscape between the city and the wilderness.[57] By locating their manufactories in the countryside and instituting a strict but benevolent system of labor relations, du Pont and his neighbors sought to preserve the health and virtue of the operatives in their employ. But instead of building the detached cottages of the Jeffersonian ideal, they erected blocks and rows reminiscent of the very same British manufacturing centers they condemned. American factory owners justified their decision by pointing out that patterns of land use were considerably less dense in this country than in England, and that wage workers here earned considerably more. Industrialists who hired immigrants could also congratulate themselves for providing accommodations that in many respects surpassed the ones their operatives had known in Europe.

Compared to the typical Ulster cottage, workers' houses along the Brandywine were not only bigger, but better finished. Kitchen floors had brick or stone pavers instead of packed earth and clay. Windows had moveable sashes and protective shutters, while tightly shingled or slated roofs kept out the weather. In Ireland, the main living space opened to the rafters, and falling dirt and bugs created a considerable housekeeping problem.[58] In the powder mill community, where timber cost little, builders ceiled over interior spaces with boards or lathe and plaster. In some cases, they also used vertical, beaded-edge boards to carve several small rooms out of a single space. Multiple coats of plaster smoothed out rough stone walls, and simple moldings picked out in Spanish brown or black paint highlighted doors, windows, and mantlepieces. Like most nineteenth-century American houses, powder workers' homes also boasted built-in cupboards, closets, and stairways. Looking back on its one-room, thatch-roofed cabin, an Irish family might well have considered its new surroundings a significant improvement.

In exchange for these relatively comfortable accommodations, employees paid minimal rents. Like other industrialists in the nineteenth-century United States, managers of the du Pont company never intended their workers' houses to make a profit in and of themselves.[59] Irénée originally provided housing to all of his employees free of cost, and only reluctantly began charging rent in the 1810s, when rising operating costs forced him to do so. Between 1841 and 1859, du Pont company houses let for between $12 and $50 a year with quarterly payments the norm.[60] Elsewhere in the United States, tenants moved in on the first of May and most landlords demanded the first installment in advance as a form of surety. With high rents and low wages, however, working people often failed to make payments on time.[61] Workers in the powder mill community, by contrast, had no formal lease, began their occupancy on January first, and had payments deducted from their wage accounts at the *end* of each quarter. Moreover, 73 percent

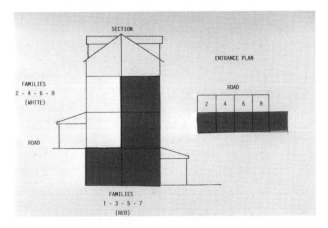

Fig. 5.8. Plan and section of back-to-back houses at Walker's Banks. Drawn by R. Howard. (Courtesy of Hagley Museum and Library)

of the full-time du Pont employees earned between $16.50 and $20 per month by 1850, an amount well above contemporary subsistence levels.[62] When combined with the income from boarders, wives, and children, even common laborers easily afforded the low rents charged by the powder company. In fact, the average rent remained at less than ten percent of the average annual income as late as 1901.[63]

Despite their low cost, Brandywine residences turned over every few months. A promotion, the birth of a child, the arrival of relatives from Ireland, or the decision to take in boarders all seemed adequate cause for moving. Some relocated to another area of the property, but many households simply moved to another unit within the same cluster. Michael Guthrie, for example, occupied house No. 25 in Squirrel Run from June to September of 1841, when he moved next door to house No. 26. Guthrie lived here for two more years and then moved to No. 2 Hiron's Bank, which he occupied for only one quarter. The next tenant of No. 2 Hiron's Bank was Michael McLaughlin, who had previously resided in unit No. 6, only four doors away. Similarly, John Stewart lived in Long Row in 1871, but had moved to Pigeon Row, the building next door, by 1877. When Stewart became foreman of the Hagley yard in 1885, his family moved to Blacksmith's Hill.

Families may also have moved to be nearer certain relatives. Given the small geographic size of the community, no one cluster of housing could really be considered far from any other, but the Irish liked to live in close proximity, and seem to have persuaded the company to place them accordingly. Consider the following examples as illustrative. In the summer of 1850, when the federal census taker paid his call, laborer Bernard McManus (38) lived on Rising Sun Lane. His brother, Patrick McManus (49), a shoe maker, occupied the house next door, while another brother, James McManus (age unknown), ran the nearby Rising Sun Tavern. Female ties linked other families. Neil Mooney (33), for example, occupied a unit in Squirrel Run with his wife, Mary (22), and their two young sons. Three doors away lived John McGonigle (30), his wife, Bridget (28), and their two children. The women were probably sisters because church records list Mary Houtton as Neil Mooney's wife and godmother to a child of Bridget Houtton and John McGonigle. Likewise, Daniel Sweeney and his wife, Mary (née Harkins), lived at the Upper Banks with their two children and six boarders, including Daniel Harkins (30). Charles Harkins (32), a laborer, lived three doors away with his wife, Mary (née Nolan), and five children ranging in age from two to twelve.

Spatial proximity enabled the preservation of bilateral extended family networks and provided an important support system for Irish households. At a time when America lacked social welfare agencies, the presence of nearby aunts, uncles, siblings, parents, and children guaranteed some measure of security to the sick, aged, injured, widowed, or orphaned members of immigrant communities.[64] Certain aspects of Irish culture and Roman Catholic doctrine reinforced these ties and imbued them with a significance that transcended economic considerations. In Ulster, families that inhabited the same clachan, townland, or parish tended to feel a kind of kinship with each other, one that reflected, in some cases, actual blood ties, but more broadly conveyed their mutual attachment to the local landscape and the traits it purportedly endowed.[65] Just as Irish men and women identified themselves as members of specific families, so they also identified themselves as residents of specific places. In some counties, intraterritorial rivalries often produced "faction fights" that pitted members of one community against another. In America, similar conflicts frequently erupted over competition for jobs and scarce resources.[66] The powder mill community did not experience this problem, but residents remained sensitive to the power of physical geography. By maintaining spatial proximity to their kin, the du Pont Irish simultaneously sustained family networks and elements of their old world identity. At the same time, by helping individuals emigrate, get jobs, and mobilize capital for joint ventures, like the acquisition of property, their family networks also encouraged acculturation.

The ideology of social mobility in nineteenth-century America afforded the hope that anyone could purchase property if he worked hard and confined his expenditures to fulfilling "needs," not "wants."[67] Although the time needed to attain this goal varied, Irish immigrants often become homeowners after working but a short time in the powder mills. In 1848, the *Blue Hen's Chicken,* a local newspaper, proudly proclaimed:

> We are almost daily told of houses, lots, or little farms purchased by our worthy naturalized citizens, and particularly those employed by the Du Ponts on the Brandywine. There is no better evidence of the good effects of true republican government than the thrift and well doing of the foreigners who come to our shores, poor and ignorant, and who soon become among our best, and best doing citizens.[68]

George Dougherty exemplifies these worthy "citizens." A Catholic immigrant from Donegal, he became a pot man in the Hagley yard on January 1, 1826, amassed his savings, and moved with his wife and family to a farm in Christiana Hundred in 1842 or 1843. Seven years later, he held real estate worth $2000. Other powder men returned to the soil, too, including James Watson, a Presbyterian, in 1836, and John Carroll, another Catholic, in 1839.[69] Even Irish textile operatives and artisans acquired farms. These included John Donaldson, a cotton spinner, and William Baldwin, a blacksmith. Many immigrants, like these men, chose to remain near their friends and family. Others moved away from the Brandywine, buying property elsewhere in the mid-Atlantic region or in the western territories.

Though wage earners, the du Pont Irish managed to buy land because their economic situation had improved considerably after emigration. In general, historians evaluate workers' material well-being by measuring the relationship between wages, earnings, expenses, and savings. Between 1802 and 1860, nominal wages along the Brandywine increased 35.1 percent while prices fell nearly 22 percent, resulting in a 74.2 percent increase in real wages. Actual earnings (measured in terms of actual days worked) increased as well—by nearly 50 percent—while a conservative estimate shows a small family's household expenditures for food and rent declining from roughly 75 percent of its total annual income to just over 53 percent. Meanwhile, many Irish took full advantage of the company savings plan, putting away some of their new, discretionary funds at a mean rate of 15 percent each year. In theory, at this rate an enterprising hand could save the equivalent of twelve months' wages in six years or less. In reality, the antebellum economy proved dangerously volatile, and some families took longer than others to achieve the same level of security, that is, if they reached it all.[70]

To most Irish before about 1850, attaining their "independence" mandated not just property ownership, but agriculturally productive property ownership. This ambition reflected deeply rooted cultural norms: Even weavers and spinners in industrializing Ulster tilled the soil, believing, despite growing evidence to the contrary, that the land itself retained subsistence potential. From their point of view, the problem was tenancy and British rule, which together channeled the proceeds of Irish labor into the hands of "tyrannous" landlords. The answer seemed clear: emigration to a proverbial land of plenty, a place where vast tracts of cheap land and a "comfortable self-sufficiency" predicated on farming awaited. In time, a significant number of Irish emigrants did manage to buy arable property.[71] But would-be farmers also faced numerous other obstacles.

Despite their different origins and outlooks, former powder workers experienced many of the same problems that plagued nineteenth-century farmers in general. Imagine the anxious excitement felt by powder man Henry Gegan and his wife as they packed up their household and headed west to Richmond, Indiana, where at least seven former Brandywine families had already resettled and where, consequently, prospects looked good. In 1834, however, their dreams evaporated: the du Ponts received notice that "an Irishman named Guigan [sic] has died of Asiatic cholera" and that his wife and children had "little hope of recovery." As it happened, the wee ones eventually rallied, thanks to the loving care of Jane Reed, an Irish woman who once worked at the Rokeby mill. They eventually returned to their kin along the Brandywine, escorted by a company representative, but their futures had changed considerably.[72] Other Irish settlers simply found life on the frontier much more difficult than they envisioned. Writing from Chippeway in the upper Midwest, Irishman Samuel Foster admitted to Alfred du Pont that "I am not sattisfied with my move to this part of the country and if you would be so kind as to give me my old birth I will go back there to you on or about the first of April and I think that will be a good time to prepare for willow cutting work." Successful farmers like Foster's neighbor, the Irish-born former powder man John Ritchie, promised fifty cents a day for agricultural laborers, but cash proved "very scarse" and, Foster declared, "I want some money to buy other things that I want."[73] Patrick Callahan experienced a related problem. Having acquired a modest farm in Chester County, Pennsylvania, he borrowed money to improve his holdings during the boom years of the 1840s and fell victim to the Panic of 1857. After paying off his debts, he had enough left over to buy a small house in Phoenixville, and lived the rest of his life as a day laborer.[74]

Given the risks, some powder workers purchased farmsteads in rural Christiana and Brandywine hundreds, but continued to work for du Pont and live in company housing. Six of the household heads and one boarder living in Free Park in 1850 owned property ranging in value from $100 to $2500. Daniel McEvey, for example, a Catholic powder man at Hagley, owned $2500 worth of real estate. The size of his holding suggests that he probably had a farm nearby.[75] Employees living in other clusters also owned real estate. Daniel Travers, a Catholic mason living at Louviers, held land valued at $1450. His holdings compare favorably to those of Jesse Gregg, a native-born American whose $1500 farm adjoined the Upper Banks, and to Catholic laborers Peter Quigley, Sr., and James Mullen, both long-term residents of the Upper Banks, who owned $900 and $2000 worth of property, respectively. Since Mullen's wage account shows deductions of $7.13 for clover seed and $3.73 for taxes in Brandywine Hundred, it is likely that he, too, had a working farm somewhere across the river.

Because the du Pont company never actually sold land to its employees, those Irish who pursued property mobility had to move beyond the immediate bounds of the powder mill community. This fact accounts for the low rates of home ownership revealed by census records. Only 17 percent of the 444 household heads in 1850 owned real property, for example, and only 10 percent of the 350 households enumerated in the 1870 census did. These rates are considerably lower than those noted for Irish households in large cities, but they are consistent with those of other industrial villages.[76] Moreover, 58 percent of the 1850 cohort and 51 percent of the 1870 cohort were Irish-born, confirming that the acquisition of real estate remained a strong priority for emigrants. Census records also indicate that most of those fortunate enough to own property within the community itself resided in Henry Clay Village.

This cluster took its name from an imposing cotton factory erected by Duplanty, McCall and Company in 1813 and dedicated to Henry Clay, the Whig senator who favored high protective tariffs on imported goods. The "village" itself extended nearly three-fourths of a mile along the south side of the Brandywine, beginning at the lower Hagley gates and following what locals called "Main Street" or "River Road" down to and including Rising Sun Lane, a narrow street running perpendicular to the creek. By 1868, some thirty or more homes and several businesses had been built into the embankment (see fig. 5.9). There resided Paul Bogan, who had a small shop worth $2000, and James F. Toy, who ran the "Blazing Rag," a tavern located conveniently near the post office and drug store. Pat Haughey, a former powder man turned trader, lived there, too, along with Robert Kirkwood, Henry Doran, and James Blessington.

These and other Irish Catholics chose commerce over agriculture. In the 1820s and thirties, arable land in New Castle County remained within the typical immigrant's grasp. As the decades passed, however, and the industrial revolution progressed, local farmers became increasingly market oriented; that is, they consolidated their holdings, began rotating their crops, and tailored their products to meet the needs of wage-earning, salaried, and professional households in northern Delaware's burgeoning cities and industrial villages. In response, property values rose and ambitious immigrants and native-born Americans alike headed west in search of cheap farm land. Others stayed behind and shifted their hopes to small-scale entrepreneurship. This transposition occurred elsewhere in the antebellum United States as well, and by about 1850, the lexeme "property" had begun to connote not just productive *land,* but productive *capital,* which included businesses, personal savings accounts, and certain types of professional skill as well as farms and houses. Likewise, "mobility" had begun to signify not movement out of manual labor, but movement into a "propertied" state.[77] For Irishmen like Pat Haughey or James Toy, then, opening a store or tavern served the same purpose as farming: it elevated them into the ranks of freeholders and thereby assuaged their desire for "independence."

By the 1880s, definitions of "property" were shifting yet again. The concentrations of industry, banking, and commerce that characterized Gilded Age America left fewer and fewer opportunities for successful entrepreneurship, so wage-earning families, in particular, fixed on householding alone.[78] For the du Pont Irish, this often meant buying lots in the newly platted neighborhoods springing up along the Wilmington City Railway, which connected Henry Clay Village to the city. The increasingly Irish Forty Acres neighborhood experienced considerable activity, as did the

Fig. 5.9. Exterior view of Henry Clay Village, looking south from the Rokeby mansion, ca. 1890–1900. (Courtesy of Hagley Museum and Library)

Highlands, a tract sandwiched between Forty Acres and Tower Hill, the area adjacent to Henry Clay Village. Self-building accounts for the eclectic appearance of many blocks along the railway right-of-way, but some streets contained identical rows of "spec" housing. Significantly, a number of Irish families bought their row houses as rental properties, not residences. Period newspaper advertisements show rents in the city's new, westside neighborhoods ranging from $16 to $35 per annum. In 1887 the *Wilmington Every Evening* declared "that houses suited to the needs of mechanics and working men have been found to be good investments and that there are no reasons why they should not prove equally good during the coming season."[79] Perhaps this market trend is what led Big Dan Dougherty to buy 1907 Lincoln Street.

"Streetcar suburbs" attracted other powder mill veterans, as well. Thus, Edward Beacom bought one side of a two-story, semidetached, brick house located at 1813 Shallcross Avenue, right in the heart of Forty Acres. "My father thought when you married you ought to have a home to take your bride to," Elizabeth Beacom recalled. "He may have brought some money over here from Ireland because I know they had had a farm over there."[80] Married in 1881, Edward ultimately decided to rent the house in Wilmington, and his family did not occupy it until after his death in 1912.

Moreover, the Beacom residence was just around the corner from Big Dan Dougherty's. In fact, the du Pont Irish seem to have deliberately relocated near each other. Hugh Dougherty, Big Dan's son, owned a house in the Highlands, a few streets further west, and powder man Robert Peoples had two lots several blocks to the south. James Cheney, Edward Beacom's brother-in-law, built his house in the Tower Hill area, a few blocks east of Henry Clay Village, and foreman John Gibbons brought the circle to a close at 1629 Lincoln Street.[81]

As these and other Irish families left the Brandywine, immigrants from Wilmington took their places. Joseph H. Hackendorn emigrated from Alsace-Lorraine with his five brothers, their parents, and two other families, named Keinbeiter and Rohr. The Hackendorns initially lived on "Plunket's Row," a section of Chestnut Street located near the morocco shops, but when Joseph got a job in the powder graining mill, they moved to Squirrel Run. Later, they moved to Free Park, "right next to the [Episcopal] church."[82] The Keinbeiters also came to the powder mill community in the 1890s, along with other Alsatians like the Krausses and Choimers, and Italians like the Consanos and Massis. Neither population ever comprised a majority, but their arrival suggests just how mobile the Irish had become.

Whether a farm, a small business, or a modest rowhouse, real estate loomed large in the lives of Irish immigrants because it symbolized self-sufficiency and social status. Despite the Ulster custom of "tenant right," laws prevented Catholics and dissenting Protestants alike from possessing property and the autonomy that seemed to come with it. Consequently, many northerners emigrated to the Brandywine, where, with the help of family networks, they quickly secured steady and well-paid employment. Like Edward Beacom, many even came to this country with money, a specific skill, or an education. The paternalism of the du Ponts offered another impetus toward success. All employees started out as common labor, and consequently, many workmen initially postponed buying property in favor of bringing out relatives from Ireland, belonging to a church, or simply achieving a daily subsistence. In time, however, many men eventually ascended the occupational ladder and became powder workers or skilled artisans. Others became farmers, clerks, or independent businessmen. The acquisition of property did not axiomatically confine Irish laborers to manual occupations, as some historians contend, nor did it take precedence over other forms of social advancement.[83] On the contrary, having a home of one's own was an advance in and of itself. Buying a home thus functioned as part of a distinctive strategy for success, one that allowed the Irish to rise socially and economically while preserving their ethnocultural identity

CHAPTER 6

All the Goods and Chattels

On November 29, 1833, Sophie du Pont returned from one of her "pastorals" among the powder workers and recorded the following passage in her diary:

> This afternoon, Pol and I went to see M[ary] A[nn] Young's little sister. I trust I may never forget the scene we witnessed. Rebecca came to the door; I was immediately struck by the careworn expression of her face—she asked us into the room where she had been sitting, there was her chair and work beside the cradle where the baby lay, while two boys, almost infants, stood beside—the baby was breathing with difficulty but lay quite still, its large black eyes rolling around, sparkling brightly with fever. Rebecca said they had no hope of its recovery—[but] to yours she added, "Rufus there was given up once."[1]

Sophie was understandably moved by her visit with the Youngs that day, so much so that she went on to record the family's drama in considerable detail. Her entries reveal that Mrs. Young had died soon after giving birth to the feverish child in question, and Rebecca, the oldest daughter, had taken over the care of the household. Meanwhile, sixteen-year-old Mary Ann worked in a nearby textile mill. Once she had been a favored student of Sophie's, but like many Sunday school scholars, Mary Ann had withdrawn early. Her father, Robert Young, earned less than $20 a month as a common laborer, and her wages offered an important supplement.

Concerned and curious to know how Mary Ann's sister fared, Sophie returned to the Youngs' on Saturday, December 1st, where, she said:

> I knocked long without obtaining an answer. At length the father appeared. His face told me at once the answer to the faltering question, "How is the child,'" and I needed not to hear the answer, "She is dead." I hesitated about

going in from the fear of intrusion—But he begged me to do so; a neighbor was scrubbing one end of the little room, at the other all the children were grouped together by the stove. It was a truly touching scene—The eldest sister held a hymn book, from which she appeared to have been reading to the two almost baby boys at her feet—Rufus leaned apart, his torn hat slouched on his face, down which the tears were trickling rapidly—Mary Ann was reading in her testament. The two other girls were crying.[2]

Though brief, these and other passages reveal important details about everyday life in the powder mill community. Death was commonplace. Despite the child's illness and eventual demise, Robert Young still had to work, Rebecca still had her mending, and the floor still needed scrubbing. Most of the household's daily activities took place in one, primary living space that visitors entered into directly. There Rebecca sewed and tended the little patient in its cradle. There, too, the older children gathered in prayer around a stove, and eventually laid out their sibling's body. Finally, we learn that the floor of this room was bare and that a neighbor, undoubtedly female, had come to help the family during its time of bereavement. None of this information would have been new to Sophie du Pont; she recorded it because the family's story appealed to her romantic sensibilities. But in so doing, she provided a rare glimpse into the powder workers' domestic world.

While not Catholic, the Youngs' domestic arrangements typified their time and place. The family rented a unit at Simsville, the name given to a pair of back-to-back, stone blocks of workers' housing that Irénée du Pont leased to Joseph A. Sims and Company in the 1830s.[3] Living conditions here differed greatly from the Irish norm. For $40 per year, the Youngs got four rooms instead of two, smooth, plaster walls instead of rough, whitewashed stones, and wooden floors instead of packed earth. Their furnishings remained simple: a chair (they undoubtedly had several), a cradle (beds were upstairs, out of sight), and probably a table of some sort (for dining and food preparation). The stove stands out sharply from the other items. Small stoves for cooking and heating became available in the Brandywine valley in the 1830s. Yet the price remained sufficiently high to endow them with important status-bearing capabilities.[4] Exactly how and when the family managed to acquire such a costly item remains unclear; however, Irish immigrants' desire for consumer goods has been well documented. Faced with declining prospects at home, experts contend, they espoused a "streets-paved-with-gold" mentality that effectively projected their ambitions for a life of "security, ease and plenty" onto the United States.[5] Descriptions of the dazzling profusion of goods available here only reinforced this tendency, and wage-earning Irish families like the Youngs developed creative strategies to achieve their material goals.

Since few powder mill families preserved their effects for posterity, identifying and interpreting their material culture poses a difficult though ultimately rewarding challenge. In fact, little is known about the ways in which laboring Americans furnished their homes and used interior space in the nineteenth century. The relationship between what workers bought and how they thought about identity is a relatively recent area of inquiry, and most studies stress wage earners' expenditures for food, rent, clothing, or entertainment.[6] But household objects yield additional insights, and because "[g]oods assembled together in ownership make physical, visible statements about the hierarchy of values to which their chooser subscribes," artifactual analysis informs questions of cultural identity, too.[7] At Lowell, Massachusetts, for example, New England farmers' daughters-cum-mill girls consciously incorporated parlor furnishings into their boardinghouses. Through their material culture, these novice wage earners simultaneously familiarized a strange, new living situation and asserted their ties to a more dignified past and future.[8] Similarly, Italian immigrants in New York City used fabric valences and thick, feather beds to convey their triumph over the material degradation of Europe, while their Jewish neighbors deployed upright pianos as signs of upward mobility, domestic tranquility, and prospective citizenship.[9] So, too, powder mill families used carefully selected objects to modify interior spaces and define their place in a modern, industrialized society. Read as texts, then, domestic furnishings make manifest not only day-to-day living conditions, but the process of acculturation.

Irish immigrants' desire for consumer goods developed as a response to their material circumstances in rural Ireland. The predominance of one- or two-room cabins, for example, meant that most people conducted their domestic activities in one, primary living space. To maximize space and maintain order, Ulster families placed their furniture around the perimeter of the room.[10] Tables, uncommon until the early nineteenth century, ranged along the walls when not in use, and meal bins kept oatmeal, flour, and bread dough safe from marauding insects. Chairs were scarce. Instead, most country folk made do with low, three-legged stools, called creepies.[11] Baskets and trunks often functioned as seats, too. After its evening meal, a family might huddle before the hearth, the symbolic heart of the home. Directly opposite stood the dresser, the most prominent piece of furniture in the room. Rows of glazed Delftware shone brightly in its upper rack. Although wooden vessels remained the norm for everyday use, imported ceramics and other household goods could be purchased from itinerant pedlars by the end of the eighteenth century. Even the lowliest households had "ware racks" or "tin rails" for display. These might be mounted alone, but more typically hung above a table or bureau.[12]

Close quarters meant that communal sleeping patterns predominated. The poorest Ulster families slept on rush or straw pallets on the floor, but carefully organized themselves by age and sex. Middling households placed the primary bed in an outshot, a small projection or alcove built specifically for this purpose into the wall near the hearth. Beginning in the late eighteenth century, the Irish could purchase specialized items like a settle bedstead, which converted into a bench during the day, or a "press" bedstead, that is, a small cabinet with a folding canvas cot inside.[13] Some homes had a separate room for sleeping. The wealthy, of course, had multiple sleeping chambers, complete with matched sets of furniture imported from England.

As subjects of the British crown, the Irish played an active role in the consumer "boom" that swept the English empire in the late eighteenth century.[14] Numerous forces combined during this period to expand the demand for and production of a wide range of manufactured goods, especially household furnishings. In Ulster, a concomitant expansion of the linen industry created new jobs that in turn enabled wider participation in the buying frenzy. Thanks to better markets and falling prices, strong farmers and other middling sorts began to acquire items once reserved for elites. By the 1810s, "luxuries" had become mere "decencies," and "decencies" had become "necessities." But the economic prosperity of the age largely bypassed the landless cottier and laboring classes, who constituted the majority of the population.[15] Additional setbacks occurred with the collapse of linen industry in the early 1820s. As a consequence, crown officials surveying taxable goods in the parish of West Tullaghobegly, County Donegal, in 1837, found only 3 pocket watches, 8 brass candlesticks, 93 chairs, 242 stools, 2 feather beds, and no clocks or looking glasses.[16] Daniel Harkin, a future powder man, was one of the 4,000 residents living there at the time, and a strong sense of material deprivation likely influenced his decision to emigrate.[17]

Upon arrival in the powder mill community, a single man like Harkin would have boarded with an established family like the Youngs. Sophie's diaries provide important clues concerning the kinds of objects and spaces he would have encountered there. More detailed information surfaces in county probate records. When an individual died intestate, the probate judge in Wilmington appointed representatives to make a detailed inventory of all the goods and chattels the decedent possessed, including clothing, furnishings, tools, livestock, real estate, and personal effects. Over 100 of these inventories survive for the powder mill community. While not comprehensive, they represent a large cross-section of the local population, and make it possible to "refurnish" ordinary Irish wage earners' homes for the first time.[18]

Just as they had in Ireland, these households conducted most of their daily activities in one, primary living space: the kitchen. Here, the *bean a ti* prepared the family's meals. Prior to about 1830, cooking occurred over one or more small fires kindled in a large, open hearth at one end of the room. Pots, pans, kettles, griddles, and various utensils clustered within arm's reach. The far corners held tools and various kinds of work equipment, especially items like churns and reels, which in this community supported various cottage industries.[19] Other typical furnishings included five or more chairs, one large table, several small tables or stands, and at least one bench. Built-in cupboards supplied storage, but a small number of kitchens boasted moveable chests or dressers, as well. In the 1830s, more fuel-efficient wood- and coal-burning stoves appeared for both heating and cooking purposes; toward the end of the century, large, six-plate ranges became the norm (fig. 6.1). When asked to describe her family's Squirrel Run home in the 1890s, Elizabeth Beacom recalled that "[t]here was a great big kitchen which was one story. My mother had a kitchen stove, a settee and a big sideboard, about eight or ten chairs and a bench table. We ate off the table and kept our schoolbooks underneath.[20] Because it was usually the warmest place in the house, the kitchen drew people in to eat, talk, play,

Fig. 6.1. Interior view showing Mrs. Maxwell at her kitchen stove, ca. 1901. Maxwell lived in Wagoner's row. (Courtesy of Hagley Museum and Library)

and study. In the hot, humid, summer months, however, some Brandywine families shifted food preparation to an outdoor structure. Usually associated with rural southern farmsteads, separate "summer" kitchens remained in use in the powder mill community as late as 1902, when 29 of the company's 143 housing units still had one.[21] Other houses at the time had "wing" kitchens, "shed" kitchens, or "basement" kitchens, suggesting that cooking facilities could occupy ancillary spaces when necessary.

During the first half of the century, when boarders existed in large numbers, kitchens frequently contained beds and bedding. As in Ireland, Brandywine families maintained traditional sleeping patterns; that is, they slept wherever possible! Seventy percent of the probated estates noted at least one bedstead, but most had three or four. Ten percent specified high-post bedsteads, 4 percent low-post bedsteads, and another 4 percent trundle beds. The latter likely accommodated children. Only seven cradles, one crib, one child's bedstead and one boy's bedstead appeared in the entire sample.[22] After 1850, inexpensive iron bedsteads were an increasingly common alternative (fig. 6.2).[23] Feather and chaff beds appeared in high numbers but often had no corresponding bedstead at all, indicating that families simply placed them on the floor at night. Coupled with portable cot and field-post bedsteads, which appeared in fully one-fourth of the inventories, these "pallet" beds provided workers' households with the ability to lodge many individuals at one time. Powder man James McLaughlin's 1851 probate inventory exemplifies this flexibility.[24] It included two field-post bedsteads with beds and bedding, two low-post bedsteads with beds and bedding, one cot bed and bedding, and two feather beds. Privacy would have been scarce and conditions crowded; the household included McLaughlin, his wife, their four children, and from two to six boarders each month.

With space at a premium, the du Pont Irish limited bedroom furniture to a few basic pieces. Tables, usually clustered in local inventories with an oiled floorcloth, a looking glass, and a wash bowl and pitcher, clearly functioned as makeshift washstands.[25] Only 24 percent of the decedents owned a real washstand and only 4 percent had a toilet table. A few chairs and a stand or small table made up the remaining items. Most bedrooms contained an impressive array of textiles, however, including blankets, quilts, sheets, coverlets, and pillowcases. Many were specified as homemade, despite access to store-bought articles. How families stored their bedding is unclear. Only 22 percent of the inventories listed trunks or chests while only 14 percent had a case of drawers. Cupboards, clothes presses, and dressing cases also appeared, but rarely. Most families likely placed clothing on pegs and shelves.

Probate inventories yield rich quantitative data concerning the kind and number of objects in a given community, yet they can also provide

Fig. 6.2. Interior view of a typical bedroom showing metal bedstead, wooden cradle, and damage from an explosion, 1890. (Courtesy of Hagley Museum and Library)

qualitative insights into the cultural values that its members held dear. Picture John McDermott and James McGuire, two Irish-born Catholic powder men, as they prepared in 1831 to inventory the belongings of their late friend and neighbor James Bogan.[26] For each item to be recorded, McDermott and McGuire had to select appropriate terms from the myriad possibilities available in their day-to-day vocabulary: chair, table, bedstead, trunk. Objects of special significance or value required modifiers, such as "walnut," "Windsor," or "painted." To the appraisers, the use of these adjectives or "markers" served merely to distinguish between common and uncommon goods. To the historian these words or phrases situate the items described "within a culturally construed field of meaning."[27]

From the way McDermott, McGuire, and their counterparts marked and unmarked goods and chattels, it is clear that residents of the powder mill community understood which characteristics made an object "common" and which did not. By the 1830s, the adjective "common" most often described the kind of simple, functional furniture considered suitable for "cottage" life. In his highly influential 1850 work, *The Architecture of Country Houses,* Andrew Jackson Downing defined the cottage as "a dwelling of small size," intended for occupation by a single family. But, he added, "the majority of cottages in this country are occupied, not by tenants, or serfs, as in many parts of Europe, but by industrious and intelligent mechanics and working men, the bone and sinew of the land."[28] Cottages therefore differed from other types of houses by the wage-earning character of their occupants.

Downing gave considerable thought to the design of appropriate cottage furniture, and devoted an entire chapter of *The Architecture of Country Houses* to its description. Simplicity and truthfulness were the most important features of cottage architecture, and its furniture, he likewise felt, "can scarcely be too simple, too chaste, or too unpretending in its character."[29] One of the cheapest and easiest items to obtain for a cottage was the barrel chair, a high-backed, upholstered seat fashioned quite literally from found materials. Downing gave his readers full instructions for making one; however, he noted that most "cottage" pieces were machine-made. Manufacturers like Edward Hennessey in Boston joined together various inexpensive woods, then painted the exterior surfaces a uniform color. Downing praised one of Hennessey's typical bedroom sets as being "remarkable for its lightness and strength. . . . It is very highly finished, and is usually painted drab, white, gray, a delicate lilac, or a fine blue—the surface polished and hard, like enamel."[30] Some of the better sets had painted flowers, too. Downing also considered certain kinds of "Elizabethan"-style furniture appropriate for cottage use. These could usually be identified by their twisted legs, he said, though one could also buy similar pieces with legs "turned in the cheaper knotted manner shown in Fig. 284." Figure 284 showed an early spool-turned bedroom set.[31]

Originally intended for middling households, cottage furniture quickly became associated with wage earners. Part of the attraction was its relatively low price. In 1849, Godey's *Ladies' Book* devoted an entire column to the style, calling it "the cheapest and prettiest [furniture] that can be manufactured."[32] By 1867, a common cottage bedstead could be purchased for as little as $5.25 at P. P. Gustine's wholesale furniture warehouse in Philadelphia. Painted bedsteads cost only a few dollars more, while an entire cottage suite could be had for $29.00. The "Elizabethan" or spool-turned bedstead, by this date referred to as a "Jenny Lind" bed, was equally popular at $11.00. A solid walnut version, by contrast, could cost anywhere from $28.00 to $125.00.[33]

Technological innovation and mass production brought an astonishing array of goods within the price range of average laborers.[34] It is important to note, however, that lower prices diluted the ability of certain goods to convey elite status. Consequently, by 1850 writers of housekeeping and decorating manuals clearly stated that iron bedsteads, low-post bedsteads, patchwork quilts, rag rugs, and white granite, or "common Queensware" dishes suited workers only.[35] Items like upholstered chairs, ingrain carpets, and mahogany tables, by contrast, they reserved for the more affluent levels of society. To many observers, the number and quality of their interior furnishings readily distinguished low-income homes from those of the wealthy. In actuality, the emergence of a vast manufacturing and distribution system in the 1830s and 1840s ensured the slow but steady dissemination of commodities to all levels of society.

Whether in Philadelphia or Wilmington or elsewhere, Irish immigrants not only eyed fashionable furnishings and goods, but some proved more than capable of acquiring them. Between the 1810s and 1850s, real earnings in the Brandywine region doubled while prices fell. As a consequence, the typical powder mill household's expenditure for necessities like food and shelter, measured as a percentage of its annual earnings, declined substantially, thereby increasing each family's ability to obtain niceties or even luxuries. In 1850 over 73 percent of the 197 full-time du Pont employees earned between $200 and $300 a year, the same amount of money as skilled labor elsewhere in the United States.[36] Coopers, wheelwrights, and carpenters earned closer to $400. While significantly lower than the $500 to $1000 that nonmanual clerks and businessmen could expect annually, this sum enabled du Pont workers to live well above the subsistence level, especially if augmented by the wages of other household members.[37] Elsewhere in the state, their counterparts consciously deployed a portion of their rising incomes to upgrade their domestic environments. Prior to the Civil War, households in Kent County dramatically increased the number and kind of genteel objects they owned.[38] At the same time, families in southern New Castle County substantially rebuilt their agricultural farmsteads.[39] Significantly, however, these rural Delawareans did not simply imitate their economic superiors; rather, they incorporated into their homes only those things that resonated most deeply with the emerging culture of refinement. Powder workers also exhibited this selective approach to increased domestic consumption, but as tenants, much of their activity focused on parlor fittings.

Despite their Irish origins and modest incomes, du Pont workers knew enough about the "ideal" bourgeois, American parlor to identify and appropriate its most important elements.[40] Prior to the Civil War, these included a bureau, a clock, a looking glass, a stove, carpeting, and some chairs, the minimum furnishings required for entertainment and display. With 68 percent of the inventories listing at least one, a bureau seemed the most important piece for a low-income household to own. Having deep drawers and a broad, flat top, it usually served as a parlor sideboard.[41] Indeed, the anonymous author of *Hints on Houses* (1861), a popular domesticity manual imported into the United States from Britain, devoted an entire chapter to the piece, explaining that,

The chests may often be seen in the best room of a thrifty cotton spinner's house, or in a miner's cottage, and in the dwellings of those who dig and work metal. With a chest of drawers and a clock, in addition to the other articles, the furnishing of the room is generally considered complete, and the care bestowed on them is often a proof of the value in which they are held. They are kept clean and polished as brightly as a looking-glass, and on the chest of drawers all the little ornaments of the parlor are displayed.[42]

An identical pattern of use has been documented among Irish, English, and Welsh households in the anthracite-mining region of Pennsylvania.[43]

But a bureau alone did not a parlor make. James Burns, the author of a nineteenth-century volume on Irish immigration to America, explained that in his experience Irish workers usually occupied "clean, comfortable dwellings with warm stoves and 'bits of carpits on their flures.'"[44] So did Brandywine families. Fifty-eight percent of the inventoried households contained a stove, and 48 percent also had a carpet, usually valued by the amount of yards. Fully 62 percent owned a clock, often designated as an eight-day, Yankee, or twenty-four-hour clock. Twenty-six percent had a settee, sometimes with cushions, and 30 percent decorated their walls with pictures or prints. These often had mahogany or gilt frames. Fourteen percent owned books or bookcases, but only 4 percent had a Bible. Although seating furniture usually comprised a group of six or so unspecified chairs, 14 percent of the inventories listed "painted" or "Windsor" chairs and another 18 percent specified a "rocking" chair. Some Irish owned easy chairs, arm chairs, cane-seated chairs, stuffed chairs, or chairs made of a particular wood, like mahogany or cherry (fig. 6.3). Other specialized items included sofas, card tables, center tables, secretaries, desks, cupboards and window shades. Du Pont employees thus owned many of the same kinds of parlor furniture as their wealthier neighbors, albeit in fewer numbers.

Several inventories suggest how powder mill families defined parlor space within their relatively small and crowded homes. Widow Ann King Dougherty, who died in 1835, had the luxury of a combined sitting-dining room. The space contained her best bed, a round tea table, a cherry bureau, a walnut breakfast table, a looking glass, and three muslin window curtains, along with a set of china, her tea plates, decanters, and six silver tea spoons. Dougherty's husband, Richard, "went across the creek" in 1815, but a combination of boarders, his savings, and her own widow's pension of $100 a year enabled her to amass an estate worth nearly $134.[45] Most households, however, resembled that of powder man John Buchanan, whose belongings totaled $74. Although Buchanan earned less than $400 per annum in the 1860s, his estate included a bureau and two looking glasses, fifteen yards of carpet, miscellaneous dishes and glassware, a set of six chairs, a

Fig. 6.3. Interior view showing powder man Gilbert Mathewson, Jr., reading the paper in his parlor, ca. 1880–1900. (Courtesy of Hagley Museum and Library)

center table, and a workstand.[46] Kitchen furniture and bedding were the only other goods listed in his inventory, indicating that the household contained a kitchen, two bedrooms, and perhaps one room given over to entertainment and display.

By the end of the century, Brandywine families used the terms sitting room, living room, and parlor interchangeably to identify the formal, public space within their homes (fig. 6.4).[47] George Cheney's daughter, Catherine, recalled that her family's living room contained:

> A mahogany carved table with a rack underneath for books, a cowhide sofa, and three chairs. One was a wooden chair and Mother covered it. Another was that kind of chair that you raise the side that lets the back go down [a recliner?]. There was an old-fashioned chair; my Father had that one. Then we had three or four of the dining room chairs that we kept in there. They were just straight-back ordinary chairs. And then we had the four chairs that I said came from the machine shop.[48]

Ella Fitzharris's family resided in a semidetached house above Walkers' Banks, as Simsville eventually came be called. She described a combination dining room–parlor: "We just had white lace curtains at the windows and

Fig. 6.4. Interior view showing an unidentified powder mill family in its parlor in Henry Clay Village, ca. 1880–1900. (Courtesy of Hagley Museum and Library)

shades . . . comfortable chairs and a couch, a china closet with an awful lot of dishes . . . all kinds and shapes and cups, also a dining table, round, with claw legs that expanded."⁴⁹ While far from the Gilded Age domestic "ideal," these spaces and furnishings held a deep meaning for the families under consideration. Pieced together in a deliberate act of *bricolage,* they effectively conveyed not only the ability of powder workers to participate in the larger culture of consumption, but the importance they placed upon doing so.

The significance of the parlor throughout the nineteenth century reflected its perceived ability to transform behavior. For rural folk, who comprised the majority of Americans before 1920, the space instilled a sense of refinement that allowed them "to join the urban stream of American cultural life and yet retain their distinctive identity as country people."⁵⁰ The du Pont Irish had similar goals. Conditioned by the values, customs, and circumstances of life in rural Ulster, they welcomed the material benefits that an industrialized, market-oriented society offered, but they did not embrace American consumer culture in its entirety. For one thing, their family-based, communitarian ethos contrasted sharply with the acquisitive individualism that characterized the "cult of domesticity." Recognizing their financial limitations and familial obligations, powder mill households often had to choose between bringing out a relative, educating a child, saving money for a home, or buying status goods. However, the choices they made were not always rational in an economic sense. Historians have tended to interpret wage earners' spending patterns in simple, dollars-and-cents terms, yet consumer behavior actually reflects the abstract realm of needs, tastes, attitudes, and outlooks.[51] Nineteenth-century economists fully recognized this point. To them, wage earners' efforts to acquire fashionable goods seemed frivolous, even immoral, given their limited incomes.[52] To the wage earners, by contrast, the act of buying a sofa or a bureau anticipated the day when they achieved their particular ideal of gentility, comfort, and material success.

The value du Pont employees attached to parlor furnishings is perhaps best explained through the concept of displaced meaning. Coined by psychologists, the term refers to a specific psychic strategy whereby individuals come to grips with the gap that often exists between the "real" and the "ideal" of their social lives. The romanticization of one's high school or college years is a common example of displacement. Faced with a boring job, a thickening waistline, or an unhappy marriage, a person might wax nostalgic about an historic moment when he or she was indispensable, attractive, or loved. By transporting or "displacing" their ideal into the past, people protect themselves, Don Quixote-like, from psychological harm: the unattainable becomes the attained, a positive memory to recall in times of self-doubt or self-despair. Objects, because they are both tangible and durable, serve as critical "bridges" to these imagined realities, and since individuals can also displace meaning forward in time, they can be used to evoke *anticipated* states of being as well as past ones. Take the classic example of a middle-aged man who has just purchased a particularly symbolic object, like a sports car; he has done so because he covets the virtues, attitudes, opportunities, and lifestyle it evokes. If, however, the coveted object is as unrealizable as the ideal it represents, he may purchase some related items, like leather driving gloves, that are within his means. While not as satisfactory as the actual object, these ancillary goods serve him as tangible proof that the ideal actually exists, and further, that he has laid claim to it, if only in a small way.[53]

Powder mill families forged their *domestic* ideal in Ulster, then displaced it through their increasing awareness of American culture. "Ann Aiken arrived the 15th and I find her in the expected state of ignorance," wrote Meta du Pont to her sister-in-law, Eleuthera. "[B]ut as she appears willing I am in hopes I shall be able to infuse the necessary knowledge."[54] As this quote suggests, Irish women played a critical role in the acquisition and dissemination of homely norms. Domestics like Aiken became thoroughly habituated to American bourgeois domesticity during their tenures with the du Ponts, and their practice of working for only a few years before marriage ensured that dozens of Irish colleens received the same education, which they quickly passed on to others. Other Irish made trips to Wilmington, Philadelphia, and New York. Richard Dougherty, for example, "went to town" on at least six occasions between 1807 and 1809. Michael Tonner also went to Wilmington several times; then, in November 1809, he spent more than a week in Philadelphia, where he met the ship bringing his wife from Ireland. Newport and New Castle were frequent stops, as well.[55] While on their travels, Irish immigrants had ample opportunity to see and purchase fashionable consumer goods. Local newspapers and city directories confirm the availability of specialized merchandise in urban areas, and surviving inventories for general stores in the outlying mill communities attest to items at closer range.[56] Over the course of the nineteenth century, E. I. du Pont de Nemours and Company maintained agreements with at least three different local merchants who let employees charge purchases against the balance in their wage account. The company kept careful track of these purchases and periodically issued payment to the merchant in the form of a check. Wage ledgers record the amounts and frequency of these deductions, but provide no clues as to the nature of the purchase. Other sources, however, indicate that foodstuffs and small household items constituted the bulk of their stock.[57]

Furniture sources were equally diverse. By 1814, six cabinetmakers, five chair makers, and one spinning-wheel maker operated in the Borough of Wilmington.[58] Though capable of producing joined pieces "in the best manner," most of these craftsmen relied on repair work and odd jobs to make ends meet. Some made coffins and moonlighted as undertakers as well. Cabinetmaker George Whitelock, who encouraged customers to select from an assortment of "fashionable and plain" ready-made furniture, sold five coffins to E. I. du Pont for victims of an 1815 explosion.[59] At the other end of the spectrum, Whitelock's known commissions include a fine Hepplewhite-Sheraton sideboard and several tall-case clocks. As Wilmington's antebellum economy expanded, so did the competition. By 1860, *Boyd's Delaware State Directory* boasted fifty furniture manufacturers, including forty cabinetmakers, seven chair makers, and three upholsterers. Thirty-one of these businesses were located in New Castle County. Those in Wilmington, like Joseph W. Springer's "Cheap Furniture Warerooms," catered specifically to low-income clients by keeping a variety of inexpensive, ready-made furniture on hand.[60] Powder mill families had contact with several of these shops, for estate settlements record the purchase of coffins from Whitelock, Springer, and several other prominent local cabinetmakers.

Additional furniture could be found along the Brandywine. In 1853, Sophie du Pont commissioned cabinetmaker James Price to make six walnut work tables for her. Price maintained a shop in Rokeby, one of the du Pont textile mills.[61] Likewise, an 1871 rent book lists Thomas Moran as the tenant of a "furniture room at the end of Breck's mill."[62] Little is known about these men, but they likely supplied new furniture to other families in the community. The du Pont Irish, themselves, should be considered, too. William Boyd, the company's first master carpenter, possessed an impressive collection of tools at his death in 1844, including more than five dozen cornice and moulding planes.[63] Several years later, his successor, Hugh Stirling, made twenty-three benches with moveable backs for the Sunday school, and several decades after that, employees at the company machine shop made George Cheney a set of chairs to celebrate his marriage.[64] Du Pont carpenters primarily built, repaired, and maintained the various structures on the property, but they undoubtedly possessed the skills and tools needed to make furnishings. Because Ireland's rural population remained too poor to support the services of specialized furniture makers, most nineteenth-century farmers, laborers, and tradesmen knew the rudiments of cabinetmaking and joinery.[65] When they emigrated to the United States, the Irish brought these vernacular furniture-making skills with them.

Estate auctions offered yet another source of household goods. Sometimes called vendues, these sales served two important purposes. On one hand, they functioned as social events, drawing people from many local mill villages and nearby farms. In *Six Hundred Dollars a Year,* the fictional wife of a factory superintendent attended a typical "auction sale of furniture" and noted that, "Many of my friends were there also—it was quite fashionable to go to auctions in our town—and I walked through the house to see what was to be sold."[66] Primarily, however, the estate sale existed to raise money for the deceased's family. By selling goods to the highest bidder, auctions enabled local families to assist one another at a time when social relief agencies were few and far between. Newspaper advertisements attest to the frequency of their occurrence, and records pertaining to Brandywine vendues survive in county probate records. They indicate that individuals from all economic levels made purchases, including local innkeepers, farmers, coopers, clergymen, and common laborers. They also suggest the strange combination of feelings such events must have engendered: sympathy for friends and neighbors forced to sell their personal possessions; glee for having acquired a coveted item at a rock-bottom price; guilt for profiting from another's loss; and resignation to the likelihood that one's own goods might end up on sale in the future.

Because items sold at auction were second-hand, their cost usually fell well below that of new goods. When Maurice Saucain died in 1825, wheelwright Jonas Miller purchased "1 shed & all loose boards belonging" for fifty cents, a set of six chairs for $3.75, and a coal stove for $1.90. The Widow Borrell acquired a piece of carpeting for thirty cents, and powder man Thomas Holland bought a corner cupboard for $3.50.[67] Many of the items bought at auction were practical in nature, like pots and pans, but some households also acquired their finer furniture this way. James Fitzgerald, for example, bought a sofa and a clock from the estate of Thomas Fitzpatrick, a company blacksmith. The rest of Fitzpatrick's parlor furniture, including a table and a set of six sofa chairs, went to three other individuals.[68] Thus, vendues effectively increased the accessibility of status goods to Irish immigrants.

Like stoves and bureaus, ceramics served as important indicators of social status in the nineteenth century.[69] Of the Brandywine households probated, 20 percent referenced only "crockeryware." Another 16 percent used the term "Queensware." Ten percent had "china," 6 had "teawares," 4 had "edged wares," 4 had "Old Delf," and 8 mentioned "earthenware." Tinware, pewter, wooden wares, glassware and a few pieces of Brittania appeared as well. Often, however, the inventory takers merely scribbled "contents of cupboard," "common plates," or "sundries," leading to some confusion about the predominant type of ceramics used by powder mill households.

"Queensware," for example, generally described generic table wares. Josiah Wedgewood began producing a cream-colored earthenware in 1759 and named the first pattern "Queensware" in honor of Queen Charlotte. Offered as part of a deliberate marketing strategy, the term soon came to describe any cream-colored or "CC" wares. But then English potters discovered that by adding oxide of cobalt to their queensware recipes they could better imitate the white-bodied porcelains of China and Japan. By the 1810s, these lighter-colored ceramics, decorated with a variety of blue underprinted designs, were being mass-produced in Great Britain for export to America.[70] Almost pure white in color by the 1830s, CC ware closely resembled stone china, a heavier, more durable product patented by Charles James Mason in 1813.[71] Because of the visual similarities between the two types of table wares, consumers in the Delaware valley applied the term "queensware" to all common, white vessels. Thus a Philadelphia author of the period noted, "Of white crockery or common queensware, you will require plates, dishes and pitchers for the use of the kitchen; and probably pudding molds and blanc-mange molds; also cups, saucers, salt-cellar, pepper box, etc., and for the table of the domestics."[72] After the Civil War, American dealers marketed stone china as "ironstone" or "white granite," but Wilmingtonians continued to favor the older term.[73]

Powder mill families owned fine table wares, too. On Blacksmith's Hill, the area of housing associated with the Hagley Yard, archaeologists found a surprisingly large amount of Chinese export porcelain, an extremely high-status ceramic. They also excavated many pieces of imported English transfer-printed wares, plus mocha wares, pearl wares, and shell-edged wares. By the late nineteenth century, all had become commonplace, yet the shards at Hagley date to the 1840s, when some of these decorative techniques were still a novelty.[74]

To understand the meaning of these costlier ceramics, it is helpful to know who owned them. The shards excavated on Blacksmith's Hill relate to a group of three workers' dwellings known collectively as the Gibbons' House site. Although workmen's houses stood on this site by 1814, the earliest known occupancy of these particular houses is recorded in the rent book of 1841–1849. The three units—actually a stone house with two frame units adjoining—are listed as a "Row of houses near Mr. Alexis's garden, nos. 30, 31, and 32." Turnover was frequent in the 1840s. Four different households rented No. 30, and two rented No. 31. In 1844, Alex Burns and his family moved into No. 30. Burns, a former powder man, served as Alexis du Pont's gardener and had free use of the house until he moved out in 1877. Powder man John McPherson and his wife, Mary, lived in No. 31 from 1852 to 1895. As foreman of the Hagley Yard, John Gibbons and his family occupied No. 32, the three-story stone unit, from 1856 to 1885. Gibbons was succeeded by John Stewart, who still lived in No. 32 when George Cheney made his rounds of the property in 1902. By that date, Cheney himself occupied the two frame units, which had been converted into a single-family dwelling. All of the nineteenth-century residents of Blacksmith's Hill, then, held high-status positions within the company, and could have afforded to buy at least some high-status ceramics.[75]

Judging by various makers' marks and patterns, most of the ceramics recovered from Blacksmith's Hill came from Staffordshire, but residents also bought table wares manufactured in New Jersey and Ohio.[76] One archaeologist speculated from the sheer variety of shards that either powder workers could not afford matched sets, or the high number of explosions caused a greater than average amount of breakage.[77] The probate inventories point to another explanation. John Hayes, for example, a cooper who died in 1834, had "plates" and "tea ware" in his cupboard, suggesting that two different dining needs had been met. Similarly, powder man Darby McAteer had "Queensware" and "a lot of tin-ware."[78] Few families could have afforded a large set of formal dishes with matched service pieces. Still, most would have known that different kinds of ceramics had different uses. And with only a limited amount of money for luxury goods, they likely splurged on a tea set for company and scrimped on everyday dishes.

Through the discriminating and deliberate acquisition of status-bearing consumer goods, the du Pont Irish not only conveyed their increasing adaptation to a technological and commercial world, but they made a creative compromise between their previous, present, and future lives.[79] In addition, their compromise occurred much earlier than previous studies of Irish immigrants admit. Many historians contend that Erin's heirs in America did not do well materially until the 1880s, when higher incomes and lower prices increased their purchasing power.[80] The material culture of the Brandywine suggests otherwise. Powder yard foremen, clerks, and coopers were certainly in a better position to "paraphrase" the ideal parlor than common laborers and recent immigrants from Ireland, but even the households of the lowest-paid, least-skilled powder workers had *some* symbolic objects, and *some* powder workers had them as early as the 1810s.[81] Like their native-born neighbors, immigrants purchased these objects because they understood their deeper cultural meaning.

Between the end of the American Revolution and the beginning of the Civil War, "the ideal of a cultivated and refined inward life" became entrenched in American society.[82] Prevented from achieving that ideal by their lower incomes and limited knowledge, middling sorts espoused instead a kind of vernacular gentility. This version differed greatly from true gentility in that it did not require polish in every aspect of life: "[True] Gentility, for those who embraced the culture wholeheartedly, required the refinement of one part of life after another. A common person with a teacup had not made so encompassing a commitment."[83] Just so, having a few carefully selected objects did not make a powder mill household genteel. However, the *combination* of a bureau, a matched set of chairs, a looking-glass, and a tea set clearly conveys an awareness that certain furnishings and spaces signaled rising status better than others. That the du Pont Irish actively acquired refined goods suggests as well the extent to which Irish wage earners shared the culture of their economic superiors.

Above all else, the pursuit of gentility reflected a changing sense of self-image. As the paradigm spread, even laborers began to consider how they looked in the eyes of others. During the Jacksonian era, wage workers in many cities took advantage of the ready-made clothing industry to outfit themselves like fashionable ladies and gentlemen of higher status.[84] In response to this "plain, dark democracy of broadcloth," which weakened the old system of determining rank, elite Americans established new rituals and conventions specifically to reinforce sociocultural divisions. The emphasis on performance embedded within these new standards, moreover, exacerbated a tendency to criticize and exclude persons whose dress and deportment missed the mark.[85] Thus, Sophie du Pont faulted a caller, as described in the following account to her brother Henry:

> This morning our attention was attracted by an elegant gig stopping at the door. Out sprung the most dandiful youth, in a large, blue surtout, who instantly hoisted a light pink umbrella over his delicate person, and proceeded

with an air of great familiarity to have his horse put in the stable. We of course were very much puzzled to imagine who it could be, tho' at the same time we could not help roaring at the pink umbrella. At length he entered, and who should it be but William Boyd, Junior, returning from a tour of Washington, where he had the honor of being introduced and shaking hands with the President! He is of course a thousand times more conceited than ever.[86]

The passage is a telling one. Boyd, the eldest son of the company's Irish-born head carpenter, left the powder mill community as a young man, became a prosperous merchant, and deigned to pay a social call on his former employers during a return visit. Because she knew his origins (and they did not even begin to approach hers), Sophie considered his conduct unseemly. Junior clearly felt otherwise. Having risen far above the station of his birth, and having acquired sufficient polish to mingle in Washington society, he approached the du Ponts as their equal.

Fashionable consumer goods appealed to wage-earning Irish immigrants because they "offered the hope that anyone, however poor or however undignified their work, could become middle class by disciplining themselves and adopting a few outward forms of genteel living."[87] Other immigrant populations shared this conviction, as evinced by the numerous household budget studies conducted by social reformers at the turn of the century. Margaret Byington's highly regarded study of Homestead, Pennsylvania, steelworkers, published in 1910 but researched earlier, provides additional data on wage-earning immigrants' domesticity. It shows that parlor furnishings still figured prominently as a symbol of upward mobility and acculturation. As Byington explained,

> It has often been said that the first evidence of the growth of the social instinct in any family is the desire to have a parlor. In Homestead, this ambition has in many cases been attained. Not every family, it is true, can afford one, yet among my English-speaking acquaintances even the six families each of whom lived in three rooms attempted to have at least the semblance of a room devoted to sociability.[88]

Although Byington used the term "parlor" to denote this public space, most Homesteaders called it the "front room." Significantly, Lewis Hine's accompanying photograph of a representative "front room" showed a corner containing a shawl-draped, upright piano, a mantel crammed with bric-a-brac, gilt-framed family portraits, wallpaper, and carpeting.[89] No matter what the rest of the room looked like, these objects defined the space as a parlor. Similarly, at the home of an unskilled, Slavic laborer, Byington recorded:

On one side was a huge puffy bed, with one feather tick to sleep on and another for covering; near the window stood a sewing machine; in the corner,
an organ,—all these, besides the inevitable cook stove. . . . Upstairs in the second room were one boarder and the man of the house asleep. Two more
boarders were at work but at night would be home to sleep in the bed from
which the others would get up.[90]

As the presence of an organ in this home attests, immigrants understood
that certain goods conveyed social ambitions better than others.

By the 1890s, the organ had replaced the bureau as the preeminent piece
of parlor furniture. Within the dominant culture of Gilded Age America,
this instrument and its cousin, the piano, became an indicator not only of
social status but of women's civilizing influence on the family.[91] Like Margaret Byington and her readers, Brandywine families understood this dual
symbolism. Eleanor Kane, the granddaughter of "Big Dan" Dougherty
and his wife, Ellen Gibbons Dougherty, remembered what the piano
meant to the women in her family.

Oh, well, I know this matter of quality. I think I—when you think, how did
she [Ellen Gibbons Dougherty] know to buy good things that would last . . .
when I say good things, how would she, when they were down on Lincoln
Street, they bought a piano. My mother [Ann Dougherty Kane] took piano
lessons, and mother was very proud of that piano. Mother said, "Four hundred dollars, your grandmother paid $400 cash." Now, you see, that was im-
portant, it was not only the—and mother would play and sing and they
would have—but grandmother liked to just sit and listen to it.[92]

Eleanor's grandmother never learned to play, but she saw to it that her
daughters, Ann, Margaret, and Lizzie, did. "But it's the kind of thing, in
other words, wanting a piano, and you see Mag Gibbons, John Gibbons's
daughter [a cousin], had the organ and she [Eleanor's mother, Ann] played
the piano. I know she played the piano, so it seemed to be important for
them to do something like that." Trade catalogues frequently depicted a
piano or organ as the center piece of a relaxed parlor setting, where family
members gathered to sing hymns or sentimental ballads.[93] The Dougherty
family also had a music stand with all their song books, especially "old-
fashioned songs, Irish songs that they sang," and hymns for when "Mother
played the organ in church." That Jonas Miller, the company's head wheelwright, owned a cottage organ at his death in 1874, and du Pont blacksmith
Thomas Fitzpatrick's 1852 inventory included a piano, suggests that the
Doughertys' experience was not atypical.[94]

Whether steelworkers or powder workers, immigrant wage earners' ability to "paraphrase" the ideal American parlor proves how complicated determinations of status and identity can be. Other material culture studies echo this conclusion. According to public records, for example, Wilmingtonian Thomas Mendenhall had a prosperous career as a sea captain-turned-merchant. When archaeologists excavated his primary residence site, however, they found a preponderance of "common" artifacts that together indicated declining fortunes and a low-status lifestyle.[95] Similarly, many of the "common" laborers who lived and worked in mid-nineteenth-century Philadelphia owned high-status goods indicative of genteel tastes and sensibilities.[96] Like Robert Young's stove, Ann Dougherty's walnut breakfast table, William Boyd's pink parasol, or Ellen Gibbons' piano, these objects served as tangible symbols of past struggles, present achievements, and future goals. They also signaled participation in and affiliation with the dominant culture of their respective eras. To be sure, Irish households possessed far fewer icons of ideal domesticity than white-collar professionals, and the ones they did have were often second-hand or inferior models. Still, their access to items once considered "luxuries" had increased considerably since leaving Ireland. Coupled with "common" chairs and tables, often sharing the same spaces, fashionable consumer goods enabled Irish immigrants to create a more "genteel" domestic environment and served as effective symbols of shifting cultural identities.

CHAPTER 7

Porches, Yards, Gardens, Fences

☙

Peter Quigley, Jr., arrived into the world on November 5, 1827, the third child of an Irish Catholic laborer, Peter Quigley, Sr., and his wife, Mary Malloy.[1] While Peter was growing up in the 1820s and 1830s, the landscape of the lower Delaware valley changed dramatically. New Castle County remained overwhelmingly rural, yet the rise of flour, snuff, paper, powder, and textile milling industries effected an unmistakable shift in local attitudes about the economy, the environment, and the place of manufacturing enterprises in each. By 1850, when young Quigley became a cooper with the du Pont company, farms and factories stood side by side along the banks of the Brandywine. Similar developments occurred elsewhere in the United States. The combination of agriculture and industry that characterized life in the powder mill community, however, resulted from a deliberate plan to nourish and uplift the laboring classes.

Pierre Samuel du Pont de Nemours and his two sons came to the United States in hopes of establishing a utopian community called Pontiana. They intended it to be small and self-sufficient. Every member would be a free person, every man would be a landowner and a tiller of the soil, and everyone would work together to guarantee mutual security and economic well-being. Laborers would have access to land and water, the two primary sources of wealth, and by this means they would be able to rise in social status. Still, the elder du Pont envisioned a stratified society, with his family and those of his investors at the top, workers at the bottom, and a range of property holders in between. With the help of his old friend Talleyrand, Pierre Samuel drew up a prospectus, formed a joint-stock company called du Pont de Nemours, Père et Fils et Cie, and began to advertise shares of 10,000 francs each. He promised investors that the likelihood of a successful return was considerable "in a country where liberty, safety, independence really exist in a temperate climate, [and] where the land is fertile and bountiful," but Pontiana never materialized. Only a few of du Pont's influential acquaintances came forward to invest, and rising land values in America greatly exceeded the little amount of money he had amassed for the venture.[2]

The industrial community established by Irénée du Pont bore little resemblance to the ideal commune envisioned by Pierre Samuel in 1800, yet it incorporated a similar commitment to agrarianism and property mobility. Peter Quigley, Sr., for example, entered the powder yards in 1819 and accumulated $900 worth of real estate by 1850.[3] He did not reside on his property. Like other Irish families in the community, the Quigleys continued to live in a company-owned house at the Upper Banks, where, in the shadow of the powder mills, they cultivated gardens, kept livestock, and followed other agricultural pursuits. Irénée knew that raising some of their own food would help his workmen sustain themselves in times of slack production. To that end, he initially provided every married man in his employ with "a house free of rent, a good garden, and a cow pasture."[4] He further hoped that providing workers with free housing and a plot of land would reduce labor turnover. From this perspective, granting such specialized privileges seemed like nothing more than a practical business decision. Many employers offered similar benefits to their wage workers. But du Pont's policies reflected as well his belief in Physiocracy, his sense of noblesse oblige, and his faith in the economic and social benefits of manufacturing. Believing that he had a moral obligation to help "those inferior in learning, talents, and resources" become freeholders, Irénée encouraged his workmen to save their money, practice their agricultural skills, and prepare for the day when they returned to farming.

Irish families like the Quigleys favored this program for several reasons. First, having gardens and livestock enabled them to perpetuate important aspects of their ethnic identity, including traditional Irish food ways and agrarian rhythms, while they lived in an industrial setting. Second, the division of exterior space in the powder mill community resembled patterns of land use in Ulster. All of the property belonged to the du Ponts, who leased to each household an individual lot within a specific housing cluster. Yet there existed as well areas within and without the housing clusters that all tenants shared in common. As in Ulster, these spaces fostered a strong sense of camaraderie and contributed to the formation of a distinct, place-oriented identity. Finally, the ability to manipulate the environment for their own purposes worked together with other aspects of everyday life to reinforce Irish immigrants' growing sense of self-determination. At the same time, however, porches, yards, gardens, and fences also worked to foster their adaptation to American culture. Porches, for example, altered traditional, communitarian ways of regulating social traffic, and developments in domestic horticulture introduced new plants and new ways of thinking about food and cultivation. Likewise, yards and fences reinforced the mutualistic compact, and instilled a new understanding of "private" property rights. Though typically neglected by historians, the outdoor environment shaped individual and communal notions of identity in subtle yet significant ways.

₰

Ulster emigrants brought with them to northern Delaware a distinctive attitude regarding proper uses of exterior space.[5] The most common form of settlement before 1800 was the clachan, a loosely arranged cluster of cottages surrounded by concentric rings of tillage and pasture. Every clachan comprised a kin-based community that leased and worked the land in common. Under a system known as rundale, however, each *fear ti* received by mutual agreement the exclusive right to certain fields. These varied in quality and location depending upon his social status. Whenever a *fear ti* died, the clachan met to redistribute allotments, and this custom, combined with a preference for partible inheritance, produced a "crazy quilt effect": dozens if not hundreds of small, irregularly shaped fields blanketed the landscape, each one bordered by a low stone wall or hedge.[6] This pattern of land use deviated sharply from accepted British practices, and beginning in the first quarter of the nineteenth century, absentee landlords began to reorder the Irish countryside. With the help of resident agents, they disbursed residential dwellings and replaced communally held and worked fields with individual farmsteads. In the region of Ulster that produced the du Pont Irish, this process of "squaring and striping" the landscape took place in the 1830s and '40s, but survivals of the old system persisted into the twentieth century. Tenants generally received "turbary rights," for example, which allowed them to cut turf, the primary fuel, from communal bogs, and they continued "booleying," a form of transhumance wherein rural communities wintered their sheep and cattle in shared mountain pastures.[7]

The typical Ulster family occupied a one- or two-room stone cottage set amid gently rolling terrain. In keeping with the ancient, communitarian values of the clachan, the boundaries between public and private space remained permeable, not solid. Visitors approaching the domicile first encountered the "street," a paved section of earth that signaled the transition from muddy country lanes to clean kitchen floor. The door opened to the hearth, the symbolic heart of the home, and guests, rarely strangers to the family, received a warm welcome and a seat of honor near the fire. A second door, opposite the first, led to the "haggard," a functional space directly behind the house. Here, residents stored harvested crops for further processing. In most cases, stables and cow byres adjoined the main dwelling; dairies, hay sheds, turf sheds, cart sheds, poultry houses, and other "out offices" stood close by, clearly stating the farm's function. These support structures, usually facing south or east and oriented parallel or perpendicular to the house, defined the "home place." Beyond it stretched fields and pastures of varying sizes, each bordered by an appropriate enclosure.[8]

Though well-suited to the climate and culture of northern Ireland, Ulster farmsteads seemed strange and conspicuous to outsiders. Some travelers exclaimed over the "neat, pretty, cheerful looking cottages" they found. Most used words like "uncomfortable," "dirty," and "disorderly." When the Royal Engineers office sent Lieutenant R. Stotherd to survey the parish of Clogher in 1833, he reported that,

> There is very little order, cleanliness or neatness in general to be found either in the houses of the more wealthy farmers or in the cottages of the poor. The turf stack often approaches within a few yards of the door and thus intersects the view and stops the currency of air. The yard in front of the house is full of the odour of the cow house and stable, for they are often built in the very front and sometimes adjoining the dwelling house. The lanes approaching the house are narrow, rough, and filthy in the extreme.[9]

Clogher, located in western Tyrone, contained one of the richest and most fertile valleys in the region, and Stotherd conceded that, "Few parishes of the same extent can vie with Clogher in natural beauty and advantages." Since cottage industries were on the rise and agricultural lands were producing more than they ever had, he decided that messy farmsteads meant "the lower orders of inhabitants in this barony have very little concern for domestic comforts." Other surveyors drew similar conclusions about Irish character from the landscape, declaring Protestants and Catholics alike to be "generally industrious" but woefully uncivilized. In reality, Irish attitudes about the domestic environment simply differed from elite English attitudes.

Irish land ways underwent a marked change after emigration to the United States. In contrast to farms in Ulster, exterior space in the powder mill community began on the porch, a structure designed to serve as a buffer between the outside world and the private household. "We had a high porch up there [in Henry Clay Village]," Aloysius Rowe recalled. "Most of the houses did have them—overlooking those banks there."[10] Rowe, the son of an Irish immigrant, grew up in the 1880s. Porches were ubiquitous along the Brandywine by that time, having first appeared in the region in the late eighteenth century.[11] Like the center hallway of a Georgian-plan house, it served as a "social lock" between the family and outsiders at a time

of rapid social and economic change. As the evolving market economy increased the number of strangers circulating through their communities,
Americans embraced the concept and added porches to a variety of vernacular forms, including industrial housing. Rural Ulsterites, however, did not
feel a similar need to add porches to their dwellings until the 1910s and
'20s.[12] Thus, nineteenth-century immigrants to the Brandywine likely
found them perplexing.

Reached by a series of three or more steps and contained by a roof and
wooden railings, the front porch altered established modes of social interaction because it stopped humans as well as wind and rain from entering
the dwelling (fig. 7.1). In contrast to the kin-based settlements of Ulster,
the powder mill community supported a diverse population of strangers,
kith, and kin. A porch allowed residents of a given household to differentiate between them. Unknown or unfriendly persons could be turned away,
and friends ushered quickly inside. Few people lingered. Too small to hold
seating furniture, entry porches promoted movement, not rest.

Detached and semidetached units often had a second, larger porch, too,
usually located to the back or side of the dwelling. These functioned very
differently. In July 1899, for example, widow Bridget Clark specifically
asked the company to lengthen the side porch on her house so that her family could dine there. She also wanted a closet installed at one end for additional storage space:

> Will you please have it made ten feet longer and a closet put on it for we have
> no place to put Butter or milk in the warm weather, only in the kitchen closet,
> and we are obliged to have a fire there every day and the milk is souer at noon
> and the Butter like oil[.] [I]n fact, we cannot keep anything over night.[13]

Some families even used these porches for bathing. As William Buchanan
remembered, "You had a wash basin and you went out on the back porch
and that's where you done your washin'. . . . When we took a bath, that was
maybe once a week or maybe once every two weeks. Of course, in wintertime, you didn't take them quite as often."[14] The functional quality of the
side or back porch did not dissuade people from using it as an entrance, too.
The Bettys had a small porch over their front door in Wagoner's Row, but it
was "just a little portico, like," so they mostly used the back door. "Everybody came and went by the back door. There was a big porch and of course
in the summer time we practically lived on it."[15] Used for a variety of purposes, the side or back porch served as an outdoor extension of the kitchen.

Food preparation and storage required so much space that the kitchen
frequently extended beyond the porch to encompass another structure entirely. These distinctive outbuildings, called summer kitchens, especially

Fig. 7.1. Exterior view of Chicken Alley, showing front porches, ca. 1880–1900. (Courtesy of Hagley Museum and Library)

characterized households in the American South, where high temperatures and humidity necessitated the removal of cooking and baking from the primary dwelling for part of the year. Delaware has a hot, muggy climate from May through September, and consequently, the use of summer kitchens extended into southern New Castle County.[16] Typically free-standing log or frame structures with masonry foundations, they even appeared along the Brandywine. Former laborer turned du Pont farm manager-cum-innkeeper William Donnan had a summer kitchen at his home on Buck Road in Christiania Hundred. Likewise, company blacksmith William Baldwin had one on his farm in Brandywine Hundred when he died in 1845, and carpenter Neil Conley had one at his home in Henry Clay Village at his death in 1849.[17] Contractor James Goodman built two kitchens at the keg mill cluster in 1844, and he added another the following year.[18] Nearly 20 percent of the 143 dwelling units owned by the powder company in 1902 retained two distinct cooking facilities, but by that time, a lack of exterior space promoted a shift to lean-tos, instead.[19] The Buchanans' home on Breck's Lane had one of these "shed" kitchens. "That's where they done their washing," William Buchanan recalled.[20] A similar structure survives on the east side of the Hagley foreman's residence, now called the Gibbons House. The Gibbons family used it for cooking as well as laundering.

Summer and shed kitchens worked together with other outbuildings to define exterior space. These included storage sheds, poultry houses, stables, spring houses, wash houses, wagon sheds, and smoke houses.[21] Each dwelling would also have had its own outhouse or privy. These structures stood at the extreme rear of the lot, and frequently incorporated the household's wood or coal box. Any additional outbuildings ranged around the perimeter of the yard.

Generally speaking, a powder mill family's yard served as work space. In the case of back-to-back dwellings or row houses, this space comprised little more than a barren patch of earth (fig. 7.2). Larger homes had open areas to the side, as well. Some families enclosed the entire lot with a fence of whitewashed palings or pickets. Others merely fenced off a portion for a kitchen garden, a fruit arbor, or an animal pen. Like the Irish haggard, the yard offered a semiprivate place to store raw materials and process them into new forms.[22] Sketches of workers' houses by Eleuthera and Sophie du Pont in the 1830s reveal the presence of bake ovens, stacked cords of wood, potted plants, and piles of fence posts. Grass did not grow well under heavy foot traffic, but flag stones, broken shells, and board walkways provided firm footing on rainy days. Washtubs and clotheslines appeared once a week. "I remember when Mr. Whiteman was killed—it was on wash day. My mother had her washtub up on two chairs," explained Elizabeth Beacom. "In those days, they boiled their clothes in a boiler [on the stove] and stirred them with a broomstick. She told me to help her off with the boiler and just as we went out the door, my, it did rip. It was a frosty morning and something struck me on the back of the hand and I had a lump the size of a walnut on my hand."[23] Had not the explosion intervened, Beacom and her mother would have proceeded to rinse, wring, and hang out the family's laundry. By the end of the century, some women, like Ellen Gibbons Dougherty, had a retractable line that could be reeled in from the porch when the laundry was dry.[24] From spring through early fall, powder mill yards boasted vegetable and flower gardens, and in the winter, they afforded space near the kitchen for hog butchering activities. Chopping wood took place more regularly.

Because the yard accommodated a variety of tasks it required neatness and order to function effectively. "Squirrel Run was so clean," recalled one former resident.[25] Little is known about methods of trash disposal in this community, but the du Pont Irish appear to have disdained simple "broadcast scatter" of the sort that defined most households in nineteenth-century America. Instead of tossing the refuse out the kitchen door, powder workers used trash pits. That is, they dug holes, then carefully tossed

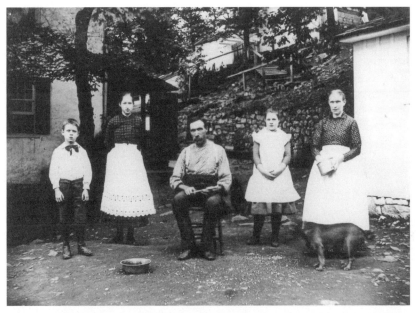

Fig. 7.2. Exterior view of Andrew Fleming and his family in their yard in Squirrel Run, ca. 1880–1900. (Courtesy of Hagley Museum and Library)

their garbage into it. Archaeologists found one pit on Blacksmith's Hill measuring approximately three feet wide, five feet long, and ten feet deep. Judging by its size, it must have served the entire cluster.[26] This practice not only preserved the neat appearance of the yard, but it ensured that members of the household would have enough space for whatever outside tasks they needed to perform.

The amount of exterior work space varied with the size, kind, and location of the family's planting beds. Most nineteenth-century industrial villages included space for workmen's gardens, but experts disagreed over how much space to allocate for this purpose. J. C. Loudon's *Encyclopedia of Gardening* (1834) recommended a half-acre or less because "the extent of the garden of the labourer ought never to be such as to interfere with his regular employment."[27] Along the Brandywine, very small gardens predominated. The average size ranged from thirty to forty feet wide by forty to sixty feet long.[28] Squeezed in wherever possible, these important patches of cultivated greenery filled interstices throughout the community. Workers living at Louviers, for example, planted their gardens near the creek, where they frequently flooded. In Squirrel Run, families had only enough space between their homes and the stream to plant small flower boxes, so the company assigned each household part of a large, communal plot at the top of nearby Keyes Hill. On Blacksmith's Hill, gardens occupied a common area across the street from the foreman's residence, only a few feet from the Hagley powder yard fence. In Free Park, each semidetached unit had its own garden directly in the rear. As these examples indicate, the size and location of powder mill gardens received little consideration, but then, their primary purpose was ideological not practical. By encouraging its employees to raise fruits and vegetables, the company helped preserve their ties to the soil and their hopes that wage labor was only temporary.

No one understood the symbolic role of the garden better than E. I. du Pont. Like his father, Irénée maintained a deep respect for the land and its associations with political independence and economic stability. He also had a curious fascination for all things related to plants, gardens, and agriculture. This interest came easily, for Irénée spent most of his childhood romping through the fields and forests of Bois-des-Fossés, the family's 4,000-acre estate. Located just south of Paris, near the city of Nemours, it included vineyards, orchards, gardens, and a large working farm, which Irénée helped manage in Pierre's absence. After completing his apprenticeship at Essone, the government's powder works, Irénée went to work at his father's printing shop in Paris. He returned to Bois-des-Fossés whenever possible, however, and when the family finally decided to emigrate to the United States in 1799, Irénée optimistically listed his occupation as "botaniste." Despite the amount of time consumed by running the powder mills, he planted a large garden at Eleutherian Mills and exchanged exotic seeds with Thomas Jefferson, Josephine Bonaparte, and other horticultural enthusiasts of the day. In 1808, the powder manufacturer joined the Philadelphia Society for Promoting Agriculture, and shortly after the explosion of 1818, he joined the New Castle County Agricultural Society. In keeping with his beliefs about the supremacy of Nature, Irénée encouraged his children to garden, collect mineral specimens, press leaves and flowers, keep unusual pets, and partake of the world around them. But more important, by instilling an appreciation of the natural world in all of his heirs, du Pont also ensured that industry and agriculture would co-exist after his death.[29]

By the time E. I. du Pont died in 1834, the farms and factories of northern New Castle County had become fully interdependent. A substantial increase in the number of people producing gunpowder, flour, and manufactured goods, rather than food for themselves, provided a ready market for the surplus fruits, grains, vegetables, and animal products that local farmers supplied.[30] In the early days of the company's existence, du Pont had to purchase food for his employees. The expansion of the company farm, expertly managed by two Irishmen, Billy Martin then William Donnan, eventually enabled him to reduce his reliance on others. Still, he could not provide everything his workmen needed. In the summer of 1815, for example, Irénée bought 235 pounds of butter from Samuel Gregg, whose property adjoined the Upper Banks. According to the company's petit ledgers, he also bought large quantities of lamb, veal, milk, and beef, which he then sold to his workmen.[31] By giving married men garden space, he reduced his need to purchase foodstuffs even further.

The du Pont Irish supplemented purchased food with homegrown produce whenever possible. Native-born Americans tended to associate gardens with women, but this community considered domestic cultivation a family affair.[32] First, the garden had to be laid out. This required the use of several stakes, a reel, and some twine. Rectangular shapes predominated, and many families left space for a two-foot path around the edge of the plot plus another that cut straight through its middle. These paths greatly facilitated digging, hoeing, weeding, and picking.[33] In March or April, when the ground had thawed sufficiently, the man of the house turned the soil with a spade or digging fork, then fertilized it with manure and lime. If necessary, he added wood ashes and bone meal to provide potassium and phosphorus. Once the ground had been readied for planting, women and children took over.[34]

Irish families preferred cheap crops that were easy to grow and store. The humble potato fulfilled all these requirements and then some. Introduced into Ireland by the late eighteenth century, the starchy tuber had become the mainstay of the Irish diet by 1840.[35] Its appeal was economic, not gastronomic: an acre of potatoes could feed twice as many people as a comparably sized crop of wheat. Such efficiency made potatoes equally appropriate for a kitchen garden. Depending upon the size of the household and its plot of land, plantings in the powder mill community ranged from one or two rows to a third or even a half of the entire garden (fig. 7.3). Although St. Patrick's Day (March 17) traditionally marked the earliest date for planting potatoes in Ireland, most Brandywine gardeners set their crops several weeks later.

Powder mill families continued the traditional planting methods that characterized Ulster. John Green emigrated from County Donegal in the early 1840s. By 1845, he and his family rented a house in Squirrel Run and tended a small kitchen garden nearby.[36] Picture him taking his spade and digging narrow furrows. The space in between, called a ridge, forms a solid foundation for the potatoes. Using the spade again, Green turns over the loosened sods in the furrow and places them on top of the ridge, grass-side down. He has just produced a typical Ulster "lazy bed," so called because inverting the sods atop the ridge spared him from breaking the ground beneath it. The next step entails blind setting the potatoes, which Green or his wife had previously cut into halves or quarters. To do this, he thrusts a

Fig. 7.3. Exterior view of the Gibbons-Seitz family standing in its potato patch in Free Park, ca. 1880–1900. (Courtesy of Hagley Museum and Library)

pointed stick into the "lazy bed" at a sufficiently sharp angle to keep rain water out and prevent the potato "sets" from rotting. Each hole receives a single set, and Green arranges the holes in a repeating pattern of rows or diamonds. Weeks later, when the tender, green shoots begin to poke through the soil, Green takes his spade again and covers or "moulds" the bed with loose dirt from the furrow. Each ridge would receive at least one more moulding later in the growing season. Ellen Green likely helped her husband set the potatoes. She also bore responsibility for watering the plants, pulling weeds, and removing pests. The children, Charles, Neal, Charlotte, John, and Margaret, helped in this effort.[37] Then, after the mature plants finished blooming, the entire family organized for the harvest. This usually occurred by the end of summer, but some of Green's neighbors specifically planted their patches early enough in March to have new potatoes for the Fourth of July holiday. "Every Fourth of July we'd have our first potatoes. We did all the preparing of the garden by hand."[38] Since late frosts are common in northern Delaware, the du Pont Irish considered new potatoes a special treat, one that attested to the skill of the gardener. The main crop did not mature until August, September, or October at the latest.

The harvesting process also followed Irish customs.[39] Working in rows, John and Ellen extricated the potatoes from their beds with digging forks, while the children gathered them into baskets and sorted them into piles. Like most families, they carefully reserved the large and medium-sized potatoes for eating. The smaller ones they saved for seed and animal feed. Since light caused harvested potatoes to become green and bitter, the entire crop had to be stored in a cool, dry place. In Ulster, farmers mounded their potatoes into a hill, which they covered with straw and sod. The du Pont Irish placed their potatoes in bushel baskets then in cellars, attics, kitchen cupboards, and unheated back rooms. Because they had gardens not farms, few households grew enough potatoes to last the entire winter. When their homegrown supply ran out, they bought more from the company. At the time of his death in January 1851, John Green had ten bushels of potatoes in reserve.[40]

The du Pont Irish also favored cabbages. Blanche McAdoo Yetter described them as being "almost as big around as a dinner plate and more flat on the top . . . as if it were a stool (fig. 7.4)." This description probably refers to a variety called the Large Flat Dutch, which nineteenth-century American experts recommended as one of the best for home cultivation; but it also characterized contemporary Ulster gardens.[41] The McAdoos would have planted their main crop in the spring and harvested it in the fall. When ready, cabbages had to be cut off whole at the root. Some families stored them indoors, but others packed them in layers of straw in an outdoor pit. These typically averaged two or three feet deep by several feet square. Tar paper covers kept out all but the heaviest rains. Ulster families, by contrast, carefully piled their cabbages into heaps, covered them with rushes, and moulded them with dirt. In this fashion, they lasted until Christmas and beyond.[42]

Powder workers generally boiled their vegetables. This method of preparation may reflect the widespread nineteenth-century fear that raw produce promoted the spread of cholera, but it more likely constituted a continuation of traditional Ulster food ways.[43] Day in, day out, landless families in northern Ireland ate little besides potatoes, oatmeal, milk, and butter. These four ingredients could be combined in several different ways. They typically appeared in the form of one-pot meals: oatmeal cooked in water or milk rendered "stirabout" or "flummery," a thick gruel especially favored in summertime; potatoes, once boiled, could be served whole with butter or mashed with milk and a little bit of chopped, wild leek as "champ." Middling households ate these staples, too, but enlivened them periodically with eggs, salt beef, dried pork or bacon, mutton, dried herring, and vegetables like cabbage.[44] As anthropologists note, food ways are among the earliest-formed aspects of a given society's culture. They not

Fig. 7.4. Exterior view of the Upper Banks showing a cabbage patch destroyed by the explosion of 1890. (Courtesy of Hagley Museum and Library)

only provide sustenance, but they "bind individuals together, define the limits of the group's outreach and identity, distinguish in-group and out-group, serve as a medium for inter-group communication, celebrate cultural cohesion, and provide a context for the performance of group rituals."[45] For all these reasons, Ulster emigrants perpetuated especially symbolic food ways in northern Delaware. Most powder mill families kept at least one cow, for example, and probate inventories frequently mention churns, butter prints, and other dairying equipment.[46] Potatoes also graced Brandywine tables. In 1811, Victor du Pont reported to his son Charles, from Louviers, that "a worker from the other side of the creek, an old Irishman named John O'Gallagher, died suddenly at table while eating his dinner." The unfortunate O'Gallagher, a powder man, choked on a potato and asphyxiated before help could arrive.[47]

Maintaining ethnic food ways certainly helped the du Pont Irish accommodate to life in a new country, but their close association with potatoes and cabbages also fueled negative stereotypes. When it came to describing Irish immigrants, nineteenth-century Americans tended to use adjectives like "dirty," "unkempt," "brutish," "blundering," "quarrelsome," and "lazy."[48] These words reflect a common practice whereby members of a given society ascribe to certain humans traits associated with animals. The traits are not assigned arbitrarily; rather, they reflect a complex system wherein animals are categorized according to whether they are fit for human consumption, whether they can consume humans, or whether they are in contention with humans for basic resources. In English-speaking cultures, those animals "feared and rejected as a food resource are drawn upon as a symbolic resource" and routinely used to distinguish insiders from outsiders.[49] Consider the prevailing attitude in the United States toward raccoons and possums. Most people agree that both species are edible, but they regard them as "strange food" and therefore unfit for "normal," everyday consumption. Nocturnal and tree-dwelling, these animals are not only difficult to hunt and therefore eat, but they like *human* food, so much so that they sometimes seem to be competitors. As a result, they are typically considered "varmints," that is, sly creatures that creep around under cover of night, invade domestic spaces, steal that which rightfully belongs to others, and contaminate whatever they touch. Given these profoundly negative associations, it is little wonder that those who hunt and consume these "critters" are labeled "strange" and "varmint-like" themselves. A similar process explains the animalistic adjectives used to characterize Irish immigrants. In their case, however, the attributed behaviors mimicked those of swine.

The close association between the Irish, their food ways, and pigs has a factual basis. Food scholars contend that Sir Walter Raleigh introduced potatoes and cabbages into Ireland as animal fodder.[50] Thereafter, raising hogs for export to England became a major cottage industry, but a widespread belief that these vegetables were poisonous to people prevented their consumption until the end of the eighteenth century, when a dramatic rise in population forced Europeans to find new sources of human food as well. Cheap and close at hand, potatoes and cabbages seemed to the Irish logical substitutes. They became permanent fixtures once Irish cottiers realized how vastly they surpassed other crops in terms of average yield per acre.[51] A similar food shortage occurred simultaneously in England and in France, yet residents of these countries found pig fodder much more difficult to swallow. Although potatoes and cabbages quite literally became "peasant" fare throughout much of western Europe, the continued association of these foods with a reduced standard of living and with rutting hogs meant they never had the same function or meaning elsewhere that they had in Ireland.[52]

Much has been written on the way food serves as a boundary marker between in-groups and out-groups.[53] It was not a coincidence, then, that Irish cottiers, who ate more pig food than anyone else and who often shared their habitations with pigs, came to be seen as pig-like during a period of economic hardship. Members of the Anglo-Protestant ascendancy initially attributed porcine behaviors to the Irish as part of a broader effort to justify their monopoly of Ireland's resources. Then they retained this negative conception of the Irish as both "other" and "inferior" because it enhanced their own sense of self-identity. The stereotype eventually followed Erin's heirs throughout the English-speaking world. By the late antebellum era, the common verbal description of the Irish in America emphasized physical features like dark eyes (which bespoke sensuality and ardor), red hair (which implied an excitable personality), a ruddy complexion (which suggested hearty, animal passions), a short, robust figure (which implied inactivity or sloth), prominent cheekbones, an upturned nose, and protruding teeth. Historians generally describe this physiognomy as Simianized, a term intended to convey the influence of Darwin's theory of evolution. But Darwin's first published work on the subject, *On the Origin of Species,* did not appear in print until 1859. By that time, the Irish had been flooding into American cities for nearly two decades. Compared to earlier migrations, the Famine Irish seemed especially threatening. Poor and unhealthy, they exhibited all sorts of questionable behaviors, from drinking and fighting to venerating the Pope. Most of all, they competed with native-born wage earners for jobs, housing, and food. Given this context, it is not surprising that the stereotype found a new audience, one desperate to distance itself from the "others" in its midst.

The assumed link between Irish immigrants, potatoes and cabbages, and swinish behavior proved so persuasive that it even colored the attitudes of those who knew better. Sophie du Pont grew up surrounded by the Irish, taught their children the ABC's, visited them at home, and worshiped beside some of them at Christ Church. But when the company's former storekeeper, Andrew Fountain, announced plans in 1832 to restore a local textile mill and staff it with Irish laborers, she fell back on convention. The "present ruinous and wild appearance of the place" suited her just as it was, she grumbled to Henry, and "when it will be filled with Irish men & women, & troops of squalling dirty brats, and surrounded by pigpens & cabbage patches, cela ira comme de cheveaux sur la soupe, to make use of a very elegant proverb."[54] On St. Patrick's Day that year she waxed nostalgic: "Do you remember what *paddies* we used to dress in our younger days, with necklaces of roasted potatoes?"[55] A final example makes the connection explicit: "The youngies on the *place* devour acorns! Did you ever hear of such little *swine?* They bring them to S[unday] school & throw the *husks* on our floor, making it look like a pig stye."[56] Other nineteenth-century Americans labeled the Irish pigs, too. Writers frequently referred to Irish homes as "sties," for example, and engravings of Irish interiors invariably showed hogs sharing the family's main living space.[57] These tropes gave special meaning to the saying "You are what you eat."

In reality, the du Pont Irish ate a great deal more than pig food. Antebellum probate inventories list barrels of dried or salted fish, like shad and mackerel, and the presence of cider suggests an important use of nearby fruit trees. E. I. du Pont planted a large orchard beside his mansion, and other orchards survived on the former Hirons and Dawes properties downriver at Hagley. These featured apples, peaches, cherries, and chestnuts, which the du Ponts allowed their tenants to pick in limited quantities.[58] Brandywine families also helped themselves to an abundant supply of wild berries, like the blackberries that grew in the vicinity of Squirrel Run. Edward B. Cheney fondly remembered how he and the other Irish children used to go out to Winterthur, Henry Algernon du Pont's nearby estate. There they gathered "blackberries and cherries and wild cherries and dewberries, and the mothers would preserve them. That's were they got their preserves for winter. Of course, we picked up a lot of poison ivy, too!"[59]

Beans offered additional fare for cold winter months. Ulster families did not typically eat legumes, but Americans did, and bean poles became a common garden fixture along the Brandywine. Made from saplings, they averaged seven or eight feet long and had to be sunk into the ground at least twelve inches deep to stand erect. Since many bean seeds failed to germinate, gardening manuals recommended planting several in a small hill of earth at the base of the pole.[60] The du Pont Irish culled out the weaker shoots to foster one hardy vine per pole. One Irish woman recalled that, "the pole beans were a mess . . . a whole row of poles that you had to put in the ground. Each plant went up a pole."[61] Popular varieties included lima, shell, string, and green snap beans, which families generally ate fresh, in season. They planted lima beans, for example, in May and picked them in August or September. Any beans left over got dried on racks and stored in bushel baskets for use during the winter. By the end of the century, canning afforded another storage option.[62]

The Irish diet also encompassed a variety of animal products. A "Straggler's Notebook, 1807–1809" indicates that powder men often missed work because they had to slaughter their cattle. As in Ulster, however, pork prevailed over beef. Hogs' ability to forage freed workers from the necessity of feeding them for much of the year, but they sometimes created a public nuisance.[63] In 1824, Sophie du Pont noted in her diary that, "Alexis and I took a very pleasant walk the other day—in Gregg's Woods, which I have named Cochin, on account of the large armies of pigs which inhabit it."[64] "Cochin's" or Pig's Woods stood adjacent to the Upper Banks, on the property of farmer Samuel Gregg. By 1831, swine also rutted in the woods above Hagley. "On Monday, Nora and I walked over to the old factory on Squirrel Run, to see a S[unday] scholar of mine—We were attacked in turns by pigs, cows, curs & bulldogs, fell in with men blowing rocks & at last reached home, rather *fatigued* from the expedition."[65] Specially cut ear notches indicated which hog belonged to which household. In late fall, the Irish rounded them up, placed them in pens, and fattened them up on potato peelings and table scraps.

A communal event, hog butchering took place between October and December. Thanks to "a most mysterious circumstance" that occurred when Irish carpenter William Boyd slaughtered his hog, a description of the process survives:

> This gentleman killed his swine right in the street with the assistance of many friends and neighbors. Having beheaded a pig, he put the head down near him and was proceeding to the dissection of the trunk, when his lady[,] having some use for the severed part, could not see it anywhere and applied to her husband, to know, "Where his head was[.]" "My head," answered he (blowing his nose), "It cannot be far."[66]

According to Sophie, who probably heard about the event second-hand, Boyd then asked, "Where is my head?" His friends happily told him to "look on his shoulders." The missing part was never recovered.

Home-butchering is further documented by the contents of wage records and probate inventories. Powder man Michael Tonner's estate, for example, recorded in March 1818, listed one barrel with soft soap and six pieces of pork, suggesting that he must have slaughtered a hog the previous winter. A Frenchman, Maurice Saucain, left a lot of ashes and a tub, one tub of pork and a cover, three shoulders, two hams, a sausage cutter, one basket of chops, and a set of candle rods. James McLaughlin, Jr., must have owned several hogs, for he sold seventy-eight pounds of lard to the du Pont company in 1845.[67] McLaughlin received the money, but the lard was probably rendered by his wife. Like gardening, slaughtering an animal required the labor of both sexes. While men performed the actual killing and eviscerating, the work of preserving the meat, rendering the fat, and making the candles, soap, and sausage fell to women.

Once butchered, fresh meats had to be salted, pickled, or smoked to preserve them. Techniques and recipes varied greatly. One late-nineteenth-century Brandywine recipe for corning beef required a "pickle" made by boiling together "two gallons of water, four pounds of salt, one and a half pounds of brown sugar, one and half ounces of saltpetre, and half an ounce of saleratus."[68] Weighted and submerged in the brine, the meat kept indefinitely. Cuts of pork usually received a thick coating of salt, sugar, and saltpeter. The curing process could last from one to seven weeks, while the mixture penetrated the flesh. Some families then smoked their hams and bacon to provide extra flavor and protection.[69]

Eggs and poultry provided another important source of animal protein. They also brought in extra income. Fanny Martin, who ran the company dormitory, sold between four and twelve dozen eggs to the powder company each month during the 1820s.[70] Although Martin raised hens for profit, most families kept only enough for their own use. Chickens rarely appear in probate inventories; however, the presence of feather beds is another good indicator of poultry growing. When widow Ann Dougherty died in 1830, for example, her estate included a forty-five-pound feather bed worth $9, a thirty-nine-pound bed worth $7.80, and a thirty-five-pound bed worth $8.75. Dougherty must have used two different kinds of down, since the estate's enumerators rated the feathers in this last, smaller bed at a higher cost per pound than the other two.[71] As they did in Ulster, the du Pont Irish considered feeding chickens, gathering eggs, and plucking feathers women's work: "Mother had charge of the chickens. She had leghorns and Rhode Island Reds, for eating and for eggs."[72] Chickens usually occupied a small structure near the kitchen. Turkeys, ducks, and geese waddled freely throughout the community.

With so many free-ranging birds and animals wandering about, the du Ponts gave considerable attention to the placement and care of fences. Rocky and well forested, the land bordering the Brandywine initially provided ample materials for the construction of both houses and fences. A low, stone wall defined the outermost perimeter of the company's property, and a series of wooden barriers divided the space within it. In the 1810s, Irénée paid a man named Pierce Neals to keep the community's enclosures in good, working order.[73] By 1835, the company's holdings in Christiana and Brandywine hundreds had expanded so much that he required the labor of four fence makers, instead of one. At least two were Ulster natives.[74]

By separating the Brandywine community from the world at large, the social and physical barriers erected by the du Ponts reinforced ties between management and labor. Outsiders coming to visit used Buck Road, which led directly to Eleutherian Mills and the company office. Their carriages followed a straight route to the mansion, past neatly fenced fields and woodlands, through an imposing alley of oak trees, to a circular drive at its end. E. I. du Pont's prized gardens and orchards occupied a visible place of honor to one side of the drive, but a willow lot on the opposite side readily proclaimed the chief source of the family's income. Plain yet elegant, the house that Irénée built marked the seat of a vast industrial and agricultural complex. To reach this seat and its powerful master, guests had to pass through a series of symbolic barriers, beginning with the dry-laid stone fences that defined the outermost perimeter of his property, and most likely ending with a meal at his table.[75] The du Pont Irish were not subject to the same formalities. Simultaneously a part of the processional landscape and a portion of its intended audience, workmen and their families used different routes, especially shortcuts that enabled them to come and go at will. They fully grasped the symbolism of their surroundings, however. Generations of living in northern Ireland had well acquainted these people with the language of great Georgian manors and picturesque estates. Here, though, tenants enjoyed the benefits of mutualism.

Within the vast system of fences that marked the powder mill community as private property, the company designated certain areas as public spaces. These included spring houses, and later in the century, wells. Most Brandywine Valley spring houses were small, stone structures built into the bank of a hill. Water bubbled up from below the ground and into a paved, sunken trench about three inches deep. A raised platform led from the doorway into the center of the trench, and wooden benches and shelves provided storage for food and equipment.[76] Every cluster of workers' housing had its own water supply. Over in Squirrel Run, water flowed from a common source into a series of spring houses. Each spring house contained multiple compartments and each family had its own place to keep perishables.[77] Rain provided another source of water. Nearly all houses had gutters and spouts that directed the run-off into tubs and barrels. After the Civil War, the company dug a series of wells around the property. Ella Fitzharris vividly remembered how her mother and other Irish women gathered at the Keg Mill cluster's pump to get water and talk.[78] Like porches and gardens, the community's water sources served cultural as well as practical uses.

Brandywine residents enjoyed the use of many other exterior spaces as well. In 1832, Sophie informed her brother Henry that "Alfred is having a pretty little fence made to enclose that part of the wood between his house & [Eva]Lina's & walks cut through it."[79] Footpaths and walkways crisscrossed the hillsides, connecting du Pont mansions and workers' houses alike. Over time, the Irish co-opted other areas for their exclusive use. Impromptu social gatherings occurred right in the streets, as when the community staged "willow peeling parties." These events included competitions to see who could peel the most, along with dancing and, of course, "refreshments."[80] Wedding celebrations also entailed outdoor activities. When Joseph Peoples married Jenny Simpson sometime in the 1850s, for example, his friends indulged in the time-honored custom of chivaree, that is, they gathered under cover of darkness and gave him "a great serenade of gunshots." The nuptials took place soon thereafter, and the newlyweds "went off in a small carriage" followed "in the same sort of vehicles" by the wedding party. The procession likely wound its way from the church to the bride's parents' home. Other kinds of processions occurred for funerals and special holidays, as when the Irish paraded from St. Joseph's to Keyes Hill in Squirrel Run, where they held the annual Fourth of July picnic. Elsewhere in the community, residents went fishing and swimming from a low-lying stretch of land along the river. "They used to call that Poor Man's Beach."[81] In the wintertime, when the Brandywine froze, skaters transformed its icy surface into a makeshift rink. These uses of exterior space helped foster a deep sense of entitlement among the residents. In many ways, the land belonged to them as much as it belonged to the du Ponts.

Although the company's position as landowner technically obligated it to maintain the landscape, the Irish often did the work themselves. When the local supply of fencing materials began to dwindle in the 1820s, Irénée began to experiment with ditches and hedgerows. His Irish-born fence makers had a lot of experience with these forms of enclosure. In Ulster, farmers routinely dug ditches to drain the region's numerous grasslands and separate fields from pastures. They then built up the grazing side of the ditch with sod and lined it with thorn bushes, shrubs, and young trees. Though less durable than walls of stone, these plantings endowed the ditches with a "near-permanence" that successfully divided fields, reinforced property boundaries, and kept livestock out.[82] Hedgerows characterized much of rural New Castle County by the 1840s. After an infestation of apple borers in 1847 killed many of the so-called "live" fences, enclosures of posts and rails took their place.[83] The Irish quickly made the transition. Carpenter William Boyd, for example, had a lot of fence posts and a post-boring machine listed among his goods and chattels in 1844. Other employees built and repaired fences, too. Powder man Thomas Holland owned a lot of posts at his death in 1847, and other men left mauls, axes, and wedges.[84] Self-repairs persisted through the century. In the 1890s, druggist George Frizell wrote to Francis Gurney du Pont requesting some lumber with which to fix his garden fence. "The fence is old and rotten, and several weeks ago the wind blew one side of it entirely down. As far as I am able to estimate, it will take ten new posts, twenty pieces of scantling, and about one bundle of palings. I will do the work myself if you will kindly grant this request."[85] By this time, the powder company owned approximately 2,500 acres of land in northern New Castle County, all neatly platted and paled.[86]

Fences received a lot of attention in the nineteenth century because they symbolized changing ideas about private property, landscape management, and the place of agriculture in American society.[87] On paper, a man might own "all that lot bounded on the east by the Brandywine Creek, on the south by the land of Rumford Dawes," and so on, but without a physical barrier of some sort to prevent people from trespassing, the resources captured within the platted lines fell easily into common use. A fence made ambiguous legal descriptions tangible. Whether made of fieldstones, hedges, or split-rails, these structures indicated to the general public that the property they enclosed was privately held, and that the freeholder had a legal right to reserve whatever advantages the property possessed to himself. And because the fence served such an important social and economic purpose, the owner typically considered any breach a personal offense.[88]

This belief often led landowners into open conflict with the rural poor, their tenants, and their neighbors. In antebellum New Castle County, roaming dogs caused so much damage to local flocks of sheep that breeders repeatedly petitioned the state legislature for legal redress. Their concerns reflected not merely the economic loss caused by the dog owners' negligence, but the danger that such disrespect posed to the freehold concept and to local attitudes about private property. The determination of blame proved difficult in these conflicts, and it took more than thirty years to pass an "act to prevent injury by dogs."[89] Similar conflicts plagued farmers and hog owners in Kent and Sussex counties. Anxious to maximize the productive capacity of their unimproved holdings, they endeavored to enclose them with fences and bring more acres under cultivation. They received immediate challenges from their economic inferiors, who had traditionally been allowed to let their hogs forage in undeveloped woodlands. These cases pitted a customary "right" of the people against the statutory "right" of the farmer to manage his private holdings as he saw fit.[90] By passing new fence legislation, Delaware courts upheld the right of landholders to preclude public use of their private property. In the process, fences came to represent the growing gap between the Haves and the Have Nots.

Similar tensions emerged along the Brandywine. As tenants, the du Pont Irish enjoyed free access to virtually all of their employer's land, but they understood the benefits that private property conferred, and took steps to assert their own rights when they became independent farmers. Powder man Hugh Bogan, for example, paid $1.44 on May 20, 1829, "for recording a deed." He moved to the farm around 1833, and in 1839, the New Castle County Commissioner of Roads laid out a new, public route through one edge of it. The novice Irish Catholic landowner did not oppose the new road; rather he contested the amount of money he would receive in exchange for the timber the county had to fell to build it. Well aware of the going rate for timber, and knowledgeable, too, of his right to "fair" compensation for his resources, he sought legal redress via his former employer.[91] A related conflict involving two Irish immigrants arose in 1843. Former foreman William Green purchased a farm from widow Elizabeth Walter and then learned that another Irishman, a wagoner named James Campbell, drove through the property on a regular basis. When Green told him to stop, Campbell explained that he had enjoyed "right of road" from Walter for many years, and further, that length of use gave him the "right" to continue his customary route. Green insisted, so Campbell applied to Alfred du Pont for legal advice. Du Pont consulted an attorney in Wilmington and reported back that Campbell's right of use ended with Walter's demise.[92]

This kind of behavior suggests the extent to which Irish immigrants' attitudes toward land and cultivation changed after emigration. In keeping with the accepted relationship between agriculture and republican virtue, antebellum Americans viewed cultivation as an important expression of civic virtue. By the 1820s, however, they no longer expected yeomen farmers to be entirely self-sufficient. The rise of modern capitalism had "grafted a new meaning of public duty onto the beliefs of the classical republican agriculturalist."[93] To remain virtuous in a society that increasingly stressed competition and individual productivity in a free market, the Jacksonian-era husbandman had to increase his output. In New Castle County, farmers responded to these pressures by expanding their holdings, diversifying their agricultural products, rotating their crops, raising livestock, or specializing in a particular commodity like orchards or dairy cows.[94] These market-driven behaviors did increase profits, but they also raised land values. By 1850, the value of farmland in Brandywine Hundred reached approximately $63 per acre.[95] John Green owned $900 worth of real property that year. His fourteen-odd acres could not provide the same level of income as George Miller's fifty-five. Miller, another Irish immigrant and former du Pont employee, acquired his land in the 1820s, before the cost of land rose so high. After 1850, the number of individual farms in northern Delaware continued to increase, but the ability of wage earners to buy them declined.[96] As a result, Irish families increasingly turned to new forms of real estate and embraced new attitudes about farming. By 1870, "property" no longer meant cultivable land. A modest house and yard sufficed to make immigrants freeholders.

As the forces of urbanization and industrialization accelerated after mid-century, the use and meaning of exterior space in the powder mill community changed again. The Wilmington Street Railway extended its horse-drawn trolley line to Rising Sun Lane in 1864, and the Wilmington and Northern Railway built a spur line to Wagoner's Row in 1884. More and more Irish families did their shopping in the city, where they patronized large-scale, commercial seed houses and nurseries.[97] Farmers at the King Street Market in Wilmington sold seedlings to many would-be gardeners, and advertisements in local newspapers attest to other sources of seeds and equipment. Few vegetables could take the place of potatoes or cabbages, however. Annie Gibbons and her husband, Jacques Seitz, had a border of asparagus around their potato beds, for example, and the plant was known to grow wild in certain spots, but most families considered it an exotic item, "one the rich people had."[98] Spinach, peas, cucumbers, and squash also appeared infrequently, as they proved difficult to grow. Tomatoes thrived in Delaware's humid summers, although the Irish usually ate them cooked or canned. Additional vegetables included parsley, corn, onions, radishes, turnips, carrots, celery, rhubarb, and lettuce.

While cheap rail service afforded some families an opportunity to experiment with new species of plants, it allowed others to buy fresh vegetables from wholesale grocers and lessen their dependence on Brandywine vendors. Many Irish gave up their kitchen gardens altogether. Frank L. Mathewson, a fourth-generation employee, proudly noted that his parents never grew their own food. The family had a big yard behind their home on Breck's Lane, but "that was too much work for my father and too much for me, too." Instead, the Mathewsons got fresh produce from Wilmington or Alfred I. du Pont's garden across the road. "He didn't supply work people but he did supply my father and his other personal employees."[99] By 1902, only 17 percent of the 143 households living on company property still had a garden.

The changing attitude of Irish families along the Brandywine paralleled attitudes elsewhere in the United States.[100] With increased access to urban markets at the end of the century, Americans purchased more of their food than ever before. The widespread growth of the meat-packing industry made it easier and cheaper to buy mass-produced, brand name pork and beef products at local stores. Few households had cows or pigs, but some women still kept chickens. Maria Abrahams Beacom, for example, bought her eggs from Kate Deery, who lived in the Upper Banks and only charged ten or twelve cents a dozen. Beacom usually bought her fresh meat from an itinerant butcher, however. Edward Devenney grew up at Walker's Banks and recalled Irish women gathering, plates in hand, whenever the butcher came to the area.[101] Other items purchased from Wilmington deliverymen included ice, ice cream, milk, baked goods, dry goods, shoes, and fish.[102]

The nineteenth century thus witnessed a complete turnabout in Irish land and food ways. In 1815, E. I. du Pont jubilantly reported to a business associate that "the face of the country is changed, old fields formerly covered with what is called here poverty grass are now rich in clover; the farms are well fenced, new barns and new stone houses are rapidly rising—the price of new produce has increased in proportion with the wants of new consumers."[103] Manufactories like his played a critical role in the transformation of northern Delaware's landscape. Wage workers needed food, farmers needed consumers. For at least fifty years, circumstances along the Brandywine contributed to the perception that du Pont employees could and should become farmers themselves. To this end, they planted gardens,

kept livestock, and preserved their agricultural skills. These activities enabled the Irish to preserve important aspects of their ethnic heritage despite
the forces of change swirling around them. In Wilmington, manufacturing
enterprises expanded swiftly in the decades immediately before and after
the Civil War. Area textile mills, iron-rolling mills, morocco shops, ship-
yards, and railroad car shops provided new opportunities for employment
and tightened the symbiotic relationship that linked farmers and wage
earners. Although many of the du Pont Irish did manage to buy land of
their own, the number who did so declined sharply after 1850, partly because land values rose significantly and partly because the Irish began to
embrace new attitudes about exterior space. These ranged from the simple
(porches serve a variety of practical functions) to the complex (property
ownership in America confers specific rights and privileges). They continued to eat potatoes and cabbages, but an array of foods now graced Irish
dinner tables, and the traditional fare of Ireland took on a new symbolism.
No longer a sign of Irish "otherness," it became by 1900 a bridge to the
agrarian past.

CHAPTER 8

Linen Tablecloths and Lace Curtains

❧

Catharine Dougherty Gibbons always said "she would rather have tea and a piece of bread on a linen tablecloth than she would a banquet on oilcloth." This *bean a ti* had a special attachment to Irish linen, which she took pains to acquire and maintain. When she died, the collection passed first to her daughter, Maggie, then down through daughter Annie's family to a granddaughter. "I had the linen from the family, loads of it," Margaret Seitz said. "Irish linen tablecloths. And the one that I gave the [Hagley] museum, with the Lord's Supper on it, is about 150 years old, I guess (fig. 8.1). But they were great for the linen. Sort of liked to show off a little bit, too."[1]

Women like Gibbons felt much the same about lace curtains. When asked a deliberately leading question concerning the use of "draperies" by the du Pont Irish, Blanche McAdoo Yetter responded, "[W]e never had draperies. Maybe in the bedroom we might have had lace curtains. Maybe in the parlor they had lace curtains. But we didn't have any particular curtain in the kitchen other than the window shade."[2] Yetter, a powder man's daughter, could not confirm the presence of lace curtains in all Irish homes, but she knew that some families had them. Ella Farren Fitzharris, by contrast, recalled them vividly: "We just had white lace curtains at the windows and shades." Her mother, Ella Lowther Farren, also collected linens: "It seemed like a lot of, I'm not saying stealing, but it seemed like a lot of things just disappeared, you know, after Mother died," Fitzharris explained. "Like linen tablecloths. I remember Mother used to entertain a lot on Sunday. I don't particularly remember the tablecloths, but I know my aunts had been talking about them. But after I got about ten years old, we just had the ordinary cotton damask tablecloths."[3] Clearly, some other person or persons valued Farren's tablecloths, too, despite their second-hand condition. Among the du Pont Irish, as among other Irish at other times

Fig. 8.1. Irish linen tablecloth owned by Catharine Dougherty Gibbons and donated to Hagley by her granddaughter, Dr. Margaret Seitz. (Courtesy of Hagley Museum and Library)

and places, white linen worked in tandem with white lace to symbolize respectability and upward mobility.

Such behavior reveals the conundrum of class in America. On one hand, scholars of the Irish in America routinely use qualifiers like "lace curtain" and "shanty" to categorize their subjects.[4] These terms, rooted in the way Irish communities historically differentiated themselves, convey a certain sensitivity to the role domestic life plays in determinations of social status. On the other hand, most historians define people primarily on the basis of job titles.[5] Very few Irish could be labeled "middle class" by this standard: as manual laborers, the vast majority belonged to the "working class," they contend, and generally lacked the *will* to advance, let alone the skills or income. Yet a sizeable proportion of every Irish community did experience some form of upward mobility. By 1870 roughly 60 percent of all Irish immigrants living in the United States had achieved decent, steady employment of the sort associated with skilled craftsmen and small proprietors; by 1900 they enjoyed relative occupational parity with their native-born, white neighbors.[6] Moreover, falling prices and rising incomes over the course of the nineteenth century meant that Irish families managed to acquire many of the things that signified bourgeois identity without benefit of white-collar work. These included lace curtains, linen tablecloths, parlor fittings, fashionable clothes, and fine tablewares. The question is whether these gains, coupled with modest advances in other arenas of life, constituted for the Irish an elevation in social status. Or, put another way, did Catharine Gibbons' linen tablecloths compensate for the fact that her highly skilled, well-paid husband wore a blue-collar shirt every day and returned sweaty and dirty from his labors every night?

From her standpoint, the answer is yes. Catharine had little difficulty reconciling this seeming contradiction because her sense of social status did not derive from occupation alone. Whereas sociological theories posit two or three rigid, mutually antagonistic strata, she and her neighbors in the powder mill community saw a fluid social structure ordered by subjective, contested terms like "producer" or "non-producer," "low-born," and "high-born," "middling," "gentry" and "higher stations in life."[7] In Ireland, years of political and cultural repression limited the ability of Catholics to advance beyond their positions at birth. But no such institutionalized obstacles existed in the United States, as Catharine's own experiences could attest. Born in County Donegal in 1821, she emigrated to the Brandywine as a young woman and married John Gibbons in 1846. As John's fortunes rose, so did hers. When he became foreman of the Hagley Yard in 1863, for example, the couple moved with their five children to a three-story, six-room, stone house adjacent to the powder yard gates (fig. 8.2). There they lived for nearly twenty years, during which time Catharine acquired for her second-floor parlor a matching suite of walnut seating furniture, an expandable dining table, and a press for her precious linens. Catharine may even have earned some of the money to purchase these items herself, for she regularly sewed powder bags and peeled willow. After John's death in 1885, she moved to a house they owned on Lincoln Street in Forty Acres, and at her own death in 1895, she left assets totaling more than $5000.[8] True, she never committed her feelings about her own socioeconomic status to paper, but that propensity to "show off a little bit," displayed especially when she used her fine linens, nicely conveys a perception of and pride in her own advancement.

Nor was Catharine's story unique. Nearly every Irish immigrant in the powder mill experienced upward mobility in some form or another. Men frequently climbed the occupational ladder from common laborer to pow-

Fig. 8.2. Exterior view of the Hagley Yard foreman's residence, now interpreted as the Gibbons house, ca. 1886–1900. The family shown is that of John Stewart, who became foreman after John Gibbons died in 1886. (Courtesy of Hagley Museum and Library)

der worker. Some served apprenticeships and rose to become master crafts-men. Still others became clerks, storekeepers, clergymen, or farmers. But there were other ways to measure status in the nineteenth century besides work. During the Jacksonian era, the traditional markers of social position, wealth and title, gave way to gentility and sincerity.[9] Countless ordinary people took advantage of the change and the opportunity it afforded for voluntary self-definition. Moreover, the climate of public opinion encour-aged them to do so by linking self-improvement to civic virtue and upward mobility.[10] Though limited by economic and cultural constraints, the du Pont Irish endorsed the new ideology of social and individual betterment, which flourished until at least the 1890s, and took pains to refine their be-havior *while* they labored for wages in manual occupations. By partaking of "self-culture," they came to reconceptualize their place in the social order. For just as people in this community forged new ethnic and religious iden-tities, so they developed a new sense of status consciousness, one that priv-ileged "quality of life" and personal autonomy over work and income.

❧

Immigrants like Catharine Dougherty and John Gibbons came to the United States seeking opportunities denied them at home. Rapid commercialization after the 1790s initially brought great prosperity to Ulster's nine counties. It also altered important cultural values. Rural folk began to define their goals in entrepreneurial or proto-capitalistic terms. Most notably, they aspired increasingly to "independence," a subjective, ambiguous term that generally signified a kind of self-sufficiency. The end of the Napoleonic wars disrupted their endeavors, however. As Ireland plunged into a severe depression, newly profit-minded landlords saw an opportunity to implement sweeping reforms. The market-oriented variety enclosed their holdings, evicted tenants, and converted arable fields to pasture. The rest simply shortened leases and prohibited partible inheritance, a time-honored practice that had allowed a tenant to subdivide the property amongst multiple offspring.[11] As a result of falling crop prices and wages, problems still plagued the countryside in the 1830s, and official reports by government investigators portray a frustrated population. Though generally considered "industrious" and "anxious to improve," Ulstermen faced a considerable obstacle to success: "I think if they were not oppressed with heavy rents they would soon be comfortably situated," wrote one observer; "Want of capital and high rent prevent the people from any turn for improvement," concluded another.[12] The Irish tenant's inability to profit substantially from his own labor persisted until the 1880s, when Parliament passed a series of historic Land Acts that slowly transferred ownership back to the Catholic peasantry.[13] In the meantime, those predisposed to pursue an "independence" projected their ambitions across the sea, sadly mindful that, in Ireland, "prosperity is not . . . commensurate with the exertions made."[14]

The upwardly mobile immigrants who reached the Brandywine entered a community divided into myriad levels. Hezekiel Talley, the federal census taker, documented its inhabitants for posterity when he visited the Brandywine in the summer of 1850. That year marked the first time enumerators gathered detailed data concerning occupation, literacy, marital status, age, property ownership, and place of birth. Congress authorized them to collect this information in an effort to assess scientifically the state of the union.[15] The United States had been experiencing rapid change for several decades by this point; the year 1850, marking as it did the half-century, seemed a propitious time to expand the function of the census beyond representative purposes. The schedules can also be used to assess the state of the powder mill community. Nearly fifty years old, it had reached a mature phase of development, and its inhabitants enjoyed a relatively stable social order.

At the pinnacle of Brandywine society in 1850 clustered a small group of industrialists, gentlemen farmers, and their kin. Six textile mills dotted the local landscape, and the would-be capitalists who operated them profoundly affected everyday life. Woolens manufacturer John Siddall sponsored the original Sunday school, for example, an informal series of meetings that Irénée du Pont formalized upon Siddall's departure.[16] Landed elites, like members of the Gregg, Husbands, and Hendrickson families, occupied vast tracts in Brandywine and Christiana hundreds and owed their livelihoods to agriculture. Although frequently in debt, especially before the Civil War, the du Ponts dominated this tier. Far better connected than their neighbors, they moved easily between the great plantations of South Carolina, the banking houses of New York and Philadelphia, the smoke-filled back rooms of Washington, D.C., and the sophisticated salons of France. For the most part, however, family members passed their days contentedly in Delaware, where they received an impressive list of callers, including the Marquis de Lafayette, Whig leader Henry Clay, President James Monroe, and architect Benjamin Latrobe.[17] Always cognizant of Pierre Samuel's patent of nobility, his heirs remained somewhat aloof from their economic equals in the United States. The family coat of arms suggests the source of their collective reserve: it bears a lone Ionic column surmounted by a helmet and the words "Rectitudine Sto," or Upright I Stand.[18]

Far below the aristocratic du Ponts were the degraded poor, a transient, largely female group that eluded Hezekiel Talley's notice, but not the community's. Anna Morris, for example, came "begging" at Louviers several times in 1851. Each time she appeared, Sophie gave the "colored" woman some change and carefully recorded the amount and day. Other beggars in the 1850s included a "German woman," an "Italian woman," an "old, deaf woman, Mary Smith alias Anderson," and Mary Ann Richardson, another African American. Itinerant pedlars like "Mr. Makin" also visited the area. Though lame, Makin made regular trips to sell buttons, pins, and similar items.[19] Whether these individuals approached other Brandywine households remains unclear. Du Pont employees voluntarily contributed to all sorts of relief efforts, from subscriptions for "the poor of Ireland and Scotland" to ones favoring injured neighbors and orphaned children.[20] Memories of hard times likely encouraged their charity toward those less fortunate.

A wide range of occupational categories and income levels filled the space between these two extremes. Some 2,000 individuals lived and worked in the area in 1850. Not counting women "keeping house" or children "at home," 558 of these individuals claimed a specific occupation. Their job titles reflect the community's distinctive industrial character. First in numerical importance came the "laborers" (36 percent), then "manufacturers" (10 percent), a generic term that identified those tending the powder rolling, stamping, and graining mills. A collier, two sulphur refiners, and eight "powder makers" rounded out the du Pont company's chief production staff, while coopers, carpenters, stone masons, blacksmiths, and teamsters handled maintenance and distribution. Spinners, fullers, carders, warpers, weavers, finishers, dyers, machinists, and wool sorters marked the local textile industry, and a waiter, a coachman, six gardeners, and an assortment of female servants represented those in domestic service. Additional occupations included a baker, a match maker, a plasterer, a painter, three tailors, and twenty-two shoemakers, who likely made and mended the special, wooden footwear worn in the powder yards. As table 8.1 indicates, Irish immigrants dominated this level of society.

TABLE 8.1

Occupational and Ethnic Data from the 1850 Census

	Number	Number Irish
Gentlemen	2	0
U.S. Navy	1	0
Powder manufacturers	6	0
Farmers	38	16
Merchants/storekeepers	10	7
Clerks/bookkeepers	6	4
Innkeepers	5	3
Medical doctors	3	0
Chemists	1	0
Teachers	1	0
Clergy	3	1
Powder workers	68	35
Skilled tradesmen	138	61
Textile workers	38	21
Domestics	41	27
Laborers	203	182

The community also had its share of "middling sorts." This group included shopkeepers, innkeepers, publicans, doctors, teachers, clergymen, and clerks, plus yeomen farmers whose fields abutted company property, and master craftsmen like wheelwrights and millwrights. Irish immigrants prevailed over this tier, too, and closer inspection reveals how hard they worked to get there. The job title "bookkeeper," for example, cannot possibly convey the sense of accomplishment Peter N. Brennan, Jr., must have felt in 1850. Brennan fled Ireland with his parents and began working in the Louviers textile mill as a teenager in the 1820s. After an unspecified accident left him crippled, he rejoined Charles I. du Pont and Company as a clerk and slowly took charge of day-to-day operations. By mid-century, he had become a prominent member of the Catholic community in New Castle County, helping to found and serving as treasurer of both St. Joseph on the Brandywine and St. Mary's College in Wilmington. "Farmer" John Coile could take similar pride in his experiences. The Irish-born Coile rose from common laborer to powder man, saved enough money to purchase a sizeable farm in Christiana Hundred, and had enough discretionary income to finance the passage of at least twenty emigrants during the Famine years. And then there was "Trader" James Toy. The son of a powder man, Toy started out as a teamster, hauling powder kegs to company agents as far away as Massachusetts and Ohio. He later opened a grocery store-cum-saloon in Henry Clay Village. After the churches let out on Sundays, he blithely tended bar in the "Blazing Rag," dispensing Irish wit and whiskey to his former colleagues until the wee hours.

The successes that these and other Irish achieved stemmed partly from the company's in-house promotion policy. Recall Alfred du Pont's 1843 explanation of it:

> [After] our works were begun in 1802, the following rules were then fixed in relation to employment. 1st Never to admit a man to work within the mills until he had been a considerable time at outdoor work with us; We therefore when help is wanted at the powder mills, take in the hands according to their date of entering our employment, the hand the longest on the place entering the mills when a vacancy occurs; in this way hands have generally from one to two years working with us previous to being admitted into our mills for we usually have from 50 to 60 outdoor hands.[21]

At mid-century, a typical outdoor laborer's stint lasted two years. Once sent "to the powder," he began his instruction as a glorified "Go Fer," moving materials and equipment from mill to mill. If his work proved satisfactory, he eventually advanced to "helper." Then, working under the close supervision of a senior employee, he gradually learned the mysteries of refining saltpeter or sulphur, making charcoal, or operating one of the specialized mills. To competitors who hoped to lure his workmen away, Irénée claimed that powder men understood "nothing of the principles and nature of the work they are about," but, really, the opposite was true. Despite various efforts to mechanize production, the manufacture of black powder in the nineteenth century required the kind of specialized knowledge gained only through years of experience. The men who ran the rolling mills had to monitor the revolutions of the great wheels, judging by hand and eye when to add water, change speeds, or stop mixing. Because of their great skill and nerve, these men represented an elite corps among the powder workers, and their names informally graced the mills they tended.[22] Rarely did one become foreman, however. No matter how talented or loyal a man might be, four yards meant four positions.

Then again, some hands never made it to the powder at all. The du Ponts only promoted those who seemed to them steady and compliant. Employees who drank on the job, deliberately used improper tools, skipped work, or disregarded orders soon lost their positions. Yet others withdrew voluntarily. Willow cutters, for example, worked on a purely seasonal basis.[23] These men, both Irish and not, typically lived on farms in the surrounding countryside and considered wage work temporary and supplementary. Even members of the powder mill community came and went as personal circumstances dictated. Francis Lynch, a Famine refugee, worked only from April 7 to October 10, 1847. During that brief time, however, he saved $90, enough to pay back his subscriber and start over elsewhere. Peter Quigley, by contrast, remained an outdoor laborer for more than twenty years. Perhaps he eschewed industrial work, or perhaps he recoiled from the threat of explosions. Either way, his experience suggests the wide range of laborers' work patterns.

The fact that powder men tended to have much longer work histories influenced the high rate of turnover among laborers. Consider the forty-three powder men and nineteen common laborers who worked for du Pont in 1820. Fifteen of the former retained their positions in 1829 (35 percent), but only four of the latter did (21 percent).[24] A similar disjuncture emerged among the men employed in 1835. Of the seventy-six powder workers that year, thirty-nine (51 percent) persisted until 1850 compared to twenty-two (37 percent) of the sixty laborers. Peer even closer at the men working just at Hagley in 1850. Nearly half of the sixty-nine powder men in that yard worked more than ten years after their initial promotion, and their rate of turnover was 6 percent compared to 27 percent for the entire workforce. And the number of employees with long terms of service only increased over time. In 1902, a substantial 70 percent of the 249 hands who signed the centennial petition had at least ten years' service, and 31 percent had a quarter century or more.[25]

Still, enough common laborers advanced to reinforce a high expectation of achieving occupational mobility, especially before the Civil War. While the company lost fifteen out of the nineteen common hands it employed in 1820, it gained by 1829 some seventy-two others of whom fifty-one eventually became powder men. The du Ponts hired during that same period twenty-one craftsmen, too, including eight carpenters, five millwrights, and three blacksmiths. Much of this growth reflects the opening of a third powder yard (lower Hagley) in 1828, but a similar increase took place with the addition of a fourth (Brandywine Mills or Lower Yard) in 1835. Of the forty men who persisted from 1835 to 1850, moreover, 63 percent improved their status in life: laborer Daniel McEvey acquired $2,500 worth of real estate, for instance, while his counterparts, James McKenna and James Stewart, become a machinist and a powder worker, respectively.[26]

A high rate of turnover characterized the powder workers, too. Like the outdoor laborers, their attitudes and experiences varied considerably. John Lynch offers an intriguing case in point. An Irish Catholic emigrant from Donegal, he went to the powder on August 1, 1835, closed his account on April 17, 1836, then recommenced nearly two months later. In July of that year, he became a powder cart man, and received a raise to $20.50 per month. That job lasted until June 13, 1839, when he left to work for Charles I. du Pont and Company across the creek. The wild rover re-entered the powder yards in 1842, but left again in 1844. At mid-century, he tended the grounds at Sophie du Pont's home, Louviers, and listed his occupation as "gardener."[27] Other leavetakers abandoned the community altogether. The thirty-one Hagley powder workers who quit between 1850 and 1860 averaged thirty-nine years of age.[28] With so much of their productive lives still ahead, these men presumably left to find an "independence" elsewhere.

Nineteenth-century Americans had great wanderlust, and du Pont employees eagerly joined the movement west.[29] These Irish pioneers included the first Hagley foreman, John McDermot, Sr., who in 1825 acquired a farm in Westmoreland County, just forty miles beyond Pittsburgh. Shortly thereafter, McDermot's eldest daughter, Rosanna, informed her former Sunday school teachers that the family had "a very comfortable situation to live on which contains 228 acres of land, [and] more than 1600 shocks of wheat, rye, and oats, with 10 head of cattle, 7 head of horses and 30 sheep." All of this, her father allowed, "was earned by the great prosperity he had making powder on the Brandywine." Significantly, she later reported that a man had offered John $600 to start a powder works for him. "My father said he had now a good property by making powder and i will not risk myself one year to start mills for you[.] when i want to make powder i will return to the gentleman that learned me to make powder."[30] Other Irish preferred agriculture, too. Joshua Gibbons, a former Sunday school teacher, also bought several acres in southwestern Pennsylvania and proudly boasted to Victorine du Pont Bauduy that, "My vocation is farming, the exercise of which has restored me to good health."[31] Similar reports arrived from as far away as Davenport, Iowa, and as late as the 1870s.

Western expansion provided opportunities for commerce, too. As the nation's leading supplier of black powder, a critical commodity on the frontier, the du Pont company's extensive network of agents provided many men with the contacts they needed to get started in business. Others advanced on their own merits. In 1844, John McDermot, Jr., returned to Delaware and began working in the powder yards. After his father died the following year, he went back west and secured a white-collar position in a grocery store, where he quickly advanced from clerk to bookkeeper. In 1857 he became a partner in the same firm.[32] Likewise, S. B. Brown found employment with a firm called Hood, Bonbright & Company. In 1872 he informed Eleuthera du Pont Smith that,

> I came here in 1864 on a salary of $300 a year, not knowing anything about the business. I had of course to begin at the bottom of the ladder and climb up. I am now their buyer of white goods, linens, flannels and blankets, and manager of a Department of about a million dollars business. My salary is now $4,500 with a prospect of continual advancement from year to year.[33]

Irish-born Edward Baxter landed in Nashville in 1860. When the Civil War erupted, he put his knowledge of powder manufacture to good use making "the first shell or shot in Tennessee for the Rebels." The arrival of federal troops in 1862 ended this venture, but the would-be entrepreneur soon found another opportunity: "I went into others Business and it was the best thing I ever done. . . . I have a store and am doing very well."[34]

Aspiring artisans also braved the uncertainty of life beyond the Brandywine. Because of its relatively small and invariable size after 1835, the company's demand for skilled craftsmen remained low. It employed in 1850, for example, nearly a hundred men in the yards, but only thirty-two coopers, twenty-seven carpenters, fourteen masons and stone cutters, fourteen blacksmiths, six machinists, six wheelwrights, and five millwrights.[35] In addition, the major crafts tended to be family affairs. Witness the aptly named Millers. Their story begins with George, a native of Bernally, County Derry, who came to Delaware in the early part of the century and briefly worked, like so many other Ulstermen, for Irénée du Pont. He later operated Brandywine Hundred's famed Blue Ball Tavern and farmed an adjacent sixty-eight-acre tract. Two of his six sons, George L. and Jonas W., served apprenticeships with company millwright Richard Rambo. George L. eventually bought Jonas' share of the family farm and took over his father's tavern. Jonas spent fifty years working for the du Ponts, becoming head millwright in the process. Meanwhile, his sons, John S. and William H., called Henry, served their apprenticeships and became journeymen. After twenty-one years with the company, John opened a general store in Henry Clay Village, but Henry eventually assumed their father's position.[36] While nepotism certainly helped these men get ahead in life, the custom forced many a young craftsman to seek work elsewhere.

Irish fathers often encouraged their sons in this regard. Master carpenter Billy Boyd's son, Andrew, plied the same trade in Philadelphia, but then headed south to Mobile in 1825. After several months had passed, E. I. du Pont sent a letter of introduction to his Mobile agents, McLockey, Hagan and Company, presumably at Billy's request. Other employees also sought letters of reference for their offspring. In 1890, for example, Frank du Pont wrote to the managers of the Jackson and Sharp Railroad Car Works in Wilmington to recommend "the son of Dennis McCarthy, an 18 yr. employee," for an apprenticeship. "I have had the boy employed here in our metallic keg factory, and the foreman has spoken well of him. He left us about a year ago, to get employment in a store. As far as I know the boy, there is nothing to discredit his past record."[37] Powder man Neil Toy's son, James, sought work as a carpenter. Trained by the du Pont company, James Toy went on to build railroad cars at Harlan and Hollingsworth, then Pusey and Jones in Wilmington. "You couldn't get him into powder," his son recalled.[38] For various reasons, then, most of the Irish boys who served apprenticeships with du Pont company craftsmen did not remain in the community as adults. Moreover, the vast majority of these apprentices were Protestant.

Religious beliefs profoundly shaped Irish attitudes toward occupational and social mobility. Though the percentages of Presbyterians, Episcopalians, and Catholics in the community remained fairly even over time, each sect more or less claimed a different calling. Catholics controlled the powder yards. In 1845–46, for example, only 135 (41 percent) of the 329 men working for the company subscribed to St. Joseph's, but at least sixty-one (62.2 percent) of the ninety-eight full-time powder workers did. Similarly, 110 (47 percent) of the 234 men on the company books in 1885 paid pew rent to the Catholic Church compared to some seventy-six (63 percent) of the 120 powder men.[39] Presbyterians dominated the textile mills, and Episcopalians gravitated to the trades. These patterns undoubtedly reflect the importance of consanguineous kin networks. Nevertheless, work "in the powder" may have held special appeal for Irish Catholics: Despite the dangers, it allowed them to secure high wages and high-status work without jeopardizing their ties to home and family.

The Catholic work ethic differed sharply from the mainstream Protestant version. Like the powder men, Romanists in America valued work for its own sake, and generally strove to balance regular, steady employment with their familial and religious obligations. They also tended to define success in group, not individual terms, and subordinated personal goals for the good of the family. This perspective deviated sharply from America's evolving "gospel of wealth," yet it did not constitute a pure "gospel of resignation" as some scholars contend. Mindful that every parish depended on the prosperity of its laity, Catholic leaders actively encouraged upward mobility. However, they condemned the pursuit of money alone, certain that followers of Mammon would ultimately abandon their families and their faith. They also discouraged the close association of material wealth and masculinity that increasingly characterized American culture. Because it denied women and children a place in the domestic economy, the Protestant ideal of home life had to stress male acquisitiveness. Catholics, by contrast, expected every member of the household to contribute, whether male or female.[40]

Although Irish women pursued occupational mobility, too, the sexual division of labor along the Brandywine, coupled with their different sense of obligation to family, severely constrained their options. They could operate machines in the local textile mills, pack powder kegs, paste labels, or enter domestic service. A skilled needle-woman might become a seamstress, or a medically inclined one a midwife. Toward the end of the Jacksonian era, teaching emerged as another acceptable female vocation. Fewer than 2 percent of the 1,186 pupils enrolled at the Sunday School between 1817 and 1850 went on to teach themselves, however. Like Mary Green and Mary Jane Cavender, the daughters of Irish powder men William Green and Henry Cavender, most of these individuals were female, Presbyterian, and taught for only a year or two before marriage. Catholics, by contrast, became educators by entering religious orders.[41]

Ann McGran's case reveals the tensions this choice often created. Born in 1814, she attended the Sunday School while her father, Patrick, toiled in the powder yards, and then she worked as a domestic in Irénée du Pont's home, Eleutherian Mills. After Patrick's death around 1830, Ann moved with her mother and five siblings to Philadelphia, where she became a textile operative, but she kept in close contact with her former teachers. Indeed, her mind dwelled often on those happy Sundays spent in the little Brandywine schoolhouse, and in 1834 she informed Sophie and Victorine that she intended to join the Sisters of Charity, a teaching order that ran a college in Emmitsburg, Maryland. Because she ultimately planned to take the veil, the Sisters agreed to defray Ann's tuition, but Mrs. McGran strongly disapproved of her daughter's plan to leave home, and in deference to her mother, the would-be novice continued to work in the textile mill for several more years. Eventually, she and her sister, Mary, both joined the Sisters, and though the decision brought both women social mobility, it did so by severing their ties to home and family: the order sent Ann to its orphanage at Vincennes, Indiana, where she ultimately became Mother Superior, and Mary ended up in St. Louis, while the rest of the McGrans remained in faraway Philadelphia.[42]

With limited opportunities for gainful and respectable work of their own, most of Erin's daughters in Delaware enhanced their prospects for social mobility through marriage. The most obvious examples are the wives of powder yard foremen, like Maria Green, Rebecca Hurst, and Catharine Gibbons, who advanced alongside their spouses. Of course, young women could not predict which men would move up the occupational ladder, which ones would fail, and which would meet an untimely death. When Ann Toy married Paul Bogan around 1836, for instance, he was just a laborer; by the time the couple celebrated their twentieth anniversary, Paul had a successful store in Henry Clay Village.[43] Mary McCartney Wilkinson offers another example of mobility by marriage. She enjoyed a regular correspondence with Eleuthera du Pont Smith, and in 1864 and 1865 she wrote several letters that describe her changing social status in detail. Mary's husband, identified only as "J.," served an apprenticeship in the Henry Clay factory machine shop, then went to work for Merrick & Son of Philadelphia, where, she reported, "he was employed at the time of our marriage in the Spring of 1851." J. soon secured an even better position as an engineer with the Pascal Iron Works. The newlyweds then "went to housekeeping" in nearby Camden, New Jersey, but Mary considered the location unsuitable, and they quickly purchased "a neat cottage" on Woodbine Street in Philadelphia. J. continued to change jobs, working variously as an engineer in Cuba and entering the Merchant Marine. In 1858, he received an appointment as Chief Engineer for the State of Georgia, but the outbreak of the Civil War forced him back into marine service. By the early 1870s, he and Mary had moved to Washington, D.C., where presumably his engineering skills would have provided the family with an acceptably elevated lifestyle.[44]

Occasionally, a Brandywine woman went directly from the altar to a higher station in life. Wagoner Francois Petitdemange's daughter, Elizabeth, married a substantial farmer named William Husbands, while farmer Samuel Gregg's daughter, Mary, wed the du Pont company's first actual chemist, Charles Le Carpentier.[45] Maria McCullough's story suggests how serendipitous such matches could be. Born in 1815, she lived at Mount Airy, a farm in Christiana Hundred, just beyond the powder yards. At the age of nineteen, she gained a serious suitor-cum-poet: "Mariah Dear, my precious gem / my jewel, most devine / I'd give my life, my life I'd give / If I could but call thee mine." Maria saved the verse, which went on in like fashion for several pages, but married Walter Lackey, an Irish immigrant nearly ten years her senior. Lackey rented a mill and several associated buildings from the du Pont company, and may have seemed a better catch. At any rate, he provided a relatively comfortable existence for his bride and the two children who arrived in due time. But in 1841 he took ill and died, leaving Maria to sell most of their household goods to pay off his debts. Undaunted, the young widow rented a house in Walker's Banks and opened her doors to boarders. The powder company quickly sent over several young men, including an enterprising English cooper named Henry Danby. As fate would have it, Henry began to court his landlady and the couple finally wed in 1846. In time, the Danbys had four children of their own and enough savings to buy a house and shop in Wilmington, where Henry continued to ply his trade. When Henry died in 1882, the value of his estate exceeded $35,000. As executrix and primary heir, the former Maria McCullough had become a wealthy woman indeed.[46]

Generally speaking, the degree of social mobility achieved by an Irish household has been attributed to the male breadwinner's skills and abilities, but an ambitious wife could enhance the process by the way she "domesticated" her family.[47] During the 1820s and 1830s, the American home became the targeted destination for a voluminous flow of consumer goods. As household managers, married women assumed primary responsibility for acquiring, arranging, and maintaining these items. Their choices had an importance far beyond cost. For in addition to symbolizing her family's status, niceties like lace curtains and linen tablecloths created polite surroundings that in turn demanded polite behavior. Period cartoons suggest that men suffered particularly: they could no longer spit tobacco, drink from a saucer, belch in public, talk loudly, slouch, or fidget with their high, starched collars. Infants might be excused from such rigid rules of conduct, but mothers reminded even small children to mind their manners, sit up straight, and hold a spoon properly. When they habituated their families to prevailing standards of gentility, middling and wage-earning women alike acknowledged that advancement required more than a steady job and decent pay.

That powder mill families understood the relationship between genteel behavior and upward mobility is revealed by the nature and number of other refinements they pursued. The Martins, for example, arranged for their seventeen-year-old daughter, Fanny, to receive instruction in French from a private tutor.[48] Born in Ireland, Billy Martin started out as a common laborer in the powder yards and worked his way up to become manager of the du Pont company farm while his wife managed the company dormitory. Foreign language skills had no effect on a woman's ability to run a household and raise a family—Fanny's ultimate future—but like the possession of parlor furniture, they symbolized a commitment to self-cultivation and "bourgeois" identity. So, for that matter, did English language skills.

In northern Delaware as elsewhere, those who could demonstrate even basic literacy stood out sharply from the "inarticulate" masses. While a significant minority of Irish workers subscribed to newspapers like the *Delaware Sentinel* and the *Intelligencer,* few owned books and many could not sign their names.[49] Their children were another story. Thanks to the presence of the Sunday school, virtually every boy and girl in the community received some formal education, and many performed so admirably they received regular "premiums," including pen wipers, books, and ink stands, items that by their very nature spurred further erudition and study. After 1827, children and their parents alike could borrow reading materials from a special lending library set up by Victorine Bauduy. In addition to moral tracts like "Christian Politeness" and "Why I Should I Obey My Mother," which the American Sunday School Union published and distributed, they could read popular fiction like *Robinson Crusoe* or nature books like *The History of Beasts.*[50]

An especially promising individual might seek higher education. Thus James Gallagher sent his son from the Sunday school to St. Mary's College, an elite school for boys in Wilmington.[51] Founded in 1841 by Rev. Patrick Reilly, then pastor of St. Peter's Church, its trustees included Rev. John S. Walsh, the parish priest at St. Joseph on the Brandywine, and Alfred Victor du Pont, as well as Peter N. Brennan, Jr. By 1857, St. Mary's boasted 120 students, some of whom came from as far as New Orleans and South Carolina to attend.[52] Patrick A. Lynch, by contrast, learned to read and write as a child in Ireland. Born around 1830, he emigrated to the Brandywine in 1846, toiled as a common laborer for nearly ten years, and entered St. Charles Seminary outside Philadelphia as a mature man of thirty-one.[53] By the end of the century, local boys and girls regularly completed the eighth grade, and a growing number pushed on to twelfth and beyond. Business school became an increasingly popular choice, especially after the Du Pont Company's incorporation in 1902, when the number of clerical positions within the firm increased dramatically.[54]

The du Ponts favored office workers who could demonstrate both literacy and loyalty—a preference that had a long history. Between 1802 and 1902, the du Ponts employed thirty-eight full-time clerks; Irishmen made up roughly a third of them and most had been promoted from blue-collar positions. The son of a powder man in the Lower Yard, John Peoples joined this rank in 1835, after a brief stint as a common laborer. Picture him seated at his tall desk, carefully crediting and debiting the appropriate amounts in each workman's account. Then see him dip his pen and witness the signature or mark of every employee, wife, or widow who came in to withdraw cash. In exchange for his skill and tact, Peoples received about $540 a year, but his status in the community stemmed from his "genteel" and "solicitous" nature.[55] During the Famine years, for example, Peoples used a considerable portion of his personal savings to secure the passage of dozens of persons unrelated to him. He eventually moved to Wilmington, where he became an independent powder agent.

Other clerks followed similar career paths. In 1884, Presbyterian James Cheney entered the powder yards as a common laborer. One day soon after, his son recalled,

> He was digging a ditch and the foreman told him he was going away for a while. If one of the du Ponts, who was in charge, came along, he was to tell him where the foreman had gone. My father wrote it down on a slip of paper and when Mr. du Pont came along he gave it to him. Mr. du Pont said, "Did you write that?" He said, "Yes." "Well, you shouldn't be down in there." And so he was taken out.[56]

Cheney eventually became an assistant clerk in the company's equipment storehouse, then head storekeeper. His story parallels that of John A. Dougherty, an Irish-born, Catholic collier's son who started work at the Eagle Packing House in 1895, but continued to practice his penmanship, developed "a fairly good hand," and so "got the job of mailing out [promotional] calendars." During the company's reorganization in 1902, he asked Eugene du Pont for an office position:

> Gene said he'd see what he could do. He walked into T. Coleman du Pont's office, the president. About an hour afterward he came out and said, "T.C. wants to see you." The first thing [Coleman] told me, "First of all, you know, when you're in the office, you keep your mouth shut." I said, "I'm well aware of that, Mr. du Pont. That's been a Brandywine characteristic. Keep your mouth shut [about company business practices]. Don't hear anything, don't see anything, don't talk." He says, "That's it."

John got the job and remained in white-collar work until his retirement.[57]

Educated men like Peoples, Cheney, and Dougherty seem atypical only when compared to the Famine refugees. In fact, Irish literacy rates rose steadily over the course of the nineteenth century. Penal laws prohibiting the education of Catholics in Ireland had been largely repealed by 1800, and in 1831 Parliament passed a National School Act, which provided money for the repair and maintenance of existing structures as well as the construction of new ones. The act had minimal impact at first, especially in western counties like Donegal, where rural folk looked askance at state regulations of any sort. Since, however, management of the schools came under clerical control and varied according to the dominant faith of the local population, Catholics slowly began to attend classes.[58] The devastation of the Famine temporarily derailed this development, but its effects could eventually be seen on both sides of the Atlantic. By 1870, for example, fully 70 percent of Irish immigrants living in the borough of Wilmington claimed the ability to read and 64 percent said they could write.[59]

Perhaps the greatest benefit of rising literacy was the exposure it brought to new ideas, new modes of living, and new visions for the future. Immigrants hoping to improve their social position, for example, could choose from an array of domesticity manuals and etiquette books that claimed to supply effective strategies for success.[60] They could even purchase special Catholic versions, like *The Youth's Director, or, Familiar Instructions for Young People* (1856) and *Sister Mary Francis' Advice to Irish Girls* (1872). Though clearly moral in tone, these works covered a wide range of secular topics, including how to dress, speak, and act. Catholic newspapers and magazines offered similar advice in weekly columns.

Still, for those Brandywine residents interested in refining their behavior, nothing could match the simple act of observing the du Ponts. Male members of the family appeared frequently in the powder yards, where they supervised the workmen and chatted informally with them during breaks. Their wives and daughters, by contrast, engaged the community at large, directing classes at the Sunday School, greeting fellow parishioners at Christ Church and St. Joseph's, tending the injured after explosions, and visiting workers in their homes. As they moved through the landscape, skirts swaying and parasols bobbing, these paragons of nineteenth-century American femininity served as crucial role models; ensconced once again in their own homes, they offered yet another level of instruction. The Irish had no compunction about calling upon their former employers or teachers, and when they did, they encountered the "ideal" parlor in all its glory. Irish maids and cooks developed an even greater familiarity with bourgeois domesticity while they worked at Eleutherian Mills, Louviers, Hagley, Winterthur, Nemours, and Swamp Hall, the du Pont family homes. Victorine, Sophie, Meta, and their female kin frequently commiserated about the problems they had finding decent "help" along the Brandywine. "We have a new abigail, Rebecca McGarvey, a perfect ignoramus of an Irish girl," announced a typical intrafamily note. "She only came day before yesterday & tho' she appears a good soul yet of course requires some directing."[61] Like their brothers, fathers and cousins in powder yards, Irish "abigails" proved quick studies. Indeed, some of these women mastered bourgeois standards of cleanliness, taste, and manners so well that their mistresses hated to see them go.

Irish wage earners learned proper modes of dress and deportment, too. On October 22, 1840, for example, Sophie received a call from two former pupils, Eliza Jane Reed and E. Russell, both of whom she pronounced "very elegantly dressed." They were followed the next day by two more Irish women, S. Walsh, who wore an "unbecoming" wool garment of apple-green, and E. Fleming, who seemed "very pretty & genteel in appearance & manners."[62] Men also favored stylish clothing. In addition to their coarse woolen work pants and cotton shirts, powder workers owned silk handkerchiefs, gold and silver pocket watches, patterned vests, and fine woolen surtouts.[63] These garments differed noticeably from the clothes people wore in Ulster. There, women typically dressed in short gowns of coarse, homespun wool, shapeless cloth bonnets, and heavy, knitted shawls. Those in the western part of Tyrone especially favored bright red cloaks and shawls, a "peculiarity of costume" that gave "a great air of liveliness and brilliance" to the local fairs.[64] Men wore old-fashioned cutaway coats, knee-britches, and heavy brogans. A soft, peaked hat and shillelagh or walking stick completed the ensemble. British officials found versions of this "indifferent" style of dress throughout the region, but a new "passion for dress" had emerged in many parishes by the 1830s. "The dress of the women is much gayer than it used to be," noted one surveyor, "and young women going to the market with lace veils and fine ribbons, with their shoes and stockings tied up in a handkerchief, is still an everyday sight."[65] A few even appeared "well-dressed" and "smart" by comparison to their neighbors, but it was not until the Irish reached the United States that they really had the means to follow fashion.

By abandoning their native dress for stylish, ready-made clothes and accessories, Irish immigrants announced their intention to acculturate. After about 1830, circumstances in the United States made it remarkably easy for working people to outfit themselves like ladies and gentlemen.[66] Because they enjoyed good, steady wages, residents of the powder mill community could afford more and better quality goods than existed in Ireland. In addition to broadcloth, for example, Andrew Fountain's store stocked "Superfine bombazines" and "elegant Jaconets," which nimble female fingers transformed into stylish garments.[67] Manufactured items, like corsets or hats, had to be purchased in nearby Wilmington. Some Irish received fashionable trifles as gifts, however. Victorine liked to give young girls embroidered or lace-edged collars to adorn their Sunday-best dresses. Sophie gave a favorite pupil two capes, and Eleuthera sent Jenny Simpson "an elegant sponge cake . . . three night caps & a pretty needle case" on the occasion of her marriage to powder man Joseph Peoples.[68] But how wage earners obtained these items is ultimately less important than the meaning they attached to them. Consider the surprising behavior of an Irish woman named Margaret and two of her friends one day in February 1857. Margaret's employer, Joanna du Pont, informed her son, Eugene, that "Miss Margaret was married in grand style on Sunday afternoon. She never bid any of us goodbye but when the hour arrived, she & Nancy & Mrs. Belin's girl went & seated themselves on the sofa in the parlor & waited till the two carriages drew up & the gentlemen entered & joined them & then they all went off together."[69] Under ordinary circumstances, no domestic would dare sit in Joanna's parlor, but that particular day was Margaret's wedding day, and having dressed carefully for the occasion, the women confidently appropriated the most refined space in the house.

Manners, literacy, clothing—by modifying their behavior in these specific areas, the du Pont Irish effectively communicated their engagement with the ideology of social and individual betterment that pervaded nineteenth-century America. Prior to the industrial and transportation revolutions of the antebellum era, most people in this country lived in small communities and reckoned rank on the basis of personal, face-to-face knowledge. Despite the anti-aristocratic rhetoric of the revolutionary era, many insisted that social position was predestined and fixed. Protestants in the Reformed (Calvinistic) tradition, who comprised a sizeable proportion of the populace, maintained that an individual's material worth—or lack thereof—reflected his innate godliness, a view based on the widespread belief in a benevolent and fair-minded deity who rewarded the virtuous and punished the amoral. The tides of modern capitalism slowly altered this way of thinking. As the populations of rural communities ebbed, dislocated strangers, increasingly Catholic immigrants from Europe, flowed into newly platted towns and urban neighborhoods. Meanwhile, ordinary people came to possess the goods and behavior once strictly associated with elites. Old methods of fixing social rank did not function effectively in this context, and the presumed relationship between personal morality, material prosperity, and social prestige began to break down. Thus, there emerged in the 1830s a new conception of status wherein Americans evaluated each other in terms of *sentimentality,* that is, the specific combination of intellectual, emotional, and moral qualities that signaled right character.[70] Unlike grace, however, character neither inhered naturally nor persisted immutably. On the contrary, "proper" Americans, expanding upon the evangelical doctrine of perfectionism, exhorted each other to cultivate their true selves to the fullest extent possible. In 1838, William Ellery Channing, the notable Unitarian minister, gave a famous lecture to that effect, saying, "We have a still nobler power, that of acting on, determining, and forming ourselves. We have the power not only of tracing our powers, but of guiding and impelling them; not only of watching our powers, but of controlling them; not only of seeing our faculties grow, but of applying to them means and influences to aid their growth."[71] Channing called his version of character-development "self-culture;" others preferred the term "self-improvement." Either way, adherents created an entirely new array of analytical activities, including physiognomy (interpreting facial features), phrenology (decoding the cranium), and chirography (handwriting analysis).[72] Historians link these and other introspective practices to the formation of a distinct "middle class," but wage earners embraced them, too. Indeed, it does working people a disservice to argue otherwise.[73] Nineteenth-century advocates of self-improvement specifically included working people in their exhortations, and they increasingly acknowledged its relationship to upward mobility. In theory, people of good character would always recognize each other; thus a poor but sincere fellow must inevitably attract the attention of his tender-hearted betters, and with their approbation advance like Horatio Alger's famous bootblack, Ragged Dick. In reality, the continuing dissemination of goods and information made it very difficult to tell who was really sincere and who was not.[74]

The magnitude of the change that resulted can be inferred from the behavior of William Boyd, Jr., the Irish-born son of the du Pont company's first master carpenter. Boyd left the Brandywine in the 1820s and became a merchant in New York City. Urbane in appearance and demeanor as well as occupation, he felt sufficiently confident to call on Sophie du Pont during a brief sojourn home in 1828. She lampooned him as a "dandiful youth," as did her brother Henry who, as a cadet at West Point, received a similar visit from Boyd, minus the pink parasol, in 1832. Fashion sense aside, the real problem was a perceived deficiency of character:

> [Men like him] do deserve credit for rising in the world as they have done, but they spoil the merit of their industry and exertion, by appearing ashamed and wishing to pass off for what they are not. I will excuse the vanity of dressing a la dandy, it is only proof of a weak mind. But to be ashamed of his family and former friends, as William is, shows a bad heart. I can understand very well that William Boyd Junior[,] who has been accustomed to see very excellent society in New York, should find his mother and father a very unpleasant contrast in manners and his father[']s dirty habitation not [a] very agreeable residence—tout cela est naturelle. But a young man of good sense and good feeling would never forget that it was to that unrefined mother he was indebted for the tender care which preserved and cherished him from helpless infancy. What mattered if she spoke English or the Irish brogue,

when she watched untired beside his bed of sickness. And vulgar as his father is[,] if that father had not worked with his own hands to be able to pay for his son[']s education, where would Billy Boyd be now! Certainly not the dashing[,] genteel[,] young merchant of New York. This ingratitude is what renders him contemptible to me.[75]

In contrast to Boyd, Sophie placed Irish individuals like Joe Martin, who had risen high in his own profession, who held his parents in esteem, and whose manner toward the du Ponts, though "easy," remained respectful. Eliza Fleming also merited approval. She, too, had acquired a suitably genteel manner and appearance, yet it was her lack of "airs & assumption" that made the difference between acceptance and condemnation.

Like their employees, the du Ponts shared the widespread American belief that anyone could rise above the station of his birth. They also felt that workmen should never forget from whence they came or who helped them rise. This way of thinking, which emphasized honesty, sincerity, and humility, fit well the new emphasis on character and "self-culture," but it also reflected an older, hierarchical view of the social order, and probably the family's aristocratic heritage, too. In the tradition of noblesse oblige and in recognition of their own method of ascent, the du Ponts vowed to help their workmen advance, yet they could never accept people like Boyd, Fleming, and Martin as their social equals. Spatial proximity reinforced this belief. Having once lived along the Brandywine and having benefited from their benevolence, the Irish would always remain "workers" to the du Ponts, no matter how far they advanced. In truth, the family required a degree of servility as a condition of employment. Most employees willingly complied. Perhaps some felt genuinely subordinate. "The du Ponts were so nice to us," recalled a typical employee. "We did respect them very much; it was like seeing the President of the United States or the King of England when any of them came along. It was always 'Mr. Alfred,' or 'Mr. Frank,' or 'Mr. Henry,' or 'Mr. Eugene,' and 'Miss Louise,' and 'Miss Joanna.'"[76] Perhaps others considered social deference a small price to pay for the assurance of protection and promotion they received in exchange. Within the community, the abiding paternalism of the du Ponts frequently worked to an individual's advantage, as when the Irish received direct assistance in the form of loans and letters of recommendation. Beyond the Brandywine, however, the transformation of American society increasingly challenged the relevance of this arrangement. The growth and corresponding anonymity of American cities, in particular, offered new opportunities for success and sanctioned different avenues for social mobility. Thus, the man known in Delaware as Billy Boyd, the "contemptible" carpenter's son, elsewhere became Mr. William Boyd, the gallant entrepreneur.

The ability that self-culture afforded to refashion personal identity, coupled with advances in other spheres of life, promoted Irish immigrants' association with those higher up the occupational ladder. At the same time, bonds of kinship and a shared sense of ethnoreligious heritage perpetuated ties to those below. A complicated sense of socioeconomic "two-ness" resulted, one akin to yet different from the dual racial consciousness expressed by prominent African Americans at the time.[77] On the one hand, residents of this community clearly knew they were workers. Every day confirmed it. Bells roused them from sleep at precisely 6:00 A.M. The men donned their denim work shirts and overalls, laced up their wood-soled shoes, and labored for wages for ten or more hours before returning home. Their womenfolk contributed to the domestic economy by sewing powder bags, peeling willow, and hosting boarders, but mainly they reared the young, cooked the meals, and kept house. Nearly all of the Irish occupied company-owned houses. Still, their homes were larger than the ones they had occupied in Ireland, and furnished with more and better quality things. Their children could go to school, and both Protestants and Catholics could worship as they saw fit. Then, too, they had money in the company "bank," and the likelihood of property ownership. Perhaps most important, the du Pont Irish now had choices. In Ulster, law and custom limited the ability of Catholic tenant farmers to become their imagined, idealized selves. In northern Delaware, by contrast, circumstances combined to expand individual opportunities for self-determination. Powder mill families regulated the importation of other immigrants into the community, created their own religious and educational institutions, participated in the democratic process, acquired real property, and maintained critical folkways indicative of their ethnic heritage. As wage earners, these people suffered no illusions about their occupational status, yet they never asserted an identity as workers over and beyond the other identities they fashioned. If anything, the sum total of their experiences, as revealed by close attention to their "private" sphere, points to a common *mentalité* that prevented feelings of alienation and powerlessness: the du Pont Irish held a sufficient array of bourgeois values and exercised sufficient control over their own lives to feel a part of the dominant culture. This sense of cultural belonging, in turn, enabled them to partake in a limited but very real way in the cultural aspects of power.[78]

Gleaned from their collective behavior, this sense of cultural belonging belies any attempt to categorize the du Pont Irish as simply or even primarily "working class." The term grossly simplifies the complexity of human consciousness, and it bears little relationship to the way nineteenth-century Americans defined social strata. The social taxonomy of "class," rooted in the Roman word *classis,* had already evolved significantly by the Federal era.

While a majority of people thenceforth acknowledged the existence of multiple "classes," they could not agree on how many there were or what criteria should be used to define them. A simple distinction between producers and nonproducers sufficed for most discourse. True, a few political economists eventually utilized Marx's terms *proletarians* and *bourgeoisie*, but they, like Marx, himself, also believed in the existence of intermediary groups.[79] Nor could nineteenth-century Americans decide whether the fundamental relationship between the various strata was essentially harmonious or antagonistic. In large measure this question reflected their unique history and environment. To many Europeans, especially those in Germany and England, the evidence clearly pointed to a deep-seated, mutual enmity, and the absence of overt, class-based conflict in the United States puzzled them greatly. Even Marx went to his grave doubting that American workers would ever recognize their alienation from the means of production. In 1886, a year of extreme unrest, his close friend and co-author, Friedrich Engels, rejoiced to see at last the emergence of a "true" labor movement in the United States, and he lamented that Marx had not lived to see it; in the 1890s, however, Engels recanted, having concluded that the turmoil of the previous decade had been aberrant.[80]

Various experts have since contended that no unified "working class" ever existed in the United States.[81] Some argue that access to the franchise derailed any efforts to form a cohesive class consciousness. Others insist that the ethnic and racial heterogeneity of America's laboring population precluded unification. More persuasive is the argument that widespread access to property ensured that wage earners never felt alienated. This conclusion has particular resonance because it underscores the relationship between economic security, upward mobility, and self-determination. It is important to note that the property did not have to be agricultural, nor did workers actually have to own it to feel enfranchised; opportunity alone proved sufficient for the purpose. In addition, definitions of "property," like definitions of "class," shifted over time. By 1831, when Alexis de Tocqueville visited the United States, "property" for many Americans included goods and chattels: "Most inhabitants of a democracy have property," he observed. "But the men who have a competency, alike removed from opulence and from penury, attach an enormous value to their possessions. . . . [B]etween poverty and themselves there is nothing but a scanty fortune, upon which they immediately fix their apprehensions and their hopes."[82] Paradoxically, to Tocqueville's mind, this "passion for physical comforts," like Americans' desire for land, served not to drive people apart, but to bring them together. "The love of well-being is now become the predominant taste of the nation; the great current of human passions runs in that channel and sweeps everything along in its course."[83] The aristocratic

Frenchman ultimately deplored this tendency toward conformity, but Americans embraced it and tailored it to suit an axiom of social harmony that persisted well into the 1890s.[84]

Close attention to daily life at the powder mills suggests that a third category of property existed alongside land and things: knowledge. Nineteenth-century Americans generally considered the diffusion of information essential to the well-being of society.[85] In a republic, everyone needed some education because everyone had civic responsibilities of one sort or another. Whereas the establishment of public day schools worked to promote basic literacy, the market revolution expanded *cultural* literacy; that is, it greatly increased the number of people who comprehended and espoused the evolving, modern ideology of social and individual betterment. Sometimes patterns of belief and behavior shifted quite abruptly and publicly, sometimes they changed gradually and inconspicuously.[86] In the case of the du Pont Irish, learning accumulated simultaneously with goods and real estate, and contributed to their sense of self-improvement in much the same way. As such, cultural knowledge functioned as a kind of intellectual property.

Interpreting a group's identity in terms of their behavior, that is, their displayed knowledge, helps explain how residents of the powder mill community came to affiliate with "middle-class" Americans, despite real differences in income and earning potential. As full and active participants of the larger society, all Irish immigrants learned which cultural traits eased admission into and advancement within the social order. At one extreme were those who made a wholesale transition. Significantly, these individuals often announced their intentions by adopting a more "American-sounding" name.[87] At the other extreme were those who resisted any attempt to acculturate. Homesick, disconsolate, and unwilling or unable to adapt to their new country, they lived out their lives as exiles from Erin.[88] Most of the du Pont Irish, like their counterparts in other times and places, fell somewhere between the two poles.

Their efforts to create meaningful lives stand as testaments to human resilience and genius. Despite hostility from native-born Americans, the du Pont Irish practiced chain migration, waked their dead, grew potatoes, drank large quantities of whiskey, displayed crucifixes, named children for saints, and sanctioned assertive female behavior, practices that clearly articulated a distinct "Irish" identity. Yet powder mill families also expressed a strong sense of patriotism. In 1824, for example, du Pont employees erected a floral arch to celebrate the return of Lafayette, whose visit that year commemorated American Independence, and they faithfully celebrated the Fourth of July.[89] The Brandywine Irish also became naturalized citizens. In times of war, they enlisted in the armed services, as Anthony

Dougherty and others did in the 1860s. In peacetime, they participated in the democratic process. They did not join workingmen's parties. Instead, they believed in mutual interests between management and labor, and voted consistently for pro-business, pro-capitalist candidates.[90] In all of these ways, they demonstrated their identity as "Americans."

Acculturation also explains why residents of this community never displayed a single, coherent sense of "class" consciousness. Like John Gibbons, the men earned their bread by the sweat of their brows. While possessed of an identity as "wage workers," they never organized effectively to resist the power of their employers. On the contrary, some identified with their employers so thoroughly that they named children for them. Despite limited opportunities for occupational advancement, du Pont employees avidly pursued social mobility and, under the civilizing influence of women like Catherine Gibbons, came to exhibit many behaviors commonly associated with their white-collar counterparts. Specifically, they transformed their methods of social reproduction, founded churches, sent their children to school, became homeowners, acquired status-bearing goods, and adopted genteel modes of dress and deportment. Not every family shared these goals, to be sure. Nor did every family follow the same path. Some slid backward, while others never advanced at all. Still, a sizeable number achieved sufficient success to consider themselves "bourgeois."

Lace curtains and linen tablecloths symbolized the intersection of these two axes perfectly. Both items were critical to bourgeois domesticity in the nineteenth century. Both were used by native-born Americans as well as immigrants from other countries. But *Irish* lace and *Irish* linen held unique meanings for this population because they represented ties to the old world as well as the new. Indeed, their cultural importance far outweighed whatever market value they might have had, so much so that some people apparently resorted to theft to obtain them.[91] However they may have acquired fine fabrics, powder mill families took pains to clean and maintain them. Heirloom pieces descended from generation to generation, with special emphasis on the relationship between mother and daughter, and new ones appeared in every bride's dowry, where they anticipated the establishment of another branch of the family.[92] Then, too, linen and lace had links to Roman Catholicism. White linen swaddled Irish corpses, and white lace edged baptismal, confirmation, and wedding dresses. In the early days of the century, when most rituals occurred in private homes, itinerant priests like Fr. Kenny celebrated the Mass on a common table covered with a linen tablecloth; after 1840, Brandywine Catholics had their own church, but Irish women retained responsibility for ecclesiastical linens through the altar guild. These and other associations imparted to delicate textiles the power to shape and symbolize complex personal identities.

Fig. 8.3. Studio portrait of Annie Gibbons and her husband, Jacques Seitz, ca. 1890–1900. (Courtesy of Hagley Museum and Library)

    Now imagine Catharine Gibbons spreading out her Last Supper table-cloth on a Sunday afternoon in 1894. She carefully smooths a small wrinkle and pauses to reflect on her past experiences: humble beginnings in a small Irish village, a harrowing journey in a leaky boat, a loving marriage and happy times spent with good friends and neighbors. Sure, she had had her share of sorrow, too. Her dear husband, John, passed away nearly ten years ago. She had also buried her youngest child, a sweet-tempered, hunch-backed little boy named Patrick, who died in 1876. Another son, Willie, lan-guished in prison. Once a skilled carpenter, he had been laid off for drink-ing on the job and soon joined the Never Sweats, the small group of disgruntled employees who burned the company barns in 1890. Her re-maining children, by contrast, were well settled. Annie had married a pow-der man and lived in Free Park, just a few feet away from her childhood home on Blacksmith's Hill (fig. 8.3). Charles, the eldest, was a powder man, too, and dedicated his bachelor life to the du Pont company. Meanwhile, Maggie, a spinster, shared her mother's comfortable house in the Forty Acres neighborhood of Wilmington. Purchased in 1872 with the help of a $500 loan from Sophie du Pont, it became Catharine's primary residence in 1885. In addition to the formal dining room, where she currently stood, it had *two* parlors, each with its own lace curtains and center table, a spacious entrance hall, and three fully furnished bedrooms upstairs. Maggie did not know it yet, but according to the terms of Catharine's will, drawn up earlier that week, she stood to inherit the house and all its contents, including her mother's prized linens and bone china. The others would be provided for as well.

Catharine Gibbons' quiet pride in her achievements was like that of any number of du Pont Irish. Born into a family of tenant farmers in County Donegal, she was, by the time of her death in December 1894, a woman of substantial property and a United States citizen. Ignorant of Roman Catholic doctrine as a child, she wed her husband before the altar at St. Joseph's, watched each of her children receive the sacraments of baptism and confirmation, and committed her earthly remains to the parish cemetery. Her descendants continued to advance the family legacy: Five of Annie's six children pursued some form of higher education, and included a civil engineer, a pharmacist, and an accountant. Annie's granddaughter, Margaret, named for her mother, Margaret Collins, and her Great Aunt Maggie Gibbons, who had died of pneumonia in 1899, earned a doctorate and became a psychologist.[93] These successes were not confined to workers at the du Pont powder mills. Irish immigrants throughout the United States experienced similar patterns of upward mobility, and interpreted their experiences in similar ways. Lace curtains and linen tablecloths appeared throughout Irish America, from Boston to San Francisco, Chicago to New Orleans. With the influx of eastern and southern Europeans in the 1880s, however, native-born Americans of Irish extraction actively sought new ways to commemorate ethnic heritage. Among other things, they launched a Celtic revival that vaunted their ancestors' contributions and magnified similarities between the Irish and Anglo-Saxon "races."[94] In Wilmington, they staged St. Patrick's Day parades, held formal dinners, and organized fraternal associations.[95] Compared to these public assertions of identity, lace curtains and linen tablecloths seem like nothing so much as quaint relics of a bygone era. And that is clearly what they are. In 1984 Dr. Margaret Seitz donated Catharine Gibbons' linens to the Hagley Museum, where they remain, wrapped in their tissue-paper shrouds, fragile reminders of "those who did the work" and whose lives mysteriously transcend the sum of their separate parts.

NOTES

1. Report of Agent EN (11/11/1890), file 1, "Reports of Investigative Agencies," box 4, Papers of Eugene du Pont, acc. 1503. Index to the 1900 Federal Census, roll 12, v. 4, e.d. 54, sheet 7, line 54, Historical Society of Delaware, Wilmington, Del.
2. Michael Kazin, "Struggling with Class Struggle: Marxism and the Search for a Synthesis of U.S. Labor History," *Labor History* 28 (Fall 1987): 505–507.
3. Dennis Clark, *The Irish Relations: Trials of an Immigrant Tradition* (E. Brunswick, N.J.: Association of University Presses, 1982).
4. Hasia R. Diner, *Erin's Daughters in America: Irish Immigrant Women in the Nineteenth Century* (Baltimore: Johns Hopkins University Press, 1983).
5. Nan Enstad, *Ladies of Labor, Girls of Adventure: Working Women, Popular Culture, and Labor Politics at the Turn of the Century* (New York: Columbia University Press, 1999), 6–7.
6. Victoria E. Bonnell and Lynn Hunt, eds., *Beyond the Cultural Turn: New Directions in the Study of Society and Culture* (Berkeley: University of California Press, 1999), introduction.
7. William H. Sewell, Jr., "Toward a Post-Materialist Rhetoric for Labor History," in *Rethinking Labor History: Essays on Discourse and Class Analysis,* ed. Leonard R. Berlanstein (Urbana: University of Illinois Press, 1993), 15–19. No matter how nuanced their interpretations of identity, most "culturalists" end up assigning primacy to one dimension over the others. Nan Enstad, for example, ultimately stresses the way her subjects used mass consumer culture to fashion "their own particular form of radicalism" and craft "dignified identities as workers." See Enstad, 5 and 13.
8. As words, *culture* and *consciousness* have different meanings for different disciplines. I take culture to encompass all the products of a given society's shared knowledge, including language, dress, beliefs, behaviors, buildings, and so forth. This perspective has long characterized other fields, but it mainly reflects the influence of cultural anthropologists, especially ethnographers, who seek to describe the nature of various "primitive" or otherwise exotic peoples. Because their subjects are usually nonliterate, ethnographers rely on oral, visual, and material sources, which they obtain through extensive fieldwork and which they use to extrapolate values, beliefs, and folkways. If, however, the ethnographer is interested in changes that occurred in a given group over time,

or if the group existed long ago, then he may expand his methods of investigation to include the kinds of documentary analysis favored by historians. But historical ethnography, or ethnohistory as it came to be known, is not an easy task. An interdisciplinary endeavor, it "demands multiple competences where conventional academic training normally promotes one." Nor is it common. The field emerged in the 1890s as a way to study Native Americans and, aside from a few notable exceptions, most ethnohistorians today still focus on tribal culture. What I share with these scholars is a desire to reconstruct the distinctive *mentalité* (or consciousness) of their subjects through careful attention to daily life and social behavior (or culture). Social historians would find this endeavor analogous to the "action approach" popularized in the 1980s. My thinking on these matters, however, has been heavily influenced by postmodern social theory, especially the notion that discourses (which are cultural products rooted in shared knowledge) so completely permeate human societies as to make any effort to develop purely scientific, rational, or objective explanations of human reality misguided. In terms of consciousness, these theorists reject any sense of the singularity of the self, substituting instead a multiplicity of subject positions, or standpoints. Sociologist Earl Lewis finds this view "discordant" with his understanding of human beings and human nature, and offers "multipositionality" as a thoughtful corrective.

The essential concepts that contributed to my "ethnohistorical, multipositional" theoretical framework can be found in the following sources: Mary Douglas and Baron Isherwood, *The World of Goods: Towards an Anthropology of Consumption* (New York: Basic Books, 1979); Clifford Geertz, *The Interpretation of Cultures: Selected Essays* (New York: Basic Books, 1973); Peter Berger and Thomas Luckmann, *The Social Construction of Reality: A Treatise in the Sociology of Knowledge* (New York: Anchor Books, 1966); James Axtell, "The Ethnohistory of Early America: A Review Essay," *William and Mary Quarterly* 35, no. 1 (1978): 120; James Henretta, "Social History as Lived and Written," *American Historical Review* 84 (December 1979): 1295, 1321–22; Rhys Isaac, *The Transformation of Virginia, 1740–1790* (Chapel Hill: University of North Carolina Press, 1982), 323–57; Earl Lewis, "Invoking Concepts, Problematizing Identities: The Life of Charles N. Hunter and the Implications for the Study of Gender and Labor," in *Labor History* 34 (Spring–Summer 1993): 292–308.

9. Timothy J. Meagher, *Inventing Irish America: Generation, Class, and Ethnic Identity in a New England City, 1880–1928* (Notre Dame, Ind.: University of Notre Dame Press, 2001).
10. William H. Sewell, Jr., "The Concept(s) of Culture," in Bonnell and Hunt, 49.
11. Kerby A. Miller, *Emigrants and Exiles: Ireland and the Irish Exodus to North America* (New York: Oxford University Press, 1985), 193, 351–52; Roger Daniels, *Coming to America: A History of Immigration and Ethnicity in American Life* (New York: Harper Perennial, 1990), 126–45.
12. See, for example, Kerby A. Miller, "Class, Culture, and Immigrant Group Identity in the United States: The Case of Irish-American Ethnicity," in *Immigration Reconsidered: History, Sociology, and Politics* (New York: Oxford, University Press, 1990), 110.

13. Kazin, "Struggling with Class Struggle," 497–514; and Ava Baron, "Gender and Labor History: Learning from the Past, Looking to the Future," in *Work Engendered: Toward a New History of American Labor,* ed. Ava Baron (Ithaca: Cornell University Press, 1991), 1–37.

14. See, for example, Alice Kessler-Harris, "Treating the Male as Other: Redefining the Parameters of Labor History," *Labor History* 34, nos. 2–3 (Spring–Summer 1993): 193, 195.

15. Kessler-Harris does not indicate what a "household-centered" study of working people would look like, but the vast body of research undertaken by material culture scholars affords many models. Representative works on the nineteenth century include: Katherine Kish Sklar, *Catherine Beecher: A Study in American Domesticity* (New York: W. W. Norton, 1976); Mary Ryan, *The Cradle of the Middle Class: The Family in Oneida County, New York, 1780–1865* (New York: Cambridge University Press, 1981); Clifford Clark, *The American Family Home, 1800–1860* (Chapel Hill: University of North Carolina Press, 1986); Colleen McDannell, *The Christian Home in Victorian America, 1840–1900* (Bloomington: Indiana University Press, 1986); Katherine Grier, *Culture and Comfort: People, Parlors, and Upholstery, 1850–1930* (Boston: The Margaret Woodbury Strong Museum, 1988); Sally McMurry, *Families and Farmhouses in Nineteenth-Century America: Vernacular Design and Social Change* (New York: Oxford University Press, 1988); Stuart Blumin, *The Emergence of the Middle Class: Social Experience in the American City, 1760–1900* (New York: Cambridge University Press, 1989); Elizabeth Garrity, *At Home: The American Family, 1750–1870* (New York: Harry N. Abrams, 1990); and Richard Bushman, *The Refinement of America: Persons, Houses, Cities* (New York: Vintage Books, 1992).

16. Quoted in Glenn Porter, *The Workers' World at Hagley,* exhibition catalog (Greenville, Del.: Eleutherian Mills–Hagley Foundation, 1981), 8.

17. Believing that "class is a relationship, and not a thing," British historian E. P. Thompson urged historians of labor to observe and trace its development over a long period of time. Although my focus is the construction of cultural identity, not class, I agree with Thompson's basic dictum that patterns of human interaction can only be understood "as they work themselves out over a considerable historical period." See E. P. Thompson, *The Making of the English Working Class* (New York: Pantheon Books, 1963), 11.

18. Miller, *Emigrants and Exiles,* 49.

19. For this study, radical is defined as the opposite of conservative, where conservative defines those interested in upholding the capitalist wage system. The triumph of liberalism in the nineteenth century resulted in a reformulation of these terms. Previously, "radical" applied to those whose beliefs and behavior signaled an opposition to a social order based on aristocracy, monarchy, deference, and classical republicanism. Over time, "radical" came to define those opposed to capitalism and its attendant modes of social and political organization. See Isaac Kramnick, *Republicanism and Bourgeois Radicalism: Political Ideology in Late-Eighteenth-Century England and America* (Ithaca: Cornell University Press, 1990).

20. John Charles Rumm, "Mutual Interests: Managers and Workers at the Du Pont Company, 1802–1915," vol. 1 (Ph.D. diss., University of Delaware, 1989), 113–15.

21. Ibid., 174–80.

22. My conclusions about the du Pont family's system of labor relations have been influenced by Philip Scranton's concept of an "accumulation matrix," or "the broad range of social and economic factors that together constitute the total situation for production and profit faced by entrepreneurs." See Philip Scranton, "Varieties of Paternalism: Industrial Structure and the Social Relations of Production in American Textiles," *American Quarterly* 36, no. 2 (Summer 1984), 235–57.

23. Catharine Davison, Seymour, Indiana, to Mrs. Smith (1/30/1873), file 21, box 6, acc. 389.

24. Recent representative works include the following: David Emmons, *The Butte Irish: Class and Ethnicity in an American Mining Town, 1875–1925* (Chicago: University of Illinois Press, 1990); Carole Turbin, *Working Women of Collar City: Gender, Class and Community in Troy, NY 1864–1886* (Urbana: University of Illinois Press, 1992); Peter Way, *Common Labor: Workers and the Digging of North American Canals, 1780–1860* (New York, 1993; reprint, Baltimore: Johns Hopkins University Press, 1997); Kevin Kenny, *Making Sense of the Molly Maguires* (New York: Oxford University Press, 1998).

25. For examples see: Stephen Norwood, *Labor's Flaming Youth: Telephone Operators and Worker Militancy* (Urbana: University of Illinois Press, 1990); Lizabeth Cohen, *Making a New Deal: Industrial Workers in Chicago* (New York: Cambridge University Press, 1990); and Lawrence Glickman, *A Living Wage: American Workers and the Making of Consumer Society* (Ithaca: Cornell University Press, 1997). One exception to this pattern is Andrew R. Heinze, *Adapting to Abundance: Jewish Immigrants, Mass Consumption, and the Search for an American Identity* (New York: Columbia University Press, 1990). Heinze, who approaches consumption from an anthropological perspective, argues that Jewish immigrants ultimately created a hybrid ethnic identity that arose from the fusion of Jewish habits and urban American ways. He does not directly address the trickier issue of class identity, although he explores the link between consumption and status.

26. This is not a revelation. Daniel Walker Howe contends that "It is unduly patronizing to assume that working-class people who professed the values of respectability cannot really have meant to do so, or must have been victims of false consciousness. Surely such values as independence, self-discipline, and self-improvement could be taken seriously by working men and women." See his book, *Making the American Self: From Jonathan Edwards to Abraham Lincoln* (Cambridge: Harvard University Press, 1997), 125. Anne Boylan offered the same conclusion several years earlier. "Although some working-class Americans may have preferred the local pub to the local church, the lessons of the Sunday school were hardly alien to people whose religious traditions had stressed order and self-discipline long before factories appeared on the landscape." See Boylan, *Sunday School: The Formation of an American Institution* (New Haven: Yale University Press, 1988), 38.

27. This point is made in John Bodnar, *The Transplanted* (Bloomington: Indiana University Press, 1985), 115.
28. On the origins of paternalism see Eugene D. Genovese, *Roll, Jordan, Roll: The World the Slaves Made* (New York: Vintage Books, 1972), 4–7; and Gerald Zahavi, *Workers, Managers, and Welfare Capitalism: The Shoeworkers and Tanners of Endicott Johnson, 1890–1950* (Urbana: University of Illinois Press, 1988), x and 1–2.
29. Daniel J. Walkowitz, *Worker City, Company Town: Iron and Cotton Worker Protest in Troy and Cohoes, New York, 1855–84* (Urbana: University of Illinois Press, 1978), 253. Walkowitz concludes that the pervasiveness of this ideology reinforced the subjective perception of Irish iron workers that they had achieved "the good life."
30. Walter Nugent, "Toqueville, Marx, and American Class Structure," *Social Science History* 12, no. 4 (Winter 1988): 325–44 passim.
31. Jerrold Seigel, "Problematizing the Self," in Bonnell and Hunt, 301–302.
32. Ibid., 284–85 and 294–95.
33. Brian Mitchell, *The Paddy Camps: The Irish of Lowell, 1821–1861* (Urbana: University of Illinois Press, 1988), 155.
34. Howe, 109.
35. Following Antonio Gramsci (the so-called "Marxist you can take home to Mother"), many social historians contend that elites' economic power endows *them* with a "preponderant influence or authority" (hegemony) over a society's culture. I respectfully disagree. Because it derives not from shared economic interests, but shared knowledge, culture exists independently of any single group of people. Yet certain *values, beliefs, and behaviors* can be said to have a dominant influence or hegemony in a given society. Thus, Jean and John Comaroff define hegemonic culture as "that order of signs and practices, relations and distinctions, images and epistomologies—situated in a cultural field—that come to be taken for granted as the natural and received shape of the world and everything that inhabits it." See their book, *Of Revelation and Revolution: Christianity, Colonialism, and Consciousness in South Africa* (Chicago: University of Chicago Press, 1999). On Gramscian theories of cultural hegemony see T. J. Jackson Lears, "The Concept of Cultural Hegemony: Problems and Possibilities," *American Historical Review* 90, no. 3 (June 1985): 567–93. On Gramscian theories as applied to the Irish in America, see Miller, "Class, Culture, and Immigrant Group Identity," 98–99.
36. Seigel, 298.

CHAPTER 1. MUTUAL INTERESTS (PP. 13–40)

1. Philip Dougherty, interview, 1955, oral history files (hereafter cited by interviewee's name and date), Hagley Museum and Library (HML). In keeping with conventions established by the Hagley Museum and Library, I use "du Pont" when referring to family members or the pre-1902 company and "Du Pont" to denote the post-1902 corporation.

2. John Charles Rumm, "Mutual Interests: Managers and Workers at the Du Pont Company, 1802–1915," vol. 1 (Ph.D. diss., University of Delaware, 1989), vii–viii.

3. "Top Fifty Employers," *The (Wilmington, Del.) Sunday News Journal,* March 10, 1996, sec. BZ, p. 25.

4. Philip Scranton, "Varieties of Paternalism: Industrial Structures and the Social Relations of Production in American Textiles," *American Quarterly* 36, no. 2 (Summer 1984): 239–42.

5. Anthony F. C. Wallace, *Rockdale* (New York: Alfred Knopf, Inc., 1978), 21.

6. Scranton, 237.

7. Kerby A. Miller, *Emigrants and Exiles: Ireland and the Irish Exodus to North America* (New York: Oxford University Press, 1985), 42–43.

8. Tamara Hareven and Randolph Lagenbach, *Amoskeag: Life and Work in an American Factory-City* (New York: Pantheon, 1978), and Jacquelyn Dowd Hall, James Leloudis, et al., *Like a Family: The Making of a Southern Cotton Mill World* (New York: W. W. Norton, 1987).

9. The party also included Sophie du Pont's brother, Charles Dalmas, Pierre Samuel's stepdaughter, Madame Bureaux de Pusy, and her son, Maurice. Maureen O'Brien Quimby, *Eleutherian Mills* (Greenville: The Hagley Museum, 1973), 9.

10. The Physiocrats believed in a system of political and economic doctrines based on the supremacy of nature, with land and agriculture as the prime sources of wealth and prosperity. Ibid.

11. Leonard Mosley, *Blood Relations: The Rise and Fall of the Du Ponts of Delaware* (New York: Atheneum, 1980), 21–22. Mosley's book contains many accepted anecdotes about the family and the company, but should be consulted with caution. More factual biographical and historical information is included throughout John Beverly Riggs, *A Guide to the Manuscripts in the Eleutherian Mills Historical Library: Accessions through the Year 1965* (Greenville, Del.: Eleutherian Mills Historical Library, 1970). The early history of the family and company is told in the *Life of Eleuthère Irénée du Pont from Contemporary Correspondence,* translated from the French by Bessie Gardner du Pont (Newark, Del.: University of Delaware Press, 1925). Among recent published works see Joseph Frazier Wall, *Alfred I. du Pont: The Man and His Family* (New York: Oxford University Press, 1990).

12. Riggs, 576; Mosley, 22.

13. J. Thomas Sharf, *History of Delaware* (Philadelphia: L. J. Richards and Co., 1888), 760–61.

14. On Quakers see Carol Hoffecker, *Wilmington, Delaware: Portrait of an Industrial City* (Charlottesville: University Press of Virginia for the Eleutherian Mills–Hagley Foundation, 1974), 8.

15. Pierre Samuel du Pont had returned to France in the spring of 1802. While there, he provided unofficial counsel to Thomas Jefferson, then president, and to the American minister in Paris, Chancellor Robert Livingston. Surviving correspondence indicates that du Pont played a significant role in the acquisition of the Louisiana Territory from France. In gratitude for du Pont's part in

securing the sale, Jefferson forwarded a July 1803 letter from E. I. du Pont de Nemours and Company to Secretary of War Henry Dearborn along with his personal recommendation. By the following year, when the powder mills had officially opened for business, Dearborn placed an order for 22,000 pounds of powder. See Riggs, 576, and Wall, 45–51.

16. Mosley, 26.
17. Victor du Pont settled in Delaware in 1810. Frustrated in his attempts to establish a diplomatic career for himself in America, Victor tried his hand at several professions before textile manufacturing. With Irénée's support, he entered into a partnership with Peter Bauduy, an émigré from San Domingo, and began producing fine, merino wool cloth at Louviers in 1811. The mill initially proved successful, and in 1813 he joined Raphael Duplanty and Archibald McCall, who were affiliated with the powder company, and began manufacturing cotton. Although Irénée was a partner in both firms, he left the daily operations to others. Riggs, 75–81.
18. E. I. du Pont to Victor du Pont (April 1803), box 2, series A, group 4, WMSS.
19. Fabrique de poudre, item 19, file 148, box 9, acc. 146.
20. Rumm, 70–71.
21. Donald Adams, "The Standard of Living during American Industrialization: Evidence from the Brandywine Region, 1800–1860," *Journal of Economic History* 42 (1982): 907–908 and 911; Linda Daur, "Domestic Servants at Eleutherian Mills, 1821–1842," unpublished research paper (1979), HML; and Peter Way, *Common Labor: Workers and the Digging of North American Canals* (1993; reprinted, Baltimore: John Hopkins, 1997), 106 and 117. Way explains that Irish canallers' wages fluctuated wildly in the 1820s–30s, but they generally received $2–3 per week. While they aspired to an "ideal" of twenty-eight working days, they typically only labored between fourteen and twenty-one.
22. Information on William Green was compiled from the following sources: petit ledgers for 1818, 1822–24, 1845–46, and 1847, acc. 500; payroll ledger, vol. 2, Nov. 1818–Jan. 1819, acc. 320; "List of Hands in 1820," file 48, acc. 146; boarding book, no. 1699, acc. 500; William Green, probate inventory, April 26, 1847, New Castle County probate records. At the beginning of 1847, Green had $1,343.76 on account with the company. He made several large withdrawls in January, and his ending balance at his death was $703.23. The Irish immigrants employed in manufacturing industries in the Brandywine region generally had a higher standard of living than canal workers or farmhands. Among other things, their wives and children could more readily find remunerative work. In the 1830s, for example, women domestics in the powder mill community earned $1–3.50 per week, while female operatives at Charles I. du Pont's cotton mill earned $2–3. See Daur, 20, and Adams, 911.
23. In "Reflections," du Pont anticipated both Adam Smith and Henry George. His two key themes were that all wealth derived from the land and that a single tax on land would provide ample revenue for the French state. He also outlined his belief that the only legitimate function of the state was to provide security for property through its police force, army, and courts. Otherwise, he felt, the state should not interfere in the lives of its citizens, who must be free

to produce and to trade unhampered by state-supported monopolies, tariffs, or regulations. Wall, 11–14.

24. Ibid., 30.

25. Quoted in Rumm, 68.

26. Ibid., 69.

27. Nuala McGann Drescher, "The Irish in Industrial Wilmington, 1800–1845" (M.A. thesis, University of Delaware, 1960), 67–68.

28. Riggs, 578.

29. Patrick Dougherty, affidavit dated June 13, 1815, New Castle County probate records.

30. Rumm, 100.

31. Ibid., 40–41, Wall, 61–62.

32. Riggs, 75–81.

33. Wall, 63.

34. Alfred I. du Pont to Andrew C. Craig (3/3/1847), du Pont Letter Book, 1846–1847, acc. 500.

35. The list is found in file 76, box 6, acc. 146. It is undated, but all of the men were killed in the explosions of 1815 and 1818.

36. McPheely, Glasgow, to E. I. du Pont & Co. (12/2/1836), item W4-1781, box 12, series D, Group 4, WMSS. John Murrell, Limavady, Ireland, to E. I. du Pont & Co. (5/25/1843), item W4-1867. Act of the Delaware General Assembly re: Henry Kyle Estate (cert. Copy) (1/31/1845), item W4-4988, box 18, series D, group 4, WMSS. Account of Henry Kyle's estate (2/15/1845), item W4-2306, box 15, series D, group 4, WMSS.

37. Wall, 71.

38. Ibid., 79.

39. Rumm, 9.

40. Population figures for the community are taken from the Seventh (1850) U.S. Census, microfilm, Morris Library, University of Delaware. The powder mill community did not constitute a separate enumeration district, so I extracted the powder mill households from the schedules for Brandywine and Christiana hundreds by modifying the work of Anthony Wallace and Glenn Uminowicz, a student who applied Wallace's methods to the powder mill community. For a description of this methodology, see Wallace, 249, n.1, and Glenn Uminowicz, "The Worker and His Community along the Brandywine: Methodology and Some Preliminary Observations," unpublished paper (1979) HML, 8–13. Like Uminowicz, I extracted the homes of the du Ponts and their employees, but my database also includes many other households, including those of former employees, independent craftsmen, textile workers, farmers, merchants, tavern keepers, innkeepers, and anyone else with an established tie to the powder mill community. Thus, my final tally for 1850 was 2,064 individuals living in 365 households.

41. Harold Hancock, "The Industrial Worker along the Brandywine," chap. 8, unpublished research report, HML (1957), 1–10.

42. Wall, 79–80.

43. Hancock, 10–28.

44. Stephen Thernstrom, *Progress and Poverty: Social Mobility in a Nineteenth-Century Industrial City* (1964; reprinted New York: Atheneum, 1975), 43.
45. Stragglers' Time Book, item 1700, acc. 500.
46. Sophie du Pont's diaries include occasional references to drinking among the Irish workers and the problems it caused at home and at work. See, for example, her entries for August 26, 1831, May 30, 1832, and May 27, 1832, series F, group 9, WMSS.
47. [Francis Gurney du Pont et al.], "Record of Explosions, 1815–1902," series C, group 5, LMSS; John Clark to "Dear Sir" (3/17/1857), photocopy, easy reference file, "Du Pont Company Employees, 19th Century," HML. The man who purportedly caused the explosion of 1852, Christopher Cowan, was a long-time employee. He started out as a common laborer. In 1850, he was thirty-eight years old and lived in the Free Park cluster of houses above the Upper Hagley Yard. According to Francis G. du Pont, who compiled the list of explosions, two Irishmen, John Devine and James McClafferty, died as a result of Cowan's actions. The company discharged Cowan on the spot, and he hanged himself two years later. John Clark, the man who offered his skills and knowledge to a du Pont competitor, worked in the Upper Hagley Yard and would likely have known Cowan. He commenced work in 1839 and went to the powder in May 1847. His letter was intercepted by persons unknown and forwarded to the du Ponts, who fired him as well.
48. The Receiving Books of the Brandywine Manufacturers' Sunday School, acc. 389, indicate when and why workmen were discharged and when and why workers moved away from the community. They also provide statistics on religious affiliation and attendance rates. Between 1816 and 1835, there were 570 children enrolled in the school. Of these, 226 or 40 percent moved away, usually with their parents. From 1835 to 1850 there were 632 children of whom 32 percent left the community. Additional data on labor turnover rates and the movement of temporary workers into and out of the powder yards are discussed in chapter 8.
49. Wall, 82–84.
50. Figures reflect wages from January to June 1863. Wage book, 1863–1865, acc. 500.
51. Wall, 98–99.
52. Hancock, chap. 9. There were a total of eight explosions in the powder yards between 1861 and 1865.
53. Riggs, 581–83; Wall, 127.
54. Rumm, 111–12, 117–18.
55. Ibid., 166.
56. Hancock, chap. 10, 61–62.
57. Rumm, 152. Various sources suggest that the close interaction between members of the du Pont family and workmen in the powder yards contributed to the feelings of loyalty, familiarity, and affection that tied management and labor. As domestics, cooks, and nannies, women also established close relationships with the du Ponts. See, for example, Rumm, 104–105; Wall, 80–81; and Glenn Pryor, "Workers' Lives at the Du Pont Powder Mills, 1877–1912" (B.A. thesis, University of Delaware, 1977), 7–8.

58. Wall, 137.
59. Ibid., 146.
60. Ibid., 148–49.
61. The events surrounding the barn-burnings are described in Rumm, 173–90, and Pryor, 50–55. Frank du Pont hired Pinkerton detectives to infiltrate the community. One of their agents, a woman who posed as a dressmaker, sent regular reports to the company. These are found in box 4, acc. 1503.
62. Pierre Gentieu, "Reminiscences" (n.d.), 13, acc. 207.
63. Hoffecker, 19.
64. James F. Toy, interview, 1964; Richard F. Rowe, interview, 1968; and Eleanor Kane, interview, 1984.
65. Quoted in Glenn Porter, *The Workers' World at Hagley,* exhibition catalog (Greenville, Del.: Eleutherian Mills–Hagley Foundation, 1981), 56.
66. Wall, 165–66.
67. Rumm, 196–97.
68. Centennial Resolution of the Du Pont Company, 1902, no. 946, part 2, series II, acc. 500.
69. Wage accounts, no. 1700, acc. 500; petit ledgers, 1812–1846, acc. 500; F. L. Mathewson, interview, 1968.
70. Rumm, 211–15.
71. Ibid., 233–35.
72. John Peoples, interview, 1952. Peoples was born in 1871 in Squirrel Run.
73. John A. Dougherty, interview, 1956.
74. A full account of the 1906 strike is found in Rumm, 265–77.
75. Porter, 15.

CHAPTER 2. THE TIES THAT BIND (PP. 41–60)

1. Elizabeth Beacom, interview, 167.
2. Tamara Hareven, *Family Time and Industrial Time: The Relationship between the Family and Work in a New England Industrial Community* (New York: Cambridge University Press, 1982); Brian C. Mitchell, *The Paddy Camps: The Irish of Lowell, 1821–1861* (Urbana: University of Illinois Press, 1988); Stanley Nadel, *Little Germany: Ethnicity, Religion, and Class in New York City, 1845–80* (Urbana: University of Chicago Press, 1990); Carole Turbin, *Working Women of Collar City: Gender, Class, and Community in Troy, New York, 1864–86* (Urbana: University of Illinois Press, 1992).
3. Roger Daniels, *Coming to America: A History of Immigration and Ethnicity in American Life* (New York: Harper Perennial, 1990), 129.
4. Kerby A. Miller, *Emigrants and Exiles: Ireland and the Irish Exodus to North America* (New York: Oxford Univeristy Press, 1985), 4.
5. Ibid., 327.
6. Daniel J. Walkowitz, *Worker City, Company Town: Iron and Cotton-Worker Protest in Troy and Cohoes, New York, 1855–84* (Urbana: University of Illinois Press, 1978), 253.

7. Miller, *Emigrants and Exiles*, 201.

8. Kerby A. Miller, "Class, Culture and Immigrant Group Identity," in *Immigration Reconsidered: History, Sociology, and Politics*, ed. Virginia Yans-McLaughlin (New York: Oxford University Press, 1990), 107.

9. Charles Tilly, "Transplanted Networks," in Yans-McLaughlin, 93.

10. Cited in Nuala McGann Drescher, "The Irish in Industrial Wilmington, 1800–1845: A History of the Life of Irish Emigrants to the Wilmington Area in the Pre-Famine Years" (M.A. thesis, University of Delaware, 1960), 32.

11. William Warner to E. I. du Pont, Co. (10/19/1809), box 6, series A, group 5, LMSS.

12. Wastebook, 1800–1813, series B, part II, acc. 500.

13. When individuals in Ireland could not come out, they usually sent others in their place but often failed to inform the agent in Philadelphia of the change. This transferring of tickets created problems for the agents in Ireland, the agents in America, the subscribers, and the du Ponts, who tried vainly to restrict their use. On May 5, 1846, Robert Taylor wrote to the company, "I enclose herein my order No. 322 for the passage of Ann McCallister *or bearer* from Liverpool—I cannot arrange it that no *other* can get a passage on this order—My correspondents could not undertake to identify the persons who present the orders—That part of the matter must be by the person sending it—If there be any doubt of its misapplication better not send it—The best way is if the person declines, just to return the order to the person who sent it—and then I make no charge to you, and if the price has been paid, I return the money when the order is returned to me—but if it be used, no matter for or by whom, the passage money is to be paid." Robert Taylor to Messrs. E. I. du Pont de Nemours & Co. (5/5/1846), file 3, box 385, acc. 500.

14. Some of the largest database files compiled for this project correlate information gathered from the immigration agents' letters. These immigration files cover the period from December 1828 to June 1853 and record the passage of 1,258 individuals. Because there are some gaps in the agents' correspondence, I cross-linked the files with du Pont company wage ledgers, which are complete for the entire century. Several of the wage ledgers also contain detailed lists of persons sent for, usually with the subscriber's name and the page number of his account noted.

15. Robert Scally, "Liverpool Ships and Irish Emigrants in the Age of Sail," *Journal of Social History* (Fall 1983), 5 and 12.

16. Ibid, 22.

17. A. J. Catherwood correspondence, n.d., box 56, acc. 500.

18. Ibid., 4/6/1848 and 1/26/1850.

19. Ibid., 12/9/1830.

20. Ibid., 3/25/1832.

21. "I have always charged full price for any that are twelve years and upwards—it is only those *under* twelve upon which allowance of half-price is made." Robert Taylor to Messrs. E. I. du Pont & Co. (11/28/1846), file 4, box, 386, acc. 500.

22. Twelve-year-olds were considered adults in 1827, when John Welsh charged $33 for an adult passage. John Welsh to E. I. du Pont (7/7/1827), box 416, acc.

500. The adult fare dropped to $23 in 1839 and rose back up to $24 in 1843. See "Miscellaneous Bills" files, box 497, acc. 500. By 1847, Robert Taylor charged $24, leading du Pont to engage the services of A. J. Craig, Taylor's former partner, who charged only $22. Robert Taylor to E. I. du Pont & Co. (3/31/1847), box 386, acc. 500, and A. J. Craig to J. Peoples (1/6/1847 and 1/9/1847), box 70, acc. 500. Additional information on fares can be found in the petit ledgers, where deductions were regularly noted.

23. A. J. Catherwood, Philadelphia, to Messrs. E. I. du Pont & Co. (5/30/1851), box 56, acc. 500.

24. Ibid., 10/28/1847.

25. Ibid., 1/26/1850 and 1/29/1850.

26. For example, Rev. Patrick Kenny noted on February 26, 1812, that, "All the letters that I brought from Coffee Run people were conveyed on yesterday 25 by a skin for Galway." Acc. 323.

27. Miller, *Emigrants and Exiles*, 271–74.

28. Robert Taylor, Philadelphia, to Mssrs. E. I. du Pont de Nemours & Co. (11/25/1846).

29. Petit ledger, 1847.

30. Margaretta Lammott du Pont to E. I. du Pont, II (5/21/?), Mrs. A. V. du Pont correspondence, 1843–47, box 48, acc. 384.

31. The number of immigrants living and working in the city did not rise again until the expansion of the leather tanning industry in the 1880s. See Drescher, 20–24, and Yda Schreuder, "Wilmington's Immigrant Settlement, 1880–1920," *Delaware History* 23 (1988–89): 143.

32. The majority of immigrants to Delaware in the nineteenth century were from Ireland. According to the U.S. Census of 1880, 3,664 of the city's 5,674 foreign-born were Irish (64 percent), compared to 768 (14 percent) of German birth, and 903 (16 percent) of British birth. See Schreuder, 140–45.

33. Miller, *Emigrants and Exiles*, 380–82.

34. Faith Betty Lattomus and Madaline Betty Walls, interview (6/12/1969). Their mother was Flemming's daughter.

35. Edward B. Cheney, interview, 1958.

36. John Maguire, *The Irish in America* (New York: D. & J. Sadlier & Co., 1868), 313–15. Whatever their motive, the Irish in America remitted £1.5 million to Ireland between 1850 and 1855. See Miller, *Emigrants and Exiles*, 293.

37. The advertisement for Grimshaw and McCabe appears in the December 17, 1866, issue of *The Delaware Republican*. They sold tickets on the Cunard Steam Weekly Line for Ireland and England, Hamburg, etc. and were also willing to send money to Ireland or England.

38. A. J. Catherwood to E. I. du Pont & Co. (5/11/1848 and 5/21/1850), box 56, acc. 500.

39. Robert Taylor to Messrs. du Pont (10/22/1842), Box 385, acc. 500.

40. This point is made in Anthony F. C. Wallace, *St. Clair: A Nineteenth-Century Coal Town's Experience with a Disaster-Prone Industry* (New York: Knopf, 1987), 150.

41. These included six entire families and four individuals, all probably relatives of Conley's employees. Data on Conley are taken from A. J. Catherwood's

correspondence, box 56, acc. 500; Andrew C. Craig's correspondence, box 70, acc. 500; and various petit ledgers. His brother and business partner, Neil Conley, sponsored three people during the same period. Conley is sometimes spelled Connelly.

42. Kevin Kenny, *Making Sense of the Mollie Maguires* (New York: Oxford, 1998), 25; and David M. Emmons, *The Butte Irish: Class and Ethnicity in an American Mining Town, 1875–1925* (Urbana: University of Illinois Press, 1989), 14–15.

43. James Toy, interview, 1964; Eleanor Kane, interview, 1984; Elizabeth Beacom, interview, 1967; Faith Betty Lattomus and Madaline Betty Walls, interview, 1969; John Peoples, interview, 1952.

44. Robert Taylor to E. I. du Pont (12/3/1832), file 1-A, box 385, acc. 500. Francis Maguire ordered her passage. See petit ledger, 1829–32, acc. 500.

45. Loose memo, Robert Taylor correspondence, file 1-A, box 385, acc. 500, and petit ledger 1834–37, p. 378.

46. See Anne Morris Mertz, "Coffee Run Cemetery," *Delaware Geneological Society Journal* 4 (April 1988): 58–62; and "Inventory of the Tombstone Inscriptions in St. Joseph's Churchyard, Henry Clay, Del.," prepared by the Historic Records Survey, Division of Women's and Professional Projects, WPA (Wilmington, Del.: typescript copy, 1939), RG 37, St. Joseph on the Brandywine, Catholic Diocese of Wilmington Archives, Greenville, Del.

47. Pamphlet, *B. R. G. Mills, County Cork* (Cork County Council, 1988); Letter from Marjorie G. McNinch, archivist, HML, to Paula Cogan, B.R.G. Mills, July 30, 1993, easy reference file, "Du Pont Company Employees, 19th Century," HML.

48. Miller, *Emigrants and Exiles,* 54 and 92.

49. Ibid., 39–40.

50. Ibid., 39–40, 112–13, 171–73, 196–230.

51. Kenny, 35.

52. Samuel Lewis, *Topographical Dictionary of Ireland* (London: S. Lewis & Co., 1877), 158.

53. Charles Dougherty was born around 1824 in the town of "Ballygorman, Parish of Cloncaugh [*sic*], County Donegal." Ballygorman was four miles north of Malin, on the extreme promontory of the peninsula. The other five people were born in Cloncha in the early nineteenth century. Further research will likely uncover additional families with ties to this area. Dennis McLaughlin, for example, died in 1872 at the age of sixty. His grave states "Ballykillin, Parish of Clencha [*sic*], County Donegal." Dennis brought out his brother, Hugh, by March 3, 1847. The next year, Hugh McLaughlin brought out his wife, Bridget, and two children, Dennis (2) and Catherine (infant). James Deery may also have hailed from Cloncha. He sent passage orders there for Nelly Callaghan, Michael Deery (8), and Mary Deery (5) in 1848.

54. Lewis, 220 and 381.

55. Angela Day and Patrick McWilliams, eds., *Parishes of County Tyrone, 1 (1821, 1823, 1831–36),* vol. 5, *Ordnance Survey Memoirs of Ireland* (Belfast: The Institute of Irish Studies, 1990), 2–14.

56. Miller, *Emigrants and Exiles,* 201.

57. Scally, 12.
58. Miller, *Emigrants and Exiles*, 38–40.

CHAPTER 3. A DISTINCTIVE FAITH (PP. 61–90)

1. Rev. Patrick Kenny, diary (7/4/1817), acc. 423. Kenny was the first Catholic priest to minister among the powder workers.
2. John Maguire, *The Irish in America* (New York: D. & J. Sadlier & Co., 1868), vii and 346.
3. Dale Knobel, *Paddy and the Republic: Ethnicity and Nationality in Antebellum America* (Middletown, Conn.: Weslyan University Press, 1986), 40–65 and 103.
4. For a review of relevant literature concerning Catholicism in nineteenth-century Ireland, see Brian Clarke, "The Parish and the Hearth: Women's Confraternities and the Devotional Revolution among the Irish Catholics of Toronto, 1850–85," in *Creed and Culture: The Place of English Speaking Catholics in Canadian Society, 1750–1930* (Montreal: McGill-Queen's University Press, 1993), 186. On the state of Catholicism in nineteenth-century America, see Sydney E. Ahlstrom, *A Religious History of the American People* (New Haven: Yale University Press, 1972).
5. Clifford Geertz, "Religion as a Cultural System," in *The Interpretation of Cultures: Selected Essays* (New York: Basic Books, 1973), 89–90.
6. On the social construction of knowledge in general, see Peter Berger and Thomas Luckmann, *The Social Construction of Reality: A Treatise in the Sociology of Knowledge* (New York: Anchor Books, 1966), 14–33, passim. Among historians, Paul E. Johnson recognized that religious beliefs are socially constructed, yet they take on an autonomous life of their own. Drawing on the works of Emile Durkeim, his book *A Shopkeeper's Millennium: Society and Revivals in Rochester, New York, 1815–1837* (New York: Hill and Wang, 1978) was an effort to explore the dialectical relationship between religion and behavior in a single community.
7. In anthropological terms, a symbol refers broadly to "any object, act, event, quality, or relation which serves as a vehicle for a conception," where a conception is the symbol's meaning or explanation. Geertz, "Religion," 91.
8. See, for example, the interpretations of Irish piety in: Jay Dolan, *The Immigrant Church: New York City's Irish and German Catholics, 1815–1865* (Baltimore: Johns Hopkins University Press, 1975); Oscar Handlin, *The Uprooted*, 2nd ed. (New York: Little, Brown and Company, 1979); John Bodnar, *The Transplanted* (Bloomington: Indiana University Press, 1985); Ken Fones-Wolf, *Trade Union Gospel: Christianity and Labor in Industrial Philadelphia, 1865–1915* (Philadelphia: Temple University Press, 1989); and Peter Way, *Common Labour: Workers and the Digging of North American Canals, 1780–1860* (Baltimore: Johns Hopkins University Press, 1993).
9. *Coffee Run: The Story of the Beginnings of the Catholic Faith in Delaware* (Hockessin, Del.: privately printed, 1960), 20. See also Gail Marie Artner, "Priest and

Parish in the Formative Years, 1800–1840: Father Patrick Kenny of the Delaware Valley" (M.A. thesis, University of Delaware, 1968).

10. Kerby A. Miller, *Emigrants and Exiles: Ireland and the Irish Exodus to North America* (New York: Oxford University Press, 1985), 22.

11. David Miller, "Irish Catholicism and the Great Famine," *Journal of Social History* 11, no. 1 (Fall 1975): 90. For the ratio of priests to people, see Sean Connolly, *Priests and People in Pre-Famine Ireland, 1780–1845* (New York: St. Martin's Press, 1982), 33.

12. Connolly, 135–48, passim.

13. Quoted in D. Miller, 92.

14. This discussion is based on Lawrence J. Taylor, *Occasions of Faith: An Anthropology of Irish Catholics* (Philadelphia: University of Pennsylvania Press, 1995), especially chap. 2.

15. Ibid., 117.

16. Ahlstrom, 531–35.

17. Joseph J. Casino, "From Sanctuary to Involvement: A History of the Catholic Parish in the North East," in *The American Catholic Parish: Volume 1, The North East, South East, and South Central States,* ed. Jay P. Dolan (New York: Paulist Press, 1987), 18–19; Patrick W. Carey, *People, Priests and Prelates: Ecclesiastical Democracy and the Tensions of Trusteeism* (Notre Dame, Ind.: University of Notre Dame, 1987), 80–81.

18. Casino, 26; Dolan, 7–8 and 56; and Connolly, 71 and 89–90.

19. D. Miller, 87.

20. "Catholic Church: Subscription charged to our hands in petit ledger, February 1818." Misc. Bills file, Jan.–June 1818, box 488, acc. 500.

21. Rev. Patrick Kenny, diary (4/5/1818), acc. 423. These payments should not be confused with funeral service fees, which are often recorded in county probate records. Thus, Kenny received $1 for performing the funeral rite of a powder worker in 1812. See John Fitzgerald (2/22/1812), Probate Records, New Castle County, Del., microfilm, Morris Library, University of Delaware, Newark, Del.

22. Quoted in *Coffee Run,* 30.

23. Historians often reduce popular religion to superstition, but most folk beliefs had important social functions that time has erased. See Conrad Arensberg, *The Irish Countryman* (1940; reprinted, Garden City: Natural History Press, 1968); E. Estyn Evans, *Irish Folk Ways* (New York: Devin-Adair, 1957); and Emmet Larkin, "The Devotional Revolution in Ireland, 1850–1875," *American Historical Review* 77, no. 3 (June 1972): 637. Herbert Gutman found evidence of a belief in fairies and holy wells in Paterson, New Jersey, as late as 1900. See his book *Work, Culture, and Society in Industrializing America: Essays in Working-Class and Social History* (New York: Vintage Books, 1977), 43–44.

24. Sophie du Pont, diary (2/4/1838), box 93, series F, group 9, WMSS.

25. Sophie du Pont to Henry du Pont (2/5/1828), box 57, series D, group 9, WMSS; and Joseph A. L. Errigo, *A History of St. Joseph's on the Brandywine* (Wilmington: William N. Cann, Inc., 1941), 32.

26. Rev. Patrick Kenny, diary (7/15/1817), acc. 423.

27. Knobel, 55.

28. Carey, 33–37, 43.
29. *Coffee Run*, 20.
30. Ibid.
31. Thus, Rev. Terence Donohoe came to baptize the infant son of powder man John Rodgers and his wife, Mary Ann Devor. Rodgers later called at Coffee Run to register the event, and, missing Kenny, left a dollar and a note explaining the circumstances. Kenny was not mollified: "One dollar or one thousand would be no credential for the above act. These roving priests will probably be soon confined to their stations." Cathedral of St. Peter, Register of Baptisms from 8/1796 to 4/1834, microfilm copy available at the Family History Center of the Wilmington Stake, LDS, Wilmington, Delaware, or the Diocese of Wilmington Archives, Greenville.
32. *Coffee Run*, 23.
33. Ibid.
34. Anthony F. C. Wallace, *Rockdale: The Growth of an American Village in the Early Industrial Revolution* (New York: Knopf, 1978), 256, 298–300, 309, 348 and 439–41. Rockdale was located along Chester Creek in southeastern Pennsylvania, just fifteen miles north of the Brandywine. The du Ponts had very close ties to this community.
35. John Wolffe, "Anti-Catholicism and Evangelical Identity in Britain and the United States, 1830–1860," in *Evangelicalism,* ed. Mark Noll, David W. Bebbington, and George A. Rawlyk (New York: Oxford, 1994), 179.
36. Ibid., 180–83.
37. Information on the religious beliefs of the Episcopal du Ponts is found in Charles A. Silliman, *The Story of Christ Church, Christiana Hundred, and Its People* (Wilmington, Del.: Hambleton Co., 1960).
38. On the differences between evangelical and Tractarian Episcopalians, see Silliman, 9–10, and Ahlstrom, 623–25.
39. Ruth C. Linton, "To the Promotion and Improvement of Youth: The Brandywine Manufacturers' Sunday School, 1816–1840" (M.A. thesis, University of Delaware, 1981), vi; and Anne M. Boylan, *Sunday School: The Formation of an American Institution* (New Haven: Yale University Press, 1988), 23 and 38.
40. BMSS Receiving books, acc. 289. The receiving books for the school list the name of each child enrolled, his class, and his religion, as well as his primary parent or guardian's name, his parent or guardian's occupation, and place of residence. A final column for "comments" recorded how often the child attended, how he or she performed, when the child left the BMSS, why the child left, and often, who and when the child married, what he did for a living, and where he resided. All of this information was entered into two database files, one for each of the first two receiving books, which together detail the entire enrollment through 1852.
41. Sophie du Pont to Henry du Pont (10/18/1830), quoted in Betty Bright-Low and Jacqueline Hinsley, *Sophie du Pont: A Young Lady in America* (New York: Harry N. Abrams, Inc., 1987), 137; Wallace, 104–13 and 312–17. On the conflation of femininity and morality among evangelical Protestants, see Mary P. Ryan, *Cradle of the Middle Class: The Family in Oneida County, New York,*

1790–1865 (New York: Cambridge University Press, 1981), and Lori D. Ginzberg, *Women and the Work of Benevolence: Morailty, Politics, and the 19th-Century United States* (New Haven: Yale University Press, 1990).

42. Victorine Bauduy, diary (11/14/1843), box 14, series A, group 6, WMSS.

43. Sophie du Pont, diary (1/6/1833), item W9-403049, box 93, series F, group 9, WMSS.

44. Sophie du Pont, diary (3/25/1832), box 93, series F, group 9, WMSS. Here we can begin to see why evangelical Protestants like Sophie du Pont frequently used the term "superstitious" to describe Irish Catholics. To non-believers, "superstitions" or "Hibernianisms" connoted repetitive, ritualized behaviors performed out of either habit, ignorance, or fear. None of these traits was conducive to the development of a sincere, personalized spirituality of the kind evangelicals encouraged. For similar statements concerning "ignorant" and "superstitious" parents see Sophie du Pont, diary (9/6/1832); and Sophie du Pont to Henry du Pont (2/5/1828).

45. Joseph Frazier Wall, *Alfred I. du Pont: The Man and His Family* (New York: Oxford, 1990), 75 and 84.

46. Ibid., 11–14.

47. Sophie du Pont, diary (1832), box 93, series F, group 9, WMSS.

48. Sophie du Pont, diary (3/15/1840), box 93, series F, group 9, WMSS.

49. Victorine du Pont Bauduy, undated note, 1840–1850 file, box 6, series A, group 6, WMSS.

50. Quoted in Sarah H. Heald, "Report on the Biographical Research for the Brandywine Manufacturers' Sunday School," unpublished mss., HML (1984), 19.

51. Sophie du Pont, diary (3/7/1841), box 93, series F, group 9, WMSS.

52. Joyce Kettaneh Longworth and Marjorie Gregory McNinch, *The Church of St. Joseph on the Brandywine, 1841–1994* (Greenville, Del.:privately printed, 1995), 16.

53. William Rowe, "St. Joseph's Church, Brandywine, Delaware," (1889). Typescript copy at St. Joseph's Parish Office, Greenville, Del. See also Errigo, 29, and Longworth and McNinch, 22.

54. Brian Mitchell has shown that the construction of new parishes at Lowell was largely financed by Irish immigrants who had achieved middle-class status and for whom the ability to build a church was an important sign of community prosperity. Brian Mitchell, *The Paddy Camps: The Irish of Lowell, 1821–1861* (Urbana: University of Illinois Press, 1988), 56.

55. An 1843 list of subscribers shows sums ranging from one dollar to $9.75. Misc. Bills file, 1843, box 497, acc.500.

56. Errigo, 33–34. The petit ledger of 1852–53 reveals that a combination of donations and subscriptions from the powder mill community financed all of these improvements. Pew rent deductions for these years were $2 in January, July, and December, compared to the $1 paid by members of Christ (Episcopal) Church every four months. Of the 410 men listed in the ledger, 42 percent paid pew rent to St. Joseph's, and some were buying new $100 shares. Petit ledger, 1852–53, acc. 500.

57. Ann Taves, "Context and Meaning: Roman Catholic Devotion to the Blessed Sacrament in Mid-Nineteenth-Century America," *Church History* 54, no. 4 (December 1985): 485–91.

58. Kevin Kenny, "The Molly Maguires and the Catholic Church," *Labor History* 37, no. 3 (Summer 1995): 346.

59. Rev. Dr. England, *The Garden of the Soul: A Manual of Fervent Prayers, Pious Reflections, and Solid Instructions* (New York: D. & J. Sadlier, 1856), 43.

60. Irénée and Alfred are listed as Jeandelle's children in the BMSS receiving books, and as his heirs in the probate accounts. Irénée Jeandelle later moved to Wilmington and became a printer.

61. F. L. Mathewson, interview, 1968. The second son, Charles Gilbert, was named for his two grandfathers, Charles Reed and Gilbert Mathewson, Sr. A third son, Frank L. Mathewson, was named for a brother.

62. Joshua V. Gibbons, Brownsville, Fayette County, Pennsylvania, to V. E. Bauduy (6/20/1835), file 21, box 6, acc. 289.

63. Catharine Davison, Seymour, Indiana, to Mrs. Thomas Mackie Smith (4/15/1872), file 21, box 6, acc. 289.

64. Eleanor Kane, interview, 1984.

65. The Holland brothers were from the Parish of Ardstraw, in County Tyrone, and there is some evidence that Irish naming patterns varied with geography. The brothers all began working in the powder yards in the 1820s. Information on the Holland family is taken from various sources, including petit ledgers, baptismal registers, immigration files, and tombstones.

66. Janet Nolan, *Ourselves Alone: Women's Emigration from Ireland, 1885–1920* (Lexington: University Press of Kentucky, 1989), 29.

67. St. Joseph on the Brandywine Roman Catholic Church, Registers of Baptism and Marriage, 9/1846 to 1895. An additional thirteen children were born out of wedlock. There is no specific evidence about prohibitions against premarital pregnancy, but the low numbers suggest that some form of social or religious control was at work. Sean Connolly found evidence of strict social sanctions against fornication and bastardy in Ireland. His analysis of a sample of marriages in six Irish parishes between 1759 and 1860 indicates that only one in ten brides was pregnant at marriage, compared to two out of every five brides in rural England. Other studies have documented the relatively low rates of illegitimate births in Ireland compared to other countries, thus attitudes in America may represent a continuance of Irish customs. On Irish marriages see Connolly, 188–90.

68. Sophie du Pont to Henry du Pont (Thursday, 9/13/1832).

69. Twenty-one-year-old David McConnell eloped with a woman ten or fifteen years his senior. Sophie du Pont, diary (5/22/1830 and 3/3/1832). For attitudes toward marriage and elopement in Ireland see Connolly, 194–215.

70. William Buchanan, interview, 1958.

71. *A Catechism of Christian Doctrine,* prepared and enjoined by Order of the Third Plenary Council of Baltimore (1885; reprinted, New York: Benzinger Bros., 1921), 233. On blessing oneself and using holy water, candles, palm

fronds, and rosaries, see pages 237–39. On the use of pictures, images, crucifixes, and relics, see pages 274–75.

72. Timothy O'Neill, *Life and Tradition in Rural Ireland* (London: J. M. Dent &
Sons, Ltd, 1977), 19; John C. O'Sullivan, "St. Brigid's Crosses," *Ulster Folklife*
11 (1973): 60–81.

73. O'Neill, 19.

74. Claudia Kinmonth, *Irish Country Furniture, 1700–1950* (New Haven: Yale
University Press, 1993), 192–94.

75. "Accounts of Rev. Patrick Kenny," acc. 323. These items came from Mathew
Carey, Philadelphia's most prominent Irishman of the antebellum era.

76. Most of these items were available locally. By the 1830s, Mathew Carey's competition included Eugene Cummiskey, whose Catholic bookstore advertised "a
very handsome assortment of religious pictures, which it offers for sale, low,"
and Patrick C. Martin, who sold Catholic prayer books, pictures, beads, and
crucifixes for a Baltimore-based company. In the 1840s, Robert Porter sold various Catholic books and objects from his store in Wilmington, as did the firm of
Wilson and Heald on Market Street. Expense accounts for the BMSS show that
Victorine du Pont Bauduy purchased Catholic catechisms and Catholic reading
and spelling books from both Porter's and Cummiskey's. In 1857, Porter and
Wilson and Heald were joined by "Messrs Cheeseman and Jones," who
"opened a store on Market Street selling bibles, prayer books, hymn books, etc.
See, *Philadelphia Catholic Herald* 4/24/1834 and 1/8/1835; BMSS account book,
1823–39 and account book, 1840–55, acc. 389; *Delaware Republican,* 7/9/1857;
James Heaney inventory (1866), James McAran inventory (1867), and Thomas
Fitzpatrick inventory (1868), New Castle County Probate Records.

77. *Harper's Weekly Magazine* 4 (June 30, 1860): 401. Another view, on December
1, 1860, showed an Irish-Catholic woman sewing in an American garret. She is
identified by the picture of a saint tacked to the wall behind her. Additional examples of Irish interiors with saints' pictures on the wall are found in vol. 18
(1874), 304, and vol. 20 (1876), 960.

78. Harold L. Peterson, *American Interiors: From Colonial Times to the Late Victo-
rians* (New York: Scribner's, 1971), plates 102 and 103, shows two woodcuts
from the *New York Illustrated News* dated February 11, 1860, which fit the pattern. Portraits of saints and statuary were found in middle-class Irish homes, as
well. William D. Griffin, *A Portrait of the Irish in America* (New York:
Scribner's, 1981), plate 318, shows a wedding in the parlor of a prosperous Irish
farmer, with appropriate religious pictures on the wall. Books also utilized this
stereotype. In describing a two-room tenement in New York City, author John
Maguire stated, "There was no actual want of essential articles of furniture,
such as a table and chairs; and the walls were not without one or two pious and
patriotic pictures, Catholic and Irish." See Maguire, 232.

79. On literary stereotypes see, Knobel, 88–93.

80. Rev. James Gibbons, Archbishop of Baltimore, *The Faith of Our Fathers* (Baltimore: John Murphy & Co., 1879), 235. See also, Rev. Dr. Challoner, *The
Catholic Christian Instructed* (Philadelphia: E. Cummiskey, 1841), 237–38.

81. Neg. No. LC-US262-11147, lot 4446-E, "Holidays," Prints and Photographs Division, Library of Congress.

82. Colleen McDannell, *The Christian Home in Victorian America, 1840–1900* (Bloomington: Indiana University Press, 1986), 55.

83. *Wilmington City Directory* (1857), 146.

84. John S. Walsh to John Peoples (1/15/1851), incoming correspondence, box 400, acc. 500.

85. John S. Walsh to John Peoples (1/1/1858).

86. John S. Walsh to James Peoples (7/12/1858).

87. Haley was not the first du Pont employee to try to leave the community without paying his debts, but he was unsuccessful. Within a week, Walsh was able to inform John Peoples that Haley had settled his account. J. S. Walsh to Henry du Pont, Esq. (2/1/1858), and J. S. Walsh to John Peoples (2/9/1858).

88. McDannell, xv–xvi and 13–14.

89. Quoted in Casino, 22.

90. William Rowe's history of St. Joseph's notes that classes were held in the basement of the church until arrangements were made to construct a school building in 1855. Rowe does not indicate when classes in the basement began. See his essay "St. Joseph's on the Brandywine (1890)," typescript copy, St. Joseph's on the Brandywine parish office, Greenville, Del.

91. Casino, 23.

92. Quoted in Longworth and McNinch, 54.

93. Ibid., 53. Victorine Bauduy died in 1861, thus the event coincides with the first efforts to promote Catholic education at St. Joe's.

94. Linton, 39.

95. As late as the 1870s, some of the men who were working in the powder yards were unable to sign their name when they received their pay. See payroll ledgers, acc. 500.

96. Casino, 24.

97. Rowe, 3; Longworth and McNinch, 54–55.

98. Rev. Joseph Deharbe, *A Full Catechism of the Catholic Religion*, trans. Rev. John Flander, ed. the Rt. Rev P. N. Lynch, 5th ed. (New York: Schwartz, Kirwin, and Fauss, 1876), 253.

99. Typescript of clipping dated 10/29/1859, file 30, RG-37, Diocese of Wilmington Archives.

100. This point will be explained in more detail in chap. 4.

101. Kenny, 370.

102. Clarke, 196–97.

103. Quoted in Glenn Porter, *The Workers' World at Hagley* exhibition catalog (Greenville, Del.: Eleutherian Mills Foundation, 1981).

104. For information on various parish activities, see: Longworth and McNinch, 24; Errigo, 38; and Harold Hancock, "The Industrial Worker along the Brandywine," typescript (August 1958), 143–44, HML.

105. Longworth and McNinch, 27–28.

106. Errigo, 63–65.

CHAPTER 4. THE *BEAN A TI* (PP. 91–111)

1. Stone 507, "Inventory of the Tombstone Inscriptions in St. Joseph's Churchyard, Henry Clay, Del." Typescript prepared by the Historical Records Survey, Division of Women's and Professional Projects, Works Progress Administration (1939), available at the Diocese of Wilmington Archives, Greenville, Del.

2. Barbara Welter, "The Cult of True Womanhood: 1820–1860," *American Quarterly* 18 (1966): 151–74.

3. Mary Ford likely moved to the Brandywine in 1859, when Peter began working for the du Pont company. Three other men named Ford already worked in the yards—John, Thomas, and Michael—and they may have arranged for Peter and Mary's passage from Ireland. Peter initially earned $18 per month as a common laborer. He also began renting a house on company property and paying pew rent to St. Joseph's at this time, and an unknown relative named Patrick Ford boarded with him and Mary. When Peter went "to the powder" in November 1862, his wages rose to $20.50 per month. He left in the middle of April 1863, although it is unclear whether he enlisted or simply sought safer work. When he died in 1894 at the age of eighty-three, his children laid him to rest beside his wife. See Petit Ledgers, 1852–53, and 1859–63.

4. Rosemary Mahoney, *Whoredom in Kimmage: Irish Women Coming of Age* (New York: Houghton-Mifflin, 1993).

5. Joseph M. Curran, *Hibernian Green on the Silver Screen* (Westport, Conn.: Greenwood Press, 1989).

6. See, for instance, Colleen McDannell, "True Men as We Need Them: Catholicism and the Irish-American Male," *American Studies* 27, no. 2 (1986): 19–33; and Ken Fones-Wolf, *Trade Union Gospel: Christianity and Labor in Industrial Philadelphia, 1865–1915* (Philadelphia: Temple University Press, 1989), 31. For a recent publication that attributes the behavior of Irish women to economic motives alone, see Carole Turbin, *Working Women of Collar City: Gender, Class, and Community in Troy, New York, 1864–1886* (Urbana: University of Chicago Press, 1990). For an overview of the ways in which labor historians have treated gender see Mari Jo Buhle, "Gender and Labor History," in *Perspectives on American Labor History: The Problems of Synthesis*, ed. Alice Kessler-Harris and J. Carroll Moody (DeKalb: Northern Illinois University Press, 1990), 55–79; and Alice Kessler-Harris, "Treating the Male as Other: Redefining the Parameters of Labor History," *Labor History* 34 (Spring–Summer 1993): 192. For specific statements regarding the materialist conception of gender held by feminist labor historians see, Alice Kessler-Harris, "A New Agenda for American Labor History: A Gendered Analysis and the Question of Class," in *Perspectives on American Labor History*, 226; and Baron, 38.

7. On the dichotomy between liberal individualism and communal or domestic values, and the relationship of each to gender, see Joan C. Williams, "Domesticity as the Dangerous Supplement of Liberalism," *Journal of Women's History* 2, no. 3 (Winter 1991): 69–88. The relationship between strictly materialist

conceptions of gender and liberalism is explored and critiqued in Tessie P. Liu, "Le Patrimoine Magique: Reassessing the Power of Women in Peasant Households in Nineteenth-Century France," *Gender and History* 6, no. 1 (April 1994): 13–36.

8. Liu, 23–31, passim.

9. Laurel Thatcher Ulrich, *Goodwives: Image and Reality in the Lives of Women in Northern New England* (1980; reprinted, New York: Vintage Books, 1991), and Christie Farnham, "Sapphire? The Issue of Dominance in the Slave Family, 1830–1865," in *To Toil the Livelong Day: America's Women at Work*, ed. Carol Groneman and Mary Beth Norton (Ithaca: Cornell University Press, 1987).

10. Turbin, 76.

11. Kerby Miller, *Emigrants and Exiles: Ireland and the Irish Exodus to North America* (New York: Oxford University Press, 1985), 12, 54–55, 239, 273.

12. On the cultural importance of the *bean a ti* in Ireland and in the United States see Patrick J. Corish, "Women and Religious Practice," in *Women in Pre-Modern Ireland,* ed. Margaret MacCurtain and Mary O'Dowd (Edinburgh: Edinburgh University Press, 1991), 213–19; and Dennis Clark, *The Irish Relations: Trails of an Immigrant Tradition* (East Brunswick, N.J.: Associated University Presses, Inc., 1982), 32. Information on the *fear ti* came from Donn Devine, archivist for the Diocese of Wilmington, and from Rev. Patrick Dineen, *An Irish-English Dictionary* (Dublin: M. H. Gill & Son, 1904).

13. Miller, 12–13 and 44–45.

14. For statistics on the number of cottiers and smallholders, see Miller, 49–51. Miller contends that "the status of women in rural Ireland has never been high" (406), yet other scholars disagree. See Hasia Diner, *Erin's Daughters in America: Irish Immigrant Women in the Nineteenth Century* (Baltimore: Johns Hopkins University Press, 1986), 13; Janet Nolan, *Ourselves Alone: Women's Emigration from Ireland, 1885–1920* (Lexington: University Press of Kentucky, 1989), 11 and 30; Joanna Burke, *Husbandry and Housewifery: Women, Economic Change and Housework in Ireland, 1890–1914* (Oxford: Clarendon Press, 1993), 39; Thomas J. Curran, "The Irish Family in Nineteenth Century Urban America: The Role of the Catholic Church," working papers, series 6, no. 2, Center for Studies in American Catholicism, University of Notre Dame (1979), 14; J. J. Lee, "Women and the Church Since the Famine," in *Women and Irish Society: The Historical Dimension,* ed. Margaret MacCurtain and Donncha O'Corrain (Westport, Conn.: Greenwood Press, 1979), 37; and Kevin O'Neill, *Family and Farm in Pre-Famine Ireland: The Parish of Killashandra* (Madison: University of Wisconsin Press, 1984), 34–36.

15. Angelique Day and Patrick McWilliams, eds. *Parishes of County Tyrone 1, 1821, 1823, 1831–6,* vol. 5, *Ordnance Survey Memoirs of Ireland* (Belfast: The Institute of Irish Studies, The Queens University, 1990), 54.

16. Miller, 372.

17. Emmet Larkin, "The Devotional Revolution in Ireland: 1850–1875," *The American Historical Review* 77 no. 3 (1972), 625–52; and Ann Taves, *The Household of Faith: Roman Catholic Devotions in Mid-Nineteenth-Century America* (Notre Dame: University of Notre Dame Press, 1986).

18. Lee, 37.

19. According to Kerby Miller, "traditional" Irish men and women dominated both the Famine and post-Famine migrations, not "modern" ones. In fact, it was their exodus, coupled with the deaths of millions of other "traditional" Irish, that allowed the strong farmers and their "modern" outlook to prevail on home soil. Miller, 308, 350–52.

20. In 200 of the 298 households headed by a married couple in 1850, the wife was younger than her spouse; in 55 households, the wife and husband were the same age; and in 43 cases, the wife was actually older. What is significant, however, is the fact that 63 percent of the same-age couples and 64 percent of the wife-older couples were Irish, while only 44 percent of the wife-younger ones were. Seventh U.S. Census (1850), Christiana and Brandywine Hundreds, New Castle County, Del.

21. For references to women cleaning on Saturdays and visiting on Sundays see Sophie du Pont, diary (2/17/1832; 3/25/1832; and 9/2/1832), series F, group 9, WMSS.

22. Joan Jensen, *Loosening the Bonds: Mid-Atlantic Farm Women, 1750–1850* (New Haven, Conn.: Yale University Press, 1986), 83–85.

23. "Expense Account book (1806–1809)," item 4, file 149, box 10, acc. 146; and "Comtes avec les ouvriers (1802–1809)," item 8, file 148, box 9, acc. 146.

24. Eighteen men were killed by the 1847 explosion, and du Pont's phrasing suggests that at least some of the women were made widows by the accident. Quoted in Nancy Soukup, "Women's Roles in the Du Pont Powder Mills in 1870," unpublished research report (1979), 17.

25. Philip Dougherty, interview, 1955.

26. In the 1830s, women domestics earned $1–3.50 per week, compared with the $2–3 per week that women earned at Charles I. du Pont's cotton mill. By comparison, men could expect to earn $3.50–4.00 as common laborers in the powder yards, or $5–6.00 per week in the textile mills. Female agricultural labor also remained an important source of income, and over 30 percent of the farming families in Brandywine and Christiana hundreds had live-in female help by 1850. See Linda Daur, "Domestic Servants at Eleutherian Mills, 1821–1842," unpublished research paper (1979), 20; and Jensen, 89. Primary sources consulted for information about women's work along the Brandywine include: "Depense," (1806–1809), item 4, file 149, box 10, acc. 146; willow books, acc. 500; petit ledgers, 1852–53 and 1863, acc. 500; wage book, Dixon and Breck textile mill (Rokeby), 1847–51, no. 191, series E, acc. 500; wage book, Charles I. du Pont & Co., no. 69,a Acc. 500; "List of domestic servants and wages (1834–36)," item W9–39838, series F, group 9, WMSS.

27. This preference has been noted by scholars of other Irish communities as well. See, for example, Carole Turbin, "Beyond Conventional Wisdom: Women's Wage Work, Household Economic Contribution, and Labor Activism in a Mid-Nineteenth-Century Working-Class Community," in *To Toil the Livelong Day: America's Women at Work, 1780–1980,* ed. Carol Groneman and Mary Beth Norton (Ithaca: Cornell University Press, 1987), 51; Brian C. Mitchell, *The Paddy Camps: The Irish of Lowell, 1821–1861* (Urbana: University of Illinois

Press, 1988), 144–45; and John Bodnar, *The Transplanted* (Bloomington: Indiana University Press, 1985), 65–79.

28. Quoted in Amy Boyce Osaki, "The Needle's Web: Sewing in One Early 19th-Century American Home" (M.A. thesis, University of Delaware, 1988), 12. Some women also sewed and mended clothing for cash. Victorine paid Mrs. Riggs fifty cents for making two baby frocks and mending another. She also paid Mrs. Finegan "for doing up my collars and dresses," and Eliza Reynolds "for sewing the carpet." See Victorine du Pont Bauduy, Memoranda File, 1850–60; diary (11/16/1843); October 1838, household account book, 1838–42; all in box 14, series A, group 6, WMSS.

29. Elizabeth Beacom, interview, 1962.

30. Boarding books (1802–46), 7 vols., series B, Production Records, acc. 500. Boarding was a widespread phenomenon in nineteenth-century America, and many historians have commented on the subject. See, for example, Tamara Hareven and John Modell, "Urbanization and the Malleable Household: An Examination of Boarding and Lodging in American Families," *Journal of Marriage and the Family* 35 (1973):, 467–68.

31. Payroll sheets, 1810–1818, box 1705-A, acc. 500.

32. Tamara Hareven used this term to describe the family members who bore the primary responsibility for arbitrating disputes, organizing assistance in "critical life situations," and reinforcing kin networks. See her book *Family Time and Industrial Time: The Relationship Between the Family and Work in a New England Industrial Community* (New York: Cambridge University Press, 1982), 105.

33. Petit ledger, 1842–44 and 1845–46; boarding book (1840–46), no. 1699, acc. 500; Seventh U.S. Census (1850), Christiana Hundred, New Castle County, Del. Baptismal register, St. Joseph's on the Brandywine Roman Catholic Church, microfilm, Wilmington Stake, LDS, Wilmington, Del.

34. For Mrs. Ferguson's purchase, see Thomas Fitzpatrick inventory (1852), New Castle County probate records. For other purchases see, "19th Century Community Stores," BSM Manual, sec. V (Supplemental Information), HML. Sam Frizzell operated a store in Henry Clay Village, but he ventured out into the community twice a week to peddle goods door-to-door. Other peddlers in the last half of the century included a butcher, an ice-cream man, a shoemaker, a milkman, and a fish monger. All came out to the Brandywine from Wilmington.

35. Wage book, no. 1703, acc. 500.

36. William Flanigan, interview, 1960.

37. Elizabeth Beacom, interview, 1962. See Blanche McAdoo Yetter, interview, May 1984, as well.

38. Victorine du Pont Bauduy to Sophie du Pont, undated, outfile, "Victorine du Pont Bauduy to friends and family," box 6, series A, group 6, WMSS.

39. Victorine du Pont Bauduy, household accounts, 1838–42, box 14, series A, group 6, WMSS. Information on Mary Jane Cavender's age is taken from the Brandywine Manufacturers' Sunday School Receiving Books, acc. 289.

40. Victorine du Pont Bauduy, diary (1/22/1843), box 14, series A, group 6,

WMSS. Within a week of this entry, an Irish widow named Isabella Baxter had replaced Mary Toy.

41. See Ruth C. Linton, "To the Promotion and Improvement of Youth: The Brandywine Manufacturers' Sunday School, 1816–1840" (M.A. thesis, University of Delaware, 1981), 9–45, passim; and Anne M. Boylan, *Sunday School: The Formation of an American Institution, 1790–1880* (New Haven: Yale University Press, 1988), 22–23, 34–38.

42. Sophie du Pont, diary (2/17/1832), item W9-40349, box 93, series F, group 9, WMSS.

43. Victorine du Pont Bauduy, "Memoranda, Diary Notes, Quotations, Compositions," file 1850–1860, box 14, series A, group 6, WMSS. Victorine's diaries also contain statements like "After school I went to see Mrs. Coyle about David," suggesting that she, too, addressed her concerns about attendance to mothers, even when the child in question was male. See her entry for Sunday, October 29, 1843.

44. Sophie du Pont, diary (2/17/1832), item W9-40349, box 93, series F, group 9, WMSS.

45. Later that same day, Sophie went to visit a girl who was sick "because I feared on Sunday we would meet so many people there." On another occasion, she visited the Alexanders in their home at Louviers. "There were a great many persons there . . . & they all were so very loquacious I had to stay a considerable time without seeing much of Martha." A different entry revealed that Martha Alexander had had to leave school because her mother needed her help on Saturday afternoons. Sophie du Pont, diary (3/25/1832, 9/2/1832, and 4/14/1833), item W9-40349, box 93, series F, group 9, WMSS

46. Sophie du Pont to Clementina Smith (6/26/1832), series F, group 9, WMSS.

47. Dr. Pierre Didier recorded the births of babies that he delivered in his account book, box 5, series A, group 10, WMSS. Dr. Thomas Mackie Smith, the husband of Eleuthera du Pont, succeeded Didier as company doctor and delivered some of the babies born on company property between 1834 and 1852. These births are recorded in his account book, item 4, "Record of Babies Delivered," part IV, series C, group 6, WMSS. Dr. Greenleaf followed Smith. None of the medical records specifically mention the presence of female friends and kin during a mother's delivery, but baptismal registers from St. Peter's and St. Joseph's show various newborns baptized *"ob periculum mortis"* (in danger of death) by women. There are also discrepancies between the number of babies delivered by the doctors and the number baptized per year. In 1821, for example, Didier delivered only one child, yet fifteen were born at the powder mills and baptized by Rev. Patrick Kenny.

48. Victorine du Pont Bauduy, "Memoranda, Diary Notes, Quotations, Compositions, 1850–1860," box 14, series A, group 6, WMSS.

49. Ella Fitzharris, interview, 1984. Ella's parents were Ella Lowther (born ca. 1880) and Michael Joseph Farren. Katie Farren, a native of County Donegal, was her paternal grandmother.

50. Richard Rowe, interview, 1968.

51. Judith Leavitt, "Under the Shadow of Maternity: American Women's Responses to Death and Debility Fears in Nineteenth-Century Childbirth," *Feminist Studies* 12 (1986): 129–54.

52. Headstones 222, 451, and 457, "Inventory of the Tombstone Inscriptions in St. Joseph's Churchyard, Henry Clay, Del.," typescript prepared by the Historical Records Survey, Division of Women's and Professional Projects, Works Progress Administration (1939), available at the Diocese of Wilmington Archives, Greenville, Del. . According to local baptismal records, Ann Curran Toy bore her husband, James, five children: Daniel (1842), John T. (1843), Thomas (1845), Martha Jane (1847), Rosanna (6/16/1848). Ann died on 6/16/1848, a date that coincides with Rosanna's birth. The little girl followed her mother to the grave thirteen months later. Likewise, Annie A. Toy, "wife William Gunn," gave birth to William F. Gunn, "son William," on December 22, 1893, and died four days later. William F. Gunn died on July 1, 1894, aged about six months.

53. Both the Boyd and Rameau cases appear in Dr. Pierre Didier's loose receipts, Bills and Cases file, box 5, series A, group 10, WMSS. The Aiken birth appears in his account book, box 5, series A, group 10, WMSS.

54. See Headstone 222, "Inventory of the Tombstone Inscriptions in St. Joseph's Churchyard, Henry Clay, Del.," typescript prepared by the Historical Records Survey, Division of Women's and Professional Projects, Works Progress Administration (1939); baptismal registers, St. Joseph on the Brandywine Roman Catholic Church; Ninth U.S. Census (1870), New Castle County, Del.

55. Victorine du Pont Beauduy, diary (5/21 and 6/4/1843), box 14, group 6, series A, WMSS

56. John Peoples, interview, 1952. Peoples was born in 1871 in County Donegal and emigrated with his parents shortly thereafter.

57. Sophie du Pont, diary 2/4/1838).

58. Quoted in Glenn Porter, *The Workers' World at Hagley*, exhibition catalog (Greenville, Del.: Eleutherian Mills–Hagley Foundation, 1981), 56.

59. *The Republican*, newspaper clipping, and "Obituary," August 17, 1904, Du Pont Company Explosions File. Ninth U.S. Census (1870), New Castle County, Del. The Doughertys, both natives of County Donegal, had at least seven children at the time of the explosion and lived in Free Park. Afterward, he received a pension from the du Pont company and they moved to a home they owned on Lincoln Street in Wilmington. Their granddaughter, Eleanor Kane, recalled that Daniel helped Ellen around the house after the explosion and that Ellen read to him every evening. Ellen's father, William G. Gibbons, was the uncle of John Gibbons, foreman of the Hagley Yard from 1856 to 1885. See Eleanor Kane, interview, 1984.

60. The probate account of powder worker James Bogan, for example, settled in April 1832, included payments to Rebecca Derrickson, Mrs. Fleming, Sarah Donnan, and Mary Russell for various funeral expenses and services including fifty cents for "making a shroud." James Bogan, New Castle County Probate Records. For descriptions of late-nineteenth-century wakes, see Aloysius Rowe, interview, 1968, and Richard Rowe, interview, 1968.

61. Sean Connolly, *Priests and People in Pre-Famine Ireland, 1780–1845* (New York: St. Martin's Press, 1982), 148–58.

62. Victorine du Pont Bauduy to Evelina du Pont Bidermann (January 1838), outfile, box 6, series A, group 6, WMSS.

63. "December 21, 1850, Annuity of $125 during life from Office of the Penn Mutual Life Insur. Co., Phila.," in Inventories and Balance Sheets file, box 18, acc. 504. This document provides a list of all widows on the company's rolls in 1850, including their names and ages. There were twenty-one women indicated.

64. Diner, 61.

65. Thomas Holland sailed from Londonderry on the ship *Israel* in late June 1827 and arrived at Philadelphia on July 7 accompanied by several relatives. He started work at the powder mills on July 13, and died in the explosion of 1847. He and his wife, Margaret Travers, had at least eight children: John (born 1832); Nicholas (1834); Thomas (1836); Eliza Ann (1837); Hugh (1839); Mary (1841); Thomas (1842); and Margaret (1844). The eldest, John, left home shortly after his father's death, and the first Thomas died before the second's birth. According to her tombstone at St. Joseph on the Brandywine Catholic Church, Margaret died on September 30, 1892, aged eighty.

66. Diner, xiv. There was no single, monolithic concept of womanhood in the nineteenth century, but historians of women agree that "there was a culturally dominant ideology of sexual spheres promulgated by an economically, socially, and politically dominant group," that this ideology was firmly grounded in the sexual division of labor appropriate to that group, and that they employed it to impose a universal definition of the female character on American society in general. See Nancy A. Hewitt, "Beyond the Search for Sisterhood: American Women's History in the 1980s," in *Unequal Sisters: A Multicultural Reader in U.S. Women's History,* ed. Ellen Carol Du Bois and Vicki Ruiz (New York: Routledge Press, 1990), 1–14; and Linda K. Kerber, "Separate Spheres, Female Worlds, Woman's Place: The Rhetoric of Women's History," *Journal of American History* 75, no. 1 (June 1988): 9–39.

67. Colleen McDannell, "True Men as We Need Them: Catholicism and the Irish-American Male," *American Studies* 27, no. 2 (1986): 19–33.

68. Although underutilized by social and labor historians, personal name analysis has a long and distinguished past. In particular, it has been employed to confirm the importance of paternal and maternal kinship ties among slaves in the American South. See, for example, Herbert Gutman, *The Black Family in Slavery and Freedom, 1750–1925* (New York: Pantheon, 1976), 113–14, 185–215; and Cheryll Ann Cody, "Naming, Kinship, and Estate Dispersal: Notes on Slave Family Life on a South Carolina Plantation," *William and Mary Quarterly* 39, no. 1 (1982): 192–211. Additional studies include: Daniel Scott Smith, "Child Naming Practices and Family Structure Change: Hingham, Massachusetts, 1640–1880," the Newbury Papers in Family and Community History, Newbury Library, Chicago, Illinois (January 1977); Richard D. Alford, *Naming and Identity: A Cross-Cultural Study of Personal Naming Practices* (New Haven: HRAF Press, 1988); and Lynn H. Nelson, "Personal Name

Analysis of Limited Bases of Data: Examples of Applications to Medieval Arogonese History," *Historical Methods* 24, no. 1 (Winter 1991): 4–15.

69. Jeffrey Burns, "The Ideal Catholic Child: Images from Catholic Textbooks," unpublished research paper, Center for the Study of American Catholicism, Notre Dame University (1978), 6.

70. Rev. Joseph Deharbe, S. J., *A Full Catechism of the Catholic Religion,* trans. Rev. John Fander, 5th ed. (New York: Schwartz, Kirwin, & Fauss, 1876), 135. On the invocation of angels and saints as protectors and role models, see also Rev. Dr. Challoner, *The Catholic Christian Instructed* (Philadelphia: Cummiskey, 1841), 218–27.

71. Rev. Alban Butler, *Lives of the Saints* (1878; reprinted, New York: Benziger Bros., 1894), 262; and Rev. Hugo Hoever, ed., *Lives of the Saints* (New York: Catholic Book Publishing Co., 1955), 284. The 1850 census shows that Annie Haughey was born in 1843. Her father, Patrick, commenced working in the powder yards as a common laborer on April 3, 1835, and became a powder man on March 30, 1836. Several years later, he opened a store in Henry Clay Village. His wife, Ann Donnelly, bore at least ten children, including Annie.

72. Butler, 163; Hoever, 166. According to St. Joseph's baptismal registers, Catherine Bogan was born on June 26, 1856, to powder man Charles Bogan, an emigrant from County Donegal, and his wife, Mary McBraerty. Her godparents were Hugh Bogan, and Catherine McBraerty. Woulfe, 208.

73. *A Christian's Guide to Heaven: Or a Manual of Spiritual Exercises for Catholics* (Philadelphia: E. Cummiskey, 1833), 198.

74. Rev. Bernard O'Reilly, *The Mirror of True Womanhood: A Book of Instruction for Women in the World,* 17th ed. (New York: P. J. Kennedy, 1892).

75. Hoever, 113.

76. Liguori's words carried substantial weight among Catholic clergy, for he was named a Doctor of the Church, and after his canonization, he became the patron saint of theologians. St. Alphonsus Liguori, *Obligations of Children and Parents Towards Each Other* (Philadelphia: H. & C. McGrath, 1851), 279.

77. McDannell, "True Men as We Need Them," 32. McDannell is correct in observing that Joseph represented the ideal of "sacred devotion to family," but at least one of the advice books she used, *True Men as We Need Them,* actually upheld St. Louis IX, King of France, as the ideal for Catholic youths, and St. Columba of Ireland as "the ideal of true manhood." See Rev. Bernard O'Reilly, *True Men as We Need Them: A Book of Instruction for Men in the World,* 4th ed. (New York: P. J. Kennedy, 1890), 310 and 267.

78. A study of naming patterns among Italian immigrants revealed that the name Mary or Maria ranked first for Italian women, and shows the cross-cultural strength of Catholic devotion to the Blessed Virgin. However, the other leading names in the Italian pool were Josephina, Rosa, Teresa, Anna, Carmela, Angelina, Filomena, and Concetta. See Susan Cotts Watkins and Andrew S. London, "Personal Names and Cultural Change: A Study of the Naming Patterns of Italians and Jews in the United States in 1910," *Social Science History* 18, no. 2 (Summer 1994): 169–210.

79. O'Reilly, *True Men,* 266.

80. Ibid., 269–70.
81. Ibid., 273.
82. John Maguire, *The Irish in America* (New York: D. & J. Sadlier & Co., 1868), 343.
83. Ibid., 335–36.
84. This story is cited in Glenn H. Pryor, "Workers' Lives at the Dupont Powder Mills, 1877–1912" (B.A. thesis, University of Delaware, 1977), 44–45. Rev. W. J. Bermingham was pastor of St. Joseph's on the Brandywine from 1894 to 1900.
85. Maguire, 333–44.

CHAPTER 5. HABITATIONS (PP. 112–140)

1. Eleanor Kane, interview, February 21, 1984. Deed (10/3/1887), book Z, vol. 13, 515, New Castle County Recorder's Office, Wilmington, Del.
2. Kerby Miller, "Class, Culture, and Immigrant Group Identity in the United States: The Case of Irish-American Ethnicity," in *Immigration Reconsidered: History, Sociology, and Politics,* ed. Virginia Yans-McLaughlin (New York: Oxford University Press, 1990), 107.
3. Richard Harris and Chris Hamnett, "The Myth of the Promised Land: The Social Diffusion of Home Ownership in Britain and North America," *Annals of the Association of American Geographer* 77, no. 2 (June 1987): 173–74; Stephen Thernstrom, *Poverty and Progress: Social Mobility in a Nineteenth-Century City* (1964; reprinted, New York: Atheneum, 1975), 161.
4. John G. Elliott to Alfred du Pont (12/16/1842), box 1, series A, group 7, WMSS. According to his letter, Elliott lived in Jay County, Indiana, near Dayton. Before heading west, he sold some land near the powder yards to the company, but never received the final payment. Elliott therefore asked Alfred to send the balance due, because, he wrote, "I have taken a lease on a farm of 160 acres for the term of 5 years from the first April next & to have possession the middle of next month & actually stand in need of money to stock with." Included in the file with the letter are two receipts showing payments to Elliott. One, for $50, bears the date March 14, 1838, perhaps the year Elliott left the Brandywine. The second, for $350, is dated only March 22, but likely documents a final payment in 1843.
5. Harris and Hamnett, 174; Thernstrom, 161.
6. David Noel Doyle, "The Irish as Urban Pioneers in the United States, 1850–1870," *Journal of American Ethnic History* 10 (Fall 1990–Winter 1991): 36–59.
7. This discussion is largely based on my previous examinations of workers' housing in America. See Margaret M. Mulrooney, *A Legacy of Coal: The Coal Company Towns of Southwestern Pennsylvania* (GPO: Washington, D.C., 1989), 10–11 and 23–27; and "Hilton Village, Virginia: The Government's First Model Industrial Community (M.A. thesis, College of William and Mary, 1990), chap. 1.
8. John S. Garner, *The Model Company Town: Urban Design through Private Enterprise in Nineteenth-Century New England* (Amherst: University of Massachusetts

Press, 1984), introduction. There was also a third type: the corporate town. Representative examples include Lowell, Lawrence, and Holyoke, Massachusetts, and Manchester, New Hampshire.

9. Nuala McGann Drescher, "The Irish in Industrial Wilmington, 1800–1845: A History of the Life of Irish Emigrants to the Wilmington Area in Pre-Famine Years." (M.A. thesis, University of Delaware, 1960), 93.

10. Quoted in Glenn Porter, *The Workers' World at Hagley,* exhibition catalog (Greenville, Del: Eleutherian Mills–Hagley Foundation, 1981), 12.

11. Walter Nugent, "Toqueville, Marx, and American Class Structure," *Social Science History* 12, no. 4 (Winter 1988): 341.

12. Kerby A. Miller, *Emigrants and Exiles: Ireland and the Irish Exodus to North America* (New York: Oxford, 1985), 201–204 and 412–15.

13. Angelique Day and Patrick McWilliams, eds., *Parishes of County Tyrone 1: 1821, 1823, 1831–1836,* vol. 5 of *Ordnance Survey Memoirs of Ireland* (Belfast: The Institute of Irish Studies, 1990), 93–103.

14. Brian De Breffny and Rosemary Ffolliott, *The Houses of Ireland: Domestic Architecture from the Medieval Castle to the Edwardian Villa* (London: Thames and Hudson, 1975), 81.

15. Most Dubliners were confined to parishes like St. Nicholas', with an average of 3.49 persons per room and 2.71 per bed. Ibid., 40, 118, 224–25.

16. For statistics on Irish emigration between 1800 and 1900 see Roger Daniels, *Coming to America: A History of Immigration and Ethnicity in American Life* (New York: Harper Perennial, 1990), 129. For additional statistics between 1851 and 1920 and information concerning emigrants' social origins see Miller, *Emigrants and Exiles,* 100–101, 193, 351–52, and appendixes.

17. De Breffny and Ffolliott, 81.

18. Miller, *Emigrants and Exiles,* 40.

19. Day and McWilliams, 96.

20. De Breffny and Ffolliott, 213, 226–28.

21. Bessie Gardner du Pont, trans., *Life of E. I. du Pont from Contemporary Correspondence, 1799–1802,* vol. 5 (Newark: University of Delaware Press, 1924), 291.

22. Ibid., 207.

23. "Inventaire general de ce qui possedent Messrs E. I. Du Pont de Nemours & Co., 1814," box 485, series M, part II, series I, acc. 500.

24. Maureen O'Brien Quimby, *Eleutherian Mills* (Greenville, Del.: The Hagley Museum, 1973), 11–12; Jacqueline Hinsley and Betty-Bright Low, *Sophie du Pont: A Young Lady in America, Sketches, Diaries and Letters, 1823–1833* (New York: Harry N. Abrams, Inc., 1987), 13.

25. John Beverly Riggs, *A Guide to the Manuscripts in the Eleutherian Mills Historical Library: Accessions through the Year 1965* (Greenville, Del.: Eleutherian Mills Historical Library, 1970), 75.

26. *Mirror of the Times,* February 23, 1803.

27. An 1808 description of the Hagley property appears in the Stephen Girard Papers, microfilm, APS, page 478. See also, "Statement of Powder, Materials, Real Estate, Utensils, etc. (1818)," box 485, acc. 500; "Division of Land Survey," J. P. Fairlamb (1826), Map Drawer VI, Manuscripts Division, HML; and

Jacqueline Hinsley, "Preliminary Research Report for Blacksmith's Hill Archaeological Dig," unpublished research report (1984), 4. These houses might also be the stone houses "below Hagley," which are mentioned in the company rent books, acc. 500.

28. William H. Pierson, Jr., *Technology and the Picturesque, The Corporate and the Early Gothic Styles*, vol. 2 of *American Buildings and Their Architects* (New York: Oxford University Press, 1978), 49.

29. On American attitudes toward the factory system, technology, republicanism, and English manufacturing centers, see John F. Kasson, *Civilizing the Machine: Technology and Republican Values in America, 1776–1900* (New York: Penguin Books, 1976), especially 55–106.

30. Jefferson is quoted in Pierson, 30–31.

31. Quoted in Gwendolyn Wright, *Building the Dream: A Social History of Housing in America* (Cambridge: MIT University Press, 1981), 58–59.

32. For a detailed description of the early industrial landscape of Great Britain, see Barrie Trinder, *The Making of the Industrial Landscape* (London: J. M. Dent & Sons Ltd, 1982), especially chapters 4, 5, and 6.

33. Franklin D. Scott, trans. and ed., *Baron Klinkowstrom's America, 1818–1820* (Evanston: Northwestern University Press, 1952), 54.

34. *Delaware State Journal,* September 7, 1844.

35. "A Ramble Through Christiana and Brandywine Hundreds," *Delaware Republican,* April 26, 1860.

36. William Cullen Bryant, ed., *Picturesque America, or, The Land We Live In,* vol. I (New York: D. Appleton & Co., 1872), 222–31.

37. Anthony F. C. Wallace, *Rockdale: The Growth of an American Village in the Early Industrial Revolution* (New York: Alfred Knopf, 1978), 13–17.

38. "Hagley Yard Housing Record," acc. 302. Cheney recorded the name of each dwelling's main tenant, the number of stories and rooms it had, the kinds of outbuildings present, the primary building and roofing materials, and the repairs needed.

39. Margaret M. Mulrooney and Stuart P. Dixon, "Frame, 2 1/2 Story, 3 or 4 Rooms with a View: Workers' Housing at Hagley," unpublished research paper (1987), 14–16 and appendixes.

40. Leifur Magnusson, "Employers' Housing in the United States," *Monthly Review of the Bureau of Labor Statistics,* no. 5 (GPO: Washington, D. C., 1917), 869–94.

41. William H. Buchanan, interview, 1958.

42. Henry Glassie, "Eighteenth-Century Cultural Process in Delaware Valley Folk Building," in *Common Places,* ed. Dell Upton and John Michael Vlach (Athens: University of Georgia Press, 1986), 400.

43. Ibid., 401–404.

44. Wallace, 14–15 and 98. The tenements at Parkmount were recently torn down, but the ones at West Branch, called "English Hill," still stand.

45. On William Donnan and family, see Sophie du Pont diary (10/20/1840 and 10/22/1840), box 93, series F, group 9, WMSS; William Donnan, will and inventory, 1828, New Castle County Probate Records, microfilm, Morris Library,

University of Delaware; petit ledgers 1815–17, 1822–24, acc. 500; and BMSS receiving books (April 1, 1826), acc. 1826. On tenants in the 1840s, see rent book no. 1687, inside cover; and petit ledgers 1845–46 and 1847, acc. 500.

46. Faith Betty Lattomus and Madeline Betty Walls, joint interview, June 12, 1969. The son of an Irish immigrant, Robert Betty started out driving a powder wagon and later succeeded his father, also named Robert, as foreman of the company farm.

47. M. W. Beresford, "The Back-to-Back House in Leeds, 1787–1937," in *The History of Working-Class Housing: A Symposium,* ed. Stanley D. Chapman (Totowa, N.J.: Rowan and Littlefield, 1971), 96–101. This early use of the cellar as a separate dwelling is likely what gave rise to the "English basement" apartment.

48. Trinder, 170–201.

49. There are actually two structures at Gladwyne. Both were originally three-and-a-half stories high, with stone walls and a gable roof. The northern one contained two semidetached dwellings, with one room per floor, but the southern one was an eight-bay, double-pile structure containing eight back-to-back units. Located in Lower Merion Township, the Gladwyne back-to-back was probably associated with one of the businesses that occupied the Rose Glen Mill in the early nineteenth century. Further research is needed to determine exactly which firm built it. Thanks to Jean Wolf of the Lower Merion Conservancy for showing the ruins to me.

50. *Delaware Gazette,* March 2, 1821.

51. Lamont Hulse, "Workers' Communities along the Brandywine" (unpublished research paper, 1984), 25; William Sisson, "A Mill Village along the Brandywine: Henry Clay" (unpublished research paper, 1980), 4–6 and 31; Thunderbird Archaeological Associates, "Archaeological Investigations of the Proposed Dualization of Rte 141 (Centre Road) from Rte 100 (Montchanin Road) to U.S. Rte 202 (Concord Pike), New Castle County, Delaware," Delaware Department of Transportation Archaeological Series No. 72 (1989), 49.

52. Rent book no. 1687, acc. 500. Between June 1850 and June 1851, the du Pont company rented the Squirrel Run mill to a firm called Stephens and Manderson for $3000 per annum. The rent book shows the rental of units 11 and 16 to A. Stephens & Co. from April 25, 1843, to December 1847. Stephens and Manderson, the successor firm, also acquired use of these two units in the "new block opposite Squirrel Run factory." Francis Ryes and Dennis Rowe were not listed in the du Pont company rent book, but the census schedule shows them as the occupants of units 11 and 16. Since they did not work in the powder yard, they were probably textile workers.

53. Hugh began working for Dixon and Breck, the textile manufacturers at Rokeby, in 1847. He may have quit in response to the explosion at Hagley that April. Peter continued to work in the powder yards until 1851, when he, too, switched to Rokeby. Both men took a pay cut: Hugh's wages dropped to $9 or $10 per month, and Peter's dropped to $6. Peter listed his occupation in 1850 as a farmer, however. They probably moved out of Squirrel Run soon after Peter

quit working for the powder company. Information on the Haughey family is taken from the following sources: petit ledger, 1837–39 and 1845–46, acc. 500; Dixon and Breck wage ledger no. 191, acc. 500; Seventh (1850) U.S. Census, Christiana Hundred, New Castle County, Delaware; rent book no. 1687, acc. 500.

54. The inside cover of the 1841–59 rent book indicates that the upper units of the "new block opposite Squirrel Run factory" let for $33 per annum and the lower units for $30. The deductions in company wage ledgers do not correspond to these figures, suggesting that rents were reduced after 1841. The difference in price probably reflects a difference in the number of rooms. Based on the only extant eight-unit block, which will be discussed in detail below, the upper units had four rooms while the lower units, like Haughey's, had three.

55. Thunderbird, 118–19. See also, "Inventory of Real Estate, Dec. 30, 1843," and "Inventory of Real Estate, Dec. 31, 1844," box 485, acc. 500. It appears that du Pont first purchased the property from the Wilmington and Brandywine Bank in 1831. By 1838, it belonged to John B. Newman, who acquired it when brothers Robert, William, and Thomas Hilton defaulted on their $8160.39 note to James Brown, William Welsh, and Lea Pusey. Newman, in turn, sold it to Andrew Adams later that year. Adams paid $3200 and proved unable to make the mill a going concern. In 1843, du Pont reacquired the site, and eventually leased it to Joseph Walker. The mill continued to operate under various tenants until 1938.

56. William Flanagan interview, 1960.

57. Kasson, 85.

58. On the interior finish of vernacular housing in Ireland, see Claudia Kinmonth, *Irish Country Furniture, 1700–1950* (New Haven: Yale University Press, 1993), 3–9.

59. Magnusson, 873. As late as 1916, the Bureau of Labor Statistics could boast that 76 percent of the houses it surveyed rented for less than $8 per month, an amount considered "well within the means of the low-paid, unskilled worker." American workers at that time could expect to spend between 15 and 20 percent of their annual income on rent. Du Pont employees spent far less.

60. Rent book no. 1687, acc. 500. There were forty-eight units listed on the inside cover, with the amount of rent charged.

61. For the national context see Elizabeth Blackmar, *Manhattan for Rent, 1785–1850* (Ithaca: Cornell University Press, 1989), 240–41.

62. Donald R. Adams, Jr., "The Standard of Living during American Industrialization: Evidence from the Brandywine Region, 1800–1860," *Journal of Economic History* 42 (1982): 903–17. In the anthracite region of Pennsylvania, by comparison, tenants of coal towns in the 1840s could expect to pay between $16.25 and $26 in rent per year. Wages ranged from $150 to $200 for a common laborer, while miners earned between $200 and $800 per year. Like powder mill households, their income varied with the number of boarders and family members who contributed. Anthony F. C. Wallace, *St. Clair: A Nineteenth-Century Coal Town's Experience with a Disaster-Prone Industry* (New York: Knopf, 1987), 144.

63. By 1900, the average wage at the powder mills was $521 per annum or about $43 per month. The average rent was $33.80. See "Statement of Repairs, Rental, etc. Tenant Houses," box 17, acc. 504.

64. Wallace, *St. Clair*, 149–50.

65. Lawrence J. Taylor, *Occasions of Faith: An Anthropology of Irish Catholics* (Philadelphia: University of Pennsylvania Press, 1995), 63.

66. On faction fights, see Miller, *Emigrants and Exiles*, 60–61; Peter Way, *Common Labor: Workers and the Digging of North American Canals, 1780–1860* (Cambridge, 1993; reprinted, Baltimore: Johns Hopkins University Press, 1997), 194–204, 217–18, 246–47; Brian C. Mitchell, *The Paddy Camps: The Irish of Lowell, 1821–1861* (Urbana: University of Illinois Press, 1988), 23–27.

67. Thernstrom, 57–79, passim.

68. *Blue Hen's Chicken*, March 10, 1848.

69. Receiving books, Brandywine Manufacturers' Sunday School, acc. 389.

70. Adams, 905, 914–15. Historian Donald Adams first calculated his figures for average household expenditure using the amount spent for food and lodging by a single, male worker. To estimate the expenditure for a small family, he multiplied the food component by 1.5. Few powder mill families could be considered "small," however, during the antebellum period. The Ordnance Survey Memoirs for County Tyrone in the 1830s estimated that Ulster families typically averaged six members, for example. Once resettled in Delaware, these nuclear families often expanded to include boarders and extended kin. While these individuals necessarily raised the household's expenditure for food, they would have reduced the per person cost of lodging, particularly if the household head enjoyed free rent. Adams' figures do not take these circumstances into account, thus the ability of a typical Irish family to save money for home ownership was greater than his figures suggest.

71. Miller, *Emigrants and Exiles*, 203, 264, and 270.

72. John D. Vaughn, Richmond, Indiana, to E. I. du Pont de Nemours and Co., box 398, acc. 500; Papers and Letters of Mrs. Jane Reed, box 4, series A, group 5, LMSS. Henry Gegan (sometimes spelled Gagan) began working for the du Ponts in 1818. He married his first wife, Mary Brady, the daughter of "Old Patrick," in 1821. She gave birth to six children (Mary, Margaret, Rosanna, Bridget, Philip, and Patrick) and died of unknown causes around 1831. Gegan then married Sara Crawford on December 15, 1833, and moved with her to Indiana, leaving $1,721.31 in his account with the company. After his death in 1834, Gegan's estate was divided among three of his children, named Patrick, Rosanna, and Frances. Patrick, born in 1829, was the last Gegan child listed in the baptismal register for St. Peter's/Coffee Run, and since Sara had no children in Delaware, the birth of Frances remains a mystery.

73. Samuel Foster, Chippeway, to Alfred du Pont (1/10/1838), incoming letters file, acc. 1993.

74. Karen Barth, email to author, June 5, 2000. Patrick Callahan is Ms. Barth's ancestor. He died in 1887.

75. Seventh (1850) U.S. Census, Christiana Hundred, New Castle County, Del. Four boarders lived with McEvey, including his son, Bernard. Since the boarders

were only engaged in the powder yards on a seasonal basis (as willow cutters), they may have helped McEvey work his farm, located somewhere in Christiana Hundred. See Glenn Uminowicz, "The Worker and His Community Along the Brandywine: Methodology and Some Preliminary Considerations," unpublished research paper (1979), 21.

76. Dennis Clark concluded that the diversification of employment opportunities in Philadelphia enabled "substantial" property holding among Irish laborers in that city by mid-century. Daniel Walkowitz found a similar correlation between regular skilled employment and property ownership in Troy, where 10 percent of the Irish iron moulders owned real estate, compared to only 5.9 percent of the native-born moulders. In the mining town of St. Clair, Pennsylvania, 19 percent of all Irish immigrants owned real estate by 1870, and many of these owned more than one property. In San Francisco, 32 percent of all forty-year-old Irish males had real property by 1850, and 57 percent had personal property. At the turn of the century, rates of Irish home ownership in Butte, Montana, ranged from 56 to 76 percent. See: Dennis Clark, "The Philadelphia Irish," in *The Peoples of Philadelphia: A History of Ethnic Groups and Lower-Class Life, 1790–1940*, ed. Allen F. Davis and Mark H. Haller (Philadelphia: Temple University Press, 1978), 136–38; Daniel Walkowitz, *Worker City, Company Town: Iron and Cotton Worker Protest in Troy and Cohoes, New York, 1855–84* (Urbana: University of Illinois Press, 1978), 41; Wallace, *St. Clair*, 374–75; R. A. Burchell, *The San Francisco Irish, 1848–1888* (Berkeley: University of California Press, 1980), 61–64; and David M. Emmons, *The Butte Irish: Class and Ethnicity in an American Mining Town, 1875–1925* (Urbana: University of Illinois Press, 1990), 80.

77. Martin J. Burke, *The Conundrum of Class: Public Discourse on the Social Order in America* (Chicago: University of Chicago Press, 1995), 114; Thernstrom, 68.

78. Harris and Hamnett, 173.

79. (Wilmington) *Every Evening*, March 31, 1887.

80. Elizabeth Beacom, interview, 1967. Elizabeth Beacom continued to live in her father's house until her death in 1976 at the age of eighty-five.

81. Alfred P. Dougherty, interview, 1968; Emily Blackwell, interview, 1970; Edward B. Cheney, interview, 1958; and Margaret Seitz, interview, 1984.

82. Samuel Hackendorn, interview, 1958.

83. Thernstrom, 161.

CHAPTER 6. ALL THE GOODS AND CHATTELS (PP. 141–161)

1 Sophie du Pont, diary (11/29/1833), item W9–40349, box 93, series F, group 9.

2. Sophie du Pont, diary (12/1/1833).

3. BMSS receiving book, acc. 389.

4. Priscilla J. Brewer, "We Have Got a Very Good Cooking Stove: Advertising, Design and Consumer Response to the Cookstove, 1815–1880," *Winterthur Portfolio* 25, no. 2 (Spring 1990): 35–54.

5. For a discussion of the "streets-paved-with-gold" mentality, see Kerby A. Miller and Bruce D. Boling, "Golden Streets, Bitter Tears: The Irish Image of

America During the Age of Mass Migration," *Journal of American Ethnic History* 10 (Fall 1990–Winter 1991): 16–35.

6. Largely uninformed by the vast body of material culture scholarship, which is rooted in historical anthropology, these works emphasize the relationship between workers' limited purchasing power, worker protest, and workers' sense of class consciousness. Recent works include: Billy G. Smith, *The Lower Sort: Philadelphia's Laboring People, 1750–1800* (Ithaca: Cornell University Press, 1990); Dana Frank, "Gender, Consumer Organizing, and the Seattle Labor Movement, 1919–1929," in *Work Engendered: Toward a New History of American Labor,* ed. Ava Baron (Ithaca: Cornell University Press, 1991), 273–95; Lawrence Glickman, *A Living Wage: American Workers and the Making of Consumer Society* (Ithaca: Cornell University Press, 1997); and Nan Enstad, *Ladies of Labor, Girls of Adventure: Working Women, Popular Culture, and Labor Politics at the Turn of the Twentieth Century* (New York: Columbia University Press, 1999). An exception is Lizabeth Cohen, who once studied with noted material culture specialist Ken Ames. Her early publications include: "Respectability at $50.00 Down, 25 Months to Pay! Furnishing a Working-Class Victorian Home," in Kenneth L. Ames, ed., *Victorian Furniture* (Philadelphia: Victorian Society of America, 1983), 231–42; and "Embellishing a Life of Labor: An Interpretation of the Material Culture of American Working-Class Homes," in Dell Upton and John Michael Vlach, eds., *Common Places* (Athens: University of Georgia Press, 1986), 261–80. Her first monograph, *Making a New Deal: Industrial Workers in Chicago, 1919–1939* (New York: Cambridge University Press, 1990), shows how the purchase and use of certain commodities by laboring Americans became politicized in the interwar period. Though she stresses the formation of a distinct working-class consciousness, her broader conclusions support what material culture scholars have long argued: people define themselves more by what they consume than by what they do for a living.

7. Mary Douglas and Baron Isherwood, *The World of Goods: Towards an Anthropology of Consumption* (New York: Basic Books, 1979), 5. Although their studies favor elite and middling households, the methods material culture scholars use to identify objects and interpret behavior are equally applicable to the "stuff" of laboring Americans. See Robert Blair St. George, ed., *Material Life in America, 1600–1800* (Boston: Northeastern University Press, 1988), especially Part I: Method and Meaning.

8. David B. Landon and Mary C. Beaudry, "Domestic Archaeology and the Boardinghouse System in Lowell, Massachusetts," paper presented at the Dublin Seminar for New England Folklife (July 1988), 11–12 and n.50.

9. Andrew Heinze, *Adapting to Abundance: Jewish Immigrants, Mass Consumption, and the Search for American Identity* (New York: Columbia University Press, 1990), 15, 137–43.

10. Claudia Kinmonth, *Irish Country Furniture, 1700–1950* (New Haven: Yale University Press, 1993), 1–27; Colleen McDannell, "Catholic Domesticity, 1860–1960," in *American Catholic Women: An Historical Exploration,* ed. Karen Kenneally (New York: MacMillan Publishing Co., 1989), 55; Dennis Clark, *The*

Irish Relations: Trials of an Immigrant Tradition (E. Brunswick, N.J.: Association of University Presses, 1982), 37.

11. Kinmonth, "Tables," 177–84, "Meal Chests," 129–32, and "Stools and Chairs," 29–34; Timothy O'Neill, *Life and Tradition in Rural Ireland* (London: J. M. Dent and Sons, Ltd, 1977), 23–24 and 30.

12. Kinmonth, "The Dresser," 99–124; O'Neill, 25–28; Henry Glassie, *Passing the Time in Ballymenone: Culture and History of an Ulster Community* (1982; reprinted, Bloomington: Indiana University Press, 1995), 365.

13. Kinmonth, "Beds," 150, 153–54, 167, "Settle Beds," 82–90, "Press Beds and Other Disguised Beds," 168–71; O'Neill, 20–21.

14. Neil McKendrick, John Brewer, and J. H. Plumb, *The Birth of a Consumer Society: The Commercialization of Eighteenth-Century England* (Bloomington: Indiana University Press, 1982).

15. O'Neill, 33. Claudia Kinmonth suggests that, "The fact that furniture was sometimes taken by landlords in lieu of rent probably deterred people from amassing it," even when they could afford to. Kinmonth, 177.

16. Robert Scally, "Liverpool Ships and Irish Emigrants in the Age of Sail," *Journal of Social History* (Fall 1983): 11.

17. Daniel Harkin sent a draft to Grace Harkin from the Brandywine in 1841, so he must have been working in the yards by 1840. Taylor correspondence, box 385, acc. 500; and petit ledger no. 971. His tombstone in St. Joseph's on the Brandywine cemetery reads: "Daniel Harkin, Parish of Tollighabigley [*sic*], County Donegal, who died 10/15/1890, aged 90." He is buried with his wife, Ann Sweeney. "Inventory of Tombstone Inscriptions in St. Joseph's Churchyard, Henry Clay, Del." Prepared by the Historic Records Survey, Division of Women's and Professional Projects, WPA (Wilmington, Del., 1939.), no. 90. Typescript copy, RG-37, St. Joseph's on the Brandywine, Diocese of Wilmington Archives, Greenville, Del.

18. A comprehensive search for individuals who resided in either Christiana or Brandywine Hundreds at the time of their decease produced over 100 decedents who lived in the powder mill community and who died intestate between 1812 and 1905. Cross-linking the inventories with company records and federal census schedules revealed that seventy-one of the decedents were employed by E. I. du Pont de Nemours and Company in some capacity at the time of death. Twenty-nine individuals were identified as local storekeepers, farmers, artisans, and workers in the affiliated textile mills. Additional Irish decedents were found in the Borough of Wilmington, and were used for comparative purposes. See New Castle County probate records, microfilm, Morris Library, University of Delaware, Newark, Delaware; population schedules, Christiana and Brandywine Hundreds, New Castle County, Delaware, Sixth U.S. Census (1840) and Ninth U.S. Census (1870), microfilm, Morris Library, University of Delaware, Newark, Delaware; "Comtes avec Divers" (1801–1805), item 4, file no. 148, box 9, acc. 146; "Account Book of Powder Workers" (1806–1809), item 2, file no. 148, box 9, acc. 146; "Powderman's Daybook" (1813–1816), item 7, file 150, box 10, acc. 146; petit ledgers (1812–1902), 64 vols., series D, Ledgers, part II, General Accounts, acc. 500.

19. Joan Jensen, *Loosening the Bonds: Mid-Atlantic Farm Women, 1750–1850* (New Haven: Yale University Press, 1986).

20. Elizabeth Beacom, interview, 1967.

21. [George Cheney], "Record of Hagley Yard Housing," (1902), acc. 302.

22. These items were the only goods specifically designated for children. The noticeable absence of children's furniture in powder workers' homes stands in contrast to the child-centered world described by Karin Calvert, and it may confirm the contention that wage-earning Americans, especially Catholics, rejected the sentimental attitude toward childhood held by their white-collar counterparts. See Karin Lee Fishbeck Calvert, *Children in the House: The Material Culture of Early Childhood, 1600–1900* (Boston: Northeastern University Press, 1992).

23. On the availability and use of iron bedsteads, see T. Webster and Mrs. Parkes, *The American Family Encyclopedia of Useful Knowledge* (New York: Derby and Jackson, 1858), 295; and Miss Leslie, *The House Book, or A Manual of Domestic Economy for Town and Country* (Philadelphia: Carey and Hart, 1841), 326–27.

24. James McLaughlin inventory (1851).

25. On the use of tables as washstands see Miss Leslie, 300–301.

26. James Bogan inventory (1831). Most of the inventory takers have been identified as company employees, local farmers, or local landowners. While each of them enjoyed a certain degree of social standing in the community, none was far removed from the person whose goods he catalogued.

27. Anne E. Yentsch, "Farming, Fishing, Whaling, Trading: Land and Sea as Resource on Eighteenth-Century Cape Cod," in *Documentary Archaeology,* 153; Beaudry, 44.

28. The other two types of country houses were the farm house and the villa. The cottage was also distinguished by its location in the suburbs, where "an industrious man, who earns his bread by his daily exertions," could enjoy the benefits of rural life in proximity to his place of employment. Andrew Jackson Downing, *The Architecture of Country Houses* (New York: D. Appleton and Company, 1850), 410. See also, William H. Pierson, Jr., *Technology and the Picturesque, The Corporate and the Early Gothic Styles* (New York: Oxford University Press, 1978), 305–307 and 389–92.

29. Downing, 372.

30. Ibid., 415.

31. Ibid., 451–52. On the popularity of spool-turned or "Jenny Lind" beds in the nineteenth century, see Ralph and Terry Kovel, *American Country Furniture, 1780–1875* (New York: Crown Publishers, 1965), 3.

32. Cited in Gail Caskey Winkler, "The Influence of *Godey's Lady's Book* on the American Woman and Her Home: Contributions to a National Culture, 1830–1877" (Ph.D. diss., University of Wisconsin, Madison, 1988), 210.

33. P. P. Gustine, *Wholesale Price List of Furniture* (Philadelphia: privately printed, 1867).

34. Archaeologist George Miller traced the excess production capacity of Staffordshire potteries to a competition in this country, which lowered the prices of ceramics throughout the nineteenth century. A similar competition appears to

have affected the American furniture industry. See George L. Miller, "Demand Entropy as a By-Product of Price Competition: A Case Study from Staffordshire," a paper presented at a seminar on "The Archaeology of Capitalism," School of American Research, Santa Fe, New Mexico, October 1993 (author's possession).

35. On iron bedsteads, see Downing, 419, and Miss Leslie, 326. Miss Leslie indicated that iron bedsteads were "much used in attics," where the servants slept. "Painted, low, bedsteads are best for rooms of domestics, who, if they had curtains, might very probably set them on fire." On patchwork quilts, rag rugs, and white granite or common Queensware, see Miss Leslie, 233, 311, and 326. On painted, low-post bedsteads, see *Hints on Houses and House Furnishings, or Economics for Young Beginners* (London: Goombridge and Sons, Ltd., 1861), 17.

36. Glenn Uminowicz, "Earnings and Terms of Service: Hagley Powdermen in 1850," unpublished research paper (1979), 6.

37. Donald Adams, "The Standard of Living During American Industrialization: Evidence from the Brandywine Region, 1800–1860," *Journal of Economic History* 42 (1982): 903–17. Other sources indicate typical incomes for other workers. Thus Juliet Corson said the average income of the "prosperous American household of the medium range of intelligence and culture" is $1500–2000, whereas "thousands of active workmen" live upon $250–500" and do not consider themselves deprived of the comforts of life." See Corson, *Family Living on $500 a Year* (New York: Harper and Bros., 1888), 1. Another source indicates that Congress considered anyone earning less than $600 a year exempt from paying income taxes during the Civil War. These "persons of the humble class" included "the large body of citizens who live on small salaries: clerks in offices and stores, mechanics, laborers, and women whose incomes from rents, interest, or dividends were just sufficient to enable them to live." See *Six Hundred Dollars a Year: A Wife's Effort at Low Living Under High Prices* (Boston: Ticknor and Fields, 1867), preface. See also Stuart Blumin, *The Emergence of the Middle Class: Social Experience in the American City, 1760–1900* (New York: Cambridge University Press, 1989), 112–16.

38. Beth Ann Twiss-Garrity, "Getting the Comfortable Fit: House Forms and Furnishings in Rural Delaware" (M.A. thesis, University of Delaware, 1983); and Richard Bushman, *The Refinement of America: Persons, Houses, Cities* (New York: Vintage Books, 1992), 229–30.

39. Bernard L. Herman, *Architecture and Rural Life in Central Delaware* (Knoxville: University of Tennessee Press, 1987).

40. Here, I draw on Katherine Grier's use of the term "paraphrasing" to describe the re-creation of "middle-class" interiors by all levels of American society. See Katherine C. Grier, *Culture and Comfort: People, Parlors, and Upholstery, 1850–1930* (Rochester, N.Y.: The Strong Museum, 1988), 2 and 13.

41. Elizabeth Garrity, *At Home: The American Family, 1750–1870* (New York: Harry N. Abrams, 1990), 68.

42. *Hints on Houses and House Furnishings, or, Economics for Young Beginners* (London: Goombridge & Sons, 1861), 45. Other nineteenth-century travelers found the cottages of British pit miners to be surprisingly well furnished. "Cottages

were kept spotlessly clean and great pride was taken in mahogany bedsteads and chests of drawers which reached the ceiling." See Barrie Trinder, *The Making of the Industrial Landscape* (London: J. M. Dent & Sons, Ltd., 1982), 189.

43. Similar patterns of consumption characterized the British, Welsh, and Irish households of St. Clair, Pennsylvania. They bought "large and expensive carved mahogany furniture—bedsteads, chests of drawers, and chairs—that graced the clean, bare interiors of humble miners' dwellings." Anthony F. C. Wallace, *St. Clair: A Nineteenth-Century Coal Town's Experience with a Disaster-Prone Industry* (New York: Alfred A. Knopf, 1987), 177.

44. James Burns, *Three Years among the Working Classes in the United States during the War* (1865), cited in Richard Stott, *Workers in the Metropolis: Class, Ethnicity, and Youth in Antebellum New York City* (Ithaca: Cornell University Press, 1990), 174.

45. Ann Dougherty inventory (1835).

46. John Buchanan inventory (1868); petit ledgers 1854–55 and 1863; payroll book no. 1703, Jan. 1863–April 1865. Buchanan commenced working in the powder yards on August 4, 1854, at $19 per month. He boarded with Gilbert Mathewson for a month, then moved his family to the Brandywine from Wilmington. On April 26, 1855, he "went to the powder," and began earning $22.50 per month. By 1863, he was earning "$32 or $20." The wage ledger is unclear here, but the former figure is more likely the correct one because he earned a total of $394 that year. The family appears to have spent most of what Buchanan earned; his wage account usually had a balance of about $20 at the end of each year.

47. Margaret M. Mulrooney and Stuart Dixon, "Frame, 2 1/2 Story, 3 or 4 Rooms with a View: Workers' Housing at Hagley," unpublished research paper (1987).

48. Catherine Cheney, interview, 1967.

49. Ella Fitzharris, interview, 1984.

50. Sally McMurry, *Families and Farmhouses in Nineteenth-Century America: Vernacular Design and Social Change* (New York: Oxford University Press, 1988), 157.

51. In addition to works previously cited, my sense of why people buy different kinds of things has primarily been shaped by the following: Colin Campbell, *The Romantic Ethic and the Spirit of Modern Consumerism* (New York: Basil Blackwell, 1987); Grant McCracken, *Culture and Consumption: New Approaches to the Symbolic Character of Consumer Goods and Activities* (Bloomington: Indiana University Press, 1988); and Cary Carson, "The Consumer Revolution in Colonial British America: Why Demand?" in *Of Consuming Interests: The Style of Life in the Eighteenth Century,* ed. Cary Carson, Ronald Hoffman, and Peter J. Albert (Charlottesville: University of Virginia Press, 1994). No matter what their period of study, recent scholars now agree that consumption is caused by the adoption of new attitudes and outlooks, which, in turn, create demand. In other words, increased supply is not a sufficient explanation for increased consumption. People have to be motivated to buy goods, and their motivations are complex.

52. Daniel Horowitz, *The Morality of Spending, 1875–1940: Attitudes Toward the Consumer Society in America* (Baltimore: Johns Hopkins University Press, 1985).

53. McCracken, 71–88 and 104–17.

54. Margaretta Lammot du Pont to Eleuthera du Pont Smith (5/2/1828), box 3, series A, group 7, WMSS.

55. "Stragglers Time Book" (1807–1809), box 1700, series I, part 5, acc. 500.

56. An indication of the goods available on du Pont company property is found in this tongue-in-cheek description from "The Tancopanican Chronicle," a family newspaper started by Victorine and Eleuthera in 1823: "Messrs. A Fountain & Co. respectfully inform their friends and the public that they have just received an assortment of the best and most fashionable fall goods among which are Rob Roy calicoes, elegant chester Jaconet, Superior calicoes of all colours, Superfine Bombazines, Children's spats and Fleecy gloves also ten fashionable mustard pots in the shape of Egyptian mummies, small black pitchers, innumerable tea pots, Salt fish, boiled cinnamon, rancid butter, and an elegant assortment of Merino shawls which they will dispose of on the most reasonable terms and unlimited credit." Quoted in Jacqueline Hinsley and Betty-Bright Low, *Sophie du Pont, A Young Lady in America: Sketches, Diaries and Letters, 1823-33* (New York: Harry N. Abrams, Inc., 1987), 127. Andrew Fountain's "emporium" was located at the ferry landing below Eleutherian Mills. Despite his limited inventory and questionable fashion sense, even the du Pont women were frequent customers.

57. Jackie Hinsley, "The Du Pont Company Store," unpublished research report, Manuscripts and Archives Division, HML. Examples of various merchants' accounts can be seen in Petit Ledger (1822–24), acc. 500. The household account books of Victorine du Pont Bauduy and Sophie du Pont detail purchases at stores in Wilmington, Philadelphia, and along the Brandywine.

58. Deborah Dependahl Waters, *Plain and Ornamental: Delaware Furniture, 1740-1890* (Wilmington: The Historical Society of Delaware, 1984), 13.

59. "Bills and receipts" file, box 44, group 5, series B, LMSS.

60. *Boyd's Delaware State Directory* (Wilmington: William H. Boyd, 1860).

61. Waters, 54.

62. Rent book (1871–77), acc. 500.

63. William Boyd inventory (1844).

64. Sarah Heald, "Report on the Biographical Research for the Brandywine Manufacturer's Sunday School," unpublished research report (1984), 60; Catherine Cheney, interview, 1967.

65. Kinmonth, 14.

66. *Six Hundred Dollars a Year,* 31.

67. Maurice Saucain inventory (1825).

68. Thomas Fitzpatrick inventory (1852).

69. Ann Smart Martin, "The Role of Pewter as Missing Artifact: Consumer Attitudes Toward Tablewares in Late 18th Century Virginia," *Historical Archaeology* 23 (1989): 1–26; George L. Miller, "A Revised Set of CC Index Values for Classification and Economic Scaling of English Ceramics from 1787–1880,"

Historical Archaeology 25 (1991): 1–25; Charles H. LeeDecker et al., "19th-Century Households and Consumer Behavior in Wilmington, Delaware," in *Consumer Choice in Historical Archaeology*, ed. Suzanne Spencer-Wood (New York: Plenum Press, 1987), 233–59.

70. Geoffrey A. Godden, *The Illustrated Guide to Mason's Patent Ironstone China* (London: Barrie and Jenkins, Ltd., 1971), 11.

71. Miller, 1; Jean Wetherbee, *A Look at White Ironstone* (Des Moines: Wallace-Homestead Book Co., 1980), 12–15; Godden, 11.

72. Miss Leslie, 233.

73. This conclusion is based on the use of the term "queensware" in post-bellum Wilmington city directories and in the inventory of powder man Darby McAteer (1870).

74. Samuel Shogren, "Lifeways of the Industrial Worker: The Archaeological Record—A Summary of Three Field Seasons at Blacksmith's Hill," unpublished research report (1986), 41.

75. William Baldwin was the blacksmith for the Hagley Yard at his death in 1845 and probably lived somewhere on the hill. William Boyd, the company's head carpenter, lived in the former Rumford Dawes house, also on Blacksmith's Hill. He died in 1844. Other residents included Alexandré Cardon, who operated the tanyard at Hagley from 1818 to 1826, and Augustus Belin, the company bookkeeper, who occupied Cardon's former house, located opposite the Gibbons site, from 1826 to his death in 1845. Belin was succeeded by his son, Henry, Sr., from 1845 to 1866, and by his grandson, Henry, Jr., from 1866 to 1870. As the next bookkeeper, Edward Collison occupied the Belin house from 1870 to 1892. Jacqueline Hinsley, "Preliminary Research Report for 1984 Archaeological Dig at Hagley," unpublished report (1984).

76. There are twenty-nine boxes of uncatalogued archaeological material. Box 23 contains the makers' marks. Most companies were from Staffordshire, East Liverpool, Ohio, and Trenton. Most of the fragments are whiteware, but some pearlware, some yellow ware, some mocha, and some blue and green shell edge are represented, as well. Box 26 contains partially reconstructed vessels, which run the gamut from ironstone to Haviland china. As in box 23, above, the high-status ceramics appear to be represented throughout the nineteenth century. Box 17 has assorted bags of transfer-printed shards, along with some very nice mocha wares. From what I can gather, some of the transfer-print colors represented in the box, like red and purple, were harder to come by than others. If this information is correct, then this box also supports the contention that powder workers had objects at the high end of the scale. Box 21 contains glass fragments. According to Shogren's report, Hagley staffers were surprised at the relatively small amount of pressed or cut glass in the ground, compared to its widespread availability. (There were a lot of strap flask fragments, however!) They surmised that workers may have disposed of glass in a different way or place. One piece that stands out is a fragment of a dolphin candleholder. A similar pair is (or was) on display at the Eleutherian Mills residence, but the fragments were found at Blacksmith's Hill.

77. Shogren, 47.

78. Most inventories merely listed tablewares under one collective label. Even Augustus Belin, whose position as the company's bookkeeper enabled him to amass more than $463 worth of household goods by 1845, only had "1 lot [of] crockery ware." John Hayes inventory (1834); Darby McAteer inventory (1870); Augustus Belin inventory (1845). Belin's total estate was worth $8,298.16.

79. The attitude of immigrants from eastern and southern Europe at the turn of the century corresponds to that of Irish immigrants in antebellum Delaware. See Cohen, "Embellishing a Life of Labor," 268–76, passim.

80. See, for example, John Modell, "Patterns of Consumption, Acculturation, and Family Income Strategies in Late Nineteenth-Century America," in *Family and Population in Nineteenth-Century America*, ed. Tamara K. Hareven and Maris A. Vinovskis (Princeton: Princeton University Press, 1978); Colleen McDannell, *The Christian Home in Victorian America, 1840–1900* (Bloomington: Indiana University Press, 1986), xvi.

81. The probate inventories collected for this study do not permit a conventional analysis of change over time. Because the practice of probating household goods had begun to die out before the Civil War, forty-two of the fifty Brandywine inventories containing furniture were taken before 1870. The level of detail also declined over time. Despite these limitations, it was clear that the most important factor influencing consumption was not large-scale, long-term change over the course of the nineteenth century, but the small-scale, short-term changes that occurred within one or two generations of a family. Again, 66 percent of the male decedents were killed in explosions and all the women were widows. Moreover, 72 percent of the decedents have been identified as emigrants from Ireland. Most of the inventories thus contain objects, clothing, and personal effects that had been purchased within a short time after the decedent's arrival in the United States.

82. Bushman, xviii.

83. Ibid., 185.

84. See Stott, 167 and 175; Sean Wilentz, *Chants Democratic: New York City and the Rise of the American Working Class, 1788–1850* (New York: Oxford University Press, 1984), 300–301; and Blumin, 140–42. Even the exaggerated parody of the Bowery B'hoys that all three authors mention would have required extensive knowledge of middle-class dress to function effectively as a critique.

85. Bushman, xv.

86. Sophie du Pont to Henry du Pont (1/19/1828), box 57, series D, group 9, WMSS.

87. Bushman, xv.

88. Margaret Byington, *Homestead: The Households of a Milltown* (1910; reprinted, Pittsburgh: University of Pittsburgh Press, 1974), 53.

89. Ibid., 57.

90. Ibid., 145.

91. Clifford Clark, *The American Family Home, 1800–1960* (Chapel Hill: University of North Carolina Press, 1986), 107; Heinze, 137–43.

92. Eleanor Kane, interview, 1984.

93. Clark, 107.
94. Jonas Miller inventory (1874); Thomas Fitzpatrick inventory (1852). Parlor organs and pianos were "common in rural and workers' homes by the 1890s." Thomas Schlereth, *Victorian America: Transformations in Everyday Life, 1876–1916* (New York: Harper-Perennial, 1992), 211.
95. Bernard L. Herman, "Multiple Materials, Multiple Meanings: The Fortunes of Thomas Mendenhall," *Winterthur Portfolio* 19 (1984): 67–89.
96. Blumin, 158–63. Simeon B. Hannold, for example, a shipwright, died owning goods with a total value of almost $70. Based on his occupation and net worth in 1861, Blumin concluded that Hannold's belongings could not have conformed to "middle-class" standards of taste and fashion. However, Hannold owned a desk, a bureau, a sofa, a set of thirteen chairs, and several tables, which could have constituted a makeshift parlor set. Peter Rodgers, a locksmith, and William Sheaff, a mason, also owned recognizable parlor furnishings, but Blumin dismissed their presence because he had already labeled Rodgers and Sheaff as "working-class" and interpreted the probate inventory data accordingly.

CHAPTER 7. PORCHES, YARDS, GARDENS, FENCES (PP. 162–185)

1. Cathedral of St. Peter, Register of Baptisms, August 1796–April 1834, microfilm copy available at the Wilmington Stake, LDS, Wilmington, Delaware.
2. Joseph Frazier Wall, *Alfred I. du Pont: The Man and His Family* (New York: Oxford University Press, 1990), 32.
3. "Roll of men in the employ of E. I. du Pont de Nemours & Co. at the powder works 11 Sept. 1835," box 1878, series I, acc. 500; Seventh U.S. Census (1850), Christiana Hundred, New Castle County, Del. Quigley was about fifty years old in 1850. The other members of his household were: his wife Mary (48); their children, Peter (23), Mary (17), and John (15); and six male boarders. According to the BMSS receiving books, Peter Quigley, Jr., moved to California in 1852, where he later died. The rest of the family may have followed him west, for they are not listed in the 1860 census.
4. Quoted in Nuala McCann Drescher, "The Irish in Industrial Wilmington, 1800–1845: A History of the Life of Irish Emigrants to the Wilmington Area in the Pre-Famine Years" (M.A. thesis, University of Delaware, 1960), 93.
5. Henry Glassie, "Irish," in *America's Architectural Roots: Ethnic Groups that Built America,* ed. Dell Upton (Washington, D.C.: The Preservation Press, 1986), 76.
6. Kerby A. Miller, *Emigrants and Exiles: Ireland and the Irish Exodus to North America* (New York: Oxford University Press, 1985), 27–28, 45–54.
7. Lawrence J. Taylor, *Occasions of Faith: An Anthropology of Irish Catholics* (Philadelphia: University of Pennsylvania Press, 1995), 62–63, 104–105; Miller, 28.
8. Henry Glassie, *Passing the Time in Ballymenone: Culture and History of an Ulster Community* (Philadelphia: University of Pennsylvania Press, 1982), 327–44.

9. Angelique Day and Patrick McWilliams, eds., *Parishes of County Tyrone 1: 1821, 1823, 1831–36,* vol. 5 of *Ordnance Survey Memoirs of Ireland* (Belfast: The Institute of Irish Studies, 1990), 59.

10. Aloysius Rowe, interview, 1968.

11. [George Cheney], "Record of Hagley Yard Housing" (1902), acc. 302. George Cheney's 1902 notebook describes the condition of 163 porches distributed unequally among 143 company-owned dwelling units. The majority were undifferentiated, but 21 percent were described as front porches, 13 percent were back porches, and 10 percent were side porches.

12. Glassie, *Passing the Time,* 394–414.

13. Bridget Clark to Mr. F. G. du Pont (July 1899), Employees File, box 17, acc. 504.

14. William Buchanan, interview, 1959.

15. Faith Betty Lattomus and Madaline Betty Walls, interview, 1969.

16. Bernard L. Herman, *Architecture and Rural Life in Central Delaware, 1700–1900* (Knoxville: University of Tennessee Press, 1987), 18–19. Herman discovered that more than 80 percent of all farms described in southern New Castle County property valuations between 1770 and 1820 had separate kitchens.

17. William Donnan inventory (1828); William Baldwin inventory (1845); and Neil Conley inventory (1849).

18. "Inventory of Real Estate, Dec. 31, 1844," and "Inventory of Real Estate, Dec. 31, 1845," box 485, acc. 500.

19. "Record of Hagley Yard Housing," acc. 302; and Margaret Mulrooney and Stuart Dixon, "Frame, 2 1/2 Story, 3 or 4 Rooms with a View: Workers' Housing at Hagley," unpublished research paper (1987), 16.

20. William H. Buchanan, interview, 1958.

21. "Record of Hagley Yard Housing," acc. 302. George Cheney's report noted the presence of at least 177 outbuildings. An exact count is impossible because Cheney often used the collective term "outbuildings."

22. Glassie, *Passing the Time,* 344. Dooryards served this function in New England. See Thomas C. Hubka, *Big House, Little House, Back House, Barn: The Connected Farm Buildings of New England* (Hanover, N.H.: University Press of New England, 1984), 77–80.

23. Elizabeth Beacom, interview, 1967.

24. Eleanor Kane, interview, 1984.

25. Quoted in Glenn Porter, *The Workers' World at Hagley,* exhibition catalog (Greenville: Eleutherian Mills–Hagley Foundation, 1984), 40.

26. Samuel Shogren, "Lifeways of the Industrial Worker: The Archaeological Record—A Summary of Three Field Seasons at Blacksmith's Hill," unpublished research report, HML (Oct. 10, 1986), 13–17.

27. Quoted in Tom Carter, *The Victorian Garden* (Salem, N.H.: Salem House, 1985), 23.

28. Karen Marie Probst, "Recommendations for a ca. 1870–85 Workers' Vegetable Garden at the Hagley Museum" (M.S. nonthesis project, University of Delaware, 1987), appendix D, 3.

29. Norman B. Wilkinson, *E. I. du Pont, Botaniste: The Beginning of a Tradition* (Charlottesville: University of Virginia Press for the Eleutherian Mills–Hagley

Foundation, 1972), 5–7, 49–55, and 67–77. The family's enthusiasm for horticulture reached its fullest expression in the extensive gardens of Henry Francis du Pont at Winterthur and those of Pierre S. du Pont II at Longwood. Henry was the grandson of Boss Henry, and Pierre was the grandson of Alfred Victor.

30. William M. Gardner and Joan M. Walker, "A Small History of the Forgotten and the Never Known," Delaware Department of Transportation Archaeology Series No. 84 (1990), 17.

31. "Depense de Menage—1811," loose receipt found in boarding book no. 1699, acc. 500; and miscellaneous receipts, Special Accounts file 1823–27, box 14, series C, group 3, LMSS. See also, Joan Jensen, *Loosening the Bonds: Mid-Atlantic Farm Women, 1750–1850* (New Haven: Yale University Press, 1986), 83.

32. Beverly Seaton, "Making the Best of Circumstances: The American Woman's Back Yard Garden," in *Making the American Home: Middle Class Women and Domestic Material Culture, 1840–1940,* ed. Marilyn Ferris Motz and Pat Browne (Bowling Green: Bowling Green State University Popular Press, 1988), 90.

33. Patricia M. Tice, *Gardening in America, 1830–1910,* exhibition catalog (Rochester: The Strong Museum, 1984), 49 and 53.

34. Probst, 3–7.

35. Timothy O'Neill, *Life and Tradition in Rural Ireland* (London: J. M. Dent and Sons, Ltd., 1977), 60.

36. Petit ledger 1840–41, 1845–56, acc. 500; Seventh U.S. Census (1850), Christiana Hundred, New Castle County, Del.; John Green inventory (1851). Green had "1 small lot of stable manure" worth $1 at the time of his death. He also owned property worth $900 in 1850.

37. On children's gardening, see Probst, 8–9. Weeds were pulled by hand, and pests were either squashed underfoot or dropped into jars of kerosene.

38. Quoted in Porter, 45.

39. On the planting and harvesting of potatoes in Ulster and in Delaware, see: Day and Williams, 54, 74, 94, 119, 129; Glassie, *Passing the Time,* 453–57; E. Estyn Evans, *Irish Heritage* (1942; reprinted, Dundalk: Dundalgan Press, 1949), 90–102; Probst, 137–40.

40. John Green inventory (Feb. 7, 1851).

41. Probst, 48–59; Glassie, *Passing the Time,* 456.

42. Glassie, *Passing the Time,* 455–56.

43. Tice, 54.

44. Day and Williams, 22, 50, 60, 90, 96.

45. Linda Keller Brown and Kay Mussell, "Introduction," in *Ethnic and Regional Food Ways in the United States: The Performance of Group Identity,* ed. Linda Keller Brown and Kay Mussell (Knoxville: University of Tennessee Press, 1984), 5.

46. "Straggler's Notebook, 1807–1809," no. 1700, acc. 500; petit ledger 1854–55, acc. 500; John Buchanan inventory (1868). Collier John McPherson bought a cow from Victorine du Pont Bauduy for $35 in 1854, and powder man John Buchanan owned a cow and calf worth $35 at his death in 1868.

47. Victor du Pont to Charles du Pont (2/24/1811), box 39, series E, group 10,

WMSS. The relevant text of Victor's letter reads, "Nous avons [illeg.] la se-maine dernière un des ouvriers de l'autre coté du creek, un viel Irlandais nommé John O'Gallagher, mort subitement à table en mangent son diner." Additional text, in English and in E. I. du Pont's hand reads, "John choked in eating a potato; and was dead before any help could arrive."

48. Dale Knobel, *Paddy and the Republic: Ethnicity and Nationality in Antebellum America* (Middletown, Conn.: Weslyan University Press, 1986), 88, 93, 121–24.

49. Roger Abrahams, "Equal Opportunity Eating: A Structural Excursus on Things of the Mouth," in Brown and Mussell, 31–34, passim.

50. Waverly Root and Richard de Rochemont, *Eating in America: A History* (New York: William Morrow and Co., 1976), 62–64. Root and de Rochemont note that potatoes were native to South America and were most likely brought back to Europe by sixteenth-century explorers. Sir Walter Raleigh is usually cred-ited with introducing the tubers to England and Ireland. He apparently began growing them on his estate in County Cork around 1588.

51. See, for example, the classic essay by L. M. Cullen, "Irish History Without the Potato," *Past and Present* 40 (July 1968): 78.

52. Michel Morineau, "The Potato in the 18th Century," in *Food and Drink in His-tory: Selections from the Annales,* vol. 5, ed. Robert Forster and Orest Ranum (Baltimore: Johns Hopkins University Press, 1979), 24. See also, Asa Briggs, *The Age of Improvement, 1783–1867* (New York: David McKay Co., Inc., 1959), 42–43.

53. Mary Douglas, "Deciphering a Meal," in *Myth, Symbol, and Culture,* ed. Clif-ford Geertz (New York: Norton, 1971), 61.

54. Sophie du Pont to Henry du Pont (2/25/1832), box 57, series D, group 9, WMSS. Translation: "then it will be like [finding] a hair in the soup."

55. Sophie du Pont to Henry du Pont (3/17/1832), box 57, series D, group 9, WMSS.

56. Sophie du Pont to Henry du Pont (9/28/1831), box 57, series D, group 9, WMSS. In this letter, Sophie informed her brother that, "Apples are scarce but the chestnut trees are loaded[.] I never saw such a fine crop as there are this year—unfortunately we have no one to gather them for us, nor to prevent the *place* urchins from stealing them, so I can't think *we* will have many."

57. Harold L. Peterson, *American Interiors: From Colonial Times to the Late Victo-rians* (New York: Scribner's, 1971), plates 102 and 103.

58. Ibid.

59. Edward B. Cheney, interview, 1958.

60. Robert Buist, *The Family Kitchen Gardener* (1847; reprinted, New York: C. M. Saxton & Co., 1856), 27.

61. Catherine Cheney, interview, 1984.

62. Probst, 18–22.

63. For a discussion of the practical and ideological problems associated with hogs in Federal Delaware, see Bernard L. Herman, "Fences," in *After-Ratification: Material Life in Delaware, 1789–1820,* ed. J. Ritchie Garrison, Bernard L. Herman, and Barbara McLean Ward (Newark, Del.: Museum Studies Pro-gram, 1988), 8–15.

64. Sophie du Pont, diary (12/8/1824).

65. Sophie du Pont to Henry du Pont (11/9/1831).

66. Sophie du Pont to Henry du Pont (12/14/1824).

67. Michael Tonner inventory (1818); Maurice Saucain inventory (1825); petit ledger 1845–46, acc. 500.

68. The recipe for corned beef was submitted to the Hagley Volunteers Cookbook Committee by a descendant of a powder mill worker. It appears along with many other nineteenth-century recipes in *The Hagley Cookbook: Recipes with a Brandywine Tradition* (Wilmington, Del.: privately printed, 1983), 155.

69. Smoke houses were commonplace in New Castle County. See Judith Quinn, "Food Ways," in Garrison, Herman, and Ward, 125–28. A former du Pont company blacksmith named Isaac Anderson had a "slaughter house" on his farm in Brandywine Hundred, and George Cheney recorded the presence of another "slaughter house" on company property in 1902. See Isaac Anderson inventory (1850); and [George Cheney], "Record of Housing in Hagley Yard" (1902), acc. 302.

70. Item L3-2873, Special Accounts file 1823–27, box 14, series C, group 3, LMSS.

71. Most feather beds were enumerated together with the bedstead, but a few were of sufficient size to be listed separately. Irishwoman Catherine Mousely valued her feather bed and bedding so highly that she willed them to her granddaughter, Catherine Pierce, in 1856. For examples, see Catherine Mousely, will, June 14, 1856; Ann Dougherty inventory (1835); John Young inventory (1846); William Boyd inventory (1857); and Elizabeth Cavender inventory (1865).

72. Aloysius Rowe, interview, 1968. Men rarely kept chickens. After he retired as gatekeeper, Alec Burns raised some "very fine Plymouth Rock chickens down there at the top of Long Row" in the 1890s. Edward Cheney, interview, 1958.

73. Miscellaneous receipt, Jan. 18, 1816, box 1705-A, acc. 500.

74. "Roll of men in the employ of E. I. du Pont de Nemours & Co. at the Powder Works 11 Sept. 1835," box 1878, series I, acc. 500. The fence makers' names were Christopher Cowan, Daniel Reilly, John Call, and Irvine McMullen.

75. Regina L. Blaszczyk, "Of Land and Water: The Republican Landscape of E. I. du Pont," unpublished research paper (1989), 12–18. See also Dell Upton, "White and Black Landscapes in Eighteenth Century Virginia," in *Material Life in America, 1600–1800,* ed. Robert Blair St. George (Boston: Northeastern University Press, 1988), 357–70.

76. Joan Jensen, *Loosening the Bonds: Mid-Atlantic Farm Women, 1750–1850* (New Haven: Yale University Press, 1986), 97.

77. Frank Zebley, *Along the Brandywine* (Wilmington, Del.: privately printed, 1940), 137. See also, William Flanagan, interview, 1960, and Elizabeth Beacom, interview, 1967.

78. Ella Fitzharris, interview, 1985.

79. Sophie du Pont to Henry du Pont (3/17/1832).

80. F. L. Mathewson, interview, 1968. Mathewson was born in 1895. He said that he learned about these events from his parents. The actual parties were "before my time."

81. Quoted in Porter, 18.

82. On fencing practices in Ulster see Day and McWilliams, 21, 54, 89, 119, and 121; and Glassie, *Passing the Time,* 439–40.

83. Paul G. Bourcier, "In Excellent Order: The Gentleman Farmer Views His Fences, 1790–1860," *Agricultural History* 58, no. 4 (October 1984): 550–52.

84. William Boyd inventory (1844); Thomas Holland inventory (1847); John Hayes inventory (1834).

85. George Frizzell to Francis Gurney du Pont, undated, employees file, box 17, acc. 504.

86. J. Thomas Scharf, *History of Delaware* (Philadelphia: L. J. Richards & Co., 1888), 764.

87. Bourcier, 546.

88. Ibid., 557.

89. Ibid., 557–58.

90. Herman, "Fences," 13.

91. E. W. Gilpin, Esq., to Alfred V. du Pont (5/9/1839), incoming file, acc. 1993; Alfred V. du Pont to E. W. Gilpin, Esq. (5/10/1839), outgoing file, acc. 1993.

92. Alfred V. du Pont to James Campbell, Wilmington (6/13/1843), incoming file, acc. 1993.

93. Bourcier, 560.

94. Thunderbird Archaeological Associates, "Archaeological Investigations of the Proposed Dualization of Rte 141 (Centre Road) from Rte 100 (Montchanin Road) to U.S. Rte 202 (Concord Pike), New Castle County, Delaware," Delaware Department of Transportation Archaeological Series No. 72 (1989), 15–16.

95. Jensen, 87.

96. Between 1850 and 1910, the number of farms swelled from 6,000 to 11,000. Thunderbird, 15–16.

97. Tice, 54–56.

98. Probst, 13.

99. Frank L. Mathewson, interview, 1968.

100. Tice, 56.

101. Edward Devenney, interview, 1984.

102. Jacqueline Hinsley, "19th Century Community Stores," Blacksmith's Hill Manual, sec. V, supplemental information (1989).

103. E. I. du Pont to Isaac Briggs (12/30/1815), box 3, series A, group 3, LMSS.

CHAPTER 8. LINEN TABLECLOTHS AND LACE CURTAINS (PP. 186–213)

1. Margaret Seitz, interview, 1984.

2. Blanche McAdoo Yetter, interview, May 1984. The prevalence of this custom cannot be determined since interviewers followed no consistent line of questioning.

3. Ella Fitzharris, interview, 1980, 1984, 1985. Fitzharris' paternal grandmother, midwife Katie Farren, had lace curtains in her home, too, and a special lace-trimmed "Sunday" apron for special occasions.

4. For examples, see Hasia Diner, *Erin's Daughters in America: Irish Immigrant Women in the Nineteenth Century* (Baltimore: Johns Hopkins University Press, 1986), 43; Kerby A. Miller, *Emigrants and Exiles: Ireland and the Irish Exodus to North America* (New York: Oxford University Press, 1985), 495; and David M. Emmons, *The Butte Irish: Class and Ethnicity in an American Mining Town, 1875–1925* (Urbana: University of Illinois Press, 1990), 77.

5. Stephen Thernstrom, *Progress and Poverty: Social Mobility in a Nineteenth-Century Industrial City* (1964; reprinted, New York: Atheneum, 1975), 83–84. Although there are many different ways to measure social status, Thernstrom concluded that occupation was the most "objective" criterion, and further, that an analysis of "the intricacies of etiquette" favored by sociologists was "of little value to the historian, for historical records rarely yield the information necessary to apply prestige categories systematically to societies of the past." This study of Newburyport is perhaps the most frequently cited study of working-class social mobility, and many social and labor historians have adopted this work-centered approach. Nevertheless, interdisciplinary research by scholars such as Rhys Isaac, Dell Upton, Jackson Lears, and Walter Susman suggests that the difficulty in assessing "prestige dimensions of class" is less an absence of historical records than a bias against certain kinds of sources and the methodologies needed to decode them.

6. Kerby Miller, "Class, Culture, and Immigrant Group Identity in the United States: The Case of Irish-American Ethnicity," in *Immigration Reconsidered: History, Sociology, and Politics,* ed. Virginia Yans-McLaughlin (New York: Oxford University Press, 1990), 107.

7. Nineteenth-century Americans generally accepted the existence of social classes, but they did not agree on how many there were or what criteria to use for categorization. Prior to the 1870s, the majority simply distinguished between the "consuming class," which meant individuals engaged in banking, speculation, and commerce, and the "producing class," an expansive category that included farmers, artisans, wage workers, and merchants. The latter term did not have the same meaning as "laboring class" or "working class" or "proletariat." Each of these categories referred to a specific subgroup. The rise of working men's parties caused additional confusion because their leaders sought to exclude merchants and professionals from "producers." Most Americans disagreed with this proposition. Despite warnings from radicals like Orestes Brownson, Charles Fourier, and Frances Wright, the majority also rejected the rhetoric of "class warfare," believing instead that the democratic process (the expansion and use of the franchise) would restore the natural "harmony of interests" by removing the "artificial" class distinctions perpetuated by the "rich and powerful." For more information, see Martin J. Burke, *The Conundrum of Class: Public Discourse on the Social Order in America* (Chicago: University of Chicago Press, 1995). Workers in antebellum Wilmington used a variety of labels, and included "manufacturers" within their definition of "producers." On this point, see Jama Lazerow, *Religion and the Working Class in Antebellum America* (Washington, D. C.: Smithsonian Institution Press, 1995), 96. For typical statements by powder workers regarding social

divisions, see Glenn Pryor, "Workers' Lives at the du Pont Powder Mills, 1877–1912" (B.A. thesis, University of Delaware, 1977), 4.

8. Last will and testament of Catharine Gibbons, filed January 23, 1895, New Castle County Probate Court. Photocopy found in "Easy reference file" for John Gibbons, HML. Born in the Parish of Conwall, County Donegal, around 1821, Gibbons emigrated to Delaware with the help of his brothers-in-law, Hugh Creeran and William McCarron. He commenced working in the powder yards as a common laborer on June 10, 1844, earning $15.50 per month. Two years later, he married Catherine Dougherty and began renting a house. On April 1, 1847, he "went to the powder," where, under the watchful eyes of Hagley Yard foreman Edward Hurst, he slowly learned the mysteries of his trade. After Hurst died in the explosion of 1863, the company made Gibbons his successor. With overtime and the wages of fourteen-year-old Charles Gibbons, the family's total income in the 1860s and 1870s usually exceeded $720 per annum. In 1873, John borrowed from Sophie du Pont $500, which he put toward the purchase of a house at 1629 Lincoln Street in Wilmington. He repaid her in regular installments, but the family continued to reside in their company-owned house until John's death on January 7, 1885. Catharine commissioned an elaborately carved set of white marble stones for his grave at St. Joseph's on the Brandywine, and the New Castle County Probate Court evaluated his estate at more than $5,000, excluding real property. He was a convincing model of the self-made man. See: Robert Taylor correspondence, series B, acc. 500; petit ledgers, 1842–44, 1845–46, 1847, 1854–55, 1863, 1872, acc. 500; boarding book no. 1699, acc. 500; Seventh (1850) and Ninth (1870) U.S. censuses, Christiana Hundred, New Castle County, Del.; Henry du Pont to Sophie du Pont (1/23/1873), item W9–29967, box 75, series E, group 9, WMSS; John Gibbons, probate inventory, February 27, 1885, New Castle County probate records; and Margaret Seitz, interview, 1984. On the ideology of the self-made man, see Mary P. Ryan, *Cradle of the Middle Class: The Family in Oneida County, New York, 1790–1865* (New York: Cambridge University Press, 1981), 146–85.

9. Karen Haltunnen, *Confidence Men and Painted Women: A Study of Middle-Class Culture in America, 1830–1870* (New Haven: Yale University Press, 1982); Stuart M. Blumin, *The Emergence of the Middle Class: Social Experience in the American City, 1760–1900* (New York: Cambridge University Press, 1989); John Kasson, *Rudeness and Civility: Manners in Nineteenth-Century Urban America* (New York: Hill and Wang, 1990); Richard Bushman, *The Refinement of America: Persons, Houses, Cities* (New York: W. W. Norton, 1992).

10. Daniel Walker Howe, *Making the American Self: Jonathan Edwards to Abraham Lincoln* (Cambridge: Harvard University Press, 1997), especially chap. 4, "The Emerging Ideal of Self-Improvement," passim.

11. Miller, *Emigrants and Exiles*, 210–13.

12. Angelique Day and Patrick McWilliams, eds., *Parishes of County Tyrone 1, 1821, 1823, 1831–36*, volume 5 of *Ordnance Survey Memoirs of Ireland* (Belfast: The Institute of Irish Studies, 1993), 96 and 91.

13. Miller, *Emigrants and Exiles*, 389–90.

14. Day and McWilliams, 121.
15. Margot J. Anderson, *The American Census: A Social History* (New Haven: Yale University Press, 1988), 32–57.
16. Ruth C. Linton, "To the Promotion and Improvement of Youth: The Brandywine Manufacturers' Sunday School" (M.A. thesis, University of Delaware, 1981), 41.
17. Betty-Bright Low and Jacqueline Hinsley, *Sophie du Pont, A Young Lady in America: Sketches, Diaries, and Letters, 1823–33* (New York: Harry N. Abrams, Inc., 1987), 15.
18. Joseph Frazier Wall, *Alfred I. du Pont: The Man and His Family* (New York: Oxford University Press, 1990), 18. Henry and Meta du Pont incorporated the family crest into their daughter's wedding invitation in 1873. See item W9-30018, Papers of Sophie du Pont, box 75, series 2, group 9, WMSS. Other members used it to mark their personal stationery.
19. Household account books, 1851–55, Papers of Sophie du Pont, series F, group 9, WMSS. See also, Diary, 1843, Papers of Victorine du Pont Bauduy, box 14, series A, group 6, WMSS.
20. In the 1830s, for example, du Pont employees pledged various sums to Francis Petitdemange, a former powder man, and his family, who lost most of their "their household furniture, wearing apparel, and also a part of his crop of potatoes some seed wheat" in a fire. "Subscription to help Francis Petitdemange," n.d., box 30, series B, acc. 384. Deductions for the Poor of Scotland and Ireland appear in the petit ledger for 1847.
21. Alfred du Pont, E. I. du Pont de Nemours and Co., to Charles McKinney, Wilkes Barre, Pennsylvania (Deccember 1843), series A, group 5, LMSS.
22. John Charles Rumm, "Mutual Interests: Managers and Workers at the Du Pont Company, 1802–1915," vols. 1 and 2 (Ph.D. diss., University of Delaware, 1989), 23–32.
23. Glenn Uminowicz, "Earnings and Terms of Service: Hagley Powdermen in 1850," unpublished research paper, HML (1979).
24. "List of Hands, 1820," file 48, acc. 146; "Population on the Property of E. I. du Pont & Co., 1829," file 143, box 9, acc. 146.
25. "Centennial Resolution of the Du Pont Company, 1902," no. 946, part 2, series II, acc. 500.
26. "Roll of Men in the Employ of E. I. du Pont de Nemours & Co. at the Powder Works 11 Sept. 1835," box 1878, series I, acc. 500; Seventh U.S. Census (1850), Christiana and Brandywine Hundreds, New Castle County, Del. Because so many employees left the community between 1835 and 1850, I also cross-checked the names of workers with the names of parents in the BMSS receiving books, acc. 389, which frequently indicate what happened to both adults and children after they moved away.
27. Petit ledgers, 1834–36, 1837–39, 1842–44, acc. 500; and ledgers 66 and 69, Charles I. du Pont and Company, acc. 500.
28. Uminowicz, 15.
29. While a complete account of this community's out-migration is impossible, documents kept by Victorine du Pont Bauduy and her sisters track the movements

of hundreds of individuals and offer important testimony to their social, geographic, and economic mobility. Between 1817 and 1850, Victorine registered 1,187 children at the Brandywine Manufacturers' Sunday School, of whom 393 (34 percent) left the community, sometimes with their parents, and sometimes as adults. The vast majority of these (34 percent) she simply listed as having "moved away." Since opportunities for skilled labor were more plentiful in urban areas, 12 percent moved to Philadelphia and 8 percent went to Wilmington. Textile manufacturing was a logical pursuit for many Catholic families from Ulster, and 22 percent resettled in places like Manayunk, Darby, and Chester, Pennsylvania. Another 13 percent of the Sunday school scholars "went West." BMSS receiving books, acc. 389.

30. McDermot family letters, file 21, box 6, acc. 389; and Rosanna McDermott, The Valley of Spruce Run, Blairsville, Derry Township, to Victorine du Pont Bauduy (7/20/1839), box 10, series A, group 6, WMSS.

31. Joshua Gibbons to V. E. Bauduy (6/20/1835), file 21, box 6, acc. 389.

32. McDermot family letters, file 21, box 6, acc. 389.

33. S. B. Brown letter (3/26/1872), file 21, box 6, acc. 389. S. B. Brown previously worked as a clerk in the du Pont company office. See entries for January 1863, item 1703, acc. 500. This individual is likely the "Samuel Brown, boy," who commenced as a common laborer on May 1, 1852, and went to the powder on October 18, 1853. A fourteen-year-old, Irish-born youth named Samuel Brown resided with the family of twenty-two-year-old Nathaniel Brown in 1850. Though a "farmer" with property in Christiana Hundred valued at $550, Nathaniel also worked for du Pont and became a powder man in 1852. An older Samuel Brown died in the explosion of 1847, leaving a widow and several children, including a namesake born in 1842.

34. A & E Baxter to Respected Mistress [Victorine Bauduy], Nashville, Tennessee (11/23/1863), file 21, box 6, acc. 389, BMSS. Four-year-old Edward Baxter emigrated to the Brandywine in February 1840 with his mother, Catharine, and two siblings. His father, Malcolm, died in an explosion on April 14, 1847, and Edward began to work as an outdoor laborer the following May. According to the Sunday school ledgers, he later served an apprenticeship in the company keg mill. "A" is likely his wife. See petit ledgers 1840–41 and 1847, acc. 500.

35. These figures are derived from the 1850 U.S. Census, which enumerates 57 powder "manufacturers," 8 "powder makers," 1 "collier," 2 "refiners." To these individuals I have added various helpers, powder cart men, and dry house men and so forth, who are mixed in with outdoor hands and assorted others as "laborers." Just five years earlier, the company employed 98 full-time powder workers, so an estimate of 100 in 1850 seems plausible. See petit ledger 1845–46.

36. William Henry Miller III, interview, 1984.

37. Francis Gurney du Pont to Jackson & Sharp Car Works (9/26/1890), recommendations file, box 3, acc. 504.

38. Francis Gurney du Pont to Harlan and Hollingsworth Co. (5/10/1899), recommendations file, box 3, acc. 504; and James F. Toy, interview, 1960. Other oral

histories attest to sons seeking work outside the powder yards. See William Buchanan, interview, 1958, and Eleanor Kane, interview, 1984.

39. Petit ledgers 1845–46 and 1885, acc. 500. Not every Catholic authorized the company to deduct pew rent payments, however.

40. On Irish Catholic attitudes toward social mobility, see: Miller, *Emigrants and Exiles,* 313–28 and 332–34; Colleen McDannell, "True Men as We Need Them: Catholicism and the Irish-American Male," *American Studies* 27, no. 2 (Fall 1986): 30–31; Jeffrey Burns, "The Ideal Catholic Child: Images from Catholic Textbooks," unpublished research paper, Center for the Study of American Catholicism, Notre Dame University (1978); and William F. Hartford, *Working People of Holyoke: Class and Ethnicity in a Massachusetts Mill Town, 1850–1960* (New Brunswick: Rutgers University Press, 1990), 63–64.

41. Ann McGran to Victorine Bauduy (4/17/1834), box 10, series A, group 6, WMSS. See also, Heald, 13–19.

42. Receiving books, BMSS, acc. 389; Sarah Heald, "Report on the Biographical Research for the Brandywine Manufacturer's Sunday School," unpublished research report, 1984.

43. BMSS receiving books, acc. 389; Seventh U.S. Census (1850), Christiana Hundred, New Castle County, Delaware.

44. "Notebook of Correspondence," file 22, box 6, acc. 389.

45. Heald, 23–26 and 37–39.

46. Heald, 78–82. Additional documents are found in the Danby Collection, folder 1, box 80, Historical Society of Delaware, Wilmington, Del. These include: Henry Danby's will; his probate inventory; the settlement of his estate; his marriage certificate to Maria Lackey; the naturalization papers of his father, John Danby; his mother's will; Maria's 1835 certificate of marriage to Walter Lackey; and an 1834 love letter sent by J. W. Caldwell to Maria McCullough, of "Mount Airy," Christiana Hundred.

47. On the relationship between women, gentility, consumption, and mobility in the nineteenth century, see Ryan, 200–203; Blumin, 183–91; Diner, 66–69; Bushman, 230–37, 273–79, 440–46; Colleen McDannell, *The Christian Home in Victorian America, 1840–1900* (Bloomington: Indiana University Press, 1986), chap. 6, passim; and Jeanne Boydston, *Home and Work: Housework, Wages, and the Ideology of Labor in the Early Republic* (New York: Oxford University Press, 1990), 102–103. While labor historians readily acknowledge that the economic strategies of immigrant families rely on women's earnings, they usually attribute social advancement to the occupational and property mobility achieved by men. For a critique of this male-centered perspective, see Carole Turbin, *Working Women of Collar City: Gender, Class and Community in Troy, NY 1864–1886* (Urbana: University of Illinois Press, 1992), 41.

48. Sophie du Pont was so impressed with their efforts to edify their daughter that she acknowledged the lessons in her diary, saying, "Now the humble Fanny Martin is receiving from the fruits of her parents' thrift an education far above what her parents had." Sophie du Pont, diary (3/5/1837), box 93, series F, group 9, WMSS.

49. See petit ledger 1845, acc. 500, and "Subscription to the Delaware Sentinel,"

n.d., box 497, acc. 500. There are fifty-one men listed, including foreman William Green, powder men James McLaughlin and Edward Dougherty, and Alexis du Pont. Since Green and McLaughlin died in the explosion of 1847, the list likely dates to the mid-1840s.

50. Linton, 60.
51. James Gallagher to Rev. Patrick Reilly (1852), collection 42, Rev. Patrick Reilly Papers, American Catholic Historic Society, Philadelphia, Pennsylvania.
52. J. Thomas Scharf, *History of Delaware, Vols. 1 and 2* (Philadelphia: L. J. Richards & Co., 1888), 689.
53. See petit ledgers 1845–46, 1847, and 1852–53; Seventh U.S. Census (1850), Christiana Hundred, New Castle County, Del.; and Patrick A. Lynch, St. Charles Seminary, to Sophie du Pont (4/11/1862), item W92666, series E, group 9, WMSS. After taking his vows, Patrick went to St. Mark's Church in Bristol, Pennsylvania, where he served a large parish and rode through the countryside much as Rev. Patrick Kenny had done several decades earlier. Lynch enjoyed a regular correspondence with Sophie in the 1870s. His father, John, served as Sophie's gardener in the 1850s and 1860s, then moved with his ailing wife, Catharine, to Bristol, where they seem to have lived in the rectory with their son.
54. Alexis I. du Pont High School opened ca. 1892. Elizabeth Beacom graduated with the class of 1908 and then attended Goldey's secretarial program in 1909. John A. Dougherty also attended Goldey. Edward Cheney attended the Wilmington Business School, which William Henry Beacom operated above Govatos Candy Store downtown. So did his sister. See Elizabeth Beacom, interview, 1967; Edward B. Cheney, interview, 1958; and John A. Dougherty, interview, 1956.
55. Wall, 87.
56. Edward B. Cheney, interview, 1958.
57. John A. Dougherty, interview, 1956. Dougherty was born at the Upper Banks in 1880. His mother had been born in the same house, shortly before her father died in an 1861 explosion. His father, an immigrant, started work in 1876. Dougherty continued to advance. He performed general clerical and janitorial work in the office at first, but the other clerks tutored him in grammar, spelling, and mathematics. In 1910 he moved downtown to the Du Pont Company's new corporate headquarters, and ended up as a statistician in the Sales Department. He retired after forty years of service.
58. Lawrence J. Taylor, *Occasions of Faith: An Anthropology of Irish Catholicism* (Philadelphia: University of Pennsylvania Press, 1995), 84–85.
59. Joseph M. Lalley, Jr., *Our Irish Ancestors and Their Descendants and the Times in Which They Lived* (Asheville, N.C.: privately printed, 2000), appendix A. Author's possession.
60. McDannell, 12.
61. Sophie du Pont to Eleuthera du Pont Smith (11/3/1830), outgoing file 1830–31, series D, group 9, WMSS.
62. Sophie du Pont, diary (10/22/1840 and 10/23/1840), box 93, series F, group 9, WMSS. An earlier diary entry, on 6/3/1832, recorded a meeting with E. Russell:

"I never met anyone in that class so interesting and lovely—She realized the description I have often read in story books & novels, of cottagers—I was delighted with her manners as well as her appearance."

63. For examples, see the following probate inventories: John Fitzgerald alias O'Gallagher, 1811; Thomas Quig, 1815; William Allison, 1818; John O'Brien, 1818; Michael Mooney, 1818; David Flinn, 1818; Hugh McCalegue, 1818; Hugh Brady, 1818; Thomas Kenaday, 1818; John Dunnery, 1818; Philip Dugan, 1818; John Donohoe, 1818; Samuel Campbell, 1825; and John McGuiness, 1835, all found in New Castle County probate records.

64. Day and Williams, 103.

65. Ibid., 18 and 124.

66. Blumin, 140–44.

67. Jacqueline Hinsley and Betty-Bright Low, *Sophie du Pont, A Young Lady in America: Sketches, Diaries and Letters, 1823–33* (New York: Harry N. Abrams, Inc., 1987), 127.

68. Victorine Bauduy to Sophie du Pont ("Wed. Evening," n.d.), 1850–60 file, box 6, series A, group 6, WMSS. For a list of clothing "premiums" given to Sunday school scholars, see acc. 389.

69. Joanna Smith du Pont to Eugene du Pont (2/24/1857), outgoing correspondence, acc. 1993.

70. Haltunnen, 194.

71. Quoted in Howe, 132.

72. Shirley Teresa Wadja, "Self-Culture in Nineteenth-Century America," paper presented to the Delaware Seminar in Art History and Material Culture, University of Delaware, Newark, Delaware (1996). Author's possession.

73. Joseph Kett, *The Pursuit of Knowledge Under Difficulties: From Self-Improvement to Adult Education in America, 1750–1990* (Stanford: Stanford University Press, 1994). Some wage-earning immigrants pursued self-culture in a naked effort to better themselves financially. But others genuinely shared the values of frugality, honesty, self-discipline, punctuality, and order that formed the heart of bourgeois American culture. In the words of Daniel Howe, "It is unduly patronizing" to assume otherwise. On this point, see Howe, 125; and Anne Boylan, *Sunday School: The Formation of an American Institution, 1790–1880* (New Haven: Yale University Press, 1988), 38.

74. Haltunnen, 193; Richard Brown, *Knowledge Is Power: The Diffusion of Information in Early America, 1700–1865* (New York: Oxford University Press, 1989), 272.

75. Sophie du Pont to Henry du Pont (8/16/1832), outgoing correspondence, series D, group 9, WMSS.

76. Quoted in Glenn Porter, *The Workers' World at Hagley*, exhibition catalog (Greenville, Del.: Eleutherian Mills–Hagley Foundation, 1981), 37.

77. W. E. B. Du Bois, *The Souls of Black Folk* (1903; reprinted, New York, Penguin Books, 1969), 45. "It is a peculiar sensation, this double-consciousness, this sense of always looking at one's self through the eyes of others. . . . One ever feels his twoness,—an American, a Negro; two souls, two thoughts, two unreconciled strivings; two warring ideals in one dark body, whose dogged strength alone keeps it from being torn asunder."

78. Dolores Hayden writes eloquently of the way public history can be used to foster a sense of cultural belonging or interconnectedness among members of the same society. See her book, *The Power of Place: Urban Landscapes as Public History* (Cambridge: MIT Press, 1995), 8–9. Other scholars reached similar conclusions about the relationship between culture and power. See, for example, Bushman, 410; and Brian Mitchell, *The Paddy Camps: The Irish of Lowell, 1821–1861* (Urbana: University of Illinois Press, 1988), 155.

79. Burke, 101–102.

80. Walter Nugent, "Toqueville, Marx, and American Class Structure," *Social Science History* 12, no. 4 (Winter 1988): 331–32.

81. For a good, clear overview of the various theories advanced for American labor's failure to organize, see Eric Foner, "Why Is There No Socialism in the United States?" *History Workshop Journal* 17 (1984): 57–80.

82. Alexis de Tocqueville, *Democracy in America,* ed. and abridged by Richard D. Heffner (New York: Mentor Books, 1956), 265.

83. Ibid., 211 and 263.

84. Burke, 161.

85. Brown, 287.

86. Ibid., 268.

87. McDannell, 30.

88. Miller, *Emigrants and Exiles,* 567.

89. Sophie du Pont, diary (7/21/1825), box 93, series F, group 9, WMSS.

90. The du Pont Irish allied with the Federalists in the 1810s and 1820s. In the 1840 election, they voted for William Henry Harrison and came home singing Whig songs. As historian Daniel Howe notes, the Whig party especially endorsed the culture of self-improvement, and some of the du Pont Irish probably found its platform genuinely appealing. The company's Irish-born, Presbyterian, master carpenter, John Q. Stirling, was such a staunch Whig that he always "stood shoulder to shoulder with the late Gen. Henry du Pont at the window of the polling place." After 1860, the du Pont Irish voted Republican. Around the end of the century, there was a greater tendency for the powder workers to vote Democratic, perhaps because company managers began to repudiate mutualism at this time. See *Delaware Gazette,* October 20, 1829 and October 27, 1829; Sophie du Pont to Frank du Pont (10/7/1840), outgoing correspondence, series E, group 9, WMSS; Howe, 135; photocopy of newspaper clipping (1889), Easy Reference file, HML; Wilmington *Every Evening,* October 19, 1888, and November 15, 1894, microfilm; Porter, 24–26.

91. Ella Fitzharris, interview, 1980.

92. Eleanor Kane, interview, 1984. Kane recalled that her grandmother, Catharine Gibbons Dougherty (as distinct from Catharine Dougherty Gibbons), helped make a trousseau for her daughter, Ann. They bought special "white goods" for the purpose at Smith and Solengers in Wilmington. Evidently, the place of purchase was just as important to the story as the creation of the items.

93. Dr. Margaret Seitz, interview by author, February 3, 2002.

94. Bluford Adams, "Ethnicity by a Different Name: Theorizing Group Identity in Gilded Age New England,"American Studies Association Annual Meeting,

Detroit, Michigan, October 2000; Timothy J. Meagher, *Inventing Irish America: Generation, Class, and Ethnic Identity in a New England City, 1880–1928* (Notre Dame: University of Notre Dame Press, 2001), chap. 4.

95. Margaret M. Mulrooney, "Delaware," in *The Encyclopedia of the Irish in America,* ed. Michael Glazier (South Bend: University of Notre Dame Press, 1999).

BIBLIOGRAPHY

MANUSCRIPT COLLECTIONS

Hagley Museum and Library, Greenville, Delaware (hereafter HML)
    Records of E. I. du Pont de Nemours and Company, 1801–1902, acc. 500
    Records of the Brandywine Manufacturers' Sunday School, acc. 289
    Papers of the Daughters of E. I. du Pont, group 6, WMSS
    Papers of Samuel Francis du Pont and his wife, Sophie Madeleine du Pont, group 9, WMSS
    Papers of Charles I. du Pont and Company, 1810–1856, acc. 500 and 501
    Papers of Francis Gurney du Pont, acc. 504
    Hagley Yard Housing Record, acc. 302
    Papers of Rev. Patrick Kenny, acc. 323
    Oral History Files
Historical Society of Delaware, Wilmington, Delaware
    Wilmington City Directories
    Danby Collection
Morris Library, University of Delaware, Newark, Delaware
    New Castle County Probate Records, mic. no. 3087
    Fifth (1830), Sixth (1840), Seventh (1850), and Ninth (1870) U.S. Censuses, mic. no. 22
Diocese of Wilmington Archives, Greenville, Delaware
    RG 37, St. Joseph's on the Brandywine
St. Joseph's on the Brandywine Roman Catholic Church, Greenville, Delaware
    Register of Baptisms, 9/1846 to 1895
Family History Center, Wilmington Stake Office, LDS, Wilmington, Delaware
    Cathedral of St. Peter, Registers of Marriages and Baptisms from 8/1796 to 4/1834; Register of Baptisms, 5/1829–1907, mic. no. 1787748, project roll no. 220–1
    St. Joseph's on the Brandywine, Registers of Baptisms and Marriages, 9/1846 to 1895, mic. no. 1822513, project roll no. 220–20.

PERIODICALS

Delaware Gazette and State Journal (Morris Library)
Delaware State Journal (Morris Library)

Mirror of the Times (Morris Library)
Delaware Republican (Morris Library)
Blue Hen's Chicken (Morris Library)
Every Evening (Morris Library)
Philadelphia Catholic Herald (American Catholic Historical Society, Philadelphia, Pennsylvania)
Harper's Weekly Bazaar (Winterthur Museum and Library)

PUBLISHED WORKS

A Catechism of Christian Doctrine, prepared and enjoined by Order of the Third Plenary Council of Baltimore. 1885; reprinted, New York: Benzinger Bros., 1921.

A Christian's Guide to Heaven: Or A Manual of Spiritual Exercises for Catholics. Philadelphia: E. Cummiskey, 1833.

Adams, Donald, Jr. "The Standard of Living during American Industrialization: Evidence from the Brandywine Region, 1800–1860." *Journal of Economic History* 42 (1982): 903–17.

Ahlstrom, Sydney E. *A Religious History of the American People*. New Haven: Yale University Press, 1972.

Alford, Richard D. *Naming and Identity: A Cross-Cultural Study of Personal Naming Practices*. New Haven: HRAF Press, 1988.

Anderson, Margot J. *The American Census: A Social History*. New Haven: Yale University Press, 1988.

Baron, Ava, ed. *Work Engendered: Toward a New History of American Labor*. Ithaca: Cornell University Press, 1991.

Beaudry, Mary C. "Words for Things: Linguistic Analysis of Probate Inventories." In *Documentary Archaeology in the New World,* ed. Mary C. Beaudry. New York: Cambridge University Press, 1988.

Beecher, Catherine. *A Treatise on Domestic Economy*. New York: Harper and Bros., 1848.

Benzinger Brothers. *Benzinger Brothers' Pontifical Institute of Art*. Catalog. New York: privately printed, 1900.

——. *Catalogue of Church Ornaments, Vestments, Materials, and Regalia*. New York: privately printed, 1881.

Beresford, M. W. "The Back-to-Back House in Leeds, 1787–1937." In *The History of Working-Class Housing: A Symposium,* ed. Stanley D. Chapman. Totowa, N.J.: Rowan and Littlefield, 1971.

Berger, Peter. *The Capitalist Revolution: Fifty Propositions about Prosperity, Equality and Liberty*. New York: Basic Books, 1986.

——, and Thomas Luckmann. *The Social Construction of Reality: A Treatise in the Sociology of Knowledge*. New York: Anchor Books, 1966.

Berlanstein, Leonard R., ed. *Rethinking Labor History: Essays on Discourse and Class Analysis*. Urbana: University of Illinois Press, 1993.

Blackmar, Elizabeth. *Manhattan for Rent, 1785–1850*. Ithaca: Cornell University Press, 1989.

Blumin, Stuart M. *The Emergence of the Middle Class: Social Experience in the American City, 1760-1900*. New York: Cambridge University Press, 1989.

Bodnar, John. *The Transplanted*. Bloomington: Indiana University Press, 1985.

Bonnell, Victoria E., and Lynn Hunt, eds. *Beyond the Cultural Turn: New Directions in the Study of Society and Culture*. Berkeley: University of California Press, 1999.

Boris, Eileen. "A Man's Dwelling House Is His Castle: Tenement House Cigar Making and the Judicial Imperative." In *Work Engendered: Toward a New History of American Labor*, ed. Ava Baron. Ithaca: Cornell University Press, 1991.

Bourcier, Paul G. "In Excellent Order: The Gentleman Farmer Views His Fences, 1790-1860." *Agricultural History* 58, no. 4 (October 1984): 546-64.

Boyd's Delaware State Directory. Wilmington: William H. Boyd, 1860.

Boydston, Jeanne. *Home and Work: Housework, Wages, and the Ideology of Labor in the Early Republic*. New York: Oxford University Press, 1990.

Boyer, Charles E. *Early Forges and Furnaces in New Jersey*. Philadelphia: University of Pennsylvania Press, 1931.

Boylan, Anne M. *Sunday School: The Formation of an American Institution, 1790-1880*. New Haven: Yale University Press, 1988.

Brewer, Priscilla J. "We Have Got a Very Good Cooking Stove: Advertising, Design and Consumer Response to the Cookstove, 1815-1880." *Winterthur Portfolio* 25, no. 2 (Spring 1990): 35-54.

Briggs, Asa. *The Age of Improvement, 1783-1867*. New York: David McKay Co., Inc., 1959.

Brown, Linda Keller, and Kay Mussell, eds. *Ethnic and Regional Food Ways in the United States: The Performance of Group Identity*. Knoxville: University of Tennessee Press, 1984.

Brown, Richard. *Knowledge Is Power: The Diffusion of Information in Early America, 1700-1865*. New York: Oxford University Press, 1989.

Bryant, William Cullen, ed. *Picturesque America, or, The Land We Live In*. New York: D. Appleton & Co., 1872.

Buder, Stanley. *Pullman: An Experiment in Industrial Order and Community Planning, 1880-1930*. New York: Oxford University Press, 1967.

Buhle, Mari Jo. "Gender and Labor History." In *Perspectives on American Labor History: The Problems of Synthesis*, ed. Alice Kessler-Harris and J. Carroll Moody. DeKalb: Northern Illinois University Press, 1990.

Buist, Robert. *The Family Kitchen Gardener*. New York: C. M. Saxton & Co., 1856.

Burchell, R. A. *The San Francisco Irish, 1848-1888*. Berkeley: University of California Press, 1980.

Burke, Martin J. *The Conundrum of Class: Public Discourse on the Social Order in America*. Chicago: University of Chicago Press, 1995.

Bushman, Richard. *The Refinement of America: Persons, Houses, Cities*. New York: W. W. Norton, 1992.

Butler, Alban, Rev. *Lives of the Irish Saints*. Dublin: J. Coyne, 1823.

———. *Lives of Saints*. New York: Benzinger Brothers, 1878; reprinted, New York: Benzinger Brothers, 1894.

[Butler, James]. *The Larger Catechism of Most Rev. Dr. James Butler*. Philadelphia: E. Cummiskey, 1841.

Byington, Margaret. *Homestead: The Households of a Milltown*. 1910; reprinted, Pittsburgh: University of Pittsburgh Press, 1974.

Calvert, Karin Lee Fishbeck. *Children in the House: The Material Culture of Early Childhood, 1600–1900*. Boston: Northeastern University Press, 1992.

Campbell, Colin. *The Romantic Ethic and the Spirit of Modern Consumerism*. London: Basil Blackwell, 1987.

Campbell, Debra. "Flannery O'Connor Is Not John Updike." *American Quarterly* 43, no. 2 (June 1991): 333–40.

Carey, Patrick W. *An Immigrant Bishop: John England's Adaptation of Irish Catholicism to American Republicanism*. New York: U.S. Catholic Historical Society, 1982.

———. *People, Priests and Prelates: Ecclesiastical Democracy and the Tensions of Trusteeism*. Notre Dame: University of Notre Dame Press, 1987.

Carr, Lois Green, and Lorena Walsh. "Inventories and the Analysis of Wealth and Consumption Patterns in St. Mary's County, Maryland, 1658–1777." *Historical Methods* 13, no. 2 (1980): 81–104.

Carr, William H. A. *The du Ponts of Delaware*. New York: Dodd, Mead and Company, 1964.

Carson, Cary. "The Consumer Revolution in Colonial British America: Why Demand?" In *Of Consuming Interests: The Style of Life in the Eighteenth Century*, ed. Cary Carson, Ronald Hoffman, and Peter J. Albert. Charlottesville: University of Virginia Press, 1994.

Carter, Tom. *The Victorian Garden*. Salem, N.H.: Salem House, 1985.

Casino, Joseph J. "From Sanctuary to Involvement: A History of the Catholic Parish in the North East." In *The American Catholic Parish: Volume I, The North East, South East, and South Central States*, ed. Jay P. Dolan. New York: Paulist Press, 1987.

Challoner, Rev. Dr. *The Catholic Christian Instructed*. Philadelphia: E. Cummiskey, 1841.

Clark, Clifford E., Jr. *The American Family Home, 1800–1860*. Chapel Hill: University of North Carolina Press, 1986.

Clark, Dennis. "The Philadelphia Irish." In *The Peoples of Philadelphia: A History of Ethnic Groups and Lower-Class Life, 1790–1940*, ed. Allen F. Davis and Mark H. Haller. Philadelphia: Temple University Press, 1978.

———. *The Irish Relations: Trials of an Immigrant Tradition*. East Brunswick, N.J.: Association of University Presses, 1982.

Cody, Cheryll Ann. "Naming, Kinship, and Estate Dispersal: Notes on Slave Family Life on a South Carolina Plantation." *William and Mary Quarterly* 39, no. 1 (1982): 192–211.

Coffee Run, 1772–1960: The Story of the Beginnings of the Catholic Faith in Delaware. Hockessin, Del.: privately printed, 1960.

Cohen, Lizabeth. "Embellishing a Life of Labor: An Interpretation of the Material Culture of American Working-Class Homes, 1885–1915." In *Common Places*, ed. Dell Upton and John Michael Vlach. Athens: University of Georgia Press, 1986.

———. *Making a New Deal: Industrial Workers in Chicago, 1919–1939*. New York: Cambridge University Press, 1990.

————. "Respectability at $50.00 Down, 25 Months to Pay! Furnishing a Working-Class Victorian Home." In *Victorian Furniture*, ed. Kenneth L. Ames. Philadelphia: Victorian Society of America, 1983.

Comaroff, Jean, and John Comaroff. *Of Revelation and Revolution: Christianity, Colonialism, and Consciousness in South Africa*. Chicago: University of Chicago Press, 1999.

Connolly, Sean. *Priests and People in Pre-Famine Ireland, 1780–1845*. New York: St. Martin's Press, 1982.

Corish, Patrick J. "Women and Religious Practice." In *Women in Pre-Modern Ireland*, ed. Margaret MacCurtain and Mary O'Dowd. Edinborough: Edinborough University Press, 1991.

Corson, Juliet. *Family Living on $500 A Year*. New York: Harper and Bros., 1888.

Crompton, Rosemary. "Class Theory and Gender." *The British Journal of Sociology* 40, no. 4 (1989): 565–87.

Cullen, L. M. "Irish History Without the Potato." *Past and Present* 40 (July 1968): 72–83.

Curran, Joseph M. *Hibernian Green on the Silver Screen*. Westport, Conn.: Greenwood Press, 1989.

Daniels, Roger. *Coming to America: A History of Immigration and Ethnicity in American Life*. New York: Harper Perennial, 1990.

Darnton, Robert. *The Great Cat Massacre and Other Episodes in French Cultural History*. New York: Basic Books, 1984.

Day, Angelique, and Patrick McWilliams, eds. *Parishes of County Tyrone 1: 1821, 1823, 1831–36*, vol. 5 of *Ordnance Survey Memoirs of Ireland*. Belfast: The Institute of Irish Studies, 1990.

————. *Parishes of County Tyrone 2*, vol. 20 of *Ordnance Survey Memoirs of Ireland*. Belfast: The Institute of Irish Studies, 1993.

De Breffny, Brian, and Rosemary Ffolliott. *The Houses of Ireland: Domestic Architecture from the Medieval Castle to the Edwardian Villa*. London: Thames and Hudson, 1975.

Deharbe, Rev. Joseph, S.J. *A Full Catechism of the Catholic Religion*, trans. Rev. John Fander. 5th ed. New York: Schwartz, Kirwin, & Fauss, 1876.

de Tocqueville, Alexis. *Democracy in America*, ed. and abridged by Richard D. Heffner. New York: Mentor Books, 1956.

Diner, Hasia. *Erin's Daughters in America: Irish Immigrant Women in the Nineteenth Century*. Baltimore: Johns Hopkins University Press, 1983.

Dolan, Jay. *The Immigrant Church: New York's Irish and German Catholics, 1815–1865*. Baltimore: Johns Hopkins University Press, 1975.

Douglas, Mary, and Baron Isherwood. *The World of Goods: Towards an Anthropology of Consumption*. New York: Basic Books, 1979.

Downing, Andrew Jackson. *The Architecture of Country Houses*. New York: D. Appleton Company, 1850.

Dubofsky, Melvyn. "Lost in a Fog: Labor Historians' Unrequited Search for a Synthesis." *Labor History* 32 (Spring 1991): 295–300.

Du Bois, W. E. B. *The Souls of Black Folk*. 1903; reprinted, New York, Penguin Books, 1969.

du Pont, Bessie Gardner, trans. *Life of Eleuthère Irénée du Pont from Contemporary Correspondence*. Newark: University of Delaware Press, 1925.

Emmons, David. *The Butte Irish: Class and Ethnicity in an American Mining Town, 1875–1925*. Urbana: University of Illinois Press, 1990.

England, Rev. Dr. *The Garden of the Soul: A Manual of Fervent Prayers, Pious Reflections, and Solid Instructions*. New York: D. & J. Sadlier, 1856.

Enstad, Nan. *Ladies of Labor, Girls of Adventure: Working Women, Popular Culture, and Labor Politics at the Turn of the Century*. New York: Columbia University Press, 1999.

Errigo, Joseph A. L. *A History of St. Joseph's on the Brandywine*. Wilmington: William N. Cann, Inc., 1941.

Evans, E. Estyn. *Irish Heritage*. 1942; reprinted, Dundalk: Dundalgan Press, 1949.

Evidence on the State of Ireland, taken before the Select Committee of the Houses of Lords and Commons. London: John Murray, 1825.

Farnham, Christie. "Sapphire? The Issue of Dominance in the Slave Family, 1830–1865." In *To Toil the Livelong Day: America's Women at Work,* ed. Carol Groneman and Mary Beth Norton. Ithaca: Cornell University Press, 1987.

Federal Writers' Project of the WPA. *Delaware: A Guide to the First State*. New York: Hastings House, 1938.

Foner, Eric. "Why Is There No Socialism in the United States?" *History Workshop Journal* 17 (1984): 57–80.

Fones-Wolf, Ken. *Trade-Union Gospel: Christianity and Labor in Industrial Philadelphia, 1865–1915*. Philadelphia: Temple University Press, 1989.

Fox-Genovese, Elizabeth, and Eugene Genovese. *The Fruits of Merchant Capitalism: Slavery and Bourgeois Property in the Rise and Expansion of Capitalism*. New York: Oxford University Press, 1983.

———. "The Political Crisis of Social History: A Marxian Perspective." *Journal of Social History* 10 (Winter 1976): 205–20.

Frank, Dana. "Gender, Consumer Organizing, and the Seattle Labor Movement, 1919–1929." In *Work Engendered: Toward a New History of American Labor,* ed. Ava Baron. Ithaca: Cornell University Press, 1991.

Fraser, Steve. *Labor Will Rule: Sidney Hillman and the Rise of American Labor*. New York: Maxwell MacMillan International, 1991.

Garner, John S. *The Model Company Town: Urban Design through Private Enterprise in Nineteenth-Century New England*. Amherst: University of Massachusetts Press, 1984.

Garrity, Elizabeth. *At Home: The American Family, 1750–1870*. New York: Harry N. Abrams, 1990.

Geertz, Clifford, ed. *The Interpretation of Cultures: Selected Essays*. New York: Basic Books, 1973.

———. *Myth, Symbol, and Culture*. New York: Norton, 1971.

Gerstle, Gary. *Working-Class Americanism: The Politics of Labor in a Textile City, 1914–1960*. New York: Cambridge University Press, 1989.

Gibbons, Rev. James. *The Faith of Our Fathers*. Baltimore: John Murphy & Co., 1879.

Glassie, Henry. "Eighteenth-Century Cultural Process in Delaware Valley Folk

Building." In *Common Places,* ed. Dell Upton and John Michael Vlach. Athens: University of Georgia Press, 1986.

———. "Irish." In *America's Architectural Roots: Ethnic Groups That Built America.* Washington, D.C.: The Preservation Press, 1986.

———. *Passing the Time in Ballymenone: Culture and History in an Ulster Community.* Philadelphia: University of Pennsylvania Press, 1983.

Glickman, Lawrence. "Inventing the 'American Standard of Living': Gender, Race, and Working-Class Identity, 1880–1925." *Labor History* 34, nos. 2–3 (Spring–Summer 1993): 221–35.

———. *A Living Wage: American Workers and the Making of Consumer Society.* Ithaca: Cornell University Press, 1997.

Godden, Geoffrey A. *The Illustrated Guide to Mason's Patent Ironstone China.* London: Barrie and Jenkins, Ltd., 1971.

Grier, Katherine C. *Culture and Comfort: People, Parlors, and Upholstery, 1850–1930.* Rochester, N.Y.: The Strong Museum, 1988.

Griffin, William D. *A Portrait of the Irish in America.* New York: Scribner's, 1981.

Groneman, Carole. "Working-Class Immigrant Women in Mid-Nineteenth-Century New York: The Irish Woman's Experience." *Journal of Urban History* 4, no. 3 (May 1978): 255–74.

Gustine, P. P. *Wholesale Price List of Furniture.* Philadelphia: privately printed, 1867.

Gutman, Herbert. *The Black Family in Slavery and Freedom, 1750–1925.* New York: 1976.

———. *Work, Culture, and Society in Industrializing America: Essays in Working-Class and Social History.* New York: Vintage Books, 1977.

The Hagley Cookbook: Recipes with a Brandywine Tradition. Wilmington, Del.: privately printed, 1983.

Hall, Jacquelyn Dowd, and James Leloudis, et al. *Like a Family: The Making of a Southern Cotton Mill World.* New York: W. W. Norton, 1987.

Haltunnen, Karen. *Confidence Men and Painted Ladies: A Study of Middle-Class Culture in America, 1830–1870.* New Haven: Yale University Press, 1982.

Handlin, Oscar. *The Uprooted.* 1951; reprinted, New York: Little, Brown and Company, 1979.

Hareven, Tamara. *Family Time and Industrial Time: The Relationship between the Family and Work in a New England Industrial Community.* New York: Cambridge University Press, 1982.

———, and Randolph Lagenbach. *Amoskeag: Life and Work in an American Factory-City.* New York: Pantheon Books, 1978

Harris, Richard, and Chris Hamnett. "The Myth of the Promised Land: The Social Diffusion of Home Ownership in Britain and North America." *Annals of the Association of American Geographers* 77, no. 2 (June 1987): 173–86.

Hartford, William F. *Working People of Holyoke: Class and Ethnicity in a Massachusetts Mill Town, 1850–1960.* New Brunswick: Rutgers University Press, 1990.

Harvey, Katherine. *The Best Dressed Miners: Life and Labor in the Maryland Coal Region, 1835–1910.* Ithaca: Cornell University Press, 1969.

Hayden, Dolores. *The Power of Place: Urban Landscapes as Public History.* Cambridge: MIT Press, 1995.

Heineman, Kenneth J. "A Catholic New Deal: Religion and Labor in 1930s Pittsburgh," *The Pennsylvania Magazine of History and Biography* 118, no. 4 (October 1994): 363–94.

Heinze, Andrew R. *Adapting to Abundance: Jewish Immigrants, Mass Consumption, and the Search for an American Identity*. New York: Columbia University Press, 1990.

Henretta, James. "Social History as Lived and Written." *American Historical Review* 84 (December 1979): 1295–1322.

Herman, Bernard L. *Architecture and Rural Life in Central Delaware, 1700–1900*. Knoxville: University of Tennessee Press, 1987.

——. "Fences." In *After Ratification: Material Life in Delaware, 1789–1820,* ed. J. Ritchie Garrison, Bernard L. Herman, and Barbara McLean Ward. Newark, Del.: Museum Studies Program, 1988.

——. "Multiple Materials, Multiple Meanings: The Fortunes of Thomas Mendenhall." *Winterthur Portfolio* 19 (1984): 67–89.

Hewitt, Nancy A. "Beyond the Search for Sisterhood: American Women's History in the 1980s." In *Unequal Sisters: A Multicultural Reader in U.S. Women's History,* ed. Ellen Carol Du Bois and Vicki Ruiz. New York: Routledge Press, 1990.

Hinsley, Jacqueline, and Betty-Bright Low. *Sophie du Pont: A Young Lady in America, Sketches, Diaries and Letters, 1823–1833*. New York: Harry N. Abrams, Inc., 1987.

Hints on Houses and House Furnishings, or Economics for Young Beginners. London: Goombridge and Sons, Ltd., 1861.

Hobsbawm, Eric. *Labouring Men: Studies in the History of Labour*. New York: Basic Books, 1964.

——. *Workers: Worlds of Labour*. New York: Pantheon Books, 1984.

Hoever, Rev. Hugo, ed. *Lives of the Saints*. New York: Catholic Book Publishing Co., 1955.

Hoffecker, Carol. *Wilmington, Delaware: Portrait of an Industrial City*. Charlottesville: University of Virginia Press for the Eleutherian Mills–Hagley Foundation, 1974.

Howe, Daniel Walker. *Making the American Self: From Jonathan Edwards to Abraham Lincoln*. Cambridge: Harvard University Press, 1997.

Hubka, Thomas C. *Big House, Little House, Back House, Barn: The Connected Farm Buildings of New England*. Hanover, N.H.: University Press of New England, 1984.

Isaac, Rhys. *The Transformation of Virginia, 1740–1790*. Chapel Hill: The University of North Carolina Press for the Institute of Early American Culture, 1982.

Jackson, Pauline. "Women in 19th-Century Irish Migration." *International Migration Review* 18, no. 4 (Winter 1984): 1004–20.

Jensen, Joan. *Loosening the Bonds: Mid-Atlantic Farm Women, 1750–1850*. New Haven: Yale University Press, 1986.

Johnson, Paul E. *A Shopkeeper's Millennium: Society and Revivals in Rochester, New York, 1815–1837*. New York: Hill and Wang, 1978.

Kasson, John F. *Civilizing the Machine: Technology and Republican Values in America, 1776–1900*. New York: Penguin Books, 1976.

—. *Rudeness and Civility: Manners in Nineteenth-Century Urban America.* Chapel Hill: University of North Carolina Press, 1990.

Kazin, Michael. "Struggling with Class Struggle: Marxism and the Search for a Synthesis of U.S. Labor History." *Labor History* 28 (Fall 1987): 497–514.

——, Alice Kessler-Harris, et al. "The Limits of Union-Centered History: Responses to Kimmeldorf." *Labor History* 32 (Winter 1991): 91–127.

Kennally, Karen, ed. *American Catholic Women: An Historical Exploration.* New York: MacMillan Publishing Co., 1989.

Kenny, Kevin. *Making Sense of the Molly Maguires.* New York: Oxford University Press, 1998.

Kerber, Linda K. "Separate Spheres, Female Worlds, Woman's Place: The Rhetoric of Women's History." *The Journal of American History* 75, no. 1 (June 1988): 9–39.

Kessler-Harris, Alice. "A New Agenda." In *Perspectives in American Labor History: The Problems of Synthesis,* ed. J. Carroll Moody and Alice Kessler-Harris. Dekalb: Northern Illinois University Press, 1989.

——. *Out to Work: A History of Wage-Earning Women in the United States.* New York: Oxford University Press, 1982.

——. "Treating the Male as Other: Redefining the Parameters of Labor History." *Labor History* 34, nos. 2–3 (Spring–Summer 1993): 190–204.

Kett, Joseph. *The Pursuit of Knowledge Under Difficulties: From Self-Improvement to Adult Education in America, 1750–1990.* Stanford: Stanford University Press, 1994.

Kimmeldorf, Howard. "Bringing Unions Back In (Or Why We Need a New Old Labor History)." *Labor History* 32 (Winter 1991): 91–127.

Kinmonth, Claudia. *Irish Country Furniture, 1700–1950.* New Haven: Yale University Press, 1993.

Knobel, Dale. *Paddy and the Republic: Ethnicity and Nationality in Antebellum America.* Middletown, Conn.: Weslyan University Press, 1986.

Knowles, Morris. *Industrial Housing.* 1920; reprinted, New York: McGraw-Hill, 1974.

Kovel, Ralph, and Terry Kovel. *American Country Furniture, 1780–1875.* New York: Crown Publishers, 1965.

Kramnick, Isaac. *Republicanism and Bourgeois Radicalism: Political Ideology in Late-Eighteenth-Century England and the America.* Ithaca: Cornell University Press, 1990.

Lalley, Joseph M., Jr. *Our Irish Ancestors and their Descendants and the Times in Which They Lived.* Asheville, N.C.: privately printed, 2000.

Larkin, Emmet. "The Devotional Revolution in Ireland." *American Historical Review* 77 (1972): 625–52.

Laurie, Bruce. *Working People of Philadelphia, 1800–1850.* Philadelphia: Temple University Press, 1980.

Lazerow, Jama. *Religion and the Working Class in Antebellum America.* Washington, D.C.: Smithsonian Institution Press, 1995.

Lears, T. J. Jackson. "The Concept of Cultural Hegemony: Problems and Possibilities." *American Historical Review* 90, no. 3 (June 1985): 567–93.

Leavitt, Judith. "Under the Shadow of Maternity: American Women's Respon to Death and Debility Fears in Nineteenth-Century Childbirth." *Feminist Stu ies* 12 (1986): 129–54.

Lee, Joseph J. "Women and the Church Since the Famine." In *Women and Irish Society: The Historical Dimension,* ed. Margaret MacCurtain and Donncha O. Corrain. Westport, Conn.: Greenwood Press, 1979.

LeeDecker, Charles H., et al. "19th-Century Households and Consumer Behavior in Wilmington, Delaware." In *Consumer Choice in Historical Archaeology,* ed. Suzanne Spencer-Wood. New York: Plenum Press, 1987.

Leslie, Miss. *The House Book, or A Manual of Domestic Economy for Town and Country.* Philadelphia: Carey and Hart, 1841.

Lewis, Earl. "Invoking Concepts, Problematizing Identities: The Life of Charles N. Hunter and the Implications for the Study of Gender and Labor." *Labor History* 34, nos. 2–3 (Spring–Summer 1993): 292–308.

Lewis, Samuel. *Topographical Dictionary of Ireland.* London: S. Lewis & Co., 1877.

Liguori, Alphonsus, St. *Obligations of Children and Parents Towards Each Other.* Philadelphia: H. & C. McGrath, 1851.

Liu, Tessie P. "Le Patrimoine Magique: Reassessing the Power of Women in Peasant Households in Nineteenth-Century France." *Gender and History* 6, no. 1 (April 1994): 13–36.

Longworth, Joyce Kettaneh, and Marjorie Gregory McNinch. *The Church of St. Joseph on the Brandywine, 1841–1994.* Greenville, Del.: Privately printed, 1995.

Magnusson, Leifur. "Employers' Housing in the United States." *Monthly Review of the Bureau of Labor Statistics.* Washington, D.C.: GPO, 1917.

Maguire, John Francis. *The Irish in America.* New York: D. & J. Sadlier & Co., 1868.

Mahoney, Rosemary. *Whoredom in Kimmage: Irish Women Coming of Age.* New York: Houghton-Mifflin, 1993.

Martin, Ann Smart. "The Role of Pewter as Missing Artifact: Consumer Attitudes Toward Tablewares in Late 18th-Century Virginia." *Historical Archaeology* 23 (1989): 1–26.

McCracken, Grant. *Culture and Consumption: New Approaches to the Symbolic Character of Consumer Goods and Activities.* Bloomington: Indiana University Press, 1988.

McDannell, Colleen. "Catholic Domesticity, 1860–1960." In *American Catholic Women: An Historical Exploration,* ed. Karen Kennally. New York: MacMillan Publishing Co., 1989.

———. *The Christian Home in Victorian America, 1840–1900.* Bloomington: Indiana University Press, 1986.

———. "True Men as We Need Them: Catholicism and the Irish-American Male." *American Studies* 27, no. 2 (Fall 1986): 19–36.

McDonnell, Lawrence T. "You are Too Sentimental: Problems and Suggestions for a New Labor History." *Journal of Social History* 17 (Summer 1984): 629–54.

McKendrick, Neil, John Brewer, and J. H. Plumb. *The Birth of a Consumer Society: The Commercialization of Eighteenth-Century England.* Bloomington: Indiana University Press, 1982.

Murry, Sally. *Families and Farmhouses in Nineteenth-Century America: Vernacular Design and Social Change.* New York; Oxford University Press, 1988.

Meagher, Timothy J. *Inventing Irish America: Generation, Class, and Ethnic Identity in a New England City, 1880–1928.* Notre Dame, Ind.: University of Notre Dame Press, 2001.

Mertz, Anne Morris. "Coffee Run Cemetery." *Delaware Geneological Society Journal* 4 (April 1988): 58–62.

Miller, David W. "Irish Catholicism and the Great Famine." *Journal of Social History* 11, no. 1 (Fall 1975): 81–98.

Miller, George L. "A Revised Set of CC Index Values for Classification and Economic Scaling of English Ceramics from 1787–1880." *Historical Archaeology* 25 (1991): 1–25.

Miller, Kerby A. "Class, Culture, and Immigrant Group Identity in the United States: The Case of Irish-American Ethnicity." In *Immigration Reconsidered: History, Sociology, and Politics,* ed. Virginia Yans-McLaughlin. New York: Oxford University Press, 1990.

——. *Emigrants and Exiles: Ireland and the Irish Exodus to North America.* New York: Oxford University Press, 1985.

——, and Bruce D. Boling, "Golden Streets, Bitter Tears: The Irish Image of America During the Era of Mass Emigration." *Journal of American Ethnic History* 10, nos. 1 and 2 (Fall 1990–Winter 1991): 16–35.

——, with Bruce Boling and David N. Doyle. "Emigrants and Exiles: Irish Cultures and Irish Emigration to North America, 1790–1922." *Irish Historical Studies* 22, no. 86 (1980): 97–125.

Mitchell, Brian C. *The Paddy Camps: The Irish of Lowell, 1821–1861.* Urbana: University of Illinois Press, 1988.

Modell, John. "Patterns of Consumption, Acculturation, and Family Income Strategies in Late Nineteenth-Century America." In *Family and Population in Nineteenth-Century America,* ed. Tamara K. Hareven and Maris A. Vinovskis. Princeton: Princeton University Press, 1978.

Montgomery, David. *Workers' Control in America: Studies in the History of Work, Technology and Labor Struggles.* New York: Cambridge University Press, 1979.

Morineau, Michel. "The Potato in the 18th Century." In *Food and Drink in History: Selections from the Annales,* vol. 5, ed. Robert Forster and Orest Ranum. Baltimore: Johns Hopkins University Press, 1979.

Mosley, Leonard. *Blood Relations: The Rise and Fall of the Du Ponts of Delaware.* New York: Atheneum, 1980.

Mulrooney, Margaret M. "Delaware." In *The Encyclopedia of the Irish in America,* ed. Michael Glazier. South Bend: University of Notre Dame Press, 1999.

——. *A Legacy of Coal: The Coal Company Towns of Southwestern Pennsylvania.* Washington, D.C.: GPO, 1989.

Nadel, Stanley. *Little Germany: Ethnicity, Religion and Class in NYC, 1845–1880.* Chicago: University of Chicago Press, 1990.

Nelson, James. *Catholic Immigrants in America.* Chicago: Nelson-Hall, 1987.

Nelson, Lynn H. "Personal Name Analysis of Limited Bases of Data: Examples of Applications to Medieval Arogonese History." *Historical Methods* 24, no. 1 (Winter 1991): 4–15.

Nolan, Janet. *Ourselves Alone: Women's Emigration from Ireland, 1885–1920.* ington: University Press of Kentucky, 1989.

Noll, Mark A., David W. Bebbington, and George A. Rawlyk, eds. *Evangelicalism* New York: Oxford University Press, 1994.

Norwood, Stephen. *Labor's Flaming Youth: Telephone Operators and Worker Militancy.* Urbana: University of Illinois Press, 1990.

Novak, Michael. *The Catholic Ethic and the Spirit of Capitalism.* New York: The Free Press, 1993.

Nugent, Walter. "Toqueville, Marx, and American Class Structure." *Social Science History* 12, no. 4 (Winter 1988): 327–47.

O'Neill, Kevin. *Family and Farm in Pre-Famine Ireland: The Parish of Killashandra.* Madison: University of Wisconsin Press, 1984.

O'Neill, Timothy. *Life and Tradition in Rural Ireland.* London: J. M. Dent & Sons, Ltd, 1977.

O'Rielly, Bernard. *The Mirror of True Womanhood: A Book of Instruction for Women in the World.* 17th ed. New York: P. J. Kennedy, 1892.

———. *True Men as We Need Them: A Book of Instruction for Men in the World.* 4th ed. New York: P. J. Kennedy, 1890.

O'Riordain, John J. *Irish Catholics: Tradition and Transition.* Dublin: Veritas Publications, 1980.

Orsi, Robert. *The Madonna of 115th Street: Faith and Community in Italian Harlem, 1880–1950.* New Haven: Yale University Press, 1985.

O'Sullivan, John C. "St. Brigid's Crosses." *Ulster Folklife* 11 (1973): 60–81.

Peterson, Harold L. *American Interiors: From Colonial Times to the Late Victorians.* New York: Scribner's, 1971.

Pierson, William H., Jr. *Technology and the Picturesque: The Corporate and the Early Gothic Styles.* Vol. 2 of *American Buildings and their Architects.* New York: Oxford University Press, 1978.

Porter, Glenn. *The Workers' World at Hagley.* Greenville, Del.: Eleutherian Mills–Hagley Foundation, 1981.

Quimby, Maureen O'Brien. *Eleutherian Mills.* Greenville, Del.: The Hagley Museum, 1973.

Quinn, Judith. "Food Ways." In *After Ratification: Material Life in Delaware, 1789–1820,* ed. J. Ritchie Garrison, Bernard L. Herman, and Barbara McLean Ward. Newark, Del.: Museum Studies Program, 1988.

Riggs, John Beverly. *A Guide to the Manuscripts in the Eleutherian Mills Historical Library: Accessions through the Year 1965.* Greenville, Del.: Eleutherian Mills Historical Library, 1970.

Root, Waverly, and Richard de Rochemont. *Eating in America: A History.* New York: William Morrow and Co., 1976.

Ryan, Mary. *Cradle of the Middle Class: The Family in Oneida County, New York, 1780–1865.* New York: Cambridge University Press, 1981.

St. George, Robert Blair, ed. *Material Life in America, 1600–1800.* Boston: Northeastern University Press, 1988.

Scally, Robert. "Liverpool Ships and Irish Emigrants in the Age of Sail." *Journal of Social History* (Fall 1983): 5–30.

arf, J. Thomas. *History of Delaware*. Philadelphia: L. J. Richards and Co., 1888.

lereth, Thomas J. *Victorian America: Transformations in Everyday Life, 1876–1915*. New York: Harper Collins, 1991.

Schreuder, Yda. "Wilmington's Immigrant Settlement, 1880–1920." *Delaware History* 23 (1988–89): 140–66.

Scott, Franklin D., trans. and ed. *Baron Klinkowstrom's America, 1818–1820*. Evanston, Ill.: Northwestern University Press, 1952.

Scranton, Philip. "Varieties of Paternalism: Industrial Structures and the Social Relations of Production in American Textiles." *American Quarterly* 36, no. 2 (Summer 1984): 235–57.

Seaton, Beverly. "Making the Best of Circumstances: The American Woman's Back Yard Garden." In *Making the American Home: Middle-Class Women and Domestic Material Culture, 1840–1940*, ed. Marilyn Ferris Motz and Pat Browne. Bowling Green: Bowling Green State University Popular Press, 1988.

Seigel, Jerrold. "Problematizing the Self." In *Beyond the Cultural Turn: New Directions in the Study of Society and Culture*, ed. by Victoria E. Bonnell and Lynn Hunt. Berkeley: University of California Press, 1999.

Silliman, Charles A. *The Story of Christ Church, Christiana Hundred, and Its People*. Wilmington, Del.: Hambleton Co., 1960.

Six Hundred Dollars a Year: A Wife's Effort at Low Living Under High Prices. Boston: Ticknor and Fields, 1867.

Smith, Billy G. *The Lower Sort: Philadelphia's Laboring People, 1750–1800*. Ithaca: Cornell University Press, 1990.

Stilgoe, John R. *Common Landscape of America, 1580–1845*. New Haven: Yale University Press, 1982.

Stott, Richard. *Workers in the Metropolis: Class, Ethnicity and Youth in Antebellum New York City*. Ithaca: Cornell University Press, 1990.

Taves, Ann. "Context and Meaning: Roman Catholic Devotion to the Blessed Sacrament in Mid-Nineteenth-Century America." *Church History* 54, no. 4 (December 1985): 482–95.

———. *The Household of Faith: Roman Catholic Devotions in Mid-Nineteenth-Century America*. University of Notre Dame Press, 1986.

Taylor, Lawrence J. *Occasions of Faith: An Anthropology of Irish Catholics*. Philadelphia: University of Pennsylvania Press, 1995.

Tentler, Leslie Woodcock. "On the Margins: The State of American Catholic History." *American Quarterly* 45, no. 1 (March 1993): 104–27.

Thernstrom, Stephen. *Progress and Poverty: Social Mobility in a Nineteenth-Century Industrial City*. 1964; reprinted New York: Atheneum, 1975.

Thompson, E. P. *The Making of the English Working Class*. New York: Pantheon Books, 1963.

Tice, Patricia M. *Gardening in America, 1830–1910*. Exhibition catalog. Rochester, N.Y.: The Strong Museum, 1984.

Trinder, Barrie. *The Making of the Industrial Landscape*. London: J. M. Dent & Sons Ltd, 1982.

Turbin, Carole. "Beyond Conventional Wisdom: Women's Wage Work, Household Economic Distribution, and Labor Activism in a Mid-Nineteenth-Century

Working-Class Community." In *To Toil the Livelong Day: America's Women's Work, 1780–1980,* ed. Carol Groneman and Mary Beth Norton. Ithaca: Cornell University Press, 1987.

——. *Working Women of Collar City: Gender, Class and Community in Troy, NY, 1864–1886.* Urbana: University of Illinois Press, 1992.

Ulrich, Laurel Thatcher. *Goodwives: Image and Reality in the Lives of Women in Northern New England.* 1980; reprinted, New York: Vintage Books, 1991.

Wallace, Anthony F. C. *Rockdale: The Growth of an American Village in the Early Industrial Revolution.* New York: Alfred Knopf, 1978.

——. *St. Clair: A Nineteenth-Century Coal Town's Experience with a Disaster-Prone Industry.* New York: Alfred Knopf, 1987.

Walker, Joseph E. *Hopewell Village: A Social and Economic History of an Iron Making Community.* Philadelphia: University of Pennsylvania Press, 1966.

Walkowitz, Daniel. *Worker City, Company Town: Iron and Cotton Workers' Protest in Troy and Cohoes, New York, 1855–1884.* Urbana: University of Illinois Press, 1978.

Wall, Joseph Frazier. *Alfred I. du Pont: The Man and His Family.* New York: Oxford, 1990.

Way, Peter. *Common Labor: Workers and the Digging of North American Canals.* 1993; reprinted, Baltimore: John Hopkins, 1997.

Warner, Sam Bass. *The Private City: Philadelphia in Three Periods of Its Growth.* Philadelphia: University of Pennsylvania Press, 1968.

Waters, Deborah Dependahl. *Plain and Ornamental: Delaware Furniture, 1740–1890.* Wilmington: The Historical Society of Delaware, 1984.

Watkins, Susan Cotts, and Andrew S. London. "Personal Names and Cultural Change: A Study of the Naming Patterns of Italians and Jews in the United States in 1910." *Social Science History* 18, no. 2 (Summer 1994): 169–210.

Webster, T. and Mrs. Parkes. *The American Family Encyclopedia of Useful Knowledge.* New York: Derby and Jackson, 1858.

Welter, Barbara. "The Cult of True Womanhood: 1820–1860." *American Quarterly* 18 (1966): 151–74.

Wetherbee, Jean. *A Look at White Ironstone.* Des Moines: Wallace-Homestead Book Co., 1980.

Wilentz, Sean. *Chants Democratic: New York City and the Rise of the American Working Class, 1788–1850.* New York: Oxford University Press, 1984.

Wilkinson, Norman B. *E. I. du Pont, Botaniste: The Beginning of a Tradition.* Charlottesville: University of Virginia Press for the Eleutherian Mills–Hagley Foundation, 1972.

Williams, Joan C. "Domesticity as the Dangerous Supplement of Liberalism." *Journal of Women's History* 2, no. 3 (Winter 1991): 69–88.

Wolffe, John. "Anti-Catholicism and Evangelical Identity in Britain and the United States, 1830–1860." In *Evangelicalism,* ed. Mark A. Noll, David W. Bebbington, and George A. Rawlyk. New York: Oxford University Press, 1994.

Worth, William. *Christian Images in Hispanic New Mexico.* Colorado Springs: Taylor Museum of the Colorado Springs Fine Arts Center, 1982.

Woulfe, Patrick. *Irish Names for Children.* Dublin: M. H. Gill and Sons, 1923.

ht, Gwendolyn. *Building the Dream: A Social History of Housing in America.* Cambridge: MIT University Press, 1981.

ntsch, Anne E. "Farming, Fishing, Whaling, Trading: Land and Sea as Resource on Eighteenth-Century Cape Cod." In *Documentary Archaeology in the New World,* ed. Mary C. Beaudry. New York: Cambridge University Press, 1988.

Zebley, Frank. *Along the Brandywine.* Wilmington, Del.: privately printed, 1940.

UNPUBLISHED WORKS

Adams, Bluford. "Ethnicity by a Different Name: Theorizing Group Identity in Gilded Age New England." Paper presented at the American Studies Association Annual Meeting, Detroit, Michigan, October 2000.

Artner, Gail Marie. "Priest and Parish in the Formative Years, 1800–1840: Father Patrick Kenny of the Delaware Valley." M.A. thesis, University of Delaware, 1968.

Beaudry, Mary C., and David B. Landon. "Domestic Ideology and the Boardinghouse System in Lowell, Massachusetts." Paper presented at the Dublin Seminar for New England Folklife, 1988.

Blaszczyk, Regina L. "Of Land and Water: The Republican Landscape of E. I. du Pont." Unpublished research paper, 1989.

Burns, Jeffrey. "The Ideal Catholic Child: Images from Catholic Textbooks." Working Papers, Center for Studies in American Catholicism, University of Notre Dame, 1978.

Curran, Thomas J. "The Irish Family in 19th-Century Urban America: The Role of the Catholic Church." Working Papers, series 6, no. 2, Center for Studies in American Catholicism, University of Notre Dame, 1979.

Daur, Linda. "Domestic Servants at Eleutherian Mills, 1821–1842." Unpublished research report, HML, 1979.

Drescher, Nuala McGann. "The Irish in Industrial Wilmington, 1800–1845: A History of the Life of Irish Emigrants to the Wilmington Area in the Pre-Famine Years." M.A. thesis, University of Delaware, 1960.

Gardner, William M., and Joan M. Walker. "A Small History of the Forgotten and the Never Known." Delaware Department of Transportation Archaeology Series No. 84, 1990.

Hancock, Harold. "Henry du Pont." Unpublished research report, HML, acc. 186.
———. "The Industrial Worker along the Brandywine." Unpublished research report, HML, 1957.

Heald, Sarah. "Report on the Biographical Research for the Brandywine Manufacturer's Sunday School." Unpublished research report, HML, 1984.

Hinsley, Jacqueline. "The Du Pont Company Store." Unpublished research report, HML, n.d.
———. "19th Century Community Stores." Blacksmith's Hill Manual, sec. V, supplemental information, HML, 1989.
———. "Preliminary Research Report for 1984 Archaeological Dig at Hagley." Unpublished research report, HML, 1984.

Hulse, Lamont. "Workers' Communities along the Brandywine." Unpublishe search paper, HML, 1984.

Linn, Mott. "The E. I. du Pont de Nemours and Company's Housing of Its Wor ers." B.A. thesis, University of Delaware, 1983.

Linton, Ruth C. "To the Promotion and Improvement of Youth: The Brandywine Manufacturers' Sunday School, 1816–1840." M.A. thesis, University of Delaware, 1981.

Miller, George L. "Demand Entropy as a By-Product of Price Competition: A Case Study from Staffordshire." Paper presented at a seminar on "The Archaeology of Capitalism," School of American Research, Santa Fe, New Mexico, October 1993.

Mulrooney, Margaret M., and Stuart P. Dixon, "Frame, 2 1/2 Story, 3 or 4 Rooms with a View: Workers' Housing at Hagley." Unpublished research paper, HML, 1987.

——. "Hilton Village, Virginia: The Government's First Model Industrial Community." M.A. thesis, College of William and Mary, 1990.

Probst, Karen Marie. "Recommendations for a ca. 1870–85 Workers' Vegetable Garden at the Hagley Museum." M.S. nonthesis project, University of Delaware, 1987.

Pryor, Glenn. "Workers' Lives at the Du Pont Powder Mills, 1877–1912." B.A. thesis, University of Delaware, 1977.

Rowe, William. "St. Joseph's on the Brandywine (1890)." Typescript copy, St. Joseph's on the Brandywine parish office, Greenville, Del.

Rumm, John. "Mutual Interests: Managers and Workers at the Du Pont Company, 1802–1915." Ph.D. diss., University of Delaware, 1989.

Shogren, Samuel W. "Lifeways of the Industrial Worker: The Archaeological Record (A Summary of Three Field Seasons at Blacksmith's Hill)." Unpublished research report, HML, 1986.

Sisson, William. "A Mill Village on the Brandywine: Henry Clay Village During the Nineteenth Century." Unpublished research paper, 1980.

Smith, Daniel Scott. "Child Naming Practices and Family Structure Change: Hingham, Massachusetts, 1640–1880." The Newbury Papers in Family and Community History, Newbury Library, Chicago, Illinois, January 1977.

Stewart, James A. "The DuPont Company and Irish Immigration, 1800–1857: A Study of the Company's Efforts to Arrange Passages for the Families of Its Workmen." Unpublished research paper, 1976.

Thunderbird Archaeological Associates. "Archaeological Investigations of the Proposed Dualization of Rte 141 (Centre Road), from Rte 100 (Montchanin Road) to U. S. Rte 202 (Concord Pike), New Castle County, Delaware." Delaware Department of Transportation Archaeological Series, no. 72, 1989.

Twiss-Garrity, Beth Ann. "Getting the Comfortable Fit: House Forms and Furnishings in Rural Delaware." M.A. thesis, University of Delaware, 1983.

Uminowicz, Glenn. "The Worker and His Community Along the Brandywine: Methodology and Some Preliminary Observations." Unpublished paper, HML, 1979.

——. "Earnings and Terms of Service: Hagley Powdermen in 1850." Unpublished research paper, HML, 1979.

a, Shirley Teresa. "Self-Culture in Nineteenth-Century America." Paper presented to the Delaware Seminar in Art History and Material Culture, University of Delaware, Newark, Delaware, 1996.

Winkler, Gail Caskey. "The Influence of *Godey's Lady's Book* on the American Woman and Her Home: Contributions to a National Culture, 1830–1877." Ph.D. diss., University of Wisconsin, Madison, 1988.

INDEX